The
Social
Fabric

Volume II

TENTH EDITION

The Social Fabric

AMERICAN LIFE FROM THE CIVIL WAR TO THE PRESENT

THOMAS L. HARTSHORNE
Cleveland State University

ROBERT A. WHEELER
Cleveland State University

JOHN H. CARY
Late, Cleveland State University

JULIUS WEINBERG
Late, Cleveland State University

PEARSON
Longman

New York San Francisco Boston
London Toronto Sydney Tokyo Singapore Madrid
Mexico City Munich Paris Cape Town Hong Kong Montreal

Executive Editor: Michael Boezi
Executive Marketing Manager: Sue Westmoreland
Production Manager: Denise Phillip
Cover Design Manager: Wendy Ann Fredericks
Cover Designer: Kay Petronio
Cover Art: *Railroad Arriving*, Stratford, Connecticut, Edward Lamson Henry (1841–1919
   American) © SuperStock, Inc./SuperStock
Photo Researcher: Photosearch, Inc.
Manufacturing Manager: Mary Fischer
Printer and Binder: R. R. Donnelley & Sons
Cover Printer: Phoenix Color Corporation

For permission to use copyrighted material, grateful acknowledgment is made to the copyright holders on the first page of the respective selections, which are hereby made part of this copyright page.

Library of Congress Cataloging-in-Publication Data

The social fabric.—10th ed. / [edited by] Thomas L. Hartshorne ... [et al.].
    p.   cm.
   Includes bibliographical references and index.
   ISBN 0-321-33382-9 (v. 1 : paperbound : alk. paper)—ISBN 0-321-33381-0 (v. 2 : paperbound : alk. paper)
   1. United States–Social conditions.   I. Hartshorne, Thomas L.

HN57S623 2006
306'.0973—dc22   2005010111

Copyright © 2006 by The John H. Cary Estate

Please visit our website at http://www.ablongman.com

ISBN 0–321–33381–0

1 2 3 4 5 6 7 8 9 10—DOC—08 07 06 05

TO JOAN

T.L.H.

Contents

I know histhry isn't thrue Hinnessy, because it ain't like what I see ivry day in Halsted Sthreet. If any wan comes along with a histhry iv Greece or Rome that'll show me th' people fightin', gettin' dhrunk, makin' love, gettin' married, owin' the grocery man an' bein' without hard-coal, I'll believe they was a Greece or Rome, but not befure.

Mr. Dooley, Finley Peter Dunne's comic Irish philosopher, expressed those sentiments in the early twentieth century, and at the time he spoke it certainly was true that "history"—that is, what the people who called themselves "historians" wrote—dealt only with politics, diplomacy, government, and famous leaders and that it ignored the daily lives of ordinary men and women. In the last few decades, however, a large section of the historical profession has staged a conscious and determined reaction against this tendency. Increasing numbers of historians have been mining a wide variety of materials to learn about the mass of men and women who tilled our fields, built our cities, and fought our wars. While it may be true, as one historian has said, that "the past is another country," reading this new sort of history can help to remind us that we have a great deal in common with the people who lived there. Furthermore, understanding what they did and why they did it can help us gain an understanding of our own lives.

This anthology of readings for college history courses was created out of the belief that adding the kind of history described by Mr. Dooley to conventional political, diplomatic, and constitutional history would make the mixture more meaningful to college students. This and Volume I of *The Social Fabric*, which covers the period from the earliest settlement of the English colonies in North America to Reconstruction, attempt to incorporate fighting and getting drunk, making love and marrying, and being in debt and desperate into the story of the American past. Covering the time from the end of the Civil War to the present, this volume includes descriptions of political violence during Reconstruction, labor conditions in the late 1800s, the impact of the Great Depression of the 1930s, and the social protest movements of the 1960s and 1970s.

In addition to offering pictures of the lives and attitudes of ordinary Americans, we have made a conscious effort to portray the diversity of American life. Thus, there are essays dealing with women as well as men, Native Americans and African Americans as well as whites, immigrants as well as the native-born, and the poor and oppressed as well as the rich and powerful. We also focus on the way in which sectional, class, racial, ethnic, and religious differences have often divided the nation and even, on occasion, threatened to tear it apart. In the end however, for all their diversity, the American people have also shown an abiding respect for values and traditions they hold in common and that bind them together.

We have prefaced each of the readings with an introductory note which explains the relation of the particular subject to broader developments in the history of the period. Each selection is also accompanied by an illustration which provides a visual commentary on the topic. At the end of each selection there are a series of questions which students may use to review what they have just read and which also suggest subjects for further reflection or class discussion. Finally, we add some suggestions for further reading for those who want to go into particular subjects more deeply.

THE TENTH EDITION

This edition of Volume II of *The Social Fabric* retains many of the readings from the previous edition. Three new selections have been added. One concerns law enforcement and criminal justice in the late 1800s. A second takes a close look at urban neighborhoods in the years immediately after World War II, and the third deals with the impact of rock 'n' roll in the 1950s.

We are extremely gratified by the response of both teachers and students to this anthology. Their comments and suggestions for improvement have been valuable aids to us in our continuing effort to make these volumes as useful and interesting as possible. We are grateful for their help.

It is also our hope that these volumes live up to the high standards established and maintained for so long by our late colleagues John H. Cary and Julius Weinberg. The original idea for this anthology was theirs, and we hope that we have succeeded in remaining true to their intention and that our efforts would meet with their approval.

T.L.H.
R.W.

Volume II

The
Social
Fabric

Part I

Expansion and Change

The quarter-century after the end of the Civil War was a period of tremendous growth in the United States. Perhaps no period in American history has seen so much profound change packed into so short a time span. It was then, for example, that the United States leapfrogged from fourth to first place among the nations of the world in terms of total industrial output, with its mills and factories turning out more goods than its three closest competitors combined. In the meantime, the nation had to face the problems, physical and emotional, stemming from the Civil War. Repairing the war's devastation was an enormous challenge. So was inventing a new status for the four million people who had been freed from slavery as one of the war's by-products.

Another challenge, and opportunity, was opening up the trans-Mississippi West, most of which was still "unoccupied" at the end of the Civil War, but had been filled with white population by 1890. And while Americans were moving west, they were moving from the countryside into the cities in even greater numbers, creating a whole new set of problems for America's urban areas.

Growing industries demanded better transportation systems, more workers, new marketing techniques, and so forth, and in meeting these demands, Americans confronted a whole new series of problems. These included the proper relationship between business and government, the proper relationship between employers and employees, and how, if at all, to attempt to control the ruthless scramble for wealth that marked the time.

Since many of these problems were new, or at least existed on an unprecedented scale, there were no effective guidelines on how to address them. Americans had to make up their responses as they went along, and frequently their ideas and institutions trailed behind the need for readjustment to rapidly changing conditions. Violence was a not infrequent result of these challenges. Racial violence, violence directed against Native Americans, the characteristic violence of the frontier, and labor violence are some examples. It is no wonder that many historians see the period not only as one of enormous growth, but also of disorganization and suffering.

The essays in this section deal with some of the trends mentioned above. The first deals with the process of Reconstruction in the post-Civil War South and shows how violence became an often used political tool. The second shows how Native Americans were pushed out of the way by advancing white settlement and had their cultures altered and nearly destroyed in the process. The subject of the third is the lives of the farmers who settled the Great Plains during this period, while the fourth and fifth deal with labor conditions in the growing industries of the time, showing the exploitation and violence that were so frequent as to become almost "normal." The last essay in the section describes methods of law enforcement and criminal justice during the period.

*Cartoonist Thomas Nast's comment on the racial violence that swept the
South during Reconstruction.*

Political Violence During Reconstruction

SAMUEL C. HYDE, JR.

When the Civil War came to an end after four long and bloody years, the United States faced the daunting problems of repairing the various damages the war had brought and creating a new foundation for the nation's future. Many of the problems centered in the defeated South. Not only had the war brought widespread physical and economic devastation to the section, but it was also necessary to fashion a new political system to replace the Confederacy, to decide how and when to readmit the Southern states to full political partnership in the Union, and, perhaps most daunting of all, to devise ways of incorporating four million ex-slaves into the economic, social, and political structure of the South on a basis other than slavery.

Shortly after the war ended, many in the North concluded that, despite their defeat, those in control in the South were determined to keep things as they had been before the war. That included keeping African Americans in a status as close to slavery as they could devise. Accordingly, under the political leadership of the Radical Republicans in Congress, the federal government created the Freedmen's Bureau to provide various kinds of aid for ex-slaves, oversaw Southern state governments, imposed qualifications for voting and other forms of political activity that temporarily excluded many prominent ex-Confederates, created stringent conditions for readmitting the Southern states to the Union, and in the meantime treated the South as conquered territory with federal troops acting as what amounted to an occupying army. All this was in the hope of creating a new political situation in the South and making secure the new rights of ex-slaves to full citizenship that supposedly became law with the adoption of the Thirteenth, Fourteenth, and Fifteenth Amendments to the Constitution.

In the end, however, the effort to impose a new social and political order on the South failed. The following selection offers some insights about the reasons for this failure. It deals with a small part of the South, the so-called Florida parishes (counties) in the "piney woods" section of southeastern Louisiana, but similar events occurred throughout the South and ultimately they meant that Reconstruction would not result in the political and social transformation of the South that some Northerners hoped to accomplish.

The catastrophe that secession and the war represented for all white social classes in eastern Louisiana . . . encouraged the plain folk to reassess their fealty to the planters. Linus Parker declared that his reflection on the events leading to secession and its results had led him to "wonder at the hollowness of the whole affair." In a chilling reference to the piney-woods tradition of political powerlessness, the Greensburg *Weekly Star and Journal* urged its readers to action by declaring, "You will have a government made for you if you do not make it for yourself." The *St. Helena Echo* reminded the people that the man who works the land has always been oppressed by "class legislation" initiated by the "lordly planters." Calls for the revival of the independent, self-sufficient life-style that characterized the region in less complicated times proved a popular theme of the piney-woods press during the immediate postwar period. The Greensburg *Journal* exhorted a revival of Jeffersonian principles to liberate the people from the manipulation that led to war, ruin, and subsequent exploitation by Yankees, proclaiming, "Home manufacturing is the true road to independence." Likewise, the Amite City *Democrat* reminded its readers of the near utopian existence inherent in the independent and self-sufficient piney-woods way of life. Many newspapers equated the prevailing deprivation with the people's abandonment of self-sufficiency for the unpredictable and dependent circumstances of the market economy. The *East Feliciana Patriot* urged farmers to plant corn, not cotton: "We never did right in so tilling our soil as to enrich others at our expense and we can never reach that level of independence as long as we allow that great mine of wealth, our soil [to] lie dormant. The surest way of relieving ourselves of debt and becoming independent is to raise everything our soil and climate can afford for human consumption."

The resurgent republican ideal demanded that piney-woods farmers free themselves from all agents of exploitation. This included their northern conquerors as well as their planter overlords, who, many plain folk appeared increasingly willing to believe, had manipulated them. Osyka resident J. W. Courtney argued that the poor had fought and suffered through the war merely to support the life-style of the rich. Proclaiming his refusal to submit further to planter selfishness, Courtney declared, "I am determined in my mind not to serve them [planters] any longer they have allways [*sic*] made laws to oppress the poor." Cotton increasingly came to be seen as the tool for exploiting the less privileged. Deliverance from the shackles of King Cotton became synonymous with independence in the piney-woods press. The *St. Helena Echo* declared, "Wealth and prosperity will come only through independence and independence will come only through agricultural diversity." Other country newspapers, such as the *East Feliciana Patriot* and the Magnolia *Gazette*, urged farmers to plant food crops in order to break the cycle of dependence and limit the wealth of rich manufacturers.

Calls for economic independence, coupled with the results of the immediate postwar elections and the commanding presence of the federal military, created conditions favorable to political realignment in eastern Louisiana. As they had in the 1850s, however, the planters would again delay the arrival of realistic democracy in the piney woods by identifying and promoting fear of another common enemy of southern whites. Planter preeminence, though now subject to an alliance with the increasingly powerful merchant-professional class, who also demanded racial unity and home rule, resurfaced in the face of a determined common enemy. Henry Clay Warmoth, a Republican organizer and successor to Governor Wells, correctly surmised that the old elite intentionally fostered hatred in order to maintain its power. According to Warmoth, Louisiana's problem lay "in the contumacy of the old ruling aristocracy, who believe that they were born to govern, without question, not only their slaves but the masses of the white people." By capitalizing on reinforced racial fears and lingering hatred for the Yankees, the elite again presented itself as the protector of the common man. Carpetbaggers, northerners who supposedly carried all their belongings in a satchel made of carpet material as they came south to exploit the defeated region, and local people who supported the efforts of the Republican party, known derisively as scalawags, provided excellent scapegoats. The old elite aggressively promoted contempt for the Republicans and their supporters. One Democratic party circular declared, "Most ill disposed negroes are not half so much deserving our aversion and non-intercourse with them as the debased whites who encourage and aid them, and who become through their votes the office holding oppressors of the people. Whatever of resentment you have should be felt toward the latter and not the colored men." Such statements, typical in the immediate postwar period, implied that the Republicans, not the freedmen, constituted the real enemy. . . . Although significant evidence demonstrates that the piney-woods aversion for rule of the elite had resurfaced, racial fears and the new common enemy would again delay the ramifications of this resentment. . . .

The prevailing perception that many among the prewar elite had been disenfranchised provided the old aristocracy with a powerful propaganda tool. Denying landholding freemen suffrage comprised a fundamental violation of the piney-woods tradition of republicanism. The old elite presented themselves as victims of tyrannical outsiders who sought not to create equality between the races but indeed to make blacks dominant in order to serve their own special ends. The transition in popular perceptions regarding the planter elite would prove decisive in determining the outcome of Radical Reconstruction in Louisiana. Racial solidarity and hostility to outsiders again secured the old elite against the potential for social upheaval. Latent antagonism between white social classes would remain dormant until the common enemy was subdued. . . .

For blacks and white Republicans the advent of Radical Reconstruction represented an unprecedented opportunity. With the future in their own hands, few would willingly relinquish their newfound power, and many would fight to retain it. Most regarded the limitations of some of their number as a product of decades of misrule and brutal oppression. Most local whites, though, viewed the changing circumstances not merely as a loss of control over their own destinies but as an affront to the very idea of order and government. And in eastern Louisiana, as in other areas of the South, the last months of the war had demonstrated an effective means of dealing with a perceived oppressor. With such a vast chasm between the opponents and such bitter lessons learned, the struggle was certain to be painful.

Violence characterized the Florida parishes from the very outset of Reconstruction. Freedmen's Bureau agents, Federal soldiers, and blacks all suffered frequent attacks. The day after the second attempt on his life, Lieutenant Edward Ehrlich reported, "Outrages are committed daily at Amite City." During the summer and fall of 1865, at least sixteen shootings and stabbings occurred in the eastern Florida parishes. Dozens of incidents of assault, battery, and intimidation also were reported. In the few cases local law enforcement sought to prosecute, it failed miserably, often in comical fashion. A jury acquitted George Story of shooting a black woman based on his assertion that he was actually shooting at another man down the street from the victim. The jury apparently not only lacked sympathy for the victim but also considered Story's intentions justifiable.

Federal authorities also proved incapable of dealing with the scope of the violence. Insufficient manpower and a sluggish bureaucracy ensured that before enough evidence could be gathered in one case, several more startling incidents had occurred. Civil authorities refused to share information from ongoing criminal investigations with federal troops and only reluctantly responded to federal demands. The vast majority of local whites refused to cooperate with federal authorities in any way. When summoned to appear before the local Freedmen's Bureau agent, Amite City resident Mark Day responded simply, "To hell with the Yankee."

Although blacks suffered greatly from acts of violence, many proved willing to defend themselves, and others resorted to violence to obtain their own ends. Many blacks who spoke in support of the Democrats became victims of black-on-black terror. Only moments after Stephen Durden, a black resident of Livingston Parish, completed a speech supporting the Democrats, a group of freedmen shot and killed him on a public highway. Such incidents increased in the wake of the September, 1867, election. After touring Washington Parish, Freedmen's Bureau agent W. H. Haugen observed that many blacks refused to work, instead resorting to theft, and were "a perfect terror to the country." Armed freedmen also seized several plantations in East Feliciana and St. Helena parishes, threatening to kill anyone who interfered with their operations. Under the heading "An Ugly Sight," the Amite City *Democrat* described the passion of a particular black woman for carrying "a tremendous navy six shooter" with her about the streets of Amite City in search of a "white man who gave her a drubbing." The article concluded, "We hope some of her colored friends will prevail upon her to leave the ugly weapon at home and use the law to protect her." White Republican officials were often accused of instigating these acts of violence. Governor Wells faced accusations that he provided immunity to those who murdered his political enemies.

The level of violence increased dramatically with the emergence of several paramilitary organizations. Prior to this development, despite the presence of numerous thinly disguised "rifle clubs" and other politically inclined groups, most violent incidents had been random acts between individuals. In the wake of the July, 1866, New Orleans race riot, which amounted to no less than a slaughter of blacks by armed whites, however, the necessity of black defensive preparations was manifest. During the spring and summer of 1867, Republican organizers from New Orleans worked aggressively to establish politically inclined self-defense organizations known as Loyal League Clubs among the blacks in eastern Louisiana. Increasing acts of violence against the freedmen, such as the seemingly daily incidents at Amite City, and inequitable labor practices encouraged a newfound militancy and willingness to defend themselves. Throughout the summer of 1867, local Freedmen's Bureau agents and federal officers reported growing political agitation among the freedmen. White residents became increasingly tense with the discovery of each new "incendiary" tract issued by the New Orleans Radical Club, headed by Warmoth and others. Warmoth created near panic in February, 1868, when he proclaimed before a black audience in New Orleans that ex-Confederates were "traitors and treason under the Constitution is punishable by death." Union army veteran A. J. Sypher confessed that his formation of a black militia in Rapides Parish "greatly exasperated the majority of the white people in the parish." By August, 1867, Freedmen's Bureau agent James Hough reported that blacks increasingly left work to attend political meetings "where incompetent negroes [created] insubordinate feelings." Hough further noted that armed groups of blacks regularly established picket posts along the public roads and that "travellers passing by [were] halted and subjected to annoyance." Suspicions of impending trouble became a reality in the volatile circumstances surrounding the September, 1867, election.

One of the most militant black paramilitary organizations emerged in western St. Helena Parish. This Loyal League Club embodied the recognition among many blacks that realistic protection from increasing racial attacks rested with themselves. Led by a mulatto farmer named Thomas Turner, the group created consternation by publicly parading with arms and threatening local whites. Hough described Turner as "very troublesome and the terror of all whites in his neighborhood." In the summer of 1867, Turner announced that he had received authority from the commanding officer of the local federal garrison "to hang all the whites." On the roads in lower St. Helena he posted pickets who loudly proclaimed their intentions. On the eve of the September 27, 1867, election, Turner mobilized his forces. Rather than marching on Greensburg as local residents expected, Turner instead headed for Amite City. During the afternoon of

September 27, he arrived outside the town at the head of an armed band, which estimates placed at anywhere from 50 to 250. Major James Offley, commanding the federal garrison, informed the militiamen that they would not be permitted to enter the town as an armed body. To the horror of local whites, Offley allowed the blacks to conceal their weapons and march into town en masse. Turner's men voted without incident, then camped on the outskirts of town for several days as a demonstration of their resolve.

In permitting Turner's militia to enter Amite City as an organized body and to camp on the outskirts of town, Offley outraged local whites, most of whom proved unwilling or unable to make the connection between black assertiveness and the daily incidents of racial violence perpetuated against the freedmen. Turner had boasted that he was authorized to hang any whites who interfered with his group, and many residents considered the federal commander's actions irrational. Many also remained incensed that Yankee planters had provided arms to some of their black laborers. The Amite City *Times* and other local newspapers angrily contrasted General Sheridan's orders to break up meetings supporting hospitals and monuments for Confederate veterans with his tolerance of secret meetings by armed blacks. The *Times,* though continuing to profess confidence in Major Offley's intentions, declared its own intentions: "The whites can not and will not sit idle and see their families butchered by barbarians. Self defense is God's gift—a deduction from the gift of existence itself."

Limited evidence does indicate that secret white paramilitary organizations functioned in Louisiana prior to the winter of 1867 or the spring of 1868. In a November, 1865, address to the state legislature, Governor Wells announced, "Secret political associations, the members of which are bound to each other by strange oaths, and recognize each other by signs and passwords, are being revived in this city [New Orleans] with affiliations in the parishes throughout the state." Wells failed to speculate on the motives of these secret organizations, nor did he provide any evidence to support his allegations. If the evidence is sparse concerning white paramilitary organizations statewide, even less exists to indicate their presence in the Florida parishes prior to the first months of 1868. It should be noted that white-on-black violence remained so universal and difficult to prosecute that prior to 1868 there was no need for organized white terrorist groups. Substantial evidence indicates that the explosive conditions surrounding the elections in the fall of 1867 and the spring of 1868 promoted the rapid growth of white secret societies across Louisiana. Although many supporters of these groups insisted that they emerged as a response to black assertiveness, they clearly functioned less for self-defense and more as mechanisms for the maintenance of white supremacy. The Knights of the White Camellia and the Ku Klux Klan emerged as the principal groups to fulfill this mission.

Historians have frequently misunderstood the relationship between these two white supremacy organizations. Despite the recurrent misconceptions, both groups functioned separately, with different methods, if not different purposes. In the winter of 1867 and 1868, the first reports of a Ku Klux Klan in Louisiana began to circulate. Organized in Tennessee in 1866, the Klan initially functioned as a social club for Confederate veterans. By early 1867 Klan members had recognized that their secrecy enabled them to function effectively as regulators as well. Ample evidence suggests that by the spring of 1868 several Klan dens existed in the Florida parishes as well as in upstate Louisiana and southwestern Mississippi. The Klan combined an unqualified commitment to white supremacy with a murderous contempt for aspiring blacks and white Republicans. Terror served as the weapon of choice for Klansmen. Murder, arson, and intimidation all played an integral role in the Klan's nightly adventures. Their violent activities demanded absolute secrecy; few ever admitted membership. Klansmen in eastern Louisiana conformed to the stereotype of white-hooded and shrouded specters who traveled late at night and terrorized with impunity.

The Ku Klux Klan's obsessive secrecy has caused some historians to question its existence in Louisiana during Reconstruction or to assume that it functioned as the more popularly recognized Knights of the White Camellia. In contrast to the Klan, though, the White Camellia originated in Louisiana with slightly different intentions. Whereas the former combined fealty to white superiority with a determination to terrorize its enemies into submission, the latter incorporated a similar commitment to white supremacy into a political and economic agenda. Although equally brutal in their condemnation of assertive blacks and white Republicans, the Knights of the White Camellia who operated in the Florida parishes seldom engaged in terror. Instead, they typically incorporated menacing persuasion with economic intimidation to achieve political ends. The combination of the terror of the Klan and the economic strangulation of the Knights proved a powerfully persuasive arrangement.

Members of the White Camellia openly admitted their affiliation, though the very same men denied any knowledge of the Klan. Local residents apparently felt justified in their determination to preserve the superiority of the white race but proved reticent in discussing an organization that encouraged murder. When congressional investigators in the spring of 1869 repeatedly insisted that the Knights of the White Camellia constituted nothing more than a pseudonym for the Ku Klux Klan, prominent Tangipahoa merchant Charles Kennon exploded: "I know that it is not the Ku Klux. I have never heard it called so." Some residents belonged to both, but the different oaths they took for these groups indicate their contrasting emphases. In swearing loyalty to the White Camellia, one committed himself to "defending the social and political superiority of the white race and in all places to observe a marked distinction between the white and African races." Furthermore, initiates pledged to "vote for none but white men for any position of honor, profit or trust, and to protect and defend persons of the white race against the encroachments and aggressions of an inferior race." Although it contained an extreme commitment to racial superiority and required an apparent willingness to defend that principle, the oath did not include an overt call to violence. A Klansman pledged to "reject and oppose the principles of the radical party in all its forms, and forever maintain that intelligent white men shall govern this country." After swearing to protect "females, widows and their households," the Klansman further pledged his life: "[I will] obey all instructions given me by my chief, and should I ever divulge or cause to be divulged any secrets, signs or passwords of the Invisible Empire, I must meet with the fearful and just penalty of the traitor, which is death, death, death, at the hands of my brethren." Although abundant evidence demonstrates the violent activities of the Klan, no available evidence indicates that the Knights of the White Camellia participated in violent activities in the Florida parishes.

During the course of Reconstruction, Florida-parish blacks endured constant physical assaults, continual efforts to retain them as virtual slaves, sustained discrimination in all areas, and universal denial of long-overdue civil rights. Without the backing of guns, their desire to enjoy the fruits of liberation from bondage would have ensured their destruction in eastern Louisiana. Yet their organized efforts to protect themselves did result in extreme racial sensitivity on the part of whites long accustomed to black passivity and subordination. By fanning the flames of this racial hysteria, the old elite recovered much of their influence. The near universal support among whites attained by the postwar leadership enabled these men aggresively to pursue their primary purpose, recovery of political control. As in the antebellum period, though, not all whites shared the same priorities. If most whites feared black empowerment and demanded government led by native conservatives, the divergence in priorities exemplified by the nebulous distinctions between the White Camellia and the Klan symbolized a contrast between the white groups that was central to the chaotic conditions of the late nineteenth century. The two organizations shared many of the same ideals and members, but in eastern Louisiana political control proved primary to the White Camellia, whereas Klansmen typically regarded racial dominance as preeminent. The differences in the priorities and methods of these two groups contributed to a growing schism between piney-woods whites in the late nineteenth century from which emerged violently competitive factions.

The distinctions between the two organizations sharpen when their day-to-day operations are examined. The membership of the White Camellia represented the best elements of white society. Most of their leaders in eastern Louisiana, including Tom and John Ellis, John Pipes, and J. B. McClendon, represented the emerging business and professional class, which provided leadership in the immediate postwar period. Others, such as former state senator and Washington Parish patriarch Hardy Richardson, exemplified the old elite's commitment to the movement. The Klan's obsessive secrecy makes identifying members difficult, but the few in eastern Louisiana whose membership is certain differed from the Knights: they were younger, less affluent, and largely detached from sources of power. Tom Ellis referred to the Klansmen simply as "drinking characters." Other possible Klansmen, such as Robert Babington, a Franklinton businessman and postmaster, represented those associated with both organizations.

In the weeks preceding the November, 1868, election, both white societies initiated offensives that exemplified their respective practices. Having failed in the spring of 1868 to achieve victory through legal means, the Democrats determined to triumph through extralegal activities. The *Daily Picayune* declared in the immediate aftermath of the April election, "The next time an election takes place we will be prepared, and their [Republicans'] intimidation game will not be a very safe one." The most hotly disputed contest in addition to the presidential election and a few local races involved the selection of a congressman from eastern Louisiana. That race pitted an aging Louis St. Martin against a carpetbagger general J. H. Sypher, in a bitter contest characterized by massive fraud and violence.

The white conservative campaign incorporated economic intimidation, psychological terror, and murder. One technique involved a systematic economic lockout of blacks who voted Republican. Acting at the behest of the Knights of the White Camellia, local Democratic executive committees issued protection papers to freedmen who voted Democratic. The papers identified the individual as a Democratic voter who was therefore entitled to retain his employment and to receive valuable services provided by Democrats such as corn grinding and credit extension. Local newspapers and power brokers promoted this effort relentlessly in the weeks preceding the November election. According to congressional testimony, the owners of the Magee Mill and Lumber Company in Washington Parish distributed flyers informing the freedmen that the mill would no longer grind their corn or cut their timber if they failed to vote Democratic. Isham McGee, a black resident of Washington Parish, confirmed that many freedmen voted Democratic simply to avoid losing their jobs or essential services. The Democrats circulated a petition among whites getting them to pledge that they would not buy from or sell to blacks who failed to vote Democratic. Those who refused to sign came under immediate suspicion. In the Florida parishes as in other regions of the South, voting Republican carried a stiff price.

Another part of the Democratic strategy involved the use of terror. This aspect of the multifaceted campaign of intimidation fell to the Ku Klux Klan. To fulfill their part of the scheme, the Klan employed tactics designed to eliminate black leadership and inspire fear in their Republican opponents. During the interim between the April and November elections, the Klan sought to "turn over" Republican activists. Johnson E. Yerks, a leading St. Helena Parish Republican, informed a congressional investigating team that several prominent blacks presented letters urging them to "turn over" or face death. Yerks himself received a menacing letter signed only "KKK." Headed "Crow Hall Midnight," the letter warned that Yerks was suspected of Radical principles and should beware the hour of midnight. Other prominent Republicans received similar letters. H. H. Bankston testified that the Klan placed cards with mystic warnings on his door and those of other known Republicans. As the election neared, the Klan began making nightly raids in full costume. Black Washington Parish residents Isham Buckhalter and Isham McGee received midnight visits from large groups of Klansmen. Both declared that the Klansmen "dressed in sheets from the top of their heads to their horses' heels" and "wore false faces." The nightriders warned the blacks to vote Democratic or die. Buckhalter testified that blacks knew the Klan members were men and not ghosts but added that most believed they would be killed if they voted Republican.

Republican activists had good reason to fear the Klan. In the two weeks preceding the November election, armed Klansmen in groups fifty to one hundred strong made nightly rides through the streets of Greensburg and Franklinton, creating fear and consternation among friend and foe alike. Other groups of Klansmen made discreet yet menacing midnight rides near the homes of Republican organizers. Even more disturbing, Klansmen unexpectedly dynamited trees late in the evening near Republican homes, greatly heightening the anxiety of the inhabitants. William H. Wilder and H. H. Bankston both declared that the "tree burstings" created extreme fear among local Republicans, black and white. Wilder described panicked families huddled in their homes, waiting to be attacked and afraid to venture out for sustenance, much less to vote. Word circulated later that the tree burstings served as a signal to Klansmen that the election should proceed without violent interruption, indicating that the Klan recognized their campaign of terror had been successful. With little physical harm, the Klan's nocturnal activities effectively neutralized a significant portion of the Republican electorate.

Some black leaders, however, refused to "turn over," so in the days immediately preceding the election, the Klan, seemingly exasperated by their intransigence, systematically eliminated the black and significantly weakened the white Republican leadership. Congressional candidate J. H. Sypher emerged as the principal candidate for elimination. Sypher, widely regarded as ruthless and opportunistic, along with his brother had engineered the appointment to local office of numerous Republicans in eastern Louisiana. His frequent speeches to largely black audiences encouraging self-defense and support for the Republican party enraged many whites in the Florida parishes.

Ten days before the November election, armed groups of whites broke up Republican meetings at Greensburg and Tangipahoa, where Sypher had planned to speak. Rumors circulated that prominent Republicans, including Sypher and John Kemp, president of the local black Republican club, would be killed that night. Learning of the rumors, Sypher wisely cut short his visit to Greensburg and canceled his appearance at Tangipahoa. Kemp received a final warning, which he answered with a telegram to Governor Warmoth requesting troops. Unfortunately for Kemp, his message fell into the hands of Klansmen, who intercepted the youth attempting to send it in a nearby village. Late that evening a body of Klansmen crossed the state line below Osyka, Mississippi, heading south. The Klan routinely employed neighboring dens in extreme cases in order to hamper identification. The nightriders entered the village of Tangipahoa and inquired at the hotels for Sypher. Learning of the absence of their prize, they proceeded to Kemp's home outside of town and murdered him. Six days later, Jim Beekham, leader of a black militia forming in western Washington Parish, met a similar fate. Black Republican organizers Squire Roberts and Mumford McCoy barely escaped with their lives. The Republican mayor of Amite City placed Roberts under arrest for disturbing the peace on election day and probably saved his life. McCoy, a Greensburg blacksmith and legislative candidate, received a postelection visit from a group of white men who denounced his activism. The visitors warned McCoy that if any whites should be harmed, he would be held personally responsible and that as retribution the Klan would cut off his head. McCoy understandably fled the parish the same day. Many other less prominent freedmen suffered similar abuses, including Bill Wheeler, whose eyes were gouged out at Greensburg, and Daniel Lee and Marshall Thompson, both bushwhacked near Amite.

In addition to Sypher, the Klan also targeted other prominent white Republicans. James B. Wands, a former Union naval officer from New York, aroused the ire of Democrats by securing from Warmoth appointments as local tax collector and state representative. If the onerous burden of Reconstruction taxation did not in itself condemn Wands, his aggressive support of the Republican cause did. In the days preceding the November election, Wands distributed Republican ballots in Livingston, St. Helena, and Washington Parishes. Warned of a plot to kill him, Wands fled Franklinton the evening before the election and camped in the woods as Klansmen searched the area. David Hennessy, a member of Warmoth's newly created Metropolitan Police Force and a registrar of voters in Washington Parish, was not so lucky. The day before the election, the third attempt to kill Hennessy proved successful. Mass torchlight counterdemonstrations by Republicans and Democrats in Clinton and Jackson avoided bloodshed only because both sides recognized the horrific casualties that could result. Describing a provocative Democratic procession near Olive Branch in East Feliciana Parish that stumbled into a similar Republican procession, Willie Dixon declared, "We came very near having a bloody battle with them." A timely absence from the region was all that saved Republican congressman J. P. Newsham of West Feliciana from death at the hands of an outraged mob. Numerous bloody encounters between individuals contributed to an incredibly high level of tension by election day in the Felicianas and East Baton Rouge. In the wake of massive election-day violence and fraud, Freedmen's Bureau agent J. W. Coleman reported from Baton Rouge that "the Bureau appears to be the only protection the freedmen have."

The pressure applied to black voters came from friend and foe alike. To counter Democratic threats and intimidation, white Republicans warned that blacks who failed to vote, and vote Republican at that, would not receive their share of land and mules. Republicans routinely promised the freedmen that once they were in power, their supporters would be appropriately compensated. Moreover, the federal garrisons increasingly demonstrated an unwillingness to intervene on behalf of black Republicans. Prominent Republican William Wilder declared, "The soldiers are worse on the negroes than anybody else." Thus, blacks had the option of risking their lives by voting Republican or of forfeiting their only realistic hope for economic advancement by voting Democratic. Unfortunately for the freedmen, this unenviable predicament would only get worse.

The 1868 Democratic campaign of terror proved remarkably successful. By employing the lessons in brutality learned from the war, the Democrats effectively neutralized much of their opposition. Political violence claimed the lives of at least 204 black and white Republicans statewide. Rowdy, armed Democrats congregated about most precincts, intimidating all who sought to vote Republican. Colorized ballots made a voter's preference easily identifiable, thus expediting coercive efforts. Only precincts guarded by federal troops recorded any Republican votes. White and black Republicans voted Democratic at most polling stations in St. Helena and Washington Parishes or faced the consequences of failing to vote. Their votes contributed to huge Democratic majorities in both parishes. On the other side, the extent of their defeat alarmed both state and national Republican leadership. Barely 40 percent of the region's Republicans cast ballots for their party's ticket. Except in West Feliciana, where the Republicans scored a substantial victory, every parish in eastern Louisiana returned a Democratic majority. The margin of victory ranged from slightly more than one hundred votes in East Baton Rouge to a 100 percent Democratic vote in Washington.

The Republicans' two-to-one majority among registered voters in the plantation parishes easily offset a similar Democratic majority in the piney woods. Despite the regional preponderance of Republicans, what the Democrats had failed to accomplish through persuasion in April, 1868, they achieved splendidly only seven months later. The key to success remained the unqualified application of violence. Moreover, Democratic efforts contributed to an emerging societal phenomenon. The secret societies, and nightriding in particular, promoted an important camaraderie among country whites. With a dearth of opportunity for fraternizing in rural areas, Republican bashing became an important outlet and social activity. Ominously, violence was at its core. With startling alacrity, violence progressed from a common element in the piney woods of Louisiana and southwestern Mississippi to an integral aspect of every resident's very existence. Long acceptable in affairs of honor, unrestrained brutality emerged as the principal means of societal regulation and governance. Significantly, violence became an aspect of behavior not merely accepted but expected. The events of the 1860s clearly demonstrated that the old adage "violence does not solve anything" was nonsense. . . .

Despite the fact that their leadership had plunged the region into war and catastrophe, during Reconstruction the old elite again emerged dominant. By promoting racial fears and encouraging popular contempt for the Republican government, antebellum power brokers identified another enemy common to the white population, Republicans and assertive blacks, who provided a focus to rally the commoners behind the elite. Again the aspirations of the plain folk would be subsumed by the necessity for unity behind the natural leadership of the planters. But the contest for political dominance between the old elite and the Republicans produced some important lessons that would have an impact on regional development. Planter attacks on Republican leadership seemed to confirm the intrinsic corruption of government, and their calls for the violent overthrow of the Republicans reinforced an inclination toward extralegal means in eastern Louisiana. . . .

For Further Study

1. Who were the so-called "carpetbaggers"? "Scalawags"? What was the attitude of most white Southerners toward the people to whom they applied these terms?

2. According to the author, at the end of the war there was some indication that lower class Louisianans were inclined to challenge the continued leadership of the planter elite. Why do you suppose they wanted to do this? Why did the challenge prove unsuccessful?

3. Many of the actions the author describes were clearly illegal, but few of those who committed these acts were even prosecuted, let alone convicted. How do you explain this? Why were the perpetrators usually able to get away with what they did?

4. What were the main similarities and differences between the Ku Klux Klan and the Knights of the White Camellia in regard to such things as goals, membership, and tactics?

5. One of the implications of the selection is that the recent experience of war made violence a more thinkable and usual way of dealing with problems than it had been. Bear this in mind when you consider the other wars in which the United States has been involved. Did they result in an increase in the amount of internal violence?

For Further Reading

Two general histories of Reconstruction are Kenneth Stampp, *Era of Reconstruction, 1865–1877* (1965) and Eric Foner, *Reconstruction: America's Unfinished Revolution, 1863–1877* (1988). The subject of political violence is dealt with in George Rabel, *But There Was No Peace: The Role of Violence in the Politics of Reconstruction* (1984). Ted Tunnell, *Crucible of Reconstruction: War, Radicalism, and Race in Louisiana, 1862–1877* (1974) offers another perspective on and a more detailed treatment of events in the state this selection deals with. On race relations see Vernon C. Wharton, *The Negro in Mississippi* (1965), Herman Belz, *Emancipation and Equal Rights* (1978), and Howard Rabinowitz, *Race Relations in the Urban South* (1978). Allen W. Trelease provides a general history of the Ku Klux Klan in *White Terror: The Ku Klux Klan Conspiracy and Southern Reconstruction* (1971). The people who came to the South from the North in the days after the Civil War are the subject of Richard N. Current, *Those Terrible Carpetbaggers: A Reinterpretation* (1988).

Chapter 2

Montana Historical Society

Native American camp, Pine Ridge, South Dakota.

The Reservation and the Destruction of Indian Culture

ROBERT M. UTLEY

Westward expansion has been a feature of American history from its very beginnings. Never was that expansion more rapid—one might almost say frenzied—than in the quarter-century after the Civil War. It encountered many obstacles, some natural, some human. One of the human obstacles was the presence of Native Americans, defending their lands and ways of life against the inroads of whites.

Whites dealt with the problem with the same basic strategy they had used from the early 1600s on: get the Native Americans out of the way, peacefully if possible, with violence if necessary, but in any case do not allow them to block the path of "progress." In the late 1800s this strategy resulted in a series of confrontations, often violent, ending in the confinement of the remaining populations of Native Americans to reservations in those areas that whites had no interest in. While not all whites agreed with General Philip Sheridan when he reportedly said, "The only good Indian is a dead Indian," and while some contemporaries protested against what they saw as the injustices being done to Native Americans, resistance to the policy of removing them from the path of white advance was never effective.

The following selection deals with only one of the many tribes of the trans-Mississippi West, the Sioux. Their culture and history differ in some ways from those of other tribes, but their experiences on reservations are broadly similar. For one thing, they all had to deal with the Indian agents who served as the link between them and the United States government. Some of them, like James McLaughlin and Valentine McGillycuddy (referred to in the following selection), were sincerely devoted to doing the best job they could, but others were political hacks who were often corrupt or incompetent, or both. A more important shared feature of the reservation experience is that it altered or even destroyed traditional Native American ways of life.

Sioux Falls, South Dakota, sported a festive air as the United States District Court opened on April 23, 1891. The streets teemed with townspeople, farmers, rough-hewn frontiersmen, and reporters from eastern newspapers come to cover the trial of a bewildered Sioux youth of twenty-two named Plenty Horses. He stood charged with the murder of an army officer during the recent Ghost Dance troubles on the Pine Ridge Reservation. His acquittal on the grounds that he acted as a combatant during a state of war made legal history. . . . But the trial also set the stage for a scene somberly symbolic of what had happened to the Indians of the American West in the short span of a decade.

On the edge of town an imaginative entrepreneur had built a corral and succeeded in assembling a herd of seventeen buffalo. The eastern visitors and, for that matter, the local residents themselves came to gawk at the shaggy, lumbering animals. Most had never seen one in the flesh. Among the viewers was a delegation of Sioux brought from Pine Ridge Agency to testify in the trial. The sight of the buffalo gave such joy to the Indians that they cavorted about like excited children. Broken Arm and He Dog even climbed into the pen and tried to hug the animals, only to be thrown roughly aside by a surly shake of the head. They then, as a reporter described it, "scampered about, although at the risk of their lives, and in general made so free with the animals that the latter looked around as though dazed at the proceedings."

Scarcely twenty-five years earlier, perhaps thirteen million buffalo darkened the Great Plains. They provided the Plains Indians with food and almost every other material want and contributed vitally to the shape of their political and social institutions and spiritual beliefs. They made possible the nomadic way of life that had endured for more than a century. In 1867–68 the Union Pacific Railroad divided the buffalo into two great herds, northern and southern. In 1871 an eastern tannery hit upon buffalo hides as a source of commercial leather. By the hundreds "hide hunters" spread over the Plains, slaughtering the buffalo at the rate of three million a year. By 1878 the southern herd had been obliterated. By 1883 a scientific expedition could find only two hundred buffalo in all the West.

For the Plains Indians, the disappearance of the buffalo was a shattering cultural catastrophe, and it had another portentous consequence: it left no alternative to the reservation. Now a breakout from the reservation no longer held the hope of old that food could be found and pursuing bluecoats eluded or fought off. For the first time the reservation actually offered a testing ground for the gov-

---

From *The Indian Frontier of the American West 1846–1890,* by Robert Utley. Copyright © 1984 by the University of New Mexico Press. Reprinted by permission.

ernment's civilization program. In other parts of the West, too, outside the buffalo ranges, Indians confronted a similar reality. Game and other resources that supported a roving life of freedom—not least of these resources open land itself—shrank as swiftly as the country filled up with white settlers.

"All our people now were settling down in square gray houses, scattered here and there across this hungry land," recalled the holy man Black Elk of the Teton Sioux Reservation in the 1880s, "and around them the Wasichus had drawn a line to keep them in. . . . The people were in despair. . . . Hunger was among us often now, for much of what the Great Father in Washington sent us must have been stolen by Wasichus who were crazy to get money. There were many lies, but we could not eat them. The forked tongue made many promises."

Life was every bit as bleak as Black Elk remembered, and it grew bleaker as nostalgia burnished yet more brightly the memory of the old free life that had been lost. It could never be recaptured, for now the line that so disturbed Black Elk truly locked the people in, forcing them to cope with rather than run from the efforts of government agents to destroy all vestiges of the old life. On most of the reservations the story was basically the same, varied only by personality, plot, and tempo. Black Elk's people, the Sioux, offer graphic personification of a process repeated among Indians all over the West. . . .

No matter what the reaction of individuals or factions, the government programs relentlessly chewed up the old ways. . . . The tribal identity, the tribal character, began to change, abruptly and swiftly, as soon as the Sioux faced the reality of reservation confinement. Almost overnight, a whole way of life had vanished, and thus whole clusters of habits and customs, activities, attitudes, values, and institutions lost relevance and meaning and likewise began to vanish.

Once warfare had consumed much of the men's time and thought and energy. With fidelity to prescribed ritual, they had fashioned and decorated weapons, planned and carried out raids on enemy tribes and invading whites, celebrated success, and mourned failure. War societies united men in common purpose, triumph, tragedy, and loyalty. Warfare opened the way to prestige, honor, wealth, and high rank. Now warfare no longer provided a foundation for this elaborate cultural edifice, and it crumbled.

Once the hunt had given order and organization to the yearly life cycle of band and tribe. The tribal circle, the police societies (Akicitas) that regulated its movement and configuration and saw that the hunt proceeded according to approved custom, the deeply embedded beliefs that formed a spiritual connection between Sioux and buffalo, and the constant preoccupation of women with the preparation of meat and hides and the crafting of clothing, tipis, utensils, and artwork—all ended as the buffalo and the life it supported vanished.

Pathetically, the Sioux tried to preserve a faint taste of the hunt. Like the buffalo of old, steers issued as rations were gunned down by breech-clouted horsemen, after which the women moved in to butcher the carcasses. But a visiting government commission saw this as "a disgrace to our civilization" that could only "perpetuate in a savage breast all the cruel and wicked propensities of his nature," and the Indian Bureau moved to stamp out the practice.

To take the place of the buffalo and the hunt, the agents constantly demanded that the Sioux turn to farming. For the time being, there would be the beef, coffee, sugar, and other rations promised in the treaties. But these would not last forever, and the Indians must learn to till the soil. These Indians had not tilled the soil since drifting out onto the Plains generations before. Labor of this sort demeaned Sioux manhood. As Red Cloud informed [Valentine] McGillycuddy, "the Great Spirit did not make us to work. He made us to hunt and fish." And, he added, not illogically, "the white man owes us a living for the lands he has taken from us." Besides, it required little foresight to see that growing crops would put an end to free rations. And so the Sioux resisted. But as the years passed, more and more moved out from the agencies and scattered over the land, built rude cabins, broke a patch of sod, and planted just enough seed to keep the agent from hounding them. . . .

The Sioux political system did not collapse as quickly as the economic, but it endured severe stresses that contributed greatly to the cultural breakdown. Some political institutions simply disappeared because the context in which they had existed, the tribal circle, had disappeared. Others persisted but came under vigorous government attack—none more so than the chieftainship.

The war on the chiefs bewildered the Sioux. On the one hand, the agents tore down the chiefs. On the other hand, they did things that built them up. McGillycuddy, for example, "deposed" Red Cloud and declared every man his own chief. Instead of chiefs drawing rations and redistributing them among their people, now every man might draw rations for his family. Yet when McGillycuddy needed Indian cooperation or acquiescence in some especially unpopular measure, the Oglalas [a branch of the Sioux] observed that he dealt through Red Cloud. In fact, the government provided Red Cloud with a shiny black carriage, built him a frame house more imposing than the agent's own, and periodically brought him to Washington for a state visit replete with all the ceremony accorded a foreign potentate. As if this were not confusing enough, the government still could not resist manufacturing chiefs. . . . There were so many chiefs, real and counterfeit, strong and weak, that one never knew where authority actually resided—if indeed anywhere.

Theoretically, supreme authority resided in the agent, and with strong agents like [James] McLaughlin and McGillycuddy this was largely true. But agents came and went, and more were weak than strong. During the tenure of weak agents, the established chiefs usually asserted themselves, only to be suppressed when a strong agent inherited the post. Agents enjoyed a number of advantages in the contest for supremacy. For example, rations could be withheld to enforce conformity in a wide range of official demands, such as requiring that children be placed in school or that crops be planted. Another advantage lay in the Indian police force. Police service involved enough attributes of the old life to be popular and to inculcate in the policeman a sense of duty and loyalty to the agent. In the hands of a forceful agent, the police proved highly effective. Finally, the slow but steady dispersal of the people in family groups across the reservation weakened the chieftainship simply because a chief's hold depended in part on the proximity of families in band groups. By the close of the 1880s the chieftainship still existed, but it had been badly weakened and subjected to such mishandling by whites and Indians alike that a chaos of authority plagued the Sioux.

In the reservation environment the spiritual life of the Sioux also eroded. Here, too, the passing of the old ways undermined established beliefs and practices. The vision quest, for example, once marked a boy's passage to manhood and determined intensely personal and intensely sacred meanings and habits that guided his course through life. Their relevance, however, depended in large part on war and the hunt, and these no longer occupied the Sioux.

The more visible expressions of the Indian spiritual world drew direct government fire when the Indian Bureau issued its "List of Indian Offenses" in 1883. Now a medicine man could be hauled before the Court of Indian Offenses for providing his people with spiritual counsel or for practicing the rituals and incantations of his calling. One by one the old-time shamans died without passing their lore to apprentices.

But the hardest blow came with the ban on the Sun Dance. Once the centerpiece of the social and religious fabric of the Sioux, the Sun Dance provided an annual forum for spiritual communication and comfort. No other institution afforded so pervading a sense of religious security. No other event so strengthened the values and institutions of society. Of all the voids that settled into Sioux life in the early reservation years, this emotional void was the worst.

Missionaries hastened to fill the void. Except at Standing Rock, with its Catholic agent, Episcopalians led the field, followed closely by Congregationalists and Presbyterians. They contradicted one another in their teachings and forever ridiculed the old Indian ways, but they made progress. They were kind, they conducted rituals that the Sioux liked, and their churches were about the only place where Indians actually experienced the Christian precept that all people, even Indians, stood equal in the eyes of God. But the main explanation for the spread of Christianity lay in the nature of the Indian spiritual belief, which did not bar the new from living comfortable next to the old—so long as the Christian holy men did not demand too insistently that the old be cast aside. The Indian spiritual life centered on a quest for personal power. The white man quite visibly possessed power. Therefore, his God might also be petitioned for power along with all the traditional Sioux deities.

Explaining his own religious experience, one of Pine Ridge's staunchest progressives, George Sword, also explained what had happened to many of his people under the influence of missionary teachings:

> When I believed the Oglala Wakan Tanka was right I served him with all my powers. . . . In war with the white people I found their Wakan Tanka the Superior. I then took the name of Sword and have served Wakan Tanka according to the white people's manner with all my power. I became the chief of the United States Indian police and held the office until there was no trouble between the Oglala and the white people. I joined the church and am a deacon in it and shall be until I die. I have done all I was

able to do to persuade my people to live according to the teachings of the Christian ministers.

I still have my Wasicun [ceremonial pouch containing personal sacred objects] and I am afraid to offend it, because the spirit of an Oglala may go to the spirit land of the Lakota.

Like Christianity, education elicited ambivalent reactions from the Sioux. On the one hand, they sensed its importance in helping them to cope with the white people in the new world forced upon them. On the other hand, they feared what it would do to the hearts and minds, indeed the Sioux identity, of their children. On both counts, of course, they were right.

The Oglalas and Brules [another branch of the Sioux] had hardly settled at their new agencies in 1879 when Captain Richard H. Pratt descended on them to recruit pupils for his new school at Carlisle, Pennsylvania. He left with sixty boys and twenty-four girls—and left behind parents anguished over the parting and fearful for their children's fate in a far-off place peopled only by whites. Spotted Tail visited Carlisle a few months later and had his worst fears confirmed: his own children, locks shorn, Indian garb discarded in favor of tightly buttoned military dress, engaged in chores no Indian had ever done before. After an angry scene with Pratt, he stormed out with his children and thereafter set his influence against Carlisle. Even so, Sioux continued to enroll and receive a rudimentary classroom and industrial education. But then they came home to find themselves almost aliens among their own people and with no place to apply their newly acquired skills and learning. One such Carlisle graduate was Plenty Horses, the youth arraigned for murder but acquitted in the federal court at Sioux Falls in 1891. To the jurors he explained his motive:

> I am an Indian. Five years I attended Carlisle and was educated in the ways of the white man. . . . I was lonely. I shot the lieutenant so I might make a place for myself among my people. Now I am one of them. I shall be hung and the Indians will bury me as a warrior. They will be proud of me. I am satisfied.

Day schools and boarding schools proved less repugnant than Carlisle and its sister institutions because the children stayed closer to home. Even so, parents found many of the rules and routines deeply offensive, and they resisted. Agents frequently had to resort to suspension of rations to fill the classrooms. At Standing Rock in 1884, for example, McLaughlin assigned quotas to the various bands and stopped issues until they were met. "But I afterward learned," he later confessed, "that there was not an *orphan child* over five years of age left in the camps after this 'conscription.' " And so, like the churches, the schools had their effect whether the Sioux resisted or not. By the close of the 1880s, the adults were confused and resentful, and the children, exposed to both white and Indian environments, were torn by conflicting values. . . .

And so the Teton Sioux ended the decade of the 1880s depressed, despairing, and drained of hope for improvement. The old values, the old verities, the old ways, and the old institutions fell irrevocably away. Nothing solid or satisfying took their place. That the people could not help giving up the old, that they could not help sampling or even embracing some of the new, only deepened the malaise. The long and exhausting battle over land, ending in defeat accompanied by a dramatic show of government bad faith—or so it appeared to the Indians—made matters even worse. The winter of 1889–90 brought hunger and perhaps even some starvation, which was in part a consequence of the ration cut. Epidemics of measles, influenza, and whooping cough swept the reservation with fatal effect. Summer drought in 1890 blasted into total ruin such crops as had been planted. Never had the fortunes of the Sioux reached lower ebb. Never had their sense of who they were been more blurred.

Other Indian tribes endured similar though usually less demoralizing stresses during the 1880s. The reservation program tore down the traditional culture without substituting the new at which it aimed. The Dawes Act set in motion a concerted drive for allotment in severalty and the cession of surplus lands. All over the West, Indians closed the decade beset by more or less cultural disintegration and by feelings of helplessness and hopelessness. Symptomatic of their condition was the fervor with which most greeted the stirring message that came out of the west in 1890, bringing with it the promise of a way out of the morass into which the white people had forced them.

A prophet had appeared among the Paiutes of Nevada. He preached a new religion. It was a religion that offered hope for the Indian race—hope not dependent upon promises of the white men. He held forth a vision of paradise in which all Indians would at last be free of the white burden and reside for eternity in a blissful land, a land without white people, a land inhabited by all the generations of Indians that had gone before, a land bounteous in game and all the other riches of the natural world, a land free of sickness and want, a land where all peoples dwelt in peace with one another. It was a religion that combined many of the old spiritual beliefs with the new teachings of the Christian missionaries. The injunction to live in peace, for example, drew on Christian dogma. Indeed, the prophet [Wovoka] came to be known as the Messiah, and when pilgrims from reservations all over the West gathered at his brush lodge he showed them scars on his hands where centuries before the whites had nailed him to a cross. But his promise was of an exclusively Indian world, and it could be simply attained by practicing the tenets of his faith and dancing a prescribed "Ghost Dance.". . .

No Indian agency exhibited a more conspicuous personification of the evils of the spoils system than Pine Ridge. . . . Pine Ridge was recognized as "Pettigrew's Place." Richard F. Pettigrew, senator from the new state of South Dakota, pledged the post to Daniel F. Royer, physician, pharmacist, and local politician of Alpena, South Dakota. Middle-aged, with thinning hair, stringy mustache, and cherubic face, Royer had fallen on bad times and now needed a chance to recoup his finances. Although he wanted to be registrar of the Huron land office, Pettigrew could offer only an Indian agency. But another candidate with good Republican credentials and equal need appeared in the person of Bishop J. Gleason. Not until the middle of 1890 did Pettigrew work out a solution: Royer would get the agency and would at once appoint Gleason his chief clerk. With understandable though not necessarily inaccurate bias, the man fired as chief clerk recalled of Royer and Gleason: They were "broken down small politicians . . . overwhelmingly in debt. They came to the reservation as political adventurers in search of fortunes."

Royer installed himself at Pine Ridge Agency on October 1, 1890, just in time to confront the Ghost Dance. The Sioux pilgrims to Nevada had returned with word of the new Messiah during the previous March, but not until after a summer of cascading afflictions did the Sioux turn seriously to the hope he held forth. Cannily, old Red Cloud steered his usual ambiguous course. If the story were true, he said, "it would spread all over the world." If false, "it would melt like the snow under the hot sun." Little Wound agreed, but he spoke for most of the chiefs in urging the people not to take a chance. "You better learn this dance," he warned, "so if the Messiah does come he will not pass us by."

And they did learn the dance. All over Pine Ridge Reservation, and on the others as well, the people abandoned their cabins and pitched their tipis in the cottonwood groves. Hypnotically, in slow shuffling cadence, they danced around sacred prayer trees. As the intensity and excitement mounted, some fell to the ground, to die and go to heaven and there talk with the Indian Messiah and see the beautiful new world foretold. They came back to describe their experiences and to urge others to dance with a passion that would reveal to them, too, a vision of the promised land.

Unhappily for Royer and the other Sioux agents, the apostles who preached the new religion among the Sioux, chief among them Short Bull and Kicking Bear, added a feature that formed no part of Wovoka's message. The prophet taught nonviolence, even in thought. The millennium would occur through divine instrumentality; Indians need only follow the rituals and precepts of the new religion. But among the Sioux the travail and resentment of recent events allowed the priests to twist Wovoka's pacifistic doctrine. Now they suggested that the time of deliverance might be advanced by direct action, and that the people should not fear such a drastic course because the special "Ghost Shirt" worn by the dancers would turn the white man's bullets. With this assurance, the Sioux, in contrast to the faithful on other reservations throughout the West, grew increasingly turbulent and defiant.

Whether a steadier agent could have contained the trouble at Pine Ridge can never be known. Suggestively, McLaughlin succeeded at Standing Rock, and McGillycuddy had weathered crises as bad. But Royer, one of the worst specimens ever produced by the spoils system, was weak, excitable, and easily panicked, so much so that the Sioux named him "Young-Man-Afraid-of-Indians." He quickly made himself a target of contempt and ridicule, and he proved utterly wanting in any ability to stem the drift to anarchy. Repeatedly he ordered the dancers to stop dancing and return to their cabins, but they simply laughed at him. Repeatedly he bombarded his superiors with frantic appeals for soldiers. At last, in late November 1890, he could no longer be denied, for the Pine Ridge Sioux and a sizable infusion from Rosebud had got so far out of hand as to threaten the lives of agency personnel and spread fear of massacre among settlers outside the reservation. . . .

Big Foot and his Miniconjou band lived on the south side of the Cheyenne River about ten miles below its forks. They belonged to the Cheyenne River Reservation, but the land agreement of 1889 had left them outside its boundaries. A leading nonprogressive, Big Foot had warmly embraced the Ghost Dance and thus had got his name on the list of troublemakers who should be arrested. Actually, his ardor for the new religion had cooled considerably, and his reputation as a peacemaker had elicited an invitation from Red Cloud and other "friendlies" at Pine Ridge to come down and help end the troubles there. When Big Foot and his people started south, . . . [Major] General [Nelson] Miles and everyone else assumed they were headed for the Stronghold to cast their lot with the dancers.

Goaded by a furious Miles, military units combed the frozen plains looking for Big Foot. They failed chiefly because Big Foot was not aiming for the Stronghold but for Pine Ridge. At last, on December 28, a squadron of the Seventh Cavalry found the fugitives. Big Foot, prostrated in a wagon with pneumonia, agreed with the officer in charge to accompany the soldiers to their camp. It lay in the valley of Wounded Knee Creek about twenty miles east of Pine Ridge Agency. That night the rest of the Seventh Cavalry rode out to Wounded Knee, and Colonel James W. Forsyth took command. Daybreak of December 29, gray with threatening storm, revealed Big Foot's tipis, sheltering some 350 people, closely surrounded by five hundred cavalrymen and commanded from a nearby hilltop by four small-caliber Hotchkiss cannon. It was not a reassuring sight.

No one on either side that morning had any thought of a fight. Certainly not the Indians, as the army later charged; they were outnumbered, surrounded, poorly armed, and had their women and children present. Certainly not the soldiers; they clearly saw their advantages, and so unconcerned was Colonel Forsyth that he failed to dispose his units so that their fire would not endanger one another. But Forsyth had orders to disarm Big Foot's people, and taking an Indian's gun from him always unleashed emotions that could override logic. That, not an outbreak of treacherous Indians or a massacre plotted by brutal soldiers, is what happened at Wounded Knee.

As the search progressed, powerful tensions rose on both sides. A medicine man pranced about inciting the men to fight; their Ghost Shirts would protect them, he said. Nervous troopers fingered their carbine triggers. One seized a deaf man and grasped his rifle. It went off. The chanting priest threw a handful of dirt into the air. A knot of Indians dropped their blankets and leveled Winchester repeaters at a rank of soldiers. Both sides fired at once, and the fight that neither side intended or expected burst upon them.

In a murderous melee at close range, soldiers and Indians shot, stabbed, and clubbed one another. Weakly, Big Foot rose from his pallet to watch. A volley killed him and most of the headmen lined up behind him. Abruptly the two sides separated, and from the hill the artillery went into action. Exploding shells flattened the Sioux tipis and filled the air with deadly shrapnel. In less than an hour most of the fighting had ended, leaving the battlefield a horror of carnage. Nearly two-thirds of Big Foot's band had been cut down, at least 150 dead and 50 wounded, and perhaps more who were never reported. The army lost 25 dead and 39 wounded. . . .

Wounded Knee was the last major armed encounter between Indians and whites in North America. A few scattered clashes occurred later, but Wounded Knee was the last of great consequence. Even so, neither Wounded Knee nor the Ghost Dance "outbreak" that formed its backdrop deserves to be viewed as an episode in the Indian Wars of the United States. More fittingly, warfare ended in 1886 at Skeleton Canyon, Arizona, with the collapse of the last armed resistance to the reservation system. Instead of armed challenge to the reservation, the Ghost Dance was a desperate bid for divine salvation where all else had failed. Among the Sioux it assumed a militant form, but still it need not have ended in violence save for an incompetent Indian agent and a tragic accident born of mutual distrust, misunderstanding, and fear.

Rather, both in fact and in symbol, Wounded Knee assumes a larger significance, for it marks the passing of the Indian frontier. A little more than two years after Wounded Knee, the young historian Frederick Jackson Turner appeared before a convention of the American Historical Association in Chicago. Pointing out that the census of 1890 had failed for the first time to trace a frontier of white settlement in the West, he expounded his provocative interpretation of "The Significance of the Frontier in American History." For generations to come the Turner thesis would profoundly influence American historical thought and spark heated controversy among historians. For more than four hundred years, Indian conflicts had flashed across the successive frontiers that Turner postulated. Coincidentally, the last serious conflict occurred in the very year, 1890, that he chose as the end of America's frontier era. . . .

More plausibly than as a single line that disappeared when whites conquered the wilderness, the Indian frontier may be viewed as zones of ethnic interaction that faded when whites established political domination over the Indians. In this formulation as well as in Turner's, the Ghost Dance and Wounded Knee signal the end of the frontier period. For the Sioux, despite a decade of reservation experience, the loss of their freedom and traditional way of life seemed unthinkable until the bullets of the Seventh Cavalry penetrated their Ghost Shirts and shattered the dream held out by the Indian Messiah. After Wounded Knee, the Sioux resignedly submitted to the reservation system and thus implicitly surrendered the last vestiges of sovereignty to the invader. In varying degree, although no other Wounded Knees dramatized the surrender, the same thing happened on reservations all over the West. Indians embraced the Ghost Dance and the last hope of salvation it offered. When the miracles failed to occur, the reality of their political subordination could no longer be denied or ignored. Thus on December 29, 1890, the Indian frontier of the American West vanished in the smoke of Hotchkiss shells bursting over the valley of Wounded Knee Creek.

For Further Study

1. The selection mentions the Dawes Act (1887). Refer to your textbook or some other source to find what this law provided and what its consequences were. How was it linked to the policy of confining Native Americans to reservations?

2. Detail the specific ways in which Sioux life and culture changed on the reservation. Consider such areas as politics, economics, and religion.

3. Native Americans did not always agree on the proper response to whites' efforts to dominate and control them. What specific evidence of such disagreements can you find in this selection?

4. Explain the appeal of the "Ghost Dance." What did it promise its followers? What was it about their current circumstances that would incline them toward it?

5. How does the "Ghost Dance" resemble and differ from Christianity?

6. Utley's account of the Battle of Wounded Knee in 1890 implies that it was a fight no one wanted and no one really started, but rather erupted out of mutual misunderstanding and suspicion. Assuming he is correct, do you think Wounded Knee was a representative example of Indian-white violence in the West? Why or why not?

For Further Reading

Robert V. Hine, *The American West* (1984), and Patricia Limerick, *The Legacy of Conquest: The Unbroken Past of the American West* (1987), are general histories that provide background for understanding the context of relations between whites and Native Americans. Books dealing specifically with Native Americans include Ralph K. Andrist, *The Long Death: The Last Days of the Plains Indians* (1964); Leonard A. Carlson, *Indians, Bureaucrats, and Land: The Dawes Act and the Decline of Indian Farming* (1981); Frederick E. Hoxie, *A Final Promise: The Campaign to Assimilate the Indians (1880–1920)* (1984); and Philip Weeks, *Farewell, My Nation: The American Indian and the United States* (1990). David Hurst Thomas, et al., *The Native Americans: An Illustrated History* (1993) provides a wealth of pictures to accompany a general account of Native American culture and history from the prehistoric past to the present. Robert M. Utley, *Lance and Shield: The Life and Times of Sitting Bull* (1993), is a biography of the Sioux leader that also says a great deal about the history and fate of his people. Helen Hunt Jackson, *A Century of Dishonor* (1885), is a vivid expression of the late nineteenth-century view that official government policy toward Native Americans was misguided and unjust. Books expressing a similar view about more recent times include Vine Deloria, Jr., *Custer Died for Your Sins* (1969), and Dee Brown, *Bury My Heart at Wounded Knee* (1971).

Chapter 3

Wisconsin Historical Society (25366)

Farmers on the Great Plains often resorted to cooperation to cope with the harsh environment, but creating settled conditions was also the result of individual drive and determination and a source of personal pride.

The Farmers' Frontier

ROBERT V. HINE

The quarter-century after the Civil War was a period of very rapid growth for the United States. A significant part of that growth was geographical. At the end of the war, the area west of the Mississippi River was sparsely populated except for the first tier of states on the west bank, Texas, and a line of settlement on the Pacific Coast. But by 1890, according to the official census of that year, this hitherto largely empty territory had been settled. It was no longer possible to draw a line on a map of the United States marking the boundary between settled and unsettled areas. The frontier, which according to Frederick Jackson Turner's theory of 1893 had been the chief determining element in forming the United States, had come to an end.

The process of settlement was filled with danger and excitement and has continued to exercise a firm hold on Americans' imaginations. We still entertain ourselves with stories of battles with Indians, of prospectors searching for the elusive big strike that would make them wealthy overnight, of cattle barons and cowboys in conflict with the elements or each other in their efforts to raise beef to feed the growing cities of the East. But while fur trappers before the Civil War, and miners and cattlemen afterwards, played vital roles in opening up the trans-Mississippi West and awakening people to its enormous possibilities, its actual settlement was accomplished by less glamorous figures in less exciting ways. It was farmers who were primarily responsible for establishing a settled society in the area from the Mississippi to the Pacific, and their story, while not having the same aura of glamour as surrounds the mountain man or the prospector or the Indian fighter or the cowboy, has its own share of human drama.

In the first place, farmers on the Great Plains had to learn to adapt to an unfamiliar and harsh environment. Bitter cold in winter, burning hot in summer, lacking timber and stone for building materials, and subject to periodic droughts, windstorms, and insect plagues, the Plains were a mighty challenge to those who chose to try their fortunes there. Further, as they learned the techniques enabling them to deal with nature, they found themselves confronted with other problems, particularly steadily falling prices for the crops they grew and large fixed debts for the land, tools, and machines they needed to grow them. Caught in this economic squeeze, farmers began to band together to seek solutions to their problems, first through the Patrons of Husbandry, or Grange, in the 1870s and then through the Populist Movement in the 1880s and 1890s. These attempts at political action enjoyed only partial success, but did pave the way for some of the reforms of the Progressive Movement of the twentieth century.

In the meantime, however, farmers on the Plains still had to learn to deal with the everyday problems created by the stringent conditions under which they had to live. The following selection from Robert V. Hine's *Community on the American Frontier: Separate But Not Alone* talks about some of the problems, including the psychological ones, they endured and the methods they devised for trying to cope with them.

"I was alone all the daylight hours with the cattle, and all around me the prairie was dying. The sound of death was in the wind that never stopped blowing across the whitening grass, or rustling the dead weeds at the edges of the fields. There was a forlorn, lonely note in the bawl of a calf for its mother and in the honking of wild geese down the pale sky." Grace Snyder's thoughts were the aftermath of death, the obliteration of a distant neighbor boy who had died while hurrying through his noon dinner. She and her family had walked the half mile to the funeral, where the glass-topped coffin exposed the bloated face of John, as lonely in death as the prairies were in life. Grace had known solitude playing among the bleached bones in the buffalo wallow, she and her sister alone because the Snyder farm was so far from neighbors. Grace's father had migrated with his proud wife and three daughters from Missouri to the Platte River Valley in Custer County, Nebraska. That was 1885, and Grace was three. Their father had preceded them and prepared housing, but Grace later remembered her first sight of "two naked little soddies" on a bare, wind-swept ridge. Nothing else. The flatness of the prairies threatened her with a child's unconscious fear of abandonment, perhaps of lost identity, perhaps even of oblivion beneath that unbroken sky. . . .

Seth Humphrey became a mortgage collector, traveling across the Great Plains in the early 1890s. Everywhere he found abandoned claims, shacks pulled apart

---

and used by others, the winds and the horizon taking their toll. Guy Divet, an Irishman who had come to Dakota with his family in the 1870s and prospered, told the story of another couple who had not. Ned and his young, pregnant wife moved into the neighborhood, and in their first winter Margie was "sick and out of her mind with loneliness and fear." So the warm, caring Divets took them in for the winter, putting up a bed in their living room.

That spring Mrs. Divet helped with the birth, but the young mother remained half-crazed, and the young father grew more and more depressed. So they left with Margie still ill. The neighbors raised thirty-six dollars to help them. The baby died on the journey, and the mother shortly after. Ned sold the wagon and team to pay for the burials. "Grist for the prairie mill," the Divets said. Ned's claim was jumped, but before that the Divets rode over to see his cabin. There were unwashed dishes and a homemade crib. The Divets piled dry weeds, lit them, and watched reverently as the cabin burned to the ground. It did not take long.

But the fire could not erase the memory, and the prairie continued to stare. Mrs. Divet herself developed a goiter, and when her husband offered a visit to her family in Wisconsin, she refused, sadly pointing to her straggly hair and sagging body and "this hideous bag that hangs at my throat." "No," she cried, "its too late now. I don't want to go." The Divet manuscripts are memorials to "the frayed ends" of these lives, "the heartstrings broken in the process of uprooting never to be brought together again."

The lives of the Snyders, the Humphreys, and the Divets were in many respects full and rewarding. Nevertheless, as with all settlers on the Great Plains between the Civil War and the close of the century, the fact of isolation underlay all other facts, social, economic, and political. Isolation was the environment in which the structure of the community must grow. Shortly after the turn of the century, when the President's Commission on Country Life asked over 100,000 rural inhabitants what could improve their lives, an overwhelming response was better roads, or, in other words, a way of overcoming isolation.

Eugene Virgil Smalley spelled out the central problem in similar terms. A newsman, he had lived and worked from Ohio to Minnesota, served in the government, and traveled abroad. "In no civilized country," he wrote, "have the cultivators of the soil adapted their homelife so badly to the conditions of nature." He saw only one solution: to draw farmers together into village communities. He knew that it would be difficult because of land laws and, even more important, American ways of thinking. There is an old western saying, he quoted, that the prairies would not produce until the Indian was beaten out of them, something savage wrested from the land by individual struggle. Smalley told of four farm families who, like many others, had decided to work more closely by building their houses and barns on the adjacent corners of their claims. But in a few years they had all moved to the far corners because, they explained lamely, when they were together their chickens had gotten mixed up. Such was the "crusty individuality" that Smalley felt had produced the inheritance of isolated lives. . . .

Some cultural identities, however, did stem from the use of, if not love of, the land. Sometimes one part of the ecology, one feature of the natural environment, can become the center of the culture, the heart of the community, like corn for the Latin-American natives or the buffalo for the Sioux. Thus on the plains cultural differences arose between wheat and corn farming. Corn cultivation spread into the plains following the water-courses, and carrying a certain life-style. The cornhusker reflected his "corn-belt mentality" when he spoke of huskings, cribs, and fodder, topics irrelevant to the wheat grower. And, more basically, he and the wheat farmer would argue over proper use of the upland plains. Each wave of newcomers to Nebraska between the 1850s and 1880s brought new and conflicting concepts of land use. In time attitudes would change, but before the late 1870s two potential cultural communities existed.

Separate crop cultures, however, did not really develop on the plains, partly because the environment was a common hazard, a common hardship, and it dictated fast, cooperative action from cornhusker, wheat grower, or cattle grazer alike. Prairie fires, for example, were a threat to all. And wolves, jackrabbits, and rattlesnakes, like fires, were more effectively controlled by cooperative drives. Cooperative coyote hunting in pioneer Nebraska was probably the only occasion when farmers, cattlemen, and sheepmen worked in concert—although afterward, eating cold pies with their wives in the nearest barn mow, in their conversations they dwelled on only safe topics like past hunts. Natural disasters such as floods could be better withstood by groups. The common threat of the environment is suggested in the tall tales and weather jokes. Why did the western farmer so love to tell of the drought when the fish in the river kicked up such a dust that the volunteer fire department had to sprinkle them down? Or why did he like to repeat the details of the well that ran so dry that a tornado lifted it from one county to another? Perhaps because the common experience welded them in a psychic community. That same drought of the tall tales, for example, brought the farmers of Roten Valley, Nebraska, to act in concert regarding their suffering livestock. Thus the environment bred cooperative action.

Prairie farmers followed a long tradition of frontier cooperation. In colonial New England all nonfarming artisans and laborers were required by law to help with the mowing and reaping. In western Pennsylvania in the eighteenth century neighbors would donate three days to build a newcomer's house, including furniture. In Kentucky about 1810 an observer described a cooperative "bond of amity." "In no other part of the world," he wrote, "is good neighborship found in greater perfection." Everywhere the tradition was built on the problem of getting big jobs done, tasks too large for the individual—clearing acres of land, house and barn raising, road building, threshing before the rains. These were situations in which men were grappling most desperately with the environment.

On the plains cooperative house raising retained its full vigor. Howard Ruede, a thin young Pennsylvania Moravian who went to Kansas in 1877, explained that neighbors would gather from miles around to construct a settler's house, and they would finish in a day. Eleven men had helped a neighbor shortly before, though Ruede was sure six could have done the job. Houses were raised frequently enough that men fell in accustomed roles based on their skills. Such raisings were not always signs of stability, for many a house soon needed moving, sometimes for long distances, as to a new homestead. More often, though, the move for which the neighbors would gather would be short, like putting Percy Ebbutt's cabin on rollers to relocate on a hilltop or dragging Faye Lewis's house on skids to a site nearer the well.

Hospitality itself was largely an exchange of goods and services. A farmer, for example, would sometimes have to ride for days to round up stray cattle, but he would never want for lodging or provender. Some distant, lonely neighbor could be found for roof, a meal, and hay. "You'll do the same for me," he would hear, "when I'm in your parts." It was an outright exchange, the neighbor expecting reciprocity. When the farmer moved on main-traveled roads, he would more likely pay for his lodging. In such a situation the Snyders were once amazed to be charged a whopping eight dollars.

The height of cooperative work came at harvest time. In those autumn days of thronging threshers and aching backs, the traditions of cooperation prospered. Crews made the rounds from farm to farm, and men sweated together over one another's fields. The men talked at dinner, cooked by women whose backs also ached. Later there was talk in the barn as the men waited for a squall to pass. One Iowa farmer described these moments as "inner neighborhood." Such was the conversational stuff of community, and it grew from simple but universal topics like the weather—the breeze from the east, the nervousness of the horses, the "sun dogs" in the west that portended storm. Or it could be the state of the crops or the advantages of this country over another region or another land.

The threshing crew was a mixed lot. In addition to the local neighbors exchanging work, there could be a few leftover hired hands, some unemployed seasonal workers like timbermen in Minnesota, perhaps a hobo, and a schoolboy or two. The nonneighbors were paid. A band cutter got $1.50 a day in Minnesota in the early 1880s. These men slept in haymows and were fed plenty of chicken and pumpkin pie. Ebbutt thought they "lived off the fat of the land."

The cooperative element in threshing should be placed in the context of a rather large, extensive operation that was partly local cooperation and barter, partly capitalistic investment, and partly involvement in wider economic markets. The threshing machine itself, for example, was usually owned by one or two of the neighbors, who would assemble the crew, arrange the schedule, and bring the rig around for a cash fee or a portion of the crop. If the machine was owned by a Swede and you were the only non-Swede in the area, your turn might well come last. But you probably had little choice, for the cost of a thresher in 1851 was $175. Few farmers could afford that, since most had already invested a minimum of $400 just to begin farming. . . .

. . . Threshing was typical of other mixes of cooperation, barter, and cash. If you exchanged work and brought along a team for a day, you got three days' work from a man without a team. In exchange for sporadic labor over many months as a hired hand, Howard Ruede received help in breaking three acres of his own land, $11\frac{1}{2}$ bushels of wheat, a few bushels of rye, and five dollars.

Reciprocal labor resulted far more often from an absence of capital than from a desire to cooperate. Anyone could offer labor, but few could offer cash. . . .

. . . Howard Ruede's Kansas neighborhood in the 1870s circulated a paper seeking help in building the school, either work or money. Eighty-one hours were pledged, but only eighteen dollars in cash. Pockets then were empty because of hard times following 1873; but in depression or not, reciprocal work expanded the cash supply. The neighbors were a reservoir of cooperative labor that assumed the nature of capital. . . .

So the plains environment and an immature economy spawned cooperative activities that could become community. Irrespective of economic forces, however, the isolation of farms called up a strong psychic yearning for companionship. Starved emotions cried for nourishment. Certainly the community was small enough in numbers, but the distances reduced practical contacts to the level of acquaintances in a large city. Neighborhoods in Kansas are measured in miles, not blocks, wrote Charley O'Kieffe, adding sadly if not typically that there was little social intermingling, and only two dances a year.

Edgar Watson Howe had an explanation for the kind of gloomy picture O'Kieffe drew. Howe thought his neighbors in Missouri in the 1850s were so habituated to isolation that they could socialize for only a short time, as in church, and then they would immediately head for their farms to resume their lives of misery. It was an immature or arrested social life. Richard Weston had earlier described a frontier party in which forty couples engaged in "puerile and frivolous sport," like kissing games, and usually in silence because the art of conversation was so little known. Of course, the preponderance of accounts of social life on the plains frontier is of vital, engaging, lively times, but the more grim commentators would say that the happier descriptions were reflections of the infrequency of the contacts, etching them in memory and exaggerating them in reminiscence.

Still there is abundant evidence of pleasurable social life among prairie farmers. In North Dakota in the 1870s a ring of eight families rotated their dances every Friday night. Even Grace Fairchild, a big woman whose strong face reflected her hard life, recalled that the dances were so popular around her house that in rapid succession they outgrew the parlor, the machine shed, and the barn. These parties were usually open, nonselective affairs. At least Percy Ebbutt always assumed that if anyone had a party everyone else was invited.

There were quilting bees, husking bees, apple bees, and "fulling bees" (for the fulling or thickening of cloth). To be sure, all these had practical ends, but they skillfully blended play with cooperative work, "a means of enlivening the spirits of old and young." As in any other true community, these occasions sparked tension. Hamlin Garland remembered Mrs. Whitwell's ostracism from the quiltings because she was too loud and told vulgar stories. There were limits to which loneliness would compel acceptance, but Garland understood as well as anyone else the gratifying cohesive force in this cooperative socialization—the vigor, the laughter, the rejoicing. Imagine what it meant even to children playing together under the frame with adults chattering and stitching on the quilt above.

At least two holidays embraced the whole community. Decoration Day combined spring with a communal memorial. Everyone picked flowers, decorated the graves, and remained for the picnic. But no community event pulled together the straggling farms as did the Fourth of July. At some nearby fort or crossroad there were flags and speeches and cold chicken, and the day was full of horse races, foot races, sack races, and baseball. There were greased pigs, greased poles, and gallons of cold drinks. At Fort Scott, Kansas, in 1859 it took four horsedrawn wagons to draw ice for the lemonade alone. Faye Lewis, a shy adolescent in South Dakota, was taken to the celebration her first year on the plains. She feared that, for families like hers, farmers who could not afford the expense or time, it would be an "irresponsible and reckless binge," but she later understood the "immeasurable benefits" from the three days, from the four-hour wagon ride, the parade, the singing, the merry-go-round, the popcorn, the fireworks. For similar reasons Friday night "literaries," often sedate enough, occasionally reverted to nonsense: Resolved that pigs are smarter than sheep; or, Resolved that it is better to be kicked by a mule than bitten by a rattler.

Between special occasions and formal gatherings, there was always visiting. In Oklahoma in the 1890s, Allie Wallace thought that her house enjoyed so many visitors because her mother owned a sewing machine; but the need being met was deeper than practicality. Grace Snyder observed an increase in visiting during a period of extended drought. The relief of tensions through social intercourse was well expressed by Grace's father, who, even when weary, wished to go visiting. He took his family, weather permitting, as often as once a week, jolting over the miles, bearing a few gifts of flowers or fresh eggs, hoping for a sip of wine and a face. For a time isolation would thaw in the warmth of human contact.

Worship services, prayer meetings, evening sings, and especially camp meetings were social events too. Small groups of neighbors could always pray together in farmhouses, but the outdoor revivals, lasting from three days to a week, provided the most highly charged release of emotion. Families came from dozens or hundreds of miles. Religion in wagons, Charles Reed called it, and like most other farmers he happily welcomed any preacher who stopped at his sod-house door. The word flew. Soon there would be "tenting tonight" in the old grove at the forks of Clear Creek. Preachings and bonfires and a few true conversions there were, but the serious reclamation of souls was overlaid with the spirit of the Fourth of July. Everyone came—Baptists, Mennonites, Catholics. The circuit rider preached to a heterogeneous congregation. Most people went, even when they had to sit under clumps of hay on poles for shade. At least, Allie Wallace said, it "broke the monotony." Whatever their backgrounds, they joined or witnessed members of their community publicly confessing sin or publicly accepting the Lord. . . .

The place as an ecological system demanded economic cooperation, and the size of the group, small but scattered, shaped the need for social gatherings; but neither would bring community without the values of sharing and caring. Such values were once held aloft by Fred Shannon as a distinctive culture revolving around cooperative rural life. Such a cooperative culture based on values might indeed be a community, but, on the other hand, group cooperation does not necessarily mean community. Was it evidence of cooperative culture when, during a measles epidemic, neighbors fed stricken families and took in their healthy children to stem the spread of the disease? Or when neighbors banded together to help the surviving families of two murdered men? Or when settlers shared the cost of a school teacher by rotating her residence among them? Or when, after a disastrous fire, the farmers near Torkel Fugelstad threshed his crop while he was away?

Was, for example, Mrs. Lockhart living the cooperative life when, unpaid, she brought her "little kit and some tools" either to deliver babies or to prepare bodies for burial? Or the "angel of mercy," who came to the smallpox house to nurse the sick while others whipped their horses to get by faster? Or Mollie Sanford, who was always feeding wanderers? Or the bachelor nursing a neighbor through a long illness? Or the neighbors in North Dakota who walked to one another's farms after severe storms to make sure everyone could get out? Or the boy in Iowa who hunted daily to feed an entire area stricken by a grasshopper plague? Or Mrs. King, who, after caring for her own twelve children, nursed the neighborhood sick, carrying their chamber pots and wet-nursing their babies?

Like exchange work, altruistic acts embodied the techniques of survival. Mollie Sanford once said that she took care of others but also expected others to care for her when she needed help. In this sense charity is individualistic, and its arena may more realistically be called the neighborhood than the community. A neighborhood is a loose collection of people, informal, unofficial, with no binding force over its members. It is reflected in many simple acts like the willingness to stop and talk over the fence. The altruism of the plains farmer, the aesthetics of the cooperative life, may have stopped at the level of neighborhood.

Of course, if there was a community on the plains, individual tensions would rise within it. There is no paucity of evidence for individualism. When John McConnell, for example, distilled from his lifetime on the Illinois prairie a composite pioneer settler, his figure was not cooperative but proud and solitary. This farmer might welcome a stranger, but he would not want him to stay long. "It was but little assistance that he ever required from his neighbors, though no man was ever more willing to render it to others in the hour of need." These were types like Jules Sandoz in Nebraska, egotistical and even antisocial. They were not likely to keep memoirs. But their figures emerge in the accounts of others. They were smudges on the record of community building. When the Wares, dirty but proud, were kindly offered some potatoes to help them over a hard time, they went to the cellar and took a bushel of the biggest and best. The Cogills, when offered chicken feed, took fine seed corn. The Fairchilds once failed to tell a neighbor that he had eaten carbolic acid in their house because they were afraid they would be blamed if he died.

A strong competitive spirit was a boon to individualism and a bane to the furthering of community. "They were always racing in those days," Garland said. Holiday rivalries were perpetuated in the shooting matches and tugs-of-war. At log rollings men struggled to build the largest piles. Harvest crews raced to the ends of the rows. And those who did not win could still tell a tall tale, for the language was peculiarly braced with competitive exaggeration. Behind the bragging was often severe privatization. Some subjects were retained for the individual or family alone, topics into which the community had no entry. Curiously, for example, bedbugs, known to be legion and battled by all, could not be discussed.

The vigorous individualism of the plains farmer has been overemphasized in the annals of the West. But it should not be dismissed. . . . Among pioneers there was a common bond, so ingrained that conformity to it was assumed, and non-conformists were instinctively ostracized. The essence of the bond was endurance, the triumph over a hostile wilderness. Although the end might be a common tie, the beginning was not in the ethics of the group but in the supreme value of the individual.

Walter Prescott Webb claimed that the 100th meridian, symbol of the passage to the Great Plains, shook to the foundation the culture of those who crossed it. In one respect Webb was wrong—the plains did not change the institution of the family. . . . The pattern of frontier family life was remarkably nuclear and similar to patterns elsewhere in the nation. James Davis, for example, in a study of ten thousand pioneer households between 1800 and 1840, found practically no one living alone. Even the few hired hands resided in the households. On the northern plains families were small—at any given time the largest number of children was only one or two, owing to birth control (abstinence), the young age of the couples, and the absence of economic incentives for large families. The pioneer farm family was nuclear in the sense that it was isolated from the community, a separate unit not subject to community controls. Of course, there were exceptions where the family appeared to be intimately linked with the community. In the Dakotas in the earliest days baptisms, weddings, shivarees, and funerals were often community affairs. Weddings in Kansas dugouts often brought so many neighbors that they had to move outside for the feasting and dancing. At Bell's Lake, Iowa, worship was held in homes before the public services, reminiscent of Puritan family prayers, but Bell's Lake was an unusual community with a religious base. Elsewhere most cases of community-oriented families came from the earliest dugout times. In the great thrust of the plains experience "the hearth of the lonely farm" was the center, with otherwise only kin and a few neighborly connections binding people together.

In fact, the family persisted through desperate circumstances. Children sometimes retained the family unit long after parents had died. A seventeen-year-old girl in early Texas, for example, maintained a house of seven brothers and sisters. A sixteen-year-old boy alone supervised two siblings. The community did not intervene in these situations unless the arrangement proved absolutely impossible.

Although often enough denied, social and economic class lines were always evident on the frontier. Some people lived in dugouts, and some in houses of pine boards. There was never any doubt in the mind of Allie Wallace that the Stewarts, who had built the biggest house in the area, were in a "different" category from the Germans and Russians in the neighborhood. She drew her "class" lines by means of the shawls of the immigrant women, their unshapely bodies from bearing babies, and the strict discipline their children received. These were hardly satisfactory guides to class distinctions, but they existed. Class consciousness was blurred, of course, by the proud equality stemming from shared hardships.

Still the community of endurance could not last indefinitely. For one thing, it was subject to invasions from outside. Think of land agents, "the wool hat people" as Grace Fairchild called them, filtering into a community's space. Mrs. Fairchild would give them a bed, meat, potatoes, and "spud varnish" for twenty-five cents, but the presence of these speculators did not please her, as if they embodied a vaguely threatening force. Seth Humphrey was playing a similarly invasive role when he came into Nebraska as a mortgage agent. He lodged with farm families but always left fifty cents on the table, symbol of the gulf between them. He noted too that as soon as a house was identified as a foreclosure the settlers quickly stole the movables. The same property was safe for months if the owner was only temporarily away. Humphrey told of a man named George who had combined with a fellow homesteader to build one house squarely across their common section line. Inside the house they dutifully slept and lived each over his own land. But the friend gave up and let the mortgage company foreclose. When Humphrey arrived, George was hitching a team to the house to pull it entirely on his own land. Humphrey protested. The man firmly explained, "I'm not touching yours; I'm pulling mine and yours is following." Knowing the climate of opinion, the mortgage man did not interfere. . . .

The environment, the place, inspired a community of hardship, but it also injected a constant dilution of community caused by separation. Even the cooperation of exchanging work and the emotionally warming social events and revivals seemed to be measures of separation rather than cornerstones in community. Altruism, heroic and soul-stirring as it was, remained individualistic, not group-oriented. The family, dominant, vital, clung to itself. Growing class distinctions, especially after the community of hardship was suspended and national economic forces pushed in, worked against unity. Thus the total experience was of limited associations, not genuine community. Grace Snyder's brooding thoughts of death as a child on the Nebraska prairie had foreshadowed the usual difficulties faced by community on the plains.

 ## For Further Study

1. According to Frederick Jackson Turner's influential essay, "The Significance of the Frontier in American History," frontier conditions created a strong sense of individualism in the people who lived there. Does Hine's account of the lives of the settlers on the Plains tend to confirm or deny that judgment?

2. What forces bred a spirit of cooperation among settlers on the Plains? Would city-dwellers of the time have more or less reason than these farmers to enter into cooperative arrangements with their neighbors?

3. Hine makes a distinction between cooperation and a true sense of community. What seems to be the essence of the distinction?

4. What did the settlers do for amusement? Which of their amusements were distinctively rural in nature and which would they have shared with people who lived in cities or small towns?

5. According to Hine, there was a conflict between the values of individualism and community on the Plains. Which predominated? Why? How, if at all, would such a conflict have been manifested in an urban setting at the time? How, if at all, is it manifested in American society today?

For Further Reading

Walter Prescott Webb's *The Great Plains* (1931) remains an instructive account of how geography and climate shaped the experience of settlers, while Everett Dick's *The Sod House Frontier, 1845–1890* (1947) provides vivid portraits of their everyday lives. Fred Shannon's *The Farmers' Last Frontier: Agriculture, 1860–1897* (1945) deals with the problems of all American farmers during the period, not just those on the Plains, and provides a good introduction to the farmers' turn to political action, a subject Lawrence Goodwyn takes further in *Democratic Promise: The Populist Movement in America* (1976). Gilbert C. Fite, *The Farmers' Frontier, 1865–1900* (1966), is a more recent treatment of the subject Shannon covers. Craig Miner, *West of Wichita: Settling the High Plains of Kansas, 1865–1890* (1986), and Joanna L. Stratton, *Pioneer Women: Voices from the Kansas Frontier* (1981), explore many of the same themes as the present selection. John C. Hudson, *Plains Country Towns* (1985), discusses urban life on the Great Plains. Finally, Hamlin Garland's stories in *Main-Travelled Roads* (1891) give insights into the inner lives of Plains settlers that cannot usually be found in conventional history books.

Chapter 4

Photography Collections, University of Maryland, Baltimore County

Women and children were a large part of the labor force in southern textile mills.

Labor in the Gilded Age

JACQUELYN DOWD HALL, JAMES LELOUDIS,
ROBERT KORSTAD, MARY MURPHY, LU ANN JONES,
AND CHRISTOPHER B. DALY

There can be no doubt that the industrialization of the United States established the foundations for economic expansion, prosperity, and a standard of living higher than Americans had enjoyed in the past and higher, too, than the inhabitants of practically any other country in the world. But there was a price to be paid for these advances. Many of the fruits of industrialization took some time to become fully ripe and could only be enjoyed in the long run. In the short run, the process often led to social dislocation, confusion, conflict, and a great deal of misery.

The growing industrial labor force, or substantial portions of it, was one group that paid the price of industrialization. Largely without the protection that unions and labor legislation would later provide, industrial workers in the late nineteenth century were overworked, underpaid, routinely subjected to dangerous or unhealthy working conditions, frequently laid off without warning, and compensated little or not at all for such layoffs or for any accidents they suffered or diseases they contracted as a result of the conditions under which they worked. All of this helped to keep labor costs low and profits high. It can reasonably be suggested that America's industrial might was built not only upon the labor of its workers, but also upon their suffering.

Despite this, America's industries continued to attract workers. Beginning in the late nineteenth century, many of them came from Europe. An even larger reservoir of industrial labor, however, was made up of native-born Americans pushed off farms by the declining economic rewards to be found in agriculture and attracted by the prospect of the more or less steady pay to be had in industry. This was particularly true in the South, where the textile industry began to grow in the late nineteenth century. There were almost no immigrants to draw on to supply the mills' needs for workers, but there was a ready supply of rural folk willing to give up farming for "public work," as the early mill workers termed it. As the following selection by Jacquelyn Dowd Hall, et al. indicates, after a while, many began to doubt the wisdom of their choice, but by that time, it was too late to return to the agricultural way of life they had left. More important, it may well have been that they had had no real choice in the first place, having been driven into the mills by sheer economic necessity.

First-generation workers in southern mills had more to learn than just the mechanics of a new job. On the farm they had chosen and ordered their tasks according to their needs and the demands of their crops. Now they drove themselves to the continuous pace of a machine. Whereas most men, women, and children had once worked together and enjoyed the fruits of their own labor, now they were "hands," working under a boss's orders and for someone else's profit. Farm work, to be sure, had been hard, but mill work took a different toll. Millhands rose early in the morning, still tired from the day before. For ten, eleven, or twelve hours they walked, stretched, leaned, and pulled at their machines. Noise, heat, and humidity engulfed them. The lint that settled on their hair and skin marked them as mill workers, and the cotton dust that silently entered their lungs could eventually cripple or kill them. At best, mill work was a wrenching change.

Chester Copeland came from a long line of farmers and carpenters in rural Orange County, North Carolina, and he remained a devoted farmer except for brief, and unhappy, sojourns in the mills. To him, mill work was "nothing but a robot life. Robot-ing is my word for it—in the mill you do the same thing over and over again—just like on a treadmill. There's no challenge to it—just drudgery. The more you do, the more they want done. But in farming you do work real close to nature. There's always something exciting and changing in nature. It's never a boring job. There's some dirty jobs in farming, but there's nothing you get more pleasure out of than planting, growing, and then harvesting. In other words, you get the four seasons just like there are in a person's life—the fall and winter and spring and summer."

Despite this loss of control, most workers stayed with the factory because it provided a steady income and the work seemed easier than farming, at least to some. Forrest Lacock found farming "a very satisfactory job—you've got no boss man."

"But," he continued, "the trouble with what we call one-horse farming, you can't have an income sufficient to take care of all your bills. A public job is more interesting because you can meet your bills." Dewey Helms's father had another reason for coming to the mill. "He wasn't worried about the income he made on the farm; he made as much as he cared about. He wanted to get rid of the harder work. Working in the cotton mill was not as hard work as running one of them mountain farms." Mill work was not for everybody, but the majority of those who came to the factories "never did want to live on the farm no more. They learned how to work in the mill."

Reliance on the family labor system meant that the southern textile industry's growth was based to a large extent on the labor of children. Between 1880 and 1910 manufacturers reported that about one-quarter of their work force was under sixteen years of age, and many more child workers went unreported. Indeed, in the industry's early years, youngsters of seven or eight commonly doffed, spun, and did all sorts of casual labor. Originally the official definition of "children" applied to youngsters up to age eight but later rose to age twelve, then fourteen, and finally sixteen; nevertheless, young people remained crucial, both to the industry's profit margins and to their own families' survival.

Child labor was by no means unique to the South. The textile industry, wherever established, tended to rely on the labor of women and children. But the technical breakthroughs that enabled the South to enter and eventually capture the market in cotton goods also encouraged a particularly intense exploitation of the young. Women and children led the first wave of migrants to the region's mills, and manufacturers matched them with the low-skill jobs created by the advent of ring spinning. A study of women and children laborers conducted by the U.S. Bureau of Labor in 1907–8 found that half the spinners were under fourteen and 90 percent were under twenty-one. As Naomi Trammel put it, "That's where they put the children. You could run a frame where you couldn't run anything else."

Technology made child labor practical, but not necessary. The practice spread primarily as a solution to problems of labor recruitment and as a system of socializing and controlling a prospective labor force. South Carolina industrialist William Gregg, founder of Graniteville, the Old South's premier cotton mill, had hoped to attract the daughters of impoverished farmers. Young single women failed to show up in large numbers, but Gregg continued to believe that the "large class of miserable poor white people among us . . . might be induced to place their children in a situation in which they would be educated and reared in industrious habits." His words captured the industry rationale: children made up a large portion of the surplus labor in the countryside; the lure of wages for everyone in the family could induce hard-pressed farmers to cast their lot with the mills; and children who went to work at an early age would eventually grow into efficient, tractable, long-term workers.

Critics of child labor were not hard to find. In the 1880s and 1890s the opposition was led by the Knights of Labor and the National Union of Textile Workers (NUTW), who complained that the low wages paid to children held down the earnings of adults. But after the turn of the century a new group of middle-class social reformers took up the banner of the child labor crusade. Educational and religious leaders such as Alabama's Edgar Gardner Murphy and North Carolina's Alexander J. McKelway organized opposition at the state level and then helped form the National Child Labor Committee (NCLC). These reformers worried that the mills' unlettered children would one day become a blight on the body politic. "In a democracy," McKelway argued, "the people all rule. Also, the people are ruled. And when it comes to the people's ruling us by their votes, electing our governors and presidents, initiating and vetoing legislation, taxing our incomes, we grow mightily concerned over the intelligence and independence of the electorate. We do not like to trust our interests now and the lives and fortunes of our children to a mass of voters who have been deprived of all opportunity for an education . . . who have been embittered by the robbery of their childhood, who are the material for the agitator, and the prey of the demagogue."

Mill men themselves were divided on the issue of child labor. Some firmly believed that hard work, commencing at a young age, was the best education available. Others championed the practice as a necessary evil in the natural progress of society. Daniel Augustus Tompkins traced the problem to the poverty caused by the Civil War, particularly to the resultant lack of educational opportunities. "In the absence of schools, the discipline of the mill and its training down to twelve years of age is much better for children than idleness and no discipline or training. . . . It would be far better to have ample school facilities and compel all children to go to school ten months in the year, and give them the other two months for vacations and recreation. But in the absence of such facilities, the discipline and training of the mill is best for the children of working people." Whatever the personal feelings of mill men, their duties to their stockholders demanded that they oppose restrictions on the employment of children. The fact of the matter, as the president of the American Cotton Manufacturers Association admitted to McKelway, was that without the labor of boys and girls under the age of fourteen, Piedmont mills simply could not operate.

Bit by bit, reformers chipped away at the opposition. By 1913 North Carolina, South Carolina, Alabama, and Georgia had laws that prohibited the employment of children under twelve and restricted the hours of labor for those below fourteen. Exemptions and lack of enforcement, however, enfeebled state regulations. The 1907–8 Bureau of Labor study found that an astounding 92 percent of the mills in South Carolina and 75 percent of those in North Carolina ignored child labor regulations. Flora McKinney's boss was one of those who paid little attention to the law. Her family moved to Lando, South Carolina, when she was nine or ten, and she soon followed her father into the mill. "When I got old enough, well, I really weren't old enough, but they'd take children to work then. We were supposed to be twelve years old before we could go to work, but I've hid from inspectors a lots of times. They'd come through and the section in front of us would send word to hide the kids, and we'd run to the water house. Then we'd all cram in there 'til they left."

Given the inadequacy of state legislation, members of the NCLC felt the need for federal action. To mobilize public opinion against child labor, the NCLC devised a highly effective propaganda campaign. Key to this effort were the photographs of Lewis Hine, which poignantly revealed the youthfulness of southern workers. Hine's images—of little girls dressed in long skirts and aprons and little boys wearing their workingmen's caps and suspenders, all swallowed up in rows of towering machines—became the crusade's symbols of the worst evils of industrialization. The NCLC convinced the public and members of Congress that the employment of children had to be stopped. In 1916 President Woodrow Wilson signed the Keating-Owen Child Labor bill to achieve that end.

Adamantly opposed to federal intervention, which might open the way to other protective laws and undermine their competitive advantage over the North, southern industrialists fought back. When federal child labor legislation was first suggested, David Clark, editor of the *Southern Textile Bulletin,* organized mill owner opposition. The son of Walter Clark, who was chief justice of the North Carolina Supreme Court and one of the South's most liberal jurists, David Clark seemed an unlikely opponent of progressive reform. But as a young man, Clark embarked on a course quite different from his father's. After earning degrees in civil and mechanical engineering from the North Carolina College of Agriculture and Mechanic Arts and Cornell University in the late 1890s, David entered the textile business, first as a mill designer and later as an investor. When his own mill failed in 1907, he turned to textile journalism. As founder and editor of the *Southern Textile Bulletin,* Clark gained a reputation as "a volunteer spokesman for an ultra-conservative philosophy in business and education matters" and "a stirrer-upper of no mean proportions." Shortly after passage of the Keating-Owen bill, he arranged to test the constitutionality of the law. At Clark's behest, a Charlotte mill worker—perhaps fearful of losing his job, his children's earnings, or a combination of the two—petitioned the courts to restrain a local mill from discharging his two underage sons. A federal judge agreed that the law violated the rights of the worker, and a year later the Supreme Court concurred. The child labor law was dead.

Despite this setback, child labor gradually did decline, largely in response to changes in the industry and the growing supply of adult workers. The trend toward finer yarns, the integration of yarn spinning with cloth-weaving operations that required more strength and skill, and the technological advances of the 1920s all worked against the practice. By World War I the number of children under sixteen employed in the Carolinas had decreased to 6 percent of the total work force, almost the level in the leading New England textile states. Yet until 1938, when the federal Fair Labor Standards Act outlawed employment of children under sixteen, many southern industrialists skirted the law so as to make use of the mill village's young, and captive, work force.

Child labor involved more, however, than the exploitation of youth. There were stories behind the expressions captured on film by Lewis Hine, stories that fit neither the rationalizations of mill owners nor the fears of reformers. Mill work was a source of pride as well as pain, of fun as much as suffering; and children made choices, however hedged about by their parents' authority and their bosses' power.

For mill children, life was paced from the outset by the ringing of the factory bell. Working women, who often had to return to their jobs within a few weeks of childbirth, adapted their nursing schedule to breaks in the workday. "People used to go out," recalled Ada Mae Wilson. "They didn't have bottle babies like they do now. They nursed the breast. A lot healthier children. You'd come out at nine o'clock, and then at twelve you'd come home for lunch. And then at three they'd let you come back, and then you'd be off at six." If labor was scarce, a woman who had neither relatives nor older children at home might take her baby to the mill. Jessie Lee Carter had a neighbor with a nursing baby who would "take a quilt and lay that baby in her roping box while she worked. And she'd bring her baby down and keep it in the mill all day long."

As children got older, the mill was like a magnet, attracting their youthful curiosity and, all too soon, their labor. Until the 1920s no barbed wire fences, locked gates, or bricked-in windows separated the factory from the village. Children could easily wander in and out of the mill, and their first "work" might be indistinguishable from play. After school and in the summers, Emma Williams accompanied her mother to the mill. "I'm sure I didn't work for the money. I just wanted to work, I reckon. Oodles of kids. All of us used to do it together. [We] didn't do much, and it was real fun. I guess maybe one reason that it was fun was because that was the only time we got with other children. When we stayed home, well, we stayed home."

Most children first learned about factory labor when they tagged along with a parent or sibling, carried hot meals to the mill at dinnertime, or stopped by after school. But this casual contact had serious consequences, for on such visits relatives began teaching children the skills they would need when they were old enough for jobs of their own. Ethel Faucette carried lunch to her sister. "While she was eating," Faucette explained, "I learned how to work her job. I was already learned when I went to work." Geddes Dodson's father gave him specific chores during his daily visits. "When I was a little fellow, my daddy was a-working in the Poinsett Mill. He was a loom fixer. He'd run the weavers' looms through the dinner hour so they could go eat their dinner. We lived about a mile and a quarter from the mill, and I'd carry his lunch every day. He'd tell me to come on in the mill, and he made me fill his batteries while he run the weavers' looms—and I was just a little fellow. See, I knew a whole lot about the mill before I ever went in one."

"Helping," then, was a family affair, a form of apprenticeship by which basic skills and habits were transmitted to each new generation. But helping was also a vital part of the family economy and the mill labor system. A child's help could increase a parent's or older sibling's piecework earnings or simply relieve the strain of keeping up production. An Englishman who reported on the American textile industry visited a mill in South Carolina where weavers who had their sons or little brothers helping could take on two additional looms. Besides, with parents working twelve-hour days in the mills, children often had no place else to go. Owners profited from such family needs. Early child labor legislation in the Carolinas only prohibited "employing" children under certain ages, so owners could stay within the letter of the law by "permitting" or "suffering" underage children to "help." A story related by a federal investigator in Georgia illustrated the system's coercive potential. "A woman reported that her little daughter ten years old worked every day helping her sisters. The child quit for a while, but the overseer said to the mother, 'Bring her in; the two girls cannot tend those machines without her.' The mother asked that the child be given work by herself, but the overseer replied that the law would not permit it."

Given the laxity of enforcement, mill owners could essentially set their own policies according to individual conscience or the bottom line of profit and loss. Allie Smith provided a child's-eye view of the confusion that often resulted. Shortly after Allie's birth, her family moved to Saxapahaw, a community in Alamance County on the Haw River. By the time they left for Carrboro, in neighboring Orange County, when Allie was eleven, she knew how to spin from having helped an older sister. But Julian Shakespeare Carr, owner of the Carrboro mill, believed that mill men should voluntarily avoid child labor in order to stave off government interference. "When we moved to Carrboro," Allie recalled, "I thought I could go in and help her, and I did. But Mr. Carr owned this cotton mill, and I hadn't been over here long when he came over and said I couldn't come in and help. I would have to be on the payroll, so they put me on the payroll. And I worked there, I don't know how long—several months—and they said I couldn't work unless my father signed me up for being twelve years old. Well, he wouldn't do it. He said he didn't want me to work. They put me out and wouldn't let me work. And then when I got to be twelve, I went in and went to work."

Playing and helping could thus shade into full-time work. But getting that first official, full-time job was a major turning point. Managers, parents, and children themselves influenced the decision. Occasionally, mills openly dictated the age at which a child had to begin work. In 1904 the owners of a South Carolina mill mandated that "all children, members of a family about twelve years of age, shall work in the mill and shall not be excused from service therein without the consent of the superintendent for good cause." More often, pressure came from supervisors, who were personally responsible for keeping a quota of workers on hand. Jessie Lee Carter was four in 1905 when her family left their Tennessee farm for the Brandon Mill in Greenville. Six of her older brothers and sisters went to work right away; eight years later Jessie joined them. "When I got twelve years old, my uncle [who was a second hand in the spinning room] come to my daddy, and daddy let me quit school and go to work." During slack times children like Jessie Lee could be sent back to school, then called in again when the need arose.

For a large family with many mouths to feed, outside pressure was often unnecessary. Lela Ranier's parents took her out of school when she was twelve and sent her to the mill. "Ma thought it was time. They thought maybe it would help 'em out, you know. They was making such a little bit. And they thought the little bit I made would help." Lacy Wright's father asked him to quit school when he reached twelve because his two oldest sisters had married and Lacy's father could not support the family on $1.25 a day. Other children realized the importance of their labor to the family's well-being and took it upon themselves to get a job. This was particularly true in families where the father was dead or disabled. Grover Hardin, for example, dropped out of school after the second grade. "I started out in the mill—the main reason—to help my mother. She wanted me to go to school until I got in the fifth grade. I told her, 'You need the help worse than I need the education, because I can get it later on, or I can do without it.' And so I went to work as quick as I possibly could. I started in as a sweeper."

Many parents wanted their children to stay in school, but youngsters often had their own plans. Ila Dodson insisted on quitting school when she was fourteen. "I wanted to make my own money. I done had two sisters go to work, and I seen how they was having money, and so I couldn't stand it no longer. My parents wanted me to go on to school, but I couldn't see that. Back then, didn't too many children go on to high school. It was just a common thing that when they'd get old enough, let them go to work. I like to worried them to death." Finally, Ila's parents relented and agreed to sign her worker's permit, required at that time in South Carolina for children under sixteen. But, she recalled, "Mama wouldn't even take me to town to get it, and my daddy wouldn't go with me. I said, 'Well, give me the Bible and give me a dime and I'll go get it.' A nickel streetcar fare up there and a nickel back, and I [took] the Bible because I had to prove my age."

Alice Evitt and Curtis Enlow also preferred mill work to schoolwork. "They'd let you go in there seven, eight years old," Alice recalled. "I'd go in there and mess around with my sisters; they'd be spinning. I liked to put up the ends and spin a little bit, so when I got twelve years old, I wanted to quit school. So I just quit and went to work, and I was twelve years old!" Both of Curtis's parents and two of his sisters worked in the card room at a Greenville mill. During summer vacation Curtis joined them there. "I was about thirteen years old, and I decided I would go to work. Well, I went to work, and my dad says if I quit when school started, he'd let me work. I went back to school, but I wasn't learning nothing—I didn't think I was. So I went and told him, and he says, 'All right, you ain't learning nothing. Well, you can go back to the mill.'"

Mamie Shue's parents had better luck keeping her in school. Although North Carolina's compulsory education law at the time required attendance only until age fourteen, Mamie's folks used it to frighten her into staying in school until she was sixteen. "I hated school all my life. But my parents told me if I didn't go to school, they'd put my daddy in jail. And I loved my daddy to death. So I went to school 'til I was sixteen." She did, however, start working after school in the spooling room. "I was fifteen when I started doing that. So when I was sixteen years old, they just give me a job, 'cause I could spool as good as the rest of them."

Learning to "spool as good as the rest of them" was often a by-product of helping in the mills, but for those who had not started out as helpers—and even for some who had—learning constituted a memorable initiation into shop floor life. Few mills had a formal training program. Instead, "they would put you with someone to train you," or "your parents would take you in and train you theirself." Parents and surrogate parents took time out from their own work, which sometimes cost money out of their pockets, to help the young learn a trade. "That's the way the whole generation in Lando learned what they knowed," remembered John Guinn, "by the older generation." From the evidence of our interviews, adults did so willingly and well.

Mill managers expected children to master their jobs within a set length of time, usually about six weeks. During that period children worked for free or for a token wage. "I don't think they paid us anything to learn. But after we learnt, we got a job, a machine of our own." Some mills used this probationary period to take advantage of young people who were eager to work in the mill. Mary Thompson saw this happen in Greenville. "When I first went to work at Slater, they had boys to put up the warps on the back of the frames because they was heavy. They'd go out there in the country and get them boys and hire them and tell them they'd have to work six weeks without money. Well, that just tickled them to death, that they'd get a chance to work in a mill. And they'd work them six weeks, and they'd find something wrong with them and lay them off, and get other boys. And they run it a long time like that."

Almost all workers recalled proudly their ability to learn their jobs despite their youth. Naomi Trammell was an orphan when she went to work in the Victor Mill at Greer, South Carolina. "Well, I didn't know hardly about mill work, but I just went in and had to learn it. Really, I had to crawl up on the frame, because I wasn't tall enough. I was a little old spindly thing. I wasn't the only one, there's a whole place like that. And they had mothers and daddies [but they] wasn't no better off than I was. They had to learn us, but it didn't take me long to learn. They'd put us with one of the spinners and they'd show us how. It was easy to learn—all we had to do was just put that bobbin in there and put it up." Children learned quickly because most entry-level jobs required more dexterity than the technical know-how. It took a while to be proficient, but most children could learn the rudiments of spinning, spooling, or doffing in a few weeks. . . .

Workers' health was another casualty of the drive for profits in a region that placed no restrictions on capital and offered workers no protection. Without unions, and without the legal and administrative apparatus that now provides a basic level of industrial health and safety, millhands were at the mercy of dangerous machinery. The threat to a worker's health could be as sudden and violent as the snapping of a bone or as insidious as the relentless clouding of a lung.

Cotton dust was a killer in the card room. "Some of that dust was terrible," Carl Durham remembered. "Whew! That dust would accumulate and you had to strip them cards out every three hours, get all that stuff out. It would get to where it wouldn't do its work, it would be so full of particles and dust. When I was coming along, and for a long time, that was all in the air. It's a wonder I can breathe, but somehow or another it didn't affect me like it did some folks. It just killed some folks." Durham's observations echoed the findings of medical researchers on both sides of the Atlantic. Cotton dust caused a number of health problems, sometimes resulting in death, but it did not affect everyone in the same way. It is now well understood that byssinosis, or brown lung, is a disease that results from prolonged exposure to cotton dust. Although the British government recognized the existence of byssinosis and began compensating victims in 1940, lack of research and resistance by the textile industry delayed any action on the disease in the United States until the 1970s.

Anyone who worked in the card room knew that the dust caused problems, but, like Grover Hardin, they "didn't pay much attention to it. See, there was a continuous fog of dust in the carding department at all times. When you hit the mill on Monday morning, you'd have a tough time. You'd cough and sneeze and fill your mouth full of tobacco and anything else to keep this dust from strangling you." This "Monday morning sickness" was the first stage of byssinosis, caused by irritation of the air passages. There would be little recurrence of the problem during the rest of the week as workers adjusted to the dust. But the coughing returned every Monday because a day or two away from the mill increased "susceptibility." After a period of ten years or more, the coughing became more persistent. Grover Hardin "got to noticing it bothering me. I took these coughs and I couldn't get over them, and I'd go home and cough and cough and cough." Rather than pay doctor's fees, he asked the advice of other workers who had the same problem—"the ones that was able to go to the doctor, I'll put it like that." Most told him they had "a little touch of asthma," so Grover took "home remedies" for asthma. "As time passed on, it'd get worse. On Mondays, I'd go in and it'd sure enough be worse by the night. Tuesday, Wednesday, it'd get a little better. I guess I'd get my lungs plugged up good. Over the weekend you'd clear your lungs up pretty good, then Monday morning, it'd be the same thing."

Like many workers with byssinosis, Hardin gradually began having difficulty running his job and started missing work. "Nothing I could take for asthma would do this breathing any good. I couldn't get no air in my lungs, and I slowed up. It got to where I had to push on the job to stay up in the mill. And when I'd get a spare minute I'd go over and lay in the windows and get all the air I could." Finally, he had to quit.

Dust was only one hazard in the card room. Accidents around the machinery mangled hands and arms; one worker called carding the "dangerousest job in the mill." In the early days, belts connected the machines to drive shafts high above, and carders had to pay careful attention as they cleaned and adjusted their equipment. "It was pretty dangerous," explained Carl Thompson. "You'd have to watch yourself. There were so many things that you could do. Even cleaning up, if maybe your brush would get caught in a belt or a pulley, it's going to jerk your hand. I've seen them jerked in the cards thataway and maybe get their whole arm and all broke and the skin pulled off, maybe slam through the bone."

One incident in particular accounted for Thompson's fears. "I'd seen so many get hurt on them, get their arms broke. That was when they had overhead pulleys, had the pulleys at the top of the mill. There was one man, his shirt or something or other got caught in the belt, and that belt throwed him to the top of the mill and busted his brains out. He just hit the ceiling of the mill. They had big beams up there, and he hit them, right at the back of his head. It killed him."

Working conditions were even more disagreeable in the weave room. The environment was dominated by the constant noise of banging looms and the eerie mist that descended from overhead sprinklers. "It was a loud, noisy place, and awful dusty and linty," remembered Edna Hargett. The moisture was particularly troublesome. "The weave room was always wet," explained Mack Duncan. "Back then, you had to have a lot of water in the weave room. The air wasn't conditioned like it is now, scientifically; there was just water being sprayed out. It was atomized and sprayed out to make the weaving run. It was wet in the back alley. There was a loom fixer taking a loom down one time, and he slipped and grabbed at the beam on the rail, and the beam probably weighed two hundred and fifty pounds, maybe more. It was above him, and it fell on him and killed him."

Less dramatic than occasional accidents, but no less threatening, were the complications that resulted from breathing warm, moist air filled with lint. Naomi Trammell was one of the fortunate ones; she had a doctor who recognized the problem. "I went to the weave room one time, and I like to took galloping TB. It'd be just wet all over, so hot, you know. And that just give 'em TB. That doctor told me when he doctored me about two weeks, 'Now, young lady, you can go back to the cloth room and live, or you can go back to the weave room and die, whichever you want to do.' So I went back to the cloth room."

Spinning had its own peculiar hazards. "Oh, it was awful hot," Alice Evitt remembered. "All that machinery a-runnin' makin' heat. It was bad. Terrible hot out here. You'd come out of there, your clothes was plumb wet." Mozelle Riddle described conditions in the Bynum mill. "It used to be so hot before they put air-conditioning in there. You could walk into the frames and burn your legs, that's how hot the heat was. Them motors'd burn you, when you'd walk around them. But we just got used to it. Didn't think nothing about it. It'd be eighty, oh shoot, it'd be ninety degrees in there in that spinning room. Work and sweat, yes sir." Eva Hopkins recalled the heat, too. "They didn't have air-conditioning in the mills and it was terribly hot. They wouldn't let you raise the windows very high: air would come in; it would make the ends come down. Sometimes they'd let you prop a bobbin under them. I'd put the window up at the end of my frame, then here'd come the section man along and take it down. When he'd leave and go off, I'd raise it again. I couldn't stand the heat."

The threat of serious injuries was all around. Most of the fast-moving machine parts were exposed, and any slip-up could have disastrous consequences. Alice Evitt remembered getting her "apron tore off two or three times a week" while running speeder frames. "Back then, they didn't wear pants. Them big flyers flyin' around, they'd grab you and just wind your apron plumb up. I was just lucky I managed to stop 'em and didn't get my arms in them. Them flyers would break your bones. I know one lady—I didn't see her get it done—but she said she wore wigs [because] she'd got her hair caught and it pulled her whole scalp out—every bit of her hair. Them speeders was bad to catch you." Evitt and her co-workers often joked about such things. "Sometimes they'd get under the frames and reach and get a-hold of somebody's dress and jerk 'em. Make 'em think the machine had 'em. Try to scare them."

When accidents did occur, there was little relief for those who suffered. "Back before now," Mack Duncan recalled, "if you got hurt on the job, you just was hurt. If you couldn't work, you had to go home; you lost your pay. Back before

World War II you didn't get much help." James Pharis remained bitter about the way he was treated when he had an accident in the mill. "I was about nine or ten years old when I got that hand hurt. I was riding on an elevator rope in the mill. My hand got caught under the wheel. That thing was mashed into jelly; all of it was just smashed to pieces. They took me down to the company store—the drug store was in the front end of the company store—never even notified my people or nothing. There were only two doctors in town at that time, and both of them was out of town on country calls. I sat there until about four o'clock. Nobody done nothing in the world for me. My people was never notified. Nothing said about it. You tear yourself all to pieces then, nothing said about getting anything out of it. Poor people like us, no use in suing. Poor people didn't stand a chance. If you done anything the company didn't like, they'd just fire you and tell the rest of [the owners] not to hire you. So there'd you be. People who lived under them circumstances, back in them days, was nothing they could do. So they didn't try to do nothing."

Lloyd Davidson summed up the situation. "The only insurance back then they had was to protect the company. They looked out for the company interest, but you didn't have any benefit. There was no retirement, no hospitalization, no benefits whatsoever, as far as for helping you. They carried insurance to protect the company. [People] probably have [sued], but it's a losing cause when you do. They have their own lawyers and they always have the upper hand, you might say. Kind of like David and Goliath. I reckon you could put it that way." . . .

 ## For Further Study

1. From this account, what would you conclude to be the most important reasons for people to be attracted to work in the mills? Were the reasons the same for children as they were for adult workers?

2. Detail the pros and cons of child labor from the point of view of mill workers, mill owners, and outsiders.

3. What specific conditions in the mills were dangerous or unhealthy for workers? To what extent do you suppose such conditions were duplicated or approximated in other industries, such as mining, steel making, or railroading?

4. How do you explain the apparent callousness of mill owners concerning the dangers their workers faced on the job? Why were the workers able to do so little to improve conditions?

5. To what extent have safety conditions in industrial work improved? Are workers in any industries today exposed to dangers comparable to those in the early textile mills?

For Further Reading

C. Vann Woodward, *The Origins of the New South, 1877–1913* (1951), is a general history of the South with particular emphasis on its economic development. Edward L. Ayers, *The Promise of the New South* (1992), is a more recent treatment of the same subject. Melton A. McLaurin, *Paternalism and Protest: Southern Cotton Mill Workers and Organized Labor* (1971), and David Carlton, *Mill and Town in South Carolina, 1880–1920* (1982), deal with the same subject as the present selection. Ronald D. Eller, *Miners, Millhands, and Mountaineers: Industrialization of the Appalachian South, 1880–1930* (1982), tells another part of the story of Southern factory labor. Stanley Buder, *Pullman: An Experiment in Industrial Order and Community Planning, 1880–1930* (1967), and Crandall A. Shifflett, *Coal Towns: Life, Work, and Culture in Company Towns of Southern Appalachia, 1880–1960* (1991), both deal with company towns similar to those described in the selection. Melvin Dubofsky, *Industrialism and the American Worker, 1865–1920* (1975), has a more general focus. The essays in Herbert Gutman's *Work, Culture, and Society in Industrializing America* (1976), also discuss the working and living conditions American workers confronted in the late 1800s. Edward C. Kirkland, *Dream and Thought in the Business Community, 1860–1900* (1956), describes the ideas and values held by most American businessmen of the time, while Daniel T. Rodgers, *The Work Ethic in Industrial America, 1850–1920* (1978), analyzes a widely held and fundamentally important set of beliefs.

Chapter 5

Pennsylvania State Archives, Charles H. Burg Collection, (MG-273)

Strikers on their way to the Lattimer mines.

Labor Violence in Industrial America

Michael Novak

Today state and federal laws protect the rights of workers to form unions and engage in collective bargaining for higher wages and better working conditions, but this was not the case in the late 1800s. Then, when workers tried to organize and act together to protect themselves against wage cuts, job insecurity, and long hours of labor, often under dangerous and unhealthy conditions, employers and others responded with fear and anger, especially when workers went on strike in the attempt to enforce their demands. This clash of interests and feelings resulted in many outbreaks of labor violence, such as the railroad strike of 1877, the strike by steel workers at Homestead, Pennsylvania in 1892, the Pullman strike in 1894, and dozens of others.

The present selection focuses on the massacre of nineteen Slavic miners in an eastern Pennsylvania coal town in 1897. The tragedy reveals elements common to many other instances of labor violence during the period. For example, when workers went out on strike, it was a fairly common practice for employers to hire armed private police. The stated reasons for this were "to preserve order" and "to protect private property," but usually the purpose was to guarantee that employers would have enough force on their side to break the strike by whatever means they thought necessary. In addition, employers usually had the support of local law enforcement officials and were often able to call on state and even the national government for help. Finally, whenever the strikers were mostly foreign-born, as they were at Lattimer, ethnic and religious prejudices intensified the hatred directed toward them.

The outcome of the story of what happened at Lattimer is also important in understanding the labor situation at the time. Although the account makes clear that the sheriff and the deputies who killed the strikers could well be considered guilty of multiple counts of outright murder, they were never

> convicted; the jury at their trial chose to overlook much of the evidence. Some of the nation's newspapers criticized the verdict, but most applauded it, sharing the sentiments of the New York *Sun*, which said that the outcome showed that "American civilization is safe under the protection of the law."

On Friday morning, the sun rose brilliant. A gang of the breaker boys from Harwood planned to go swimming. By the time the men began to assemble for the march to Lattimer Mines, some had already been out over the hills in Butler Valley to pick berries. At nine o'clock, John Hlavaty, a Slovak from Lattimer, came to the home of Thomas Racek in Harwood and said again that the men at Lattimer planned to walk out that afternoon if the men from Harwood would come to call them out. Racek took Hlavaty to Jacob Sivar's house, and they called the men together. There was still discussion as to whether a large crowd should go to Lattimer or whether they should just send a committee. Some said everyone should go, or else the company might blacklist the men on the committee. This idea was generally approved.

The men recalled John Fahy's instructions of the night before about the sheriff and his armed men. Fahy had warned them not even to take marching sticks, like the garden fence poles that walkers in these parts usually carried. He instructed them about the rights of free assembly, but also about the sheriff's use of the riot act. Yesterday, he told them, the sheriff's men had fired warning shots and were reported to be more and more hostile; great caution was necessary. Fahy did not plan to accompany the marchers to Lattimer. He said he would be posting signs in nearby Milnesville; he would come over to Lattimer later. He never took part in marches.

John Eagler, who was to lead the march, was excited. He had sent a message to Alex McMullen inviting the McAdoo men to come along. McMullen said no. Echoing Fahy, he warned Eagler again not to march without an American flag. So Eagler told the men to hold off until he could find a flag to carry. With three companions, Andro Sivar, Joseph Michalko, and August Kosko, he hiked over to Humboldt.

Those who waited behind decided that the youngest boys would not be permitted to march. It would be twelve miles or more, round trip, under a broiling sun. Only boys over fifteen would be allowed to accompany the men; these were sent inside to put on shoes and decent dress. Some of the men may have fortified themselves with a little whiskey; in any case, the sheriff was later to allege so.

From *The Guns of Lattimer*, by Michael Novak. Copyright © 1978 by Michael Novak.

Meanwhile, unknown to the marchers, someone from Harwood—possibly an employee at the company store—telephoned Sheriff Martin about the plan to march, its route, and destination.

In the days just before the march, visible signs of conflict frightened some of the American women of Harwood, who nervously embroidered on them at the trial. Thus, for example, Mrs. Catherine Weisenborn heard one foreigner threaten another: "If you don't come, we'll kill you." She also testified she heard some strikers threaten people like her: "We'll show the *white people* what we'll do when we come back!" . . .

By the time John Eagler got back, the men had had time for an early lunch. A cheer went up when they saw Eagler and Sivar return with not one, but two flags. Stragglers poured out of the houses. Steve Jurich kissed his pretty bride, and the others teased them both. The older men waved good-bye to their families. At almost every doorway and out in the street women and children waved and shouted as the men moved into position. Eagler and Joseph Michalko walked down the line, telling individuals to discard their walking sticks and suggesting that they start out four abreast. There were between 250 and 300 men. They started from two separate locations and met at the picnic grounds. Joseph Michalko and Steve Jurich walked out in front with the American flags snapping in the breeze. A crowd of breaker boys fell in behind the flags, but their elders sent them unhappily away. As this unarmed band got themselves organized to answer the request of their Italian brothers at the Lattimer Mines, many were taking part in the first civic act of their lives. Most had not been in the previous marches; Eagler hadn't; Cheslak hadn't. Most had never laid eyes on Sheriff Martin; none, perhaps, had seen the guns of the deputies. It was just after one when the command "Forward march!" was shouted by Michalko.

As they walked along, they picked up new recruits. They did not aim to create a big crowd, and they did not plan to have a large rally. Frequently, they called out to friends lined up to watch them on their route. . . . The men were relaxed and festive. For the past year, most had worked only one day out of every two, and the activities of the strike—giving promise of some small but basic changes in their lives—seemed far preferable to being out of work.

The night before, the strikers had formulated three grievances and taken them to the superintendent at Harwood. They demanded a pay raise of 10¢ a day, a reduction in the price of powder from $2.75 a keg to $1.50, and an end to the company store and the company doctor. They particularly resented the prices at the company store: a dozen eggs that cost 13¢ at an independent store cost 23¢ from the company; butter at 8¢ a pound elsewhere cost 26¢; and the powder they needed for their work came from the manufacturer at 90¢ to $1.00 a keg. On the average, excess charges to miners in the Hazleton region worked out to $217.50 per capita per annum.

Their ranks swollen by recruits from Crystal Ridge and Cranberry, four hundred men were now raising a cloud of dust on their way toward Hazleton, jackets over their arms, their handkerchiefs often in use to wipe their necks and brows.

No effort was made on this day, as there had been on others, to close down other breakers as they passed. They passed the Cranberry breaker, calling to their friends, shouting threats to scab workers. The marchers were unarmed and determined to be peaceful, in order to avoid trouble with the sheriff.

The strikers felt patriotic under the flag. They also felt protected. Marching down into the valley and up the opposite hill, the thin yellow dust rising in the still air behind them, many felt a surge of purpose and accomplishment. John Eagler, at nineteen, although walking at their head, was not really in charge; neither was Michalko. Older leaders like Anthony Novotny, Mike Cheslak, Andrej Sivar, and others quite naturally talked things through and decisions emerged among them by common consent. Each had been carefully reared not to be boastful, assertive, or proud. No one should be in the position of attracting criticism. The traditions of serfdom and peasant life operated like censors upon anyone who might stand out too far above the group. Oppression from above had been internalized. The community cut would-be leaders down to size.

Harwood lay two miles southwest of Hazleton. The plan was to proceed by the road at the bottom of Buck Mountain and on up through the city of Hazleton. This would be the shortest route to Lattimer Mines on the far northeast side of town. Even so, the march would be about six miles.

It was almost two when the marchers in the front line caught sight of armed men hurrying toward them in West Hazleton. . . .

Deputy Ario Pardee Platt boasted of ancestors who had fought in the Revolutionary War, in the War of 1812, and in the Civil War. (During 1861–65, little Hazleton had supplied almost two thousand men to the Union cause.) Platt was the chief bookkeeper of the Pardee company, and the general manager of its company stores in Hazleton, Harwood, and Lattimer Mines. It made his blood boil to see all these foreigners carrying the flag his ancestors had championed. Platt was looking for action, he had wanted action all along and was not happy with the overcareful way the sheriff had been handling things.

Thomas Hall, another deputy, was a leader in the Coal and Iron Police. He was a man who had organized the posse for the sheriff and who directed it in the sheriff's absence. Before the strike had even begun, as far back as August 12, the owners of the mine companies had called a meeting in Hazleton to discuss their dissatisfaction with the performance of the Coal and Iron Police. Even without a strike looming up before them, they were complaining that they were paying for one hundred policemen, paying well, too, and not getting the protection they needed. The police were spending too much time at Hungarian weddings, they said, and not enough time protecting property. They were paying for protection and they intended to have it. The tenor of the meeting was then leaked to the newspapers. So now, only one month later, Thomas Hall was not of a mind to occasion any further dissatisfaction from his employers. It would be his task to teach Sheriff Martin the way things were done in the lower end of the county and to keep the pressure on him to do them. His own neck was at stake.

Deputy Alonzo Dodson was a miner who lived in Hazleton. He was heard to say, "We ought to get so much a head for shooting down these strikers. I would do it for a cent a head to make money at it."

Deputies George and James Ferry—the latter known to everyone as Pinky—were also heard to say at McKenna's Corner that they would blow the strikers' brains out. Perhaps it was the power of suggestion that was working on the consciousness of the deputies, for one of them, Harry Diehl, even threatened to blow out the brains of Herman Pottunger, if he did not get off the road. Pottunger himself heard Deputy Wesley Hall say of the marchers: "I'd like to get a pop at them." . . .

Also among the deputies were Robert Tinner, the superintendent of the Central Pennsylvania Telephone and Supply Company, Willard Young, a lumber merchant and contractor, and Samuel B. Price, who held the contract to build a new breaker in Harwood, work on which was being held up by the strike. All in all about forty deputies had accompanied Sheriff Martin to West Hazleton. Nearly all these men owed their livelihood, or a portion of it, to the mining companies. Other deputies were waiting for the marchers at Lattimer.

Sheriff Martin's fondest hope seems clearly to have been to put an end to the march right at West Hazleton. But he was in something of a spot. He knew he didn't have jurisdiction inside the city, at least not without consultation, and the marchers had already reached McKenna's Corner. He was being pressured to "teach the strikers a lesson" that would get them off the roads. His own inclination still seemed to be to keep matters peaceable and under his control.

The sheriff walked directly toward the two men carrying flags, Andro Sivar and Joseph Michalko. He had his pistol in one hand. He took the nearest man, John Yurchekowicz, by the coat, brandishing the revolver in his face, and announced vigorously: "I'm the sheriff of Luzerne County, and you cannot go to Lattimer."

Steve Juszko pushed past Yurchekowicz, saying defiantly, "Me no stop. Me go to Lattimer."

The sheriff again said: "If you go to Lattimer, you must kill me first."

John Eagler, who had been fifty paces back in the line when it stopped, walked forward and now spoke up in a reedy voice. "We ain't goin' to. We are going to Lattimer. We harm no one. We are within the law."

Before the words were fully out of Eagler's mouth, Anthony Kislewicz [variants: Kascavage, etc.] bent over for a flat rock (he later said) to strike a match for his pipe during the halt. One of the deputies brought the butt of his rifle down viciously on Kislewicz's arm. Then Deputy Hall moved toward Steve Juszko, who had stepped forward, and swung through the air twice with his rifle butt, crunching across the two arms the boy raised to protect himself and hitting his head. Blood flowed. Both arms hung limp.

The sheriff pointed his pistol right and left as though holding off a legion.

Ario Pardee Platt, fired up by the bloodshed, ripped the flag from Joseph Michalko's hands, broke the stick across his knee, and stood there shredding the flag with contempt. He dropped the torn rags in the dust.

John Eagler, watching Deputy Cook raise his gun, stopped to pick up a stone. The sheriff waved his pistol and Eagler dropped the stone. Other deputies mixed it up briskly with the marchers.

Deputy Cook fired a shot into the air and the hillside reverberated. The marchers did not move. They were baffled.

John Eagler stepped forward to obtain the name of the deputy he had seen hit Juszko. Sheriff Martin held Eagler with a gesture and pulled a paper from his pocket. The sheriff had seen disorder and now had his opportunity. "This is my proclamation and you can't go any farther. It's against the law."

Then Chief of Police Jones walked forward shouting to John Eagler and the sheriff, and Sheriff Martin put his paper back in his pocket. Jones told the sheriff the strikers had a right to march peacefully, and he, the sheriff, knew it. To Novotny the chief said he had confidence in the way the marchers were conducting themselves; he would let them march around the edges of West Hazleton but not go through the city. He was willing to show them how they could go, so as to continue on to Lattimer in peace. . . .

Murderous joking, meanwhile, seems to have gripped the deputies. They had talked all morning about shooting and killing. Herman Pottunger heard a deputy say quietly to a friend: "I bet I drop six of them when I get over there." August Katski and Martin Lochar stood near the trolley car as the departing deputies were boarding. Two deputies went after them and hit them, but one said: "Let them go until we get to Lattimer and then we'll shoot them." It may have been a form of macabre humor, intended only to frighten.

William A. Evans, the reporter, arrived just after the confrontation, while the men were still standing on opposite sides of the road. He saw one of the strikers picking up a stone as Ario Pardee Platt tore the flag. No stone was actually thrown.

Doctor John Koons of Hazleton was called by the chief of police to treat the two wounded men in the jail. One of the men—Juszko—had to be examined by force. His scalp wounds required nine stitches. Juszko appears to have been listed the next day as among the wounded in the hospital. Six months later, he was still unable to use his arms.

Chief Jones did, as he offered, point the way for the marchers to cut through West Hazleton, adding another mile or so to the trip. It was after 2:30 when the marchers returned to their original plan. Now only one American flag waved in the sun, but the men were feeling vindicated and safe under the law. Mike Krupa from Crystal Ridge had joined them in West Hazleton with several of his friends, and the marchers made Krupa and his friends throw away their walking sticks. George Yamshak also joined them and was told to throw away the small stick he was carrying. The marchers had learned that their best protection was lack of arms. . . .

Later, the editorialists were not to overlook the symbolism of the day and the hour. It was almost three o'clock and the detachment of deputies assigned to wait at Lattimer was restless. A mile away, at Harleigh, Sheriff Martin and the deputies who had seen action at West Hazleton sat in the trolley and waited. Some removed plug hats to wipe away the sweat under their hatbands. Others fingered their Winchesters. A few of them were later to claim that they believed then that the miners had guns in their pockets; some even may have believed it. . . .

For the deputies sitting on that trolley in front of Farley's Hotel in Harleigh, the waiting was almost over. In a cloud of dust, the marchers were beginning to appear around the bend, the lone American flag still at their head. The deputies watched the strikers pause while eight men or so from the first two lines huddled. The other marchers broke ranks to drink water from a pump. The question for the huddled leaders, posed by John Eagler, was whether to march first to breaker Number One in Lattimer Mines or to breaker Number Three. Finally the strikers started walking again. John Laudmesser, the hotel-keeper, counted the marchers as they passed, there were 424. . . .

In the past, strikers had often changed plans in unexpected ways, and the sheriff was taking no chances. He ordered the trolley to stay right alongside the marchers. For almost a mile, deputies and strikers went along eyeing one another. A few insults may have been exchanged. At the last fork in the road, when it was plain that the strikers could be taking no other road except into Lattimer, the sheriff ordered the trolley to speed up and race ahead to the village.

In Lattimer there was by now considerable commotion. The colliery whistle sounded a warning. Those deputies and private police who had already been waiting in Lattimer had made their preparations. One of them told Mrs. Craig, "Go inside, as there may be some shooting today." Trolley cars shuttled in from Milnesville, Drifton, and points north. Doors slammed. Some mothers hurried to the school to bring their children home. Fear of the foreigners had been intense ever since the Tuesday before, when a band of noisy strikers had marched through the village.

On his arrival by trolley, Sheriff Martin took command of the assembling deputies. His force, bolstered by some of the new deputies from Drifton, now numbered almost one hundred and fifty. Some of them stood guard at the breakers and the superintendent's office. He divided the others into three companies, under Samuel Price, A. E. Hess, and Thomas Hall. He called the men down off the trolley bank and stationed them across the single road leading into Lattimer, just before it forked into Main Street and Quality Row, with the schoolhouse lane above. Dissatisfied, he then ordered all of them off the road to take up positions in an enfilading crescent on the lower, north side of the road. In this way, they would be able to cover the entire length of the march as it filed in front of them. The Craig house on the end of Main Street was surrounded by a white picket fence. Inside, Mrs. Craig fretted nervously. Outside, across the street, stood a tall gumberry tree, later to become known as "the massacre tree." Almost in its shade, Sheriff Martin stood near the house with the white fence and looked up the empty road toward Harleigh. As he did so, A. E. Hess was showing his men one last time how to fire their guns.

From where the sheriff stood, the road swept gently upward over the brow of a distant hill. Not far from where it came over the hill, the trolley track crossed over it and continued to parallel it on the south but on a raised embankment. The marchers would come over the hill and then be caught between the embankment and the line of Winchesters. In addition, the road then gradually curved closer and closer to the deputies down toward the house where the sheriff was now standing. Thus, if the marchers kept coming, their first rank would be no farther than fifteen yards from the line of deputies, and those in the last ranks would be no farther than thirty or forty yards. The sheriff was satisfied and strode up the line a little, nearer to the center of his deputies. . . .

At last the marchers came over the hill. Next door to the Craig house, John Airy watched from his home as the unarmed marchers walked in rank toward him. As at West Hazleton, so at Lattimer the marchers felt secure under the law. In the first two rows were Steve Jurich, carrying the flag, John Eagler, John Pustag, Michael Malody, Mike Cheslak, wearing an odd pointed cap, Andro Novotny, and George Jancso. All were from the two counties of Saris and Zemplin in Slovakia.

After dismissing their students when anxious mothers came to gather their youngsters, Charles Guscott and Grace Coyle, the teachers, stood at the doorway of the schoolhouse, and watched the slow-motion drama unfold. They stood about one hundred yards from the gumberry tree. About sixty of the ninety men in the deputies' line, they later recalled, had their rifles raised in firing position as the strikers, led by the flag, began to file past them.

Sheriff Martin told Hess and Price to keep an eye on him. He said he would find out the marchers' intentions. "If they say they are not going to do anything I may let them go on and we will go along with them." When the flag had come about two-thirds of the way past the far flank, Sheriff Martin strode forward as he had now done on four previous occasions to see if he could handle the situation alone. He had his revolver drawn. He held up one hand. The men kept coming as he advanced and he had his hand almost in their faces when he announced in of-ficial manner: "You must stop marching and disperse." Those a few ranks back could not hear him at all, and the others behind them could not see him. "This is contrary to the law and you are creating a disturbance. You must go back. I won't let you go to the colliery."

The front ranks stumbled, trying to halt. Someone from behind called out in English, "Go ahead!" The marchers behind kept coming. The front row was pushed forward.

Angered, the sheriff reached first for the flag. But Steve Jurich pulled it erect. Then the sheriff reached into the second row and grabbed Michael Malody by the coat, thinking that he was the one who had said, "Go ahead!" The sheriff didn't know which man was the leader. Frightened, Malody insisted he hadn't said a word. Andro Novotny, who was next to Malody, intervened in his defense. The sheriff then grabbed Novotny with one hand and pulled his revolver up, aiming it at Novotny's chest. By now, the sheriff had pulled four or more men to the deputies' side of the road. The other marchers continued on. Eagler was among those pushed partially forward down the road. Those near the sheriff—including, now, men from the rear like John Terri and Martin Shefronik (Šefronik)—were afraid and puzzled.

"Where are you going?" the sheriff asked, pulling on Novotny and beginning to panic. The front of the column was getting farther and farther past him. Novotny said in English, "Let me alone!" He swept his arms up and pushed the barrel of the sheriff's revolver away from his own chest.

George Jancso reached in and pulled the sheriff's other hand free from Novotny. The sheriff then grabbed Jancso's coat and pointed his pistol at Jancso's forehead; Jancso and Eagler heard the pistol snap—Sheriff Martin also felt it snap—but it did not fire.

In that instant, the sheriff's second in command, Samuel Price, left the line of deputies and stepped forward to come to the surrounded sheriff's assistance. Other deputies frantically called him back, since he was now in the line of fire. He stepped back.

Mrs. Kate Case from her third-floor window heard someone shout "Fire." She thought the deputies were firing over the marchers' heads. Then she saw some marchers fall. She screamed.

Novotny heard the sheriff command, "Fire," and Jancso heard him shout "Give two or three shots!" Some witnesses thought that in the struggle the sheriff had fallen briefly to his knees; others said he remained standing. His body was directly between the deputies and Jancso when a shot rang out, then three or four in unison. The sheriff raised both arms as though to stop the action. But a full volley rang out again and again.

Watching from the schoolhouse, Charles Guscott saw the first puff of smoke come from the fourth or fifth man from the farthest end of the deputies' line, Hess's men. It seemed to those closer that the whole line erupted with fire.

Steve Jurich had held the flag and was the first to fall. "*O Joj! Joj! Joj!*" he cried in the ancient Slovak cry to God. "Enough! Enough!" Bullets shattered his head and he died as he bled.

John Eagler saw Cheslak drop, his peculiar peaked hat falling from his head, so he, too, dropped to the ground. Eagler saw trickles of blood flowing in the dust toward him from Cheslak's head. He realized then that the deputies were not using blanks.

John Terri threw himself on the ground. Another striker fell on him, dead. Terri saw Cheslak beside him and tried to speak to him. Cheslak's eyes were open but he did not speak. Then Terri got up and ran.

Andro Sivar, in the fourth row, turned his back at the first shot. When the man beside him caught a bullet in the back, Sivar fell with him. Michael Kuchar, nineteen, was about ten yards from the sheriff and could neither hear nor see what was happening in front; at the loud shouting, he threw himself down. George Jancso tore himself from the hands of the sheriff and ran to throw himself in a ditch as flat and close to mother earth as he could press himself.

Martin Shefronik stood close to Jurich, and saw blood spurt out the back of Jurich's head and also from his mouth. As he dropped, Jurich was completely drenched with blood. Shefronik ran toward the schoolhouse, until he was thrown forward by the impact of a bullet in his shoulder. John Putski of Harwood also ran toward the schoolhouse until a bullet in his right arm and another in his leg spun him to the ground. Andrew Jurechek ran toward the schoolhouse and almost reached safety before a bullet struck his back and exploded through his stomach.

Watching from the schoolhouse, teachers Charles Guscott and Grace Coyle had looked on in horror as dust and acrid gunsmoke filled the air. "They're firing blanks," Miss Coyle said. "No, see them dropping," Guscott said. The firing went on for two or three minutes. Some deputies turned, wheeled, and followed running men, shooting some down at a distance of 300 yards. Many men ran toward the schoolhouse; one was hit, spinning, just before he reached the terrified teachers. Other shots crashed into the schoolhouse sending showers of splinters. Running toward the teachers, Clement Platek clutched his side; he too was crying: "*O Joj! Joj! Joj!*" The teachers saw, in addition to those mentioned: the brains of one man splattered forward; still another hapless man shot through the neck so that his head was almost severed. Grace Coyle ran forward to help Andrew Jurechek, who was clutching at the entrails slipping from his stomach and who cried out to her: "No! Me want to see wife. Before die." He died before her eyes. His wife was heavy with child.

Mathias Czaja had been standing ten or twelve feet from the sheriff. He had seen the sheriff pull his revolver and point it at the man with the flag. He had heard him say, "If you go any farther, I will shoot you." He had been frightened. He did not hear the order to fire. His back was blown open by a bullet.

Michael Srokach (Srokač) saw eight deputies run forward thirty yards or so to gain better shots. From the public road, the miners fled backward toward the trolley line and up over its bank, either up the hill west toward Harleigh or east toward the schoolhouse.

One man fled as far as a telephone pole on the trolley line when he was hit. He pulled himself up, holding to the pole. As other shots poured into him, his body buckled two or three times. He slid to the earth.

William Raught and another deputy, according to several witnesses, broke from the line of deputies in order to pursue the fleeing strikers. In order to get a line of fire, Raught and the other man climbed up on the trolley tracks, still firing. Srokach heard some deputies answer pleas from the wounded with the shout: "We'll give you hell, not water, hunkies!" Others heard: "Shoot the sons of bitches!"

The smoke from the first volley was thick. Dust was raised by men running. For a while it was difficult to see. From his home, John Airy saw deputies take careful aim and pick men off as they were running to get in the shelter of the hillside. "They shot man after man in the back," he reported. "The slaughter was awful." He estimated that the deputies fired "at least 150" shots. "They kept firing for some time. Men fell on the ground and screamed in agony and tried to drag themselves from the murderous guns. At last it was all over."

Cries of pain, groans, and shrieks remained. Andro Sivar got up from a circle of dead and wounded. Andrew Meyer—seventeen-year-old breaker boy—pleaded for help for his shattered knees. John Slobodnik, wounded in the back of the head just above the neck cried out for water. Slobodnik and John Banko, also shot in the head, were carried by friends to Farley's Hotel in Harleigh, looking for medical attention of some kind. John Eagler ran, bent over, for 150 yards before he turned. He saw one of the men from Crystal Ridge bleeding from his arm and back. The man asked him: "Butty, loosen me suspenders and collar, they hurt me much." Eagler pulled down the man's shirt and saw a big hole in the back of his neck spouting thick blood. He pushed a handkerchief in the hole. Then he bent to help Frank Tages. He pulled off his own coat, put it around his friend, led him to a trolley car for a ride to the hospital. Sick and afraid, Eagler saw some of the deputies begin to offer water to the wounded. Then he started on the long walk back to Harwood. In shock, he could not comprehend what had just happened.

Cornelius Burke was eleven years old and lived in Lattimer II, the next settlement up from Lattimer. During recess from school, he was overcome by curiosity about the commotion in town and ran down to Lattimer to see the excitement. He was part way up Main Street when he heard the terrific crack of rifles. When he got up to the site, he recalls, ". . . Oh, my God, the poor fellows were lying across the trolley tracks on the hillside, some had died and some were dying. Some were crying out for water." Connie picked up a little can and carried water to one of the dying miners. "It was a terrible sight and so much confusion existed. Everyone was running in all directions. They searched the men who were shot and found they carried no weapons."

One of the deputies, George Treible, was wounded by a bullet that creased both his arms. The Wilkes-Barre *Times* reported that he believed he was shot by one of his own men, who had wheeled to fire after the dispersing strikers. Bullets flew, Treible said, in every direction. Some of the deputies at the right end of the crescent (farthest from Lattimer), who seem to have fired most of the shots, were shooting back toward Lattimer at the strikers fleeing toward the schoolhouse. "The deputies," said the paper, "were not under control. The odor of smoke inflamed them."

The fury of some was not yet spent. Some of the deputies walked among the fallen, kicking them and cursing them. A. E. Hess told one bystander who was crying shame, "Shut up or you will get the same dose." John Terri, who had fallen beside Cheslak, went through the smoke of battle to find water for his wounded uncle and cousin. Asked for water, a deputy named Clark said, "Give them hell," grabbed Terri, kicked him, and held him prisoner for an hour. Joseph Costello, a Hazleton butcher, saw Hess kick a prostrate victim (who was in fact Andrew Meyer) and denounced Hess for the butchery. Hess told him, too, to shut up. Grace Coyle, the schoolteacher, upbraided Hess for his manner among the fallen, with his cigar in his mouth. Hess did not defend himself.

John Welsh saw Sheriff Martin after the shooting and asked him how he was.

"I am not well," Sheriff Martin said.

The sheriff was pale and shaken. He turned his revolver over to a detective. Many of his deputies had fled and some went into hiding. Some of the others were lifting the wounded into conveyances. But John Airy witnessed the most saddening scene of all: "The trolley car in which the sheriff and his deputies came was right in front of my house and the officers got in it. They were laughing and telling each other how many men they killed." Another bystander also heard them: "Yes, and one of them said he took down a dozen 'Hunks,' and knew what he was shooting at every time. He was boasting of what a fine shooter he was. They sat there for some time, joking and laughing about it, and then they rode back to the city."

 ## For Further Study

1. What impression do you get of the relationships in this mining town—between the workers and their employers, the workers and the law enforcement officers, and among the workers?

2. Is there any nativistic (anti-immigrant) sentiment in the community? If so, what evidence is there for it; if not, how do you account for its absence? Also, do the nativistic tendencies appear to be universal in the community?

3. What is the attitude of the workers toward their adopted country—the United States? Document your answer.

4. What impression do you get of the degree of professionalism of the deputies?

5. Do you feel, on the basis of the narrative, that the verdict of the jury (see the Introduction to the selection) was a fair one? If so, why; if not, why not?

6. Turn to the author of the narrative. (a) Is he dispassionate in his account, or do you sense that he has some strong feelings about what happened? Document your answer—either way. (b) Does it surprise you to learn that he is a spokesman for ethnicity in our country, the founder of a movement to promote ethnic pride among immigrant groups and their descendants? (c) What evidence is there in this essay of ethnic pride on Novak's part? Is it, in your opinion, justified, or to put the question another way: did the miners, in your opinion, act in a legal and patriotic manner? If so, on what evidence; if not, on what evidence?

For Further Reading

In addition to the book from which the preceding selection was taken, Michael Novak, *The Guns of Lattimer* (1978), the following provide information on labor, unions, strikes, and labor violence in the late 1800s: Paul Avrich, *The Haymarket Tragedy* (1984); Melvin Dubofsky, *Industrialism and the American Worker, 1865–1920* (1975), and *We Shall Be All: A History of the Industrial Workers of the World* (1969); Philip Foner, *The Great Labor Uprising of 1877* (1977). Harold Livesay, *Samuel Gompers and Organized Labor in America* (1978), is a brief biography of an important labor leader. Stuart Kaufman, *Samuel Gompers and the Origins of the American Federation of Labor* (1973), is a fuller account of Gompers' contributions to the labor movement. Milton Meltzer, *Bread and Roses: The Struggle of American Labor, 1865–1915* (1967), is a brief but valuable general history. Leon J. Wolff, *Lockout: The Story of the Homestead Strike of 1892* (1965), focuses on one of the most important labor struggles of the time. Paul Kraus, *The Battle for Homestead, 1880–1892: Politics, Culture, and Steel* (1992), is a more recent account of the same strike that provides fuller background on the steel industry and the town of Homestead. Leon Fink, *Workingmen's Discovery: The Knights of Labor and American Politics* (1983), deals with one of the important labor organizations of that era.

Chapter 6

B.W. Kilburn/ Hulton Archive/ Getty Images

African American convict laborers, late 1800s. Prisoners were often used as a source of labor at this time.

Crime and Punishment

Lawrence M. Friedman

Controlling crime has always been a matter of concern for Americans, and the rapid changes and the growing complexity of American society in the late 1800s made it a greater concern than ever. The justice system, like many other American institutions, was under considerable strain as a result of the rapid, tumultuous, and profound social and economic changes the nation was going through. The rapid growth of cities meant that more people were living closer together than ever before, and this greatly increased the chances that one would become a crime victim, or at least that one would become more aware that others were being victimized. Such experiences helped to create a greater fear of crime than had existed before. In addition, such things as the racial tumult and violence of Reconstruction and later, the violence that often attended labor disputes, the increasing ethnic and religious diversity of many American urban centers, and the widespread political corruption combined to make many Americans fear that the society was threatened by lawlessness coming from the so-called "dangerous classes." Originally this term was used to refer to derelicts, tramps, career criminals, and so on, but its meaning was increasingly broadened so that it often included African Americans, immigrants, and industrial workers. Many Americans felt a pressing need to keep these elements of society under control. The result was a demand for heightened standards of public order.

In the following essay we see how that demand was met in regard to law enforcement and the methods of punishment for crime. Standards of professionalism among the police left much to be desired, but their numbers increased. In regard to punishment, it is often said that there are four chief reasons for putting people in jail or otherwise punishing them for their crimes: justice (making those who have done injury to others suffer for their crime), separation (keeping them apart from law-abiding citizens so that they cannot do them any further damage), deterrence (making an example of criminals so that others will be less tempted to commit crimes), and rehabilitation (making the experience of punishment such as to make it unlikely that the criminal will return to a life of crime). As the following account makes clear, some of these goals were emphasized much more heavily than others, and there was little attempt to achieve a balance among them. One wonders how effective America's jails and prisons were in protecting Americans from crime.

THE POLICE . . . WERE ESSENTIALLY AN INVENTION OF THE FIRST half of the century. In the latter half of the century, police departments were all over the map, and the old, more slipshod ways of patrolling urban (as well as rural) spaces were gone forever. Big cities had big forces; little cities had little forces. New York City was, naturally, the giant; according to the census of 1880; the city, with a population of about 1,200,000, had a force of 202 officers and 2,336 patrolmen; Kalamazoo, Michigan, with a population of 11,937, had one officer and two patrolmen (they made 175 arrests); Keokuk, Iowa, with a population of 12,117 had two officers and four patrolmen (who chalked up 1,276 arrests). If we can believe the census figures, there were, all told, in 1880, 1,752 officers and 11,948 patrolmen in cities and towns with inhabitants 45,000 or more.

It was still the case—especially in big cities—that American police departments were more overtly political than, say, in England. In this country, police officers were "primarily tools of local politicians"; when the winds of politics changed, during or between elections, jobs and policy changed with it. In Cincinnati, for example, 219 of 295 patrolmen were dismissed after the election of 1880; six years later, after another election, 238 of 289 patrolmen, and 8 of the 16 lieutenants lost their jobs.

Since local politics in many big cities meant, primarily, Democratic Party politics, the Republicans, who represented business and controlled more statehouses, found the idea of state control over the police unusually attractive. The state did take control over some cities (New York in 1857, Detroit in 1865, Cleveland in 1866, for example), but when the outs (the Democrats) regained office, they turned back the clock. Local control remained the general rule.

That is, if there was any control at all. It would be a gross exaggeration to call the police "professionals." The job had no prerequisites and called for no formal training whatsoever. The man on the beat was most of the time, entirely on his own; there was no real supervision. Nothing kept a patrolman from drinking in a tavern, or sleeping on the job. There was a long struggle to bring the policeman to heel. Rule books and codes of conduct sprouted. In 1861, the police commissioners of Chicago issued orders that "prohibited mustaches, prescribed the proper style for beards, and required that all patrolmen eat with forks." A military

---

From Lawrence M. Friedman, *Crime and Punishment in American History.*

model was the ideal: clean, disciplined, regimented. Some cities instituted military drill. City after city put their police in uniform—Jersey City (1856), Washington, D.C. (1858), New Orleans (1866), Kansas City, Missouri (1874). Every big city, and most middle-sized cities, followed suit. Terre Haute, Indiana, which made the move in 1897, was one of the last.

The uniform symbolized discipline, military precision, and the like; but it had other functions. It made the police very much a *visible* presence in the community. This was in line with the basic function of the police: to keep order in public places, to deter crimes of disorder by patrolling urban spaces. People think of the police as crime-fighters; but order is, and probably was then, their prime goal.

Order is definitely the aim of the traffic cop today; and the thousands of arrests for vagrancy, drunkenness, and disturbing the peace are supposed to guarantee order and discipline on the streets, roads, and open spaces of the city. This can be rough work at times, and hardly fit the more refined notions of due process. That concept has changed a lot over the years, but even in the nineteenth century there was some grumbling about police behavior. A lawyer in Detroit, in 1880, told the press that "Men have for years been arrested . . . 'on suspicion,' confined for days and nights in a station house where nobody is allowed to . . . communicate with him, and finally . . . 'discharged' in the same arbitrary manner," while no police judge or court would take notice of the incident. In Milwaukee, in the late nineteenth century, the police "maintained a rigid policy of arresting potential criminals on 'suspicion' and running them out of town." If the police suspected a man of some property crime but could not prove it, they locked him up, investigated, and then ordered the man out of town.

One can be sure that it was not the wealthy or the powerful who were arrested "on suspicion" and thrown into jail cells. This was also true of some (but not all) arrests for drunkenness. Drunkenness was technically a minor crime or offense. The police did not treat drunks as threats to society; after all, most police got drunk themselves once in a while. But they cleared them off the streets, or dragged them out of bars where they were brawling—or even from their homes, when they made trouble for the family. When the drunken husband of Mrs. Annie Hules, of Alameda County, locked her and her baby out of the house in 1891, she, of course, called the police.

The police tended to treat the ordinary drunkard with a kind of amused, vacant paternalism. It was important to arrest drunks, sober them up, and keep the streets in shape for respectable people. Often, the police infantilized drunks, who were mostly laborers, and often immigrants; they treated their offenses with malicious humor. This was also the attitude of the newspapers, when they reported the goings on in police court. It was, in a sense, a big joke. Laughing at drunks and skid row bums was one way to avoid taking the problem seriously.

The police also acted as a kind of catchall or residual welfare agency. This was a period in which the state (from a twentieth-century point of view) was lax and anemic. Besides, the civil service closes up shop at five o'clock and is nowhere to be found on weekends and holidays, or even at lunchtime. The eye of the police never closes. Even today, when in doubt about whom to call, people call the police. All the more so in the nineteenth century. Thus, in Oakland, California, in 1894, when people in a neighborhood fell into "a state of violent excitement" because a ghost appeared in an empty house, along with much shrieking, groaning, and clanking of chains, they called the police to get rid of it.

Ghost-busting was not a common police function, of course. But the policeman's lot was a most miscellaneous one. The Boston police, during the fiscal year ending November 30, 1887, made (we are told) 30,681 arrests. But, in addition, there were

> 1,472 accidents reported; 2,461 buildings found open and made secure . . . 37 dangerous chimneys reported; 169 dead bodies cared for; 181 defective cesspools reported; 66 defective drains reported . . . 138 defective hydrants reported; 2,611 defective lamps reported; 4 defective sewers reported; 13,614 defective streets and walks reported . . . 148 intoxicated persons assisted; 1,572 lost children found; 269 insane persons taken in charge; 228 missing persons reported; 151 missing persons found . . . 7 persons rescued from drowning; 1,673 sick and injured persons assisted; 311 stray teams found; 51,302 street obstructions removed.

It was common for police to run a sort of primitive welfare program. They collected and returned lost children; they gave shelter to the homeless. How much the police did seemed to vary a good deal from city to city. In 1880, in New York City, there were 124,318 "lodgers" in the station houses; in Philadelphia, 109,673; Cincinnati, with about one-fifth the population of New York City, housed 47,658 of the homeless; St. Louis housed none. In Philadelphia, the homeless usually got tea and crackers to sustain them. Not everybody was lucky enough to find a place in the station house, even in the generous cities; the "undeserving" could be simply turned away.

The crowd of ragged, hungry people "had a dreadful impact on the station houses"; they became filthy bedlams. There is a vivid description of tramps "crashing" in a Chicago station house in the winter of 1891: "an unventilated atmosphere of foulest pollution . . . the frowzy, ragged garments of unclean men. . . . Not a square foot of the dark, concrete floor is visible. The space is packed with men all lying on their right sides with their legs drawn up"; the men used newspapers for mattresses, wet jackets and boots for pillows; the whole place was crawling with lice. Finally, toward the end of the century, cities began to build municipal lodging houses. Here conditions were often even worse; but at least it freed police stations from the job of serving as welfare hotels.

Eric Monkkonen connects the end of the lodging-house era with a major overall shift in police function: from "class control" to "crime control." At first, the police had been mainly concerned "with the orderly functioning of cities"; next, with the control of "the dangerous class," which meant, not just criminals but a motley group of people from the lower orders, including the urban poor and tramps; then, finally, at the very end of the nineteenth and into the twentieth century, came the relative shift to "crime control." The police withdrew from their intimate *working* connection with the poor and their neighborhoods. This change in the basic tasks of the police was, perhaps, a kind of side effect of one aspect of progressivism, the movement to make the police more rational, bureaucratic, and professional.

As the police gave up (hardly unwillingly) their dirty and repulsive role as landlords of the homeless, their relationship to the community became more complicated—and more ambivalent. Police and public, as Samuel Walker put it, were in a situation of "mutual disrespect and brutality." The police were sometimes brutal on the streets; and they did not treat men in the station house with kid gloves, to put it mildly. Torture and brutality—the so-called third degree—were common. The police had their ways of making people talk. We hear about the "sweat box," after the Civil War. This was "a cell in close proximity to a stove, in which a scorching fire was built and fed with old bones, pieces of rubber shoes, etc., all to make great heat and offensive smells, until the sickened and perspiring inmate of the cell confessed in order to get released." The law books said nothing about sweat boxes; they were part of a police underground. There were even more direct methods of forcing and punishing: fists, blackjacks, clubs.

All this was only semisecret. The police were, in fact, proud of their physical directness. George Walling, a former chief of New York's police, called the force "the finest organization of its kind, . . . better trained, more athletic, more resolute and hardy"; it also enjoyed "unusual liberty of action." He sneered at the British police, hamstrung by legal niceties: "A band of pickpockets may rush through a crowd at Hyde Park . . . but the police are powerless. A howling mob of ten or twenty thousand rascals may gather in Trafalgar Square with the declared intention of sacking Buckingham Palace, but the police can only stand round, waiting for the commission of some illegal act." Not so in New York! A New York police officer "knows he has been sworn in to 'keep the peace,' and he keeps it. There's no 'shilly-shallying' with him. . . . He can and does arrest on suspicion." Moreover, "the men are given to understand that their actions, when governed by a desire for the public good, will be protected and upheld by the courts."

Walling's instincts were probably sound. The respectable public, including the legal public, surely liked strong action, directness, force. Few members of the respectable middle class were arrested; hence few of them felt the blackjack or the fist of a patrolman—or suffered from police gunfire. And the opinion was abroad, that evil was strong and ubiquitous, that fire had to be fought with fire. To be sure, there were limits to public tolerance. But the public chose, in general, not to know. Police tactics also varied a good deal from place to place. In Detroit, incidents of brutality were (apparently) not very common; although in 1874, a ward collector and his sons claimed they were beaten by police. There were only fifty-two claims of physical abuse over a twenty-year period in Detroit. But drunks and hoboes, as John Schneider points out, do not usually complain about brutality; and if they do, nobody pays attention.

Many people, too, were willing to shut their eyes to a certain amount of police corruption. Again, only up to a point. In part, it depended on whose ox was goared. The party out of power was always more eager to expose corruption and brutality than the party in power. Politics was behind many police exposés, including the most famous, the so-called Lexow investigation (1894). The target here was the police department of New York City.

Whatever its motivations, the special committee of the New York legislature turned over a lot of stones and brought to light a lot of creeping, crawling creatures. Election fraud, for one thing: the police had committed "almost every conceivable crime against the elective franchise" for the sake of Tammany Hall, that is, the "dominant Democratic organization of the city of New York." The police arrested and brutalized Republican voters; they stuffed ballot boxes, or let it happen; they wallowed in "oppression, fraud, trickery [and] crime."

The Lexow Committee found widespread corruption, too, in law enforcement. In "most precincts of the city, houses of ill-repute, gambling houses, policy shops, pool rooms and unlawful resorts of a similar character" were "openly conducted" under the noses of the police. The reason, of course, was a massive pattern of payoffs. Even "legitimate business" had to pay its toll. An illegal business, like that of "Mrs. Herreman, who had kept a number of houses of ill-repute in the fifteenth precinct," had to pay even more—some $30,000 over the years, which brought Mrs. Herreman "protection." In general, brothels were subject to "blackmail"; indeed, there was a systematic scale of payments, including "initiation fees" for startups, and a monthly rate based on the number of rooms or inmates. The police also tolerated poolrooms and policy shops; they permitted "professional abortionists . . . to ply their awful trade"; they even collected from "boot-blacks, push-cart and fruit venders, as well as keepers of soda water stands, corner grocerymen, sailmakers with flag-poles extending a few feet beyond the place which they occupy," merchants who were "compelled to use the sidewalk and street"—small businesses that might be violating some minor ordinance, or who needed help or protection. All of them had to "contribute . . . to the vast amounts which flow into the station-houses, and which, after leaving something of the nature of a deposit, then flow on higher."

Some policemen were incredibly brutal and callous. Victims paraded before the committee: "The eye of one man, punched out by a patrolman's club, hung on his cheek." One journalist had been "assaulted . . . with brass knuckles while he was a prisoner in the station-house." The police, it seems, "formed a separate and highly privileged class, armed with the authority and the machinery for oppression," and yet free themselves from any criminal responsibility. In some cases, the police combined extortion with brutality: there was the case, for example, of "Mrs. Urchittel, a humble Russian Jewess, ignorant of our tongue, an honest and impoverished widow with three small children." A detective "falsely accused" her of keeping a disorderly house; she was arrested, and dragged through the streets; when she did not come up with enough money for the detective's payoff, she was arrested again, and convicted on perjured testimony. She fell ill, her children were taken by the Society for the Prevention of Cruelty to Children, and she lost her home.

Despite the scandals, the publicity, the headlines, the outrage, the exposés, police corruption and brutality had remarkable survival power. In city after city, the police were on the take. Saloonkeepers in Chicago and Boston were asked regularly for "contributions." Everywhere, police were involved "in a systematic pattern of payoffs from drinking, gambling, and prostitution," and (as in New York City) voting fraud. The system of corruption, as Samuel Walker puts it, "was inherent in the fact that the police were largely a political institution.". . . The basic problem was the demand for vice. Cities were nests of vice, because vice had a huge clientele. Enough people lusted after gambling, hard liquor, and prostitution to support the cost of buying off the law.

The Decline of the Classic Penitentiary

Ultimately, the police were a success story of sorts; police departments probably played a role in reducing serious crime and disorder in the country, despite politics, oppression, incompetence, and corruption. The penitentiary system was another story.

The *idea* of the penitentiary—grim, total, silent; a monastery for criminals—gained many new converts; the idea spread from city to city, state to state. By the time of the Civil War, the newfangled penitentiary system was in place throughout the North and Midwest; the whipping post was only a memory, except in a few places (tiny Delaware was one holdout). The gallows remained, of course, but was used only for the most serious crimes. The convicted felon was simply thrown into prison; that was his fate. And the prison was modeled after the great eastern penitentiaries. Michigan Territory, for example, built a prison at Jackson in 1839, copied from the paragons in New York. Even in the South, some states fell into line and built penitentiaries.

But decay set in almost immediately in most prisons—almost as soon as the last brick was laid and the prison opened for business. The silent system, for example, had little staying power. Silence meant one-man one-cell; but solitary confinement was an expensive luxury. Men were sentenced to prison faster than the state built new cells and cellblocks. In the Massachusetts State Prison, the silent system, in its extreme form, was gone by the 1850s. In Missouri, a prison opened in Jefferson City in 1836 with forty cells, which seemed enough at the time. By 1847, there were two and three men to a cell, and the governor was arguing that this posed no difficulty. The silent system lingered in theory in many prisons; but its classic purity—and its effectiveness—was long since gone. When Hutchins Hapgood arrived in Sing Sing, late in the nineteenth century, prisoners still ate dinner "in dead silence. Silence indeed, except on the sly, was the general rule of our day, until work was over, when we could whisper together until five o'clock, the hour to return to our cells."

Money was the problem, or one of the problems. Austere, silent prisons were expensive; it was cheaper to let them get noisy and crowded. Even worse, states could not resist the temptation to make money off prisoners, which was difficult in the classic penitentiary. Illinois passed a law in 1845 leasing the penitentiary at Alton "and the labor of the convicts" to Samuel A. Buckmaster. Buckmaster was to pay a bonus of $5,100, the "usual fees of the inspectors," and furnish "at his own expense, the necessary guards and food, clothing, beds and bedding, and necessary bills of physicians for the convicts." He could use convicts to manufacture "hempen articles." Buckmaster continued as lessee until 1857, when he was replaced by S. A. Casey. Only in 1871 was the leasing system discontinued. California tried a leasing system, too, in the 1850s; and it became standard practice in the South.

There had been flirtations with leasing in the South before the Civil War; but the golden age of leasing came afterward. Before the Civil War, most prisoners in the South were white, not black; blacks were overwhelmingly slaves, and they were whipped and sent back to work (or hanged in more serious cases). After the war, the prisons filled with blacks—to be precise, young black men. In Virginia, in 1871, there were 828 prisoners in the state penitentiary; 609 of these were black men, 63 were black women; there were 152 white men, and 4 white women. In Georgia, as of October 1, 1899, there were 2,201 state prisoners; no less than 1,885 of them were black men (68 were black women); only 3 white women were in prison, and 245 white men. The ages of prisoners ranged from eleven to seventy-three—there were twelve boys and one girl under the age of fifteen—but the bulk of the prisoners were in their late teens and twenties. Half of the prisoners were completely illiterate.

Racial facts powerfully influenced southern penal policy. In many parts of the South, it was not the prison that was put in private hands to manage, but the prisoners. Contractors got bodies, to be housed in work camps and made to slave away in mines, or swamps, or on the railroads. These prisoners were, of course, overwhelmingly black. Conditions were harsh and brutal. They slept at night in "filthy shacks. Men with capital, from the North as well as the South, bought these years of convicts' lives. The largest mining and railroad companies in the region as well as small-time businessmen scrambled to win the leases." In extreme cases, the "crumbling antebellum penitentiaries" were abandoned except for a few white murderers, black men too sick to work profitably, and women of both races. Meanwhile, in the camps, men died like flies. In 1881, in Virginia, the death rate inside the penitentiary was 1.5 percent per year; in camps run by contractors for the Richmond and Allegheny Railroad, the death rate was 11 percent. Even worse death rates . . . occurred on some southern chain gangs.

The leasing system was in local use as well. Throughout the South, prisoners convicted of petty crimes sweated their lives away in work gangs, laboring either for the county or municipality, or for private contractors. Crime . . . became a kind of asset to the counties. They made money on the deal. Conditions were, as usual, subhuman. One month in 1893, 160 black males (men and boys), along with 26 black women—and only 11 whites, 2 of them women—were working "from dawn to dark building a canal" for Chatham County, Alabama; slaving in the muck of the ditches, buried up to their knees. No wonder so many prisoners died; or that a young man (a white), who had been caught stealing a hat in a bar-room, tried to cut his throat with "an old piece of iron barrel hoop" after three days on the chain gang.

In the North and West, the prisons were still purveying, in theory, a stern, relentless system of discipline; they were supposed to be a kind of reformatory for the criminal class, severe but just. There was no thought of returning, officially, to the helter-skelter methods of the older jails. The ideology of stern but just reformation kept some of its zest. The South Dakota statute on prisons imposed on warden and officers the duty to treat their charges "uniformly" and with "kindness." This did not mean coddling. The convict was to eat "wholesome coarse food, with such proportions of meat and vegetables as the warden shall deem best." If a convict violated the rules, he could be sent to a "solitary cell" and "fed on bread and water"; on the other hand, no cruel or corporal punishment was (officially) allowed. In Rhode Island, the law required an under keeper to inspect each cell daily to see that meals were "regularly furnished" and that the "cell and all its contents" were in "good order." Each prisoner was entitled to a "change of underclothing . . . at least once a week."

Real life inside the walls was very different. In some instance the regimen broke down, and discipline turned to flab. At Sing Sing, 1870s, corruption was rife; a prisoner could buy forbidden items from guards; convicts lolled about in the yard, which had "something of the atmosphere of a village." More generally, real life meant filth and degradation. In the state prison of New Jersey, as described in 1867, prisoners lived as many as four to a cell, in cells measuring seven by twelve feet; the newer cells were only four feet wide and seven feet long. Real life was lived "in a room the size of a small bathroom, with a noisome bucket for a toilet and a cot narrower than a bathtub." A prisoner might bathe "occasionally" in a bathhouse in the yard, "which was closed in bad weather." Wardens and guards, in many prisons, whipped prisoners liberally to keep them in line, regardless of what the statutes said.

There were other ways, too, to punish the convict's body. In New York, we hear about a practice called "bucking"; the convict sat with an iron bar between his legs and his wrists fastened down with chains. In Sing Sing, some inmates in the 1870s were hanged by the thumbs. In Ohio, there was the "humming-bird," an electric shock administered while a steam whistle blew. The cold-water bath was another trick of the trade in Ohio: the convict was tied to a chair or post, and buckets of ice water were poured over his head. Or the prisoner might be "blind-folded and lifted into a large vat filled with water."

Prisoners were supposed to work; work was a tool of reformation. It was also a way to make prisons pay for themselves. The trick was to put prisoners to work on something the state could profitably sell. But this made prisoners direct competitors of organized labor; this provoked a bitter political struggle in state after state. The California constitution of 1879 included a clause against convict labor. The Illinois constitution was amended in 1866 to make it "unlawful . . . to let by contract . . . the labor of any convict." Under the Michigan Constitution of 1850, as amended, convicts were not to be taught any "mechanical trade" except the "manufacture of those articles of which the chief supply for home consumption is imported from other States or countries." A Pennsylvania statute of 1883 required convict-made goods to be branded as such, in "plain English lettering," and the brand had to be put "upon the most conspicuous place upon such article." Some states tried to turn prison labor to political or economic advantage: in Minnesota, in the 1890s, prisons were directed to manufacture twine, to be sold to farmers. In this way, farmers would be helped in their struggle with the National Cordage Company, which the farmers considered one of the worst of the "trusts."

Most often, however, it was out-and-out war between the unions and prison labor, which unions regarded as a vicious scab tactic, a strike-breaking, union-busting tool. In New Jersey, New York, and New England, prisoners manufactured hats, which made them economic enemies of hatters. In 1878, New Jersey banned hatmaking in state prison, and campaigns in New York, Connecticut, and Rhode Island in the next few years were successful in cutting down prison production. Shoe manufacturers and workers, too, put aside their industrial differences to protest against the making of shoes in prisons. . . .

Local Jails

The newfangled devices and reform institutions were at the cutting edge of American penology. They were reforms that affected, on the whole, the great northern penitentiaries and certain special categories of offenders—notably, children. But they left virtually untouched the huge squalid mass of county and local prisons: the end of the line for thousands of men and women who were picked up for drunkenness or vagrancy, as well as brawlers, petty thieves, and countless others.

The local jails, in the aggregate, housed a considerable number of prisoners. The 1880 census counted 58,609 prisoners (not including juveniles in reformatories). Of these, 30,659 were found in penitentiaries, 7,865 in workhouses and houses of correction, 12,691 in county jails, 1,666 in city prisons, 499 in military prisons, 350 in hospitals for the insane, and 4,879 leased out to private parties as laborers.

In the local jails, confusion was king, along with plain dirt and humiliation. These were the sewers and toilets of humanity. At best they were simply chaotic and neglected. In 1880, Enoch Wines described Michigan's jails as follows: "no work, no instruction, no discipline; no uniformity of structure." He pointed out, as so many had, that the innocent and the depraved were thrown together in "intimate and continuous association," the "old offender" boasting of his exploits to the "wayward youth," who drank in "the fatal poison, . . . burning with desire for similar adventures." In rural Iowa, the local lockup, or jail—called the "calaboose"—was a tiny, simple building used to store drunks and tramps; offenders waited here to be dragged off to county jails, in the days before paved roads, when snow or mud made the long trip a torture. In Grand Mound, Iowa, the lockup was even used as a makeshift hotel, rented out to travelers as "an occasional low cost bed."

In the cities, most people who were arrested never got further than a local jail; the "big house" was for serious crimes. If a person could not make bail, the first stop was a cell in a police station house. George Walling, writing in 1887 about New York, has vividly described the experience. Most of the men (and women) are hauled to the cells "in a state of beastly intoxication. They shout and scream and curse worse than any furies." Dumped in a "loathsome" room, cramped, with foul air, the prisoner has to spend the night on a "hard board," where "his limbs become lame and paralyzed" in a vain attempt to sleep. All around him, in other cells, are other objects of misery: a "howling Jezebel, . . . mad with liquor"; a "tender, refined, intelligent woman" who sinned out of "weakness" and who "moans and groans in her grief"; a "sobbing boy" spending his first night in jail, thinking of his mother; an old man, "half maniacal through the constant habit of drinking," tortured by "delirium tremens, and the strange creatures of his vision."

The next stop for a convicted criminal in New York City might be the Ludlow Street Jail. This lacked the stern uniformity of the great prisons. One class of inmates, the "aristocrats of the jail," paid the warden fifteen dollars a week; this gave them a "respectable room" instead of a cell, and the privilege of sitting at the warden's table, "eating the luxuries of the market." A few rich prisoners paid between fifty and a hundred dollars a week; this bought a "nicely furnished room with all the luxuries"; their meals were served in their rooms and, in general, they lived "in royal style."

The "non-paying boarder" was locked in a cell from seven-thirty at night, to six-thirty in the morning, when he "takes up his slop-pail and carries it down to the sink." Breakfast is brought to the cell: hunks of bread, which the prisoner grabs through the cell door as best he can, followed by coffee in a tin cup. Dinner is bread and a kind of soup, served at noon. Supper is tea and another hunk of bread.

But the worst and most notorious of the jails in New York City was the prison usually known as "the Tombs." This massive building was finished in 1838, in a crazy style of architecture that vaguely resembled someone's idea of an Egyptian tomb. It had cells for both men and women. It, too, was divided into classes: there were five or six "comfortable cells," rooms with a view (of the street) for "aristocratic rogues" who could afford to "live in style." Most of the prisoners, however, were far from "aristocratic"; they were, instead, members of the "disorderly or vagrant class." They appeared first in the police court, in the Tombs. Here they were, generally, found guilty and sentenced, in an "awful smelling court-room amid the dull and brutish stare of the assembled scum of the lower city wards." The cell that received them was small and damp, with a cement floor. The regimen was much the same as at Ludlow Street.

The Tombs was four stories high, and each floor was specialized. On the ground floor were "lunatics, *delirium tremens* cases, and . . . sentenced prisoners." The second tier was "Murderers' Row"; it also housed burglars, highway robbers, and "other desperate criminals." The third tier was for "prisoners arrested for grand larceny"; the fourth for "minor misdemeanors."

The local jails in the South were scandalous in their own right. Here is the county "prison" of Cleveland County, North Carolina, as of 1870, as it appeared to a contemporary:

> The county prison is built of brick, and is thirty by twenty-six feet in size. It is three stories high, and has four cells for prisoners, including debtor's room; iron cage, etc. The iron cage is eight feet square and six feet high, the other part of the room twelve feet by fifteen. The other rooms for prisoners, fifteen by ten and fifteen by seven. There is one window in each room and cell, four and a half by three feet in size. There is no way of heating the prison except that of giving the prisoners in cold weather, a heated rock. There have been some of the prisoners frost-bitten during extremely cold weather. Each prisoner has allowed him, a straw bed and three blankets. The males and females are confined in different apartments. They have fresh water as often as they want it, and just as much food as they wish. The excrement is removed from the prison, and tar is often burned in the cells to take away the offensive smell.

Even so, prisoners in such jails were lucky, compared to those in the work camps and chain gangs, where, as we have seen, the prisoners died like flies. In general, prison and jail conditions everywhere in the country were a scandal—hidden lesions and sores on society. They were also a lesson on the meaning of race, poverty, and lack of power—and the terrible indifference of respectable people to the miseries of life underneath their feet.

Capital Punishment in the Late Nineteenth Century

The *formal* use of the death penalty continued to decline in the late nineteenth century. Michigan had abolished it, as a territory, in 1847, except for treason (not a major offense in Michigan); Maine got rid of it in 1876, restored it in 1883, then got rid of it for good in 1887. Some states and localities continued to allow public executions, but a trend against it began in the 1830s. . . . In California, public executions were banned in the 1850s; the hangman was supposed to do his dirty work discreetly, behind the sheltered walls of prisons and jails.

Executions still fascinated the public. Public executions, where they existed, were tremendous box-office hits. "Private" executions were also popular. The word *private* has to be taken with a grain of salt. These executions were, of course, not carried out in the public square, but neither were they well screened, at first, from the curious. The execution of Sam Steenburgh, on April 19, 1878, in the village of Fonda, New York, attracted about fifteen thousand visitors. "Two special trains from the east, aggregating 12 cars, and one of 7 cars, from the west" pulled in, jammed with "curiosity seekers" dressed in "holiday attire" whose ages ranged "from the . . . bent old man or woman of 70 to the child in arms"; the "sexes were quite evenly divided."

Fonda had made elaborate preparations for this great event. The jail itself was a "small rectangular building of unhewn stone," located between the railroad track and the river. A high board fence had been built, enclosing a plot of turf 138 by 108 feet, on the western side of the jail. Inside this enclosure was the gallows, "a plain, upright structure . . . painted black." The condemned man was to be "jerked into the air by the fall of an iron weight of 310 pounds." The hanging "machine" had been built in 1871, and had been used in a number of New York executions. Near the river was a house with a peaked roof, and from here you could have "an excellent view of the scene." The owner, it was said, had rented out all the space, though "at fair rates."

Steenburgh, a black man, had been convicted of the murder of a farmer named Jacob S. Parker; he confessed to this and many other crimes. On the morning of the execution, there was a scene of pandemonium outside the jail, beginning at nine o'clock. The weather was fine: a "gentle breeze tempered the rays of the sun." The area was "blackened with people. Stands had been erected for the sale of sandwiches, gingerbread, chewing gum and ginger-pop..... Hundreds of boys were dodging among the multitude crying out copies of the 'Confession.' "

Steenburgh had "slept soundly" until nine-thirty. After he dressed and "performed his ablutions," he said a prayer. His "mistress and their child" appeared at the gate; officials refused to let the woman in "for fear of unduly exciting the prisoner"; but "little Susie" did get to see her father one last time. For the execution, Steenburgh was given a "new suit of clothes and a linen shirt." At 12:50 P.M., a drum began beating and a "procession made its appearance around the corner of the jail." Soldiers marched on either side of the doomed man. At the scaffold, two priests prayed for Steenburgh's soul. Steenburgh's wrists, thighs, and ankles were bound by leather straps. Shouts and noises came from the "more disorderly of the mob" of onlookers. The sheriff asked Steenburgh if he wanted to make a last statement; Steenburgh spoke briefly, and said he was ready to die.

The noose was fitted around his neck and a black cap placed on his head. Steenburgh begged for five minutes' grace, then for ten. The crowd wanted blood. At one o'clock, the black cap was put on again; the sheriff's assistant touched "the lever with his foot," the iron weight fell with a crash, "and Steenburgh's body was jerked sideways and upward about five feet..... As he came down he swung and swayed from left to right for a few seconds." The newspaper lovingly recorded every twitch and contraction of the body, every detail of Steenburgh's pulse rate until (after ten minutes) the doctors pronounced him dead. The body was lowered at 1:23 P.M. and placed in a coffin; the crowd pressed forward to look at the body.

Crowds were present, in fact, at many "private" executions. Charles Guiteau, the assassin of President Garfield, went to the gallows on July 1, 1882; according to a newspaper account, the "representation of morbid sightseers was remarkably small"; yet over two hundred people crowded into the jail to watch, and hundreds more stood outside the jail "staring." When Lloyd Majors was executed in the jail yard in Oakland, California, in 1884, the streets were full of people who hoped to catch a glimpse of the show. Some of the spectators climbed on roofs, a few from atop the Sagehorn Building might have been actually able to see the event itself. The jail yard was jammed with viewers. Outside, "several boys had climbed into a tall poplar tree in front of the jail, in full view of the scaffold." When an execution took place "in private" at the Tombs, in New York City, "the neighboring buildings are black with people, seeking to look down over the prison walls and witness the death agonies of the poor wretch who is paying the penalty of the law."

Of course, when all is said and done, not many people could climb trees or roofs, or watch an execution with opera glasses; but millions could read all about it in the daily press. The newspapers of the late nineteenth century adored executions; they described the major executions in lip-smacking detail. When Nathan Sutton was hanged in California, in January 1888, the *Oakland Tribune* delivered to the breathless public a blow-by-blow account. People had climbed to the house-tops in a desperate attempt to watch Sutton die an agonizing death. When Sutton was dropped, the rope cut deeply into his neck; his head almost separated from his body. According to the *Tribune* a "noise was heard . . . like the gurgle of wind"; blood was "spurting from the left side of his neck . . . bubbling from the right side . . . welling from in front—rushing in a thick crimson torrent . . . forming a sanguinary pool on the ground which sucked it voraciously. . . . The crowd stood spell-bound with horror." At least the crowd was not bored; and neither, one guesses, were the *Tribune's* readers. In a sense, then, the death penalty was perhaps as public as ever. Lynchings in the South, and vigilante executions in the West, were also often public events, where thousands watched people die.

Were executions even marginally more discreet, less primitive? It is hard to say. There was, however, a move to bring the methods up to date. New York pioneered in scientific death when it introduced the "electrical chair" in 1888, to replace the hangman, the gallows, and the noose. Experiments throughout the 1880s proved the awesome power of electricity; these experiments showed that electricity could kill animals swiftly and smoothly. Why not human beings as well? The governor of New York sent a message to the legislature in 1885, proposing the use of electricity. Hanging, he said, was a remnant of the "dark ages"; now "science" showed the way to put criminals to death "in a less barbarous manner." The law of 1888 provided that the "punishment of death must, in every case, be inflicted by causing to pass through the body of the convict a current of electricity of sufficient intensity to cause death." The electric chair was also a step in the direction of true privacy; it was housed in a small chamber in the prison, and needed considerably less space than a good, old-fashioned hanging. But the coming of "the chair" did not, of course, dampen public curiosity; it only whetted the appetite of yellow journalists.

William Kemmler had the dubious honor of being first to die in "the chair." This was in 1890. The first woman executed by this "progressive" method was Mrs. Martha Place, in 1899. Her eyes closed, and clutching a Bible, she was guided into the chamber "dressed in a black gown with big sleeves and a few fancy frills at the bosom.... She wore russet slippers." Her hair was braided, but a spot had been clipped near the crown to make room for the electrode. Another electrode was fastened to her leg. A current of 1,760 volts went through her body. It was all over in a short time; the doctors pronounced her dead and took the Bible from her motionless hand. The execution, we are told, "had been successful in every way."

For Further Study

1. What evidence do you see in the selection that law enforcement and punishment varied according to the social class of the people involved?

2. The author explains the existence of police corruption by asserting that "enough people lusted after gambling, hard liquor, and prostitution to support the cost of buying off the law." What other factors might help to explain police corruption?

3. The author's account indicates that police brutality was widespread, indeed almost routine. What conditions of the time might explain why such conduct was more acceptable then than it would be today?

4. How, if at all, do the attitudes toward crime, law enforcement and punishment described in this selection differ from the attitudes that prevail today?

For Further Reading

Samuel Walker, *Popular Justice: A History of American Criminal Justice* (1980) and David R. Johnson, *American Law Enforcement: A History* (1981) are general histories. Books that deal more specifically with the period covered in this selection are Robert M. Fogelson, *Big-City Police* (1977) and Eric H. Monkkonen, *Police in Urban America, 1860–1920* (1981). David J. Rothman, *The Discovery of the Asylum: Social Order and Disorder in the New Republic* (1971), and Adam J. Hirsch, *The Rise of the Penitentiary: Prisons and Punishments in Early America* (1992), are both somewhat outside the period dealt with in this particular selection, but they provide valuable insights into the social purposes that prisons were intended to serve in America. Elaine S. Abelson, *When Ladies Go A-Thieving* (1989), and Ruth Rosen, *The Lost Sisterhood: Prostitution in America, 1900–1918* (1982), deal with different aspects of female criminality.

Part II

The Challenges of Diversity

Many Americans were deeply disturbed by what they saw happening to their nation in the late 1800s. The fantastic economic growth the nation was experiencing carried a heavy price in human terms. Greed and callousness seemed to rule. Workers were exploited, and many small businesses were crushed in the ruthless competition that often prevailed. There was a growing gulf between the haves and have-nots, and periodic economic dislocations, such as the depression of the mid-1890s, produced a sense of insecurity and even fear. Such conditions sparked vigorous protests and demands for change, and in the first two decades of the twentieth century, the nation was swept by the Progressive Movement, a widespread and broadly based impulse toward reform.

Progressives addressed issues having to do with corruption in municipal government, child labor, regulation of hours for working women, standards of cleanliness in the production of food, the overweening power of large corporations, and many, many others. Their fundamental goal was to take steps toward solving the problems that had arisen in the years since the Civil War as a result of rapid economic expansion and the transition from a rural and agricultural to an urban and industrial nation. They relied on the power of government at all levels to control and regulate behavior believed to be illegitimate or threatening to social harmony.

As they addressed these issues, however, another set of problems emerged as the nation confronted a mighty wave of immigration that began in the mid-1880s and crested in the early years of the twentieth century. While many Progressives were sympathetic to the immigrants and were involved in efforts to extend assistance to them, other Americans, including many Progressives, were inclined to view immigrants as detrimental to the nation's social health because they represented diversity and potential disorder.

These problems, real or imagined, were intensified by the increasing presence of black Americans in northern cities as hundreds of thousands of them moved north in search of jobs, education, and freedom from the racial oppression they faced in the South.

The following selections illustrate the new problems and opportunities resulting from the growing diversity of the American people and American life. One describes both the positive and negative aspects of life in America's rapidly growing cities. One concerns the lives of Asian immigrants and their adjustment to their new homeland. The last deals with the migration of African Americans to the North and what they found when they got to "the promised land."

Chapter 7

Orchard Street, ca. 1898. Museum of the City of New York, The Byron Collection.

Street peddlers and their customers on New York City's Lower East Side.

The City at the Turn of the Century

David Nasaw

One vivid example of the expansion and change that were occurring in the United States in the late 1800s was the phenomenal growth of America's cities. Americans had been moving from the country to the city ever since the mid-eighteenth century, but never before on such a scale. The mechanization of farming lowered demands for agricultural labor while growing industries created job opportunities in urban areas. In addition, the 1880s saw the beginnings of a huge wave of immigration from Europe, with most of the new arrivals settling in cities. The result was that between 1880 and 1890 New York City's population grew by 50 percent, Chicago's by more than 100 percent, and Minneapolis-St. Paul's by 300 percent; other cities showed comparable rates of growth.

This urban explosion created an urban emergency. American cities had always suffered from crime, disease, poverty, and overcrowding, but such problems now threatened to become overwhelming. Rapidly increasing numbers both magnified existing difficulties and ensured that more people would be affected by them. It was essential to do something before cities became unlivable.

In confronting these problems, American people of the late 1800s and early 1900s essentially invented the modern American city. The story was not always pretty, being attended with considerable amounts of graft, greed, corruption, inefficiency, and failure, but in the end the foundations for many of the basic features of modern city life were laid. Public mass transit, municipal water and sewage disposal systems, the grid for generating and distributing electricity, and the telephone network, among other things, became characteristic of American urban life during this period. In addition, the problems that resulted from having so many people of diverse ethnic, racial, religious, and class backgrounds living so close together created a demand for higher

standards of public comfort and safety to be maintained by professional police and fire-fighting forces. And ethnic diversity and the cultural variety and
interaction it generated contributed to an enhanced vitality and creativity in
artistic and intellectual life.

In the following selection, David Nasaw focuses on New York City, but
much of what he says about the attractions and drawbacks of urban life there
can be applied to other American cities around the turn of the century.

The early twentieth-century city was among the wonders of the New World.
Concentrated within it were the marvels of the age. Electric lights made night into
day. Subways, streetcars, and the elevated sped commuters through the streets.
Steel-girded skyscrapers and granite railroad stations expressed its solidity and its
power. Lobster palaces, vaudeville palaces, movie palaces, and department store
palaces of consumption recreated in the present the mythic splendors of the past.

American cities had expanded in all directions in the decades surrounding the
turn of the century: up with the skyscrapers, down into the subway tunnels, out-
ward across the bridges and tunnels to the new streetcar suburbs. The central
business districts, once crowded with warehouses but not much else, had been en-
larged and subdivided into financial, government, manufacturing, warehousing,
shopping, and entertainment districts, each with its army of workers.

Every morning swarms of commuters boarded their trolleys, trains, cable cars,
elevateds, and subways for the ride to town. Three quarters of a million people
flowed daily off the elevated into the Chicago Loop. They arrived in downtown
Boston from Roxbury, West Roxbury, Dorchester, and the surrounding "streetcar
suburbs." In Cincinnati, Columbus, and Pittsburgh, they took electric streetcars
from the heights into the "flats" of the central city. In Manhattan, they trooped to
work across the bridges, on the ferries, and by streetcar, elevated train, and subway. Theodore Dreiser described the procession from his vantage point at the
Williamsburg Bridge. "Already at six and six-thirty in the morning they have begun to trickle small streams of human beings Manhattan or cityward, and by seven
and seven-fifteen these streams have become sizable affairs. By seven-thirty and
eight they have changed into heavy, turbulent rivers and by eight-fifteen and
eight-thirty and nine they are raging torrents, no less. They overflow all the streets
and avenues and every available means of conveyance. They are pouring into all
available doorways, shops, factories, office-buildings—those huge affairs towering
so significantly above them. Here they stay all day long, causing those great hives
and their adjacent streets to flush with a softness of color not indigenous to them,

and then at night, between five and six, they are going again, pouring forth over the bridges and through the subways and across the ferries and out on the trains, until the last drop of them appears to have been exuded."

Those who arrived in the central business districts came to work, but they stayed to be entertained and to shop. The city's palaces of consumption were as new, as exciting, and as spectacular as its skyscrapers and bridges. The downtown department stores, huge as factories, luxurious as the most opulent millionaire's mansions, and jammed full of goods were a relatively new phenomenon in the life of the city. Until the 1870s there had been no real downtown shopping streets. City folk did their shopping in neighborhood stores or from itinerant peddlers. Local shops were specialized: butcher, baker, and candlestick maker had their own establishments where they produced and sold their own goods.

The extension of the streetcar lines into the suburbs and the new concentration of white-collar workers downtown provided retailers with hundreds of thousands of customers. Old-fashioned dry goods stores were expanded into department stores and then relocated and rebuilt along the busiest streetcar and subway lines to make shopping as convenient as possible for suburban women, tourists, and downtown workers.

Visitors to the city joined the commuters and workers on the shopping streets where the department stores were located. In Manhattan, the first "Ladies' Mile" was situated along Broadway and Fifth and Sixth Avenues between Eighth and Twenty-third Streets. There was nothing like it anywhere in the world. Wanamaker's, a sixteen-story cast-iron giant, was at Eighth Street and Broadway, Hearn's was on Fourteenth Street, and Siegel-Cooper's on Sixth Avenue and Eighteenth Street with its main attraction, "The Fountain," a circular marble terrace surrounding a mammoth marble and brass statue of "The Republic" shooting jets of water, "illuminated by myriad colored lights." Across the street from the Big Store was B. Altman's, a short walk away were Stern Brothers, Lord and Taylor, Arnold Constable, Best and Company, Bonwit Teller's, W. and J. Sloane, and Macy's.

As the city moved northward so did the department stores. Macy's in 1901 broke ground on its new Herald Square store—with one million square feet of floor space. Within a decade all the other downtown stores had relocated on Fifth Avenue or close by.

In Chicago, State Street was as grand a tourist attraction as New York's Fifth Avenue. One could wander up and down the avenue for days without running out of stores to visit and windows to peer into. There was Marshall Field's with its forty acres of shopping and its forty-five plate glass windows; Carson, Pirie, Scott's in its new building designed by Louis Sullivan; Fair, Rothschild's, Siegel, Cooper and Company; the Boston Store; Mandel Brothers; and the Stevens Store—all within walking distance of one another.

Every city had its own special stores, stores which had grown up with the downtown areas and, in the beginning, helped lure customers from the outskirts: Jordan Marsh's and Filene's in Boston, the original Wanamaker's and Gimbel's in Philadelphia, Kaufmann's in Pittsburgh, Abraham and Straus in Brooklyn, Rich's in Atlanta, Neiman-Marcus in Dallas, Goldwater's in Prescott and then in Phoenix, Arizona, I. Magnin's in San Francisco, Hudson's in Detroit, and Lazarus in Columbus.

The department stores were more than containers of goods or huge indoor markets. They were living encyclopedias of abundance designed to overwhelm the consumer with the variety of items available for purchase. The department stores brought together under one roof an unimaginable collection of commodities, catalogued by department, arranged by floor. Furniture, rugs, and bedding were on the upper floors; ready-to-wear clothing and shoes for women and children on the middle floors; bargain goods and groceries in the basement. The street-level floors displayed clothing and accessories for men, who it was feared would not take the time to ride to the higher floors; and for the women, dozens and dozens of alluring, lower-priced items: cosmetics, notions, gloves, stationery, hosiery.

What overwhelmed was not simply the variety of goods, but the variety and abundance of luxury goods, "from silk dresses and chocolate-covered candies to bicycles, cigarettes, and pink popcorn, which consumers had not produced themselves and which they did not need."

The department stores, by so artfully juxtaposing the necessary and the frivolous, redefined and intertwined needs with desires. There was so much there, at such a range of prices, it was difficult to know what to buy. Sister Carrie, recently arrived in the city from the countryside and looking for work, was directed by a policeman to "The Fair," one of Chicago's more massive and imposing stores. "Carrie passed along the busy aisles, much affected by the remarkable displays of trinkets, dress goods, stationery, and jewelry. Each separate counter was a showplace of dazzling interest and attraction. She could not help feeling the claim of each trinket and valuable upon her personally, and yet she did not stop. There was nothing there which she could not have used—nothing which she did not long to own. The dainty slippers and stockings, the delicately frilled skirts and petticoats, the laces, ribbons, hair-combs, purses, all touched her with individual desire."

One did not have to go inside to be touched by the magic of the stores. Plate-glass windows with superbly crafted displays highlighted by "the planned adoption of electrical lighting and of a new color technology, of drapery and mechanical props, of reflectors and wax mannequins, and even, occasionally of living models . . . consciously converted what had once been dull places stuffed with goods into focused *show* windows, 'gorgeous' little theatrical stage-sets, sculpted scenes, where *single* commodities might be presented in the best possible light." The banks of show windows opened up the street, extending the interior opulence of the palaces onto the sidewalks and inviting the passers-by to pause and dream of the splendors inside. Window-shopping, in essence no more than a dignified form of loafing, became a new and acceptable pastime.

If shopping brought people downtown, entertainment establishments kept them there after dark or, to be more accurate, after the sun went down. There was, in reality, no more "dark" in the theater districts. Street lighting, first by kerosene and gas, then by electric arc and incandescent lights, extended day into night. Theater marquees, billboards, and restaurants with plate glass windows revealing and highlighting the gaiety within converted dark, deserted streets into well-lit thoroughfares of fun and fantasy. Broadway, the Great White Way, illuminated for two miles between Madison and Longacre Squares, was the prototype for the all-night entertainment district, but every city had its theaters, its restaurants, its hotels, its vaudeville palaces, and motion picture shows.

Night life, once the province of lower-class characters and men who acted as if they were, had moved out from the tenderloin and vice districts into the lights of the new and expanded "Broadways." Every city had its cheap public dance halls, saloons, and whorehouses, but for those who wanted to be entertained without shame and guilt and in the company of respectable women, there were new and proper places to do it.

The vaudeville theaters were the first establishments to, quite literally, clean up their acts. Once a men-only affair, with prostitutes cruising the aisles, profanity rampant, "girly shows" on stage, and the aroma of stale beer inescapable, vaudeville had, in the 1870s and 1880s, been transformed into acceptable, wholesome entertainment for the entire family. "Jeering, drinking, smoking, and soliciting were all but abolished by policing. Managers also clamped down on vulgar stage language and actions, creating a strict system of censorship that outlawed the uttered 'hell' and 'damn.'" Animal acts, magicians, pantomimists, and ladies who played the "concertina, banjo, and xylophone" were brought in to replace the "blue" acts that had once been standard.

Though vaudeville shows could be seen in every town, at country fairs, and at amusement parks, it was in the cities that the theaters attracted the largest number of customers. In New York City there were, by 1910, thirty-one different vaudeville houses. Chicago had twenty-two, Philadelphia thirty.

Vaudeville brought the middle classes—in the thousands—downtown for the show. It was not, however, the only attraction of the entertainment districts. There were also the variety theaters and the music halls, where on any given night one could see operettas, new musical comedies like *Little Johnny Jones* and *George Washington Junior*, melodramas, or Shakespeare. Arnold Bennett, on his trip to the United States in 1912, was astounded to find "nearly twice as many first-class theaters in New York as in London."

Within walking distance of the theaters were restaurants to wine, dine, and be seen in. Dining out, once the preserve of society people who could afford fancy hotel dining rooms and restaurants like Delmonico's and of working men who frequented taverns, chophouses, and rathskellers, had become an acceptable—and accessible—form of entertainment for middle-class men and women. In New York City, the dozens of new "Broadway" restaurants which opened their doors between 1899 and 1912 "helped make the life of conspicuous consumption available to a wider portion of the city and the nation."

Patrons were not only wined and dined but also treated like kings and queens on holiday. Restaurateurs created sumptuous new interior decors to bedazzle their customers with a taste of luxury. "In Murray's [on Broadway in New York City], patrons entered the main dining room through a black and gold mosaic-lined foyer. The main dining room was built to resemble the atrium of a Roman home, complete with an open court with colonnades on each side. Surrounded by trees and statues and gazing out on an ancient barge fronting a terraced fountain crowned by a classical temple rising clear to the ceiling, diners enjoyed the illusion of being in ancient Rome or at a villa in Pompeii. . . . The classical porticos and temples provided a sense of restful magnificence, while the enormous height of the room and open space suggested the lofty opulence and power of the diner."

Entering the room was only the beginning of the treat. Eating in a lobster palace, like shopping in a department store, was an adventure, an excitement, an event to be savored. The beginning to a proper meal in hotel dining room or lobster palace was oysters (when not in season, clams could be substituted), followed by soup, hors d'oeuvres, fish, the entrée, the main course (usually a roast), the game dish, and dessert and coffee.

For those who preferred to keep the good time rolling late into the night, there were cabarets and nightclubs, another early twentieth century addition to city night life. Fast dancing, once practiced only in the cheap dance halls and bawdy houses, was a major attraction in the new clubs. And when people danced, they danced—not waltzes or two-steps—but the turkey trot and the grizzly bear to the syncopated ragtime beat of black musicians who, had they not been playing in the band, would never have been allowed in such respectable downtown establishments.

As Lloyd Morris has noted, it was just three miles from Rector's on Broadway, where twenty dollars would buy a dinner for five with two bottles of champagne, to the lower end of Orchard Street, where another restaurant "served a dinner of soup, meat stew, bread, pickles, pie, and a 'schooner' of beer for thirteen cents."

In New York City, as in Chicago, Boston, Cincinnati, Columbus, and almost every other city in the nation, the "other half" lived close by and a world away from the downtown business, shopping, and entertainment districts. H. G. Wells noticed during his visit in 1905 that there were "moments when I could have imagined there were no immigrants at all" in American cities. "One goes about the wide streets of Boston, one meets all sorts of Boston people, one visits the State House; it's all the authentic English-speaking America. Fifth Avenue, too, is America without a touch of foreign-born." And yet, Wells recognized, the America of the immigrant and the working class, though out of sight, was just around the corner, just down the street, just over the hill, "a hundred yards south of the pretty Boston Common," "a block or so east of Fifth Avenue," an elevated stop from the Loop in Chicago.

The two urban worlds did not mingle or mix. Each recognized the presence of the other, but neither went out of its way to cross over into the other's workplace or neighborhood. As Robert Shackleton noted in Chicago, the sellers and customers in the department stores were almost all "Americans." "The great foreign population of the city lives and does its shopping mainly in its own districts."

Most residents of the working-class city had no reason to travel downtown. Why leave the neighborhood where goods were cheaper and shopkeepers spoke your own language? Why go elsewhere to be entertained when you had little free time and the local streets provided all you needed in friends, family, neighbors, social clubs, saloons, and coffee houses?

Working men and women stayed behind in their own neighborhood because they were comfortable there. While the neighborhoods were not ethnically homogeneous, there were always enough "landsmen" clustered to establish and sustain churches, lodges, patriotic groups, food shops, bakers, butchers, restaurants, theaters, banks, and newspapers.

Settlement-house workers at the turn of the century and historians, more recently, who portray the working-class immigrants as helpless, hopeless, uprooted victims misread the historical record. On the downtown business, shopping, and entertainment streets the Italian, Polish, and Russian Jewish immigrants wearing dirty overalls and speaking foreign tongues might have been out of place. But in their own communities, they were at home.

The two cities, though geographically distinct, shared the same congested, polluted urban space. There were many constants in city life. No matter where you lived or worked, you were assaulted daily by the smoke, soot, and dust in the air; the noise of clattering cobblestones, cable cars, trolleys, and the elevated; the smell of horse dung on the streets. In the working-class and immigrant residential districts, these annoyances were intensified a hundredfold. It was in the city of the "other half" that the sewers were always clogged and the streets and alleyways filled with garbage. It was here that dead horses lay for days, bloated and decaying, children poking at their eyes and pulling out their hair to weave into rings. It was here that cats roamed at will through the streets, alleyways, backyards, roofs, and interior hallways, alley cats with gaping wounds, flesh hung loosely on starving bodies, wide frightened eyes, and the look, smell, and howl of starvation. It was here that tuberculosis raged and babies died of exposure or cold or heat or spoiled milk, that pushcarts, streetcars, and horse-drawn wagons fought for space, and children were crushed to death in the duel.

The residents of the working-class districts lived in a variety of dwellings: multistory tenements, converted single-family row houses, double-deckers, triple-deckers, wooden shacks and shanties. Wherever they lived, they were likely to live piled together, several families in space designed for one, several persons to a room.

Families made the best possible use of their limited space, rearranging their flats every evening to provide maximum sleeping room for children, relatives, and boarders. On his first evening in the New World, Marcus Ravage, future historian and author of *An American in the Making,* looked on in amazement as his relatives transformed their apartment into a "camp." "The sofas opened up and revealed their true character. The bureau lengthened out shamelessly, careless of its day-light pretensions. Even the wash-tubs, it turned out, were a miserable sham. The carved dining-room chairs arranged themselves into two rows that faced each other like dancers in a cotillion. . . . The two young ladies' room was not, I learned, a young ladies' room at all; it was a female dormitory. The sofa in the parlor alone held four sleepers, of whom I was one. We were ranged broadside, with the rocking-chairs at the foot to insure the proper length. And the floor was by no means exempt. I counted no fewer than nine male inmates in that parlor alone one night. Mrs. Segal with one baby slept on the washtubs, while the rest of the youngsters held the kitchen floor. The pretended children's room was occupied by a man and his family of four."

As the population and land values in the central cities increased, working people and the poor were forced to live in spaces that should have remained uninhabited. In Washington, D.C., and Baltimore, Maryland, cities within the city were built in the alleyways. In Pittsburgh and Chicago, investigators discovered hundreds of families living below street level in cellars, basements, and dark, dreary, "cavelike" dwellings. In Chicago, where landlords had increased their profits—and the congestion—by building on every inch of land they owned, "rear tenements" and wooden shacks facing on alleyways were built in the back of long, slender lots.

Cities with massive, multistory tenements had the worst congestion. In New York City, where a higher percentage of residents lived in tenements than anywhere else in the country, the congestion inside and out was beyond belief. Theodore Dreiser, among those visitors to the Lower East Side overwhelmed by the sight, reported having seen "block after block of four-story and five-story buildings, "all painted a dull red, and nearly all . . . divided in the most unsanitary manner. Originally they were built five rooms deep, with two flats on a floor, but now the single flats have been subdivided and two or three, occasionally four or five, families live and toil in the space which was originally intended for one."

Light, air, and privacy were at a premium for the working-class and immigrant residents of the early twentieth-century cities. In the typical New York City tenement, with fourteen rooms on each floor, only four—two in front and two in back—"received direct light and air from the street or from the small yard at the back of the building." A housing inspector testified that the inner kitchens and bedrooms on the lower floors of the tenements he visited "were so dark that the lights are kept burning in the kitchen during the daytime. The bedrooms may be used for sleeping at any time within the twenty-four hours, as they exceed the Arctic Zone in having night 365 days in the year."

Lack of windows meant lack of ventilation. The front and rear windows let in a bit of air—along with the noise and stench of street and alleyway. The interior rooms had windows, but because they opened onto airshafts and courtyards stuffed with rotting garbage, most residents kept them permanently closed.

The flats were dark, the hallways darker. In most tenements, the only light in the halls came from the front door when that was opened. A tenement house inspector testified that, in his experience, "the most barbarous parts of [tenement] buildings are the halls. A person coming in from the sunlight outside, plunges into these halls just like a car filled with men plunges and disappears in the black mouth of a mine shaft. If he is fortunate in not running against anybody, he stumbles along, finding his way with his feet. . . . [H]e hurries forward as rapidly as possible and rushes out upon the roof or into some open room, because the air is so dense and stifling [in the hallway] that he wishes to escape quickly."

Privacy was as treasured and rare in the working-class districts as fresh air and light. High rents forced families to economize on space and sublet rooms and parts of rooms to boarders. City dwellers shared their flats, their rooms, even their beds and their toilets with virtual strangers. In many tenements, the water closet was located in the hall or the backyard, where it was used by several families and their boarders and relatives. In Chicago, for example, a turn-of-the-century study found that only 43 percent of families had toilets in their flats, 30 percent had to use the water closet in the yard, 10 percent had a toilet in the basement or cellar, and another 17 percent shared a hall toilet with their neighbors on the floor.

Unventilated, overused water closets and backyard privies were bound to and did overflow continually, seeping waste through the floorboards and into the yards. The odor of human excrement joined that of horse dung from the streets and stables and of garbage rotting in the airshafts, inner courtyards, streets, and alleyways.

If we were to be moved backward in time to the early twentieth-century city, we would probably be most repelled not by the lack of privacy, or toilets, or space, air, and light, but by this stench. Without proper ventilation, the interior halls and rooms of the tenements retained their odors indefinitely. Inside and out, the air was not just heavy and fetid but, at times, unbearable. Cities like Chicago, Cincinnati, and Kansas City, with their slaughterhouses, packing plants, and streets clogged with hogs, sheep, and cattle smelled the worst, but no city was free of what we today would consider an overpowering stench.

The residents of the central cities struggled as best they could to find a breath of air, cool, fresh, clean air. Men, women, and children herded themselves into streetcars and subways for interminable Sunday excursions to the parks and beaches, looking for grass to walk on and air to breathe. In the summertime, when the air was so heavy and hot "it was painful to draw one's breath," entire families—abandoning their last grasp at privacy—relocated on the docks, in the parks, at the stoops, the fire escapes or up on the roofs. As Mike Gold put it in *Jews Without Money,* "People went exploring for sleep as for a treasure." "Like rats scrambling on deck from the hold of a burning ship, that's how we poured on the roof at night to sleep. What a mélange in the starlight! Mothers, graybeards, lively young girls, exhausted sweatshop fathers, young consumptive coughers and spitters, all of us snored and groaned there side by side, on newspapers or mattresses. We slept in pants and undershirt, heaped like corpses. The city reared about us."

Light, air, and privacy were scarce commodities in the working-class districts of the cities. But to paint too grim a picture of life in the early twentieth century, to speak only of scarcity, to emphasize only poverty is to caricature the conditions of daily life for many. The city was no golden land, but it was also no desert. There was plenty mixed with the poverty, abundance interspersed with scarcity. The city was many things at the same time to the same people.

Marcus Ravage, who arrived in New York City from his native Vaslui, Rumania, at the turn of the century, tried hard to organize his perceptions of this new land. He could not resolve the contradictions. He was disappointed on his arrival, "bitterly disappointed" at the "littered streets, with the rows of pushcarts lining the sidewalks and the centers of the thoroughfares, the ill-smelling merchandise, and the deafening noise," at the congestion inside the homes, and the boarders crowded into too little space, stuffed into too few beds. (In Vaslui, he remembered, only the "very lowest of people kept roomers.") And yet, at the very same time, he was astonished at the material abundance displayed amidst the poverty. His landlady scrubbed the floor, not with sand, but with a "pretty white powder out of a metal can." "Moreover, she kept the light burning all the time we were in the kitchen, which was criminal wastefulness even if the room was a bit dark." There was "eggplant in midwinter, and tomatoes, and yellow fruit which had the shape of a cucumber and the taste of a muskmelon." There was meat in the middle of the day and "twists instead of plain rye bread, to say nothing of rice-and-raisins . . . and liver paste and black radish." And then, as if he had not seen enough such wonders in his first day in the country, the young men calling on his Cousin Rose arrived that evening "with beer in a pitcher from the corner saloon." Common people—with beer in a pitcher—at home.

The city—not just New York City, but every early twentieth-century city—overwhelmed with its abundance. There were enough goods to go around town and back again. The department stores and specialty shops got the best of the lot, but the working-class districts, according to Harry Roskolenko, a poet and journalist who grew up on the Lower East Side, were stocked with their own "massive supplies of shoddy goods . . . leftovers from other years and seasons; things that could not be sold" elsewhere; and goods produced especially for sale to "the peddlers and the peasants and the proletarians jamming the sidewalks and gutters."

The pushcarts overflowed, the shops were littered with items for sale: umbrellas, stockings, boys' sailor suits with whistles attached, suspenders, gabardine overcoats, handkerchiefs, laces and ribbons and shoes and long underwear. There were carts filled with oranges and others loaded with bananas, herring came in barrels, milk was ladled out of forty-quart cans, potatoes dug out of fifty-pound sacks. Food, drink, and sweets could be purchased from peddlers and pushcarts, from stands, butchers, bakers, and grocers who sold it in cans, in boxes, in jars, in bottles, in packages, in bags.

Newcomers might have assumed that city markets had always displayed such variety and abundance, but many of the items now prominently displayed were as new to the city as the electric streetcars and lobster palaces. The banana, for example, among the most proletarian of fruits, had until the 1880s been almost entirely absent from the working-class shops and shopping streets. On arrival in New Orleans, "each fruit was wrapped individually in tinfoil and like a rare and precious object rushed to New York or New England, where, if it survived the journey, a single banana was worth a dollar."

Oranges were also a luxury item until the 1890s when, with the completion of the Florida East Coast Railway, they could be shipped north by rail instead of being imported from the Mediterranean.

Grapefruits were entirely new to the city. The old pear-shaped fruit, distinguished by its lack of juice, coarse rind, and expensive price tag had been redesigned by Florida growers who shipped them north in refrigerated boxcars. Between 1909 and 1920, annual consumption of the new pink fruit jumped from under a pound to over five pounds per capita.

The immigrants who arrived in American cities in the early twentieth century were astounded by the number of foods for sale and the variety of ways in which they could. be purchased. Fruits, vegetables, soups, meats, even baby food, were sold fresh *and* in cans and tins. Propelled into the marketplace by new food companies alert to the advantages of national distribution, advertising, and brand name promotions, Campbell's soups, Heinz's fifty-seven varieties, and Libby's canned goods became part of the city's daily diet. Between 1909 and 1920, annual per capita consumption of canned fruits increased from under three pounds to over nine, canned soups from less than a third of a pound to two, and baby food from less than a tenth of a pound to over two.

The addition of fresh and canned fruits and vegetables to a diet that had once consisted of little more than bread, potatoes, crackers, and various forms of salted and preserved meats was no doubt beneficial. From a social standpoint, the availability of food in cans meant even more. Here was yet another item once exclusively the preserve of the wealthy (and of military expeditions which could survive on no other form of food) that had become part of the common folks' daily diet. The family that could now for the first time eat peas for dinner was certainly more pleased by the new addition to its diet than it was distressed by the nutritional loss suffered in the canning process.

Of all the foods entering the diet of the working people, none were as enticing, as aristocratic, as luxurious, and as plentiful as the sweets. One by one, luxuries like refined white sugar and chocolate and homemade delights like fresh ice cream were mass-produced, distributed, and marketed in the cities. Candy consumption increased from 2.2 pounds per capita in 1880 to 5.6 in 1914 and 13.1 in 1919; ice cream from 1.5 pounds in 1909 to 7.5 in 1920. To wash it all down, there was Coca-Cola, invented as a "remedy for headaches and hangovers" by an Atlanta dentist in 1886.

The new sweets further broadened and "democratized" the urban diet. Luxuries became commonplaces available for pennies from neighborhood shops and pushcart peddlers. And yet, there remained significant differences between the diet of the downtown gentleman and the factory worker's family. Both ate sweets and vegetables and meat. But the sirloin and spring lamb served in the lobster palaces was a far cry from the meat soup "made up of leftovers and ends and bones which the butcher sold for six cents a pound instead of throwing it away." Bananas and oranges and grapefruits were, for the first time, available downtown and in the slums, but only for the few who had the money to pay for them. For the rest, they remained as inaccessible as they had been in the days before refrigerated boats and boxcars carried them north.

In the midst of plenty, poverty and hunger remained. Within sight of the carts and shops filled with enough food to feed armies, parents struggled to provide for their families. Children grew up with what actress Ruth Gordon has called "the dark brown taste of being poor." Hy Kraft, later a successful Broadway playwright, never forgot what it was like to grow up poor. "A boy stands in front of a candy store—in front, mind you. He sees a hundred varieties of sweets, but he doesn't have a penny, one cent. Or he's in the street; a vendor pushes his cart, calling 'Icacrim sendwich, pennyapiss.' Other kids holler up to their mamas, 'Mama, t'row me down a penny' and the mama wraps the penny in paper and 't'rows' it down. This kid doesn't have a penny—one cent. And there's no mama upstairs; she's in the back of the basement."

Poverty was not unique to the metropolis, but nowhere else did it coexist with such splendor and spectacle. As Charles Zueblin, an authority on American cities, noted in the preface to his widely read volume on *American Municipal Progress,* "There is poverty in the country, sordid and ugly. But city poverty is under the shadow of wealth. Luxury flaunts itself in the city."

The city was suffused with contrasts: between the electrically illuminated magnificence of the downtown shopping and entertainment districts and the grayish squalor of the slums, between the abundance of goods offered for sale on the streets and the paucity of resources available to pay for them. Poverty and plenty lived side by side, in the same city, on the same block, in the same tenement flat. The contradictions that assailed Marcus Ravage on his first day in the city were inescapable. Wise men peddled suspenders on the streets while fools lived like millionaires. People slept crowded one on top of another, but they ate meat several times a week. Families shared toilets with complete strangers, but they were able to purchase shoes, stockings, and underwear for everyone—even for the children. It made no sense and yet it was real. It was the city.

   ## For Further Study

1. Put yourself in the shoes of someone just arriving from a rural home and getting a first glimpse of New York City. From Nasaw's account, what would you find most striking about that experience? What features of the city would have had the greatest impact on you?

2. What does Nasaw's portrait indicate as the main attractions and drawbacks of city life at the turn of the century? From your textbook or some other source, try to discover what important elements of city life he may have omitted in his depiction.

3. At the turn of the century many Americans believed that the American city was one of the nation's greatest disgraces. What evidence do you find in this selection to support or contradict that belief?

4. One of the themes in this selection is the ways in which the experience of the city differed for those who had money from those who did not. What were some of the differences? To what extent is it true that those who had little money suffered from the disadvantages of city life while unable to enjoy its advantages?

For Further Reading

Arthur M. Schlesinger, Sr., *The Rise of the City, 1878–1898* (1933), is a classic account of urban growth that contains a wealth of still valuable information. Raymond Mohl, *The New City: Urban America in the Industrial Age* (1985); Sam Bass Warner, Jr., *The Urban Wilderness* (1982); Zane L. Miller, *The Urbanization of Modern America* (1973); and Howard P. Chudacoff and Judith E. Smith, *The Evolution of American Urban Society* (4th ed., 1993), are more recent and cover a broader time span. Oscar Handlin, *The Uprooted* (2nd ed., 1973), and Alan M. Kraut, *The Huddled Masses: The Immigrant in American Society, 1880–1921* (1982), are readable accounts of the interactions between immigrants and the city. On urban culture and recreation at the turn of the century, see Lewis A. Erenberg, *Steppin' Out: New York Nightlife and the Transformation of American Culture, 1890–1930* (1981); Gunther Barth, *City People: The Rise of Modern City Culture in Nineteenth-Century America* (1980); John F. Kasson, *Amusing the Million: Coney Island at the Turn of the Century* (1978); and Kathy Peiss, *Cheap Amusements: Working Women and Leisure in Turn-of-the-Century New York* (1986).

Chapter 8

*Young Chinese-American women often found themselves trying to bridge the gap between the
traditional Chinese world and the modern American one.*

Immigration and Cultural Conflict

Judy Yung

The United States has always been a nation of immigrants, never more so than in the late 1800s and the first years of the twentieth century. The immigration of those years dwarfed anything that had happened before. It was also different in kind. Immigrants crossing the Atlantic now came mostly from southern and eastern Europe, not from northern and western Europe as before. In addition, there was a smaller, but still significant movement to the United States from across the Pacific, first from China and somewhat later from Japan as well. Contemporaries became increasingly concerned about the cultural differences between the new immigrants and the existing population of the United States as well as their sheer numbers, and the combination triggered anti-immigrant feelings among many native-born Americans and led to demands that further immigration be restricted.

Chinese first began coming to the United States in numbers at the time of the California Gold Rush in the 1850s, and they continued in succeeding decades. Chinese immigrants provided a substantial fraction of the labor for the construction of the first transcontinental railroad in the 1860s and also became an important presence in many mining communities throughout the West. Like immigrants of other nationalities, the Chinese faced a wide range of difficulties. In addition to unfamiliarity with their new country's customs, language, and laws, they had to deal with keen competition for the sort of jobs available to them, which were usually unskilled and low-paying. They were also the victims of overt prejudice and discrimination in many areas of life including housing and employment.

One of the immigrants' responses to such conditions was to form compact communities. The Chinese were no different, and by 1900 many cities along the Pacific coast had "Chinatowns," the largest of them in San Francisco. At first, the overwhelming majority of the Chinese who came to the United

States were men, but soon women began to arrive also, and the sex division among the Chinese gradually began to approach an even split. Chinese women faced an even greater set of problems than their male counterparts, for besides all the problems they had to face because of their ethnicity there were those additional ones they confronted because of their gender. This was not only because of the attitudes of native-born Americans, but also because in traditional Chinese culture there was a strong tendency to favor males over females, and Chinese women faced pressure and discrimination even within the family circle.

A second generation of Chinese women, however, those born within the United States, proved less willing than their mothers had been to accept all the restrictions placed on them by traditional attitudes within the Chinese community or by the anti-Chinese attitudes of many native-born Americans. The following selection describes the lives of some second-generation Chinese American women from San Francisco and the various ways they began to challenge prevailing notions that limited them because of their ethnicity and gender.

As young daughters, Chinese American girls had little choice but to give unquestioning obedience to their parents. However, as they became older and more exposed to a Western lifestyle and ideas of individuality and equality through public school, church, and popular culture, some began to resist the traditional beliefs and practices of their immigrant parents, even to the extent of ridiculing their "old-fashioned" ways. Like most second-generation children, Chinese Americans experienced cultural conflicts and identity dilemmas when they tried to reconcile the different value system of their home culture with that of mainstream American society. Many disagreed with their parents over the degree of individuality and freedom allowable, the proper relationship between sexes, and choice of leisure activities, education, occupation, and marriage. For young Chinese American women, the cultural clash was often compounded by stricter adherence to traditional gender roles and by the parental favoritism bestowed on the boys in the family. Depending on the family's economic circumstances, daughters were usually expected to forgo higher education in deference to their brothers. They were also expected to stay close to home and do all the housework, while their brothers were allowed greater freedom of movement and had fewer responsibilities at home. Parents frowned on their sons taking up sports and partying instead of studying, but disapproved of their daughters going out at all, dancing, or even mixing, with the opposite sex. Adhering to the double moral standards in the community, they

From Judy Yung, *Unbound Feet: A Social History of Chinese Women in San Francisco*. University of California. Copyright © 1995 by Judy Yung.

were more concerned about regulating their daughters' sexuality than their sons', of protecting their daughters' virginity and the family's upright standing in the community. . . .

. . . As the following stories of Jade Snow Wong, Esther Wong, and Flora Belle Jan (all of middle-class background) reveal, there were at least three patterns of response to the conflict over gender roles: acquiescence, resistance, or accommodation—creating a new gender identity by combining different aspects of two cultures. . . .

As she states in her first autobiography, *Fifth Chinese Daughter,* Jade Snow Wong was the fifth daughter in a family of seven children. Her father owned and ran a Chinatown garment factory and was an ordained Protestant minister on the side. Her mother was the faithful wife and benevolent mother, constantly hard at work at the sewing machine. The family was among the first in Chinatown to have a bathroom equipped with running water in their home. Although her father was progressive in many ways, he still believed in a Confucian upbringing for his children. From an early age, Jade Snow was taught her proper place as a daughter in a traditional Chinese family and insulated community:

> A little girl never questioned the commands of Mother and Father, unless prepared to receive painful consequences. She never addressed an older person by name. . . . Even in handing them something, she must use both hands to signify that she paid them undivided attention. Respect and order—these were the key words of life. It did not matter what were the thoughts of a little girl; she did not voice them.

So ingrained was this deference in her that even as an adult she chose to write her autobiography in the third person singular, signifying her understanding of her proper place in the Confucian hierarchal order:

> Although a "first person singular" book, this story is written in the third person from Chinese habit. The submergence of the individual is literally practiced. In written Chinese, prose or poetry, the word "I" almost never appears, but is understood. In corresponding with an older person like my father, I would write in words half the size of the regular ideographs, "small daughter Jade Snow," when referring to myself; to one of contemporary age, I would put in small characters, "younger sister"—but never "I." Should my father, who owes me no respect, write to me, he would still refer to himself in the third person, "Father." Even written in English, an "I" book by a Chinese would seem outrageously immodest to anyone raised in the spirit of Chinese propriety.

As was true for most of her peers, Jade Snow's parents did not spare the rod. "Teaching and whipping were almost synonymous," Jade Snow wrote. "No one ever troubled to explain. Only through punishment did she learn that what was proper was right and what was improper was wrong." It was expected that she excel in both American and Chinese schools, that she learn to cook and sew, that she look after her baby brother, work in her father's sewing factory, and help her mother with the household chores, and that she never go out unless escorted and with her parents' permission.

In the area of education, Jade Snow's father was more progressive than most other Chinese parents. As a Christian and a nationalist reformer, he believed in education for his daughters as well as his sons, at least through high school. Expressing the sentiments of a Chinese nationalist, he explained to Jade Snow:

> Many Chinese were very short-sighted. They felt that since their daughters would marry into a family of another name, they would not belong permanently in their own family clan. Therefore, they argued that it was not worth while to invest in their daughters' book education. But my answer was that since sons and their education are of primary importance, we must have intelligent mothers. If nobody educates his daughters, how can we have intelligent mothers for our sons? If we do not have good family training, how can China be a strong nation?

For the sake of a strong China, it was equally important that his children be educated in the Chinese language and have an appreciation of Chinese culture. Even before Jade Snow started kindergarten, her father began tutoring her in Chinese at home. By the time she was ready for Chinese school, she knew enough Chinese to be placed in the third grade. Jade Snow, in essence, had a bilingual and bicultural education, which would later help shape her ethnic and gender identity.

Once Jade Snow left the sheltered environment of home for public school, she began to notice subtle but significant differences between Western and Chinese ways. Creativity that had been stifled in the regimentation and rote memorization of Chinese school was given free rein in public school activities such as making butter, painting, and sports. Children were encouraged to speak their minds and expected to strike back in self-defense when hit. Whereas her parents believed in maintaining a distance and encouraging their children through negative reinforcement, her public school teachers practiced the opposite. When Jade Snow was hurt by a flying baseball bat, her teacher Miss Mullohand comforted her by embracing her. Unaccustomed to such intimacy, Jade Snow broke away in confusion and embarrassment.

Christian organizations such as the Chinese YWCA and library books also broadened her outlook on life. When she went to the Chinese YWCA for piano lessons, she experienced "American dishes of strange and deliciously different flavors" cooked by her older sister who worked there, and she found that to see other faces than those of her friends at school and at the factory, and "to play without care for an hour or two were real joys." Through reading, she discovered how different life was outside Chinatown: "Temporarily she forgot who she was, or the constant requirements of Chinese life, while she delighted in the adventures of the *Oz* books, the *Little Colonel, Yankee Girl,* and Western cowboys, for in these books there was absolutely nothing resembling her own life." Later, as a live-in housekeeper with the Kaisers, a European American family composed of husband and wife, two young children, and a large dog, she was able to observe first-hand the different lifestyle of a rich family:

> It was a home where children were heard as well as seen; where parents considered who was right or wrong, rather than who should be respected; where birthday parties

were a tradition, complete with lighted birthday cakes, where the husband kissed his wife and the parents kissed their children; where the Christmas holidays meant fruit cake, cookies, presents, and gay parties; where the family was actually concerned with having fun together and going out to play together; where the problems and difficulties of domestic life and children's discipline were untangled, perhaps after tears, but also after explanations; where the husband turned over his pay check to his wife to pay the bills; and where, above all, each member, even down to and including the dog, appeared to have the inalienable right to assert his individuality—in fact, where that was expected—in an atmosphere of natural affection.

Through these influences, Jade Snow unwittingly became acculturated into mainstream American life despite her parents' attempts to raise her according to Chinese tradition. Cultural conflict, not surprisingly, was the result. Her emerging desire for recognition as an individual erupted when her father denied her request for a college education because of limited family resources and because her brother—as the son who would bear the Wong name and make pilgrimages to the ancestral burial grounds—deserved it more. She bitterly questioned her father's judgment:

> How can Daddy know what an American advanced education can mean to me? Why should Older Brother be alone in enjoying the major benefits of Daddy's toil? There are no ancestral pilgrimages to be made in the United States! I can't help being born a girl. Perhaps, even being a girl, I don't want to marry, *just* to raise sons! Perhaps I have a right to want more than sons! I am a person, besides being a female! Don't the Chinese admit that women also have feelings and minds?

On another occasion, she dared to argue with her parents over her right to go out on a date. She was sixteen and had found a way to attend junior college by working as a housekeeper. Inspired by a sociology professor who advocated that young people had rights as individuals, Jade Snow decided not to ask her parents for permission to go out. When her father asked where she was going and with whom, she refused to tell him. "Very well," he said sharply. "If you will not tell me, I forbid you to go! You are now too old to whip." Rising to the occasion, "in a manner that would have done credit to her sociology instructor addressing his freshman class," she delivered her declaration of independence:

> That is something you should think more about. Yes, I am too old to whip. I am too old to be treated as a child. I can now think for myself, and you and Mama should not demand unquestioning obedience from me. You should understand me. There was a time in America when parents raised children to make them work, but now the foreigners [Westerners] regard them as individuals with rights of their own. I have worked too, but now I am an individual besides being your fifth daughter.

Her defiance shocked and hurt her parents, but Jade Snow had made up her mind to find her own lifestyle, to satisfy her own quest for individual freedom and accomplishment, even if it meant going against her parents' wishes. It was in the pursuit of these liberating ideas that placed the person's needs over the group's that she became an emancipated woman in the Western sense. From then on, she came and went as she pleased.

A number of fortuitous circumstances helped her along the way. She found work as a live-in housekeeper to support her college education. After completing junior college with honors (she won an award as the most outstanding student in California and was chosen to give the commencement speech), she was introduced by the family that employed her to the president of Mills College. With the president's encouragement, Jade Snow went on to attend Mills, living with the college dean and supporting herself with scholarships and domestic work. She graduated with Phi Beta Kappa honors in economics and sociology. When opportunities opened up for Chinese Americans during World War II, she landed a job as a secretary in a shipyard and wrote an award-winning essay on absenteeism that earned her the honor of launching a ship. This time she made the front pages of the Chinatown newspapers. Despite the skepticism and disapproval of the Chinese community, she also decided to start a hand-thrown pottery business in Chinatown, which proved so successful that by the third month she was driving the first postwar automobile in Chinatown.

By the end of her autobiography, Jade Snow had come to terms with her cultural conflicts by selectively integrating elements of both cultures into her life and work as a ceramicist. Not only did she come to appreciate Western thought and culture through her education and social life at Mills College, but she also returned to her community to rediscover the rich cultural heritage to be found in Chinese foods, medicine, opera, and the established artisans she came to know. Her pottery, which combined classic Chinese and Western utilitarian motifs, reflected this newfound bicultural identity. She was indeed at home in both cultures, having achieved personal autonomy and self-definition as a second-generation Chinese American woman. More important, Jade Snow had proven her worth as a daughter to her parents through her many accomplishments, which had brought honor to them and earned her their respect. Her father paid her the highest compliment when he acknowledged that her example had helped to wash away the former "shameful and degraded position into which the Chinese culture has pushed its women." Jade Snow ended her autobiography with the comforting thought that she had at last claimed her niche in life: "She had found herself and struck her speed. And when she came home now, it was to see Mama and Daddy look up from their work, and smile at her, and say, 'It is good to have you home again.'"

While most of Jade Snow's peers took the same middle road of accommodation through bicultural fusion, there were others who either acquiesced or rebelled against traditional gender roles. Jade Snow's own older half-sister Esther Wong (Jade Swallow) initially chose the acquiescing route. According to a Survey of Race Relations interview conducted in 1924, Esther was born in China and immigrated to America with her mother and younger sister, Ruth Wong (Jade Lotus), when she was five years old. As with Jade Snow, Esther's childhood was one of strict discipline and hard work. Her day started with Chinese lessons with her father at 6 A.M., followed by public school and then work at her father's overall factory from 3 to 9 P.M. every weekday, all day on Saturday. When only twelve years old, she was put in charge of supervising twenty-five male workers. She also had to help with the housework, and later, when her mother fell ill for a year, she had to nurse her at home. Esther did not resent the heavy responsibilities or her lack of leisure time, but what she found unfair was her father's lack of understanding and the preferential treatment accorded her brother.

> When I was 13 my brother was born and then he [her father] lost interest in us girls, did not care to bother teaching girls, and seemed to forget what we were like. When we were small he used to work at a machine next to ours, and when we were all busy he would tell us stories as we worked; but later he became very stern and cold and did not try to understand us at all. My brother has a great deal of spending money and a bank account of his own and can do just about as he likes. We girls were expected to do everything and to pay for our room and board, which we thought was hard, as that is not the Chinese way, usually that is given to children.

Considering herself an "old-fashioned girl," Esther was always careful about conducting herself properly in public.

> I was brought up in the very strictest Chinese way. I have never been to a dance, never had a caller that I received, although some have come, never had what is called "fun" in my life. Father did not believe in it. He was one of the prominent leaders of the Chinese National League of America, and acted as Treasurer, handling large sums of money. I used to be all alone in the office, receiving large sums, but was perfectly safe, no one ever spoke to me except when necessary, because I had the right Chinese manner, very cold and proper, which the Chinese look for in women, and so I was not ever spoken to, except in a business way. These League Teams always end in a feast, but though I was on many different teams at different times I never went to a feast, and so I could not be criticized. Perhaps you could not find a family that would better illustrate the conflict between the old and the new. We were brought up more strictly than most girls, even according to Chinese ideas, and my sister and I have kept these habits, never going to dances, or having company, always working.

What led Esther to challenge her parents' traditional expectations of her were their efforts to arrange a marriage for her to suitors she found unacceptable. The havoc that the controversy created in Esther's life led her finally to stand up for herself. "I was 17 years old, and I hated them both [the suitors], and I stood out against them all. I finally said that I would pack my suitcase and go, if they did not stop this torture." Esther did indeed move out, found a job that supported her through Mills College, and then went to China to teach, where she remained until war broke out between China and Japan in 1937.

At the other extreme of responses to cultural conflicts was the rebel who totally rejected traditional gender roles. Like the "flappers" of the 1920s jazz age, she was someone who defied social control and conventions, who was modern, sophisticated, and frank in speech, dress, morals, and lifestyle. The best-known Chinese flapper was Anna May Wong, who broke convention by becoming a Hollywood actress. She made more than one hundred films in her thirty-seven-year career, most of which typecast her in the limited role of "Oriental villainess." The image she projected in the movie magazines, however, was that of a beautiful and fashionable modern woman, who lived in her own apartment, dressed in the most up-to-date fashion, and spoke the latest slang. As for her counterpart in San Francisco

Chinatown, according to Rev. Ng Poon Chew, the Chinese flapper in her "bobbed-haired, ear-muffed, lipsticked, powder-puffed loveliness" was but an "Oriental echo of the American manifestation of youth. . . . Today she not only wants to select her own husband, but she wants the freedom of the chop-suey restaurants, the jazz cabarets, the moving pictures and long evenings with her beau, minus the chaperone, a 1,000 year old concomitant of Chinese civilization."

Flora Belle Jan can be considered such a Chinese flapper. The third child in a family of seven children, she was born in 1906 in Fresno, California. She later moved to San Francisco to attend college in 1925. Like Jade Snow and Esther Wong's parents, Flora Belle's parents were immigrants from Guangdong Province; but unlike the Wongs, they were not influenced by Christianity or Chinese nationalism in deciding how to raise their children. Although relatively well off—they owned and operated the Yet Far Low Restaurant in Fresno Chinatown—they did not encourage any of their sons or daughters to pursue higher education. They were quite strict with Flora Belle, wanting to maintain control over her comings and goings, to mold her into a "proper" Chinese woman, though they evidently failed.

Influenced more by her teachers, peers, and mainstream culture than by her tradition-bound parents, Flora Belle became a rebel at an early age. As she described herself in a Survey of Race Relations interview conducted in 1924, she was not one to hold back her true feelings:

> When I was a little girl, I grew to dislike the conventionality and rules of Chinese life. The superstitions and customs seemed ridiculous to me. My parents have wanted me to grow up a good Chinese girl, but I am an American and I can't accept all the old Chinese ways and ideas. A few years ago when my Mother took me to worship at the shrine of my ancestor and offer a plate of food, I decided it was time to stop this foolish custom. So I got up and slammed down the rice in front of the idol and said, "So long Old Top, I don't believe in you anyway." My mother didn't like it a little bit.

To expose the hypocrisy that she saw in both Chinese and mainstream American society, Flora Belle wrote scathing articles, poems, stories, and skits, some of which were published in the *Fresno Bee, San Francisco Examiner,* and *Chinese Students' Monthly.* One article, "Chinatown Sheiks Are Modest Lot; Eschew Slang, Love-Moaning Blues," used the latest slang to poke fun at her male contemporaries, while another sketch, "Old Mother Grundy and Her Brood of Unbaptized Nuns," ridiculed the American flapper.

Letters that Flora Belle wrote to her best friend, Ludmelia Holstein, from 1918 to 1949 reveal a young woman struggling with generational and cultural conflicts at home. Her parents obviously did not approve of Flora Belle's writings, her plans to go away to college, or her active social life. When they scolded her for leaving home for two weeks without permission, Flora Belle responded in anger by writing Ludmelia: "I *hate* my parents, *both,* now, and I want to show them that I can do something in spite of their dog-gone skepticism, old-fashionism, and unpardonable unparentliness."

Like many other American girls, Flora Belle was interested in the latest fashions, romance, and having a good time—values promoted by the mass media during a period of postwar prosperity and consumerism. She wrote Ludmelia about accepting automobile rides with boys, of lying to her parents in order "to keep pace with Dame Fashion," of how she would "rather be a vamp and have a Theda Bar-ist time in S.F." than spend $20 to attend a religious convention at Asilomar. She also had aspirations to be a famous writer. Both Flora Belle and Ludmelia evidently wrote poems, stories, and songs, which they submitted to newspapers and magazines for publication. She took her ambition to write seriously, for when admonished by Ludmelia for taking too much interest in boys, she wrote back:

> Oh, dear me! Please, dear chum, *don't* say such an awful, awful thing. You are going to discourage me, utterly dishearten me, and take away all my ambition. *Don't* say that I will be married before you finish college. It will be impossible to adapt myself to a settled-down condition. Oh, how can I bear it, to be a mother and take care of children and live an uneventful life, and die, "unwept, unhonored, and unsung," by the world of Fame; only by friends and relatives! No, Luddy dear, I can not, simply will not do it. You must encourage me, and tell me constantly that I must achieve fame and fortune before I consider my task is done.

Although her parents did not instill Chinese nationalism in her, she was exposed to it during her visits to the San Francisco Bay Area. In another letter to Ludmelia, she wrote about wanting to work in China: "When I went to 'B' [Berkeley] I got loaded with patriotism, and now my ambition is to graduate from U. of C. [University of California] and go back and teach. Lucy told me that (she's been back there) teachers were in terrible demand in China now." After graduating from Fresno Junior College in 1925, Flora Belle did attend the University of California, Berkeley, but only for six months. To support her college education, she worked first in an ice cream parlor and later as a check girl at the Mandarin Cafe while writing feature stories for the *San Francisco Examiner*—jobs that were not considered respectable by Chinatown standards. According to her last letter from San Francisco, too much partying, riding in automobiles, and "scandalous" columns in the *San Francisco Examiner* had earned her a bad reputation in the close-knit, conservative Chinese community of San Francisco. With the help of Robert E. Park, who had met her in the process of conducting his Survey of Race Relations on the Pacific Coast, Flora Belle left San Francisco to study journalism at the University of Chicago. There she met and fell in love with a graduate student from China. Upon graduation in 1926 she married him and, a year later, they had their first child. In 1932 she accompanied him to China, where they made their home for the next sixteen years.

The life stories of Jade Snow Wong, Esther Wong, and Flora Belle Jan demonstrate the extent of sexism and cultural conflicts faced at home by second-generation women of middle-class background. Their stories also show the different responses that women brought to bear on intergenerational conflicts over gender roles. While some, like Esther, acquiesced and accepted the traditional role for Chinese women, a few, like Flora Belle, openly rebelled and tried to become liberated women. Most, however, took the accommodation route, as Jade Snow Wong did. Caught in the webs of two cultures and the double binds of sexism and racism, they sought to define their own ethnic and gender identity, to find their own cultural niche by selectively adopting a bicultural lifestyle that allowed them to enjoy what they felt was the best of two worlds. . . .

. . . Like their mothers before them, second-generation women generally had to work because of the denial of a family wage to most Chinese men. Indeed, as Evelyn Nakano Glenn points out in her study of Chinese American families, the small-producer family in which all family members, including children, worked without wages in a family business—usually a laundry, restaurant, grocery store, or garment shop—predominated from the 1920s to the 1960s. For those families in San Francisco that did not own a small business, a family economy in which individual family members worked at various jobs to help make ends meet still prevailed. It was not uncommon for daughters to work part-time throughout their public school years and quit school in their teens to work full-time to help out their families. May Kew Fung, for example, began working at the early age of seven to help her widowed mother support a family of seven children. "I never had a childhood like other kids," May told her grandson Jeffrey Ow many years later. "I had nothing as a child. No toys, no place to go." She started out peeling shrimp, shelling clams, and stringing stringbeans, then moved on to sewing in her uncle's garment shop. At fifteen, although she enjoyed school and wanted to become a stenographer, May put the family's interest first. She quit school to work full-time sewing blue jeans during the day, and at night she worked as an usher in a Chinese opera house for an extra dollar.

Second-generation daughters, less encumbered by traditional gender roles that dictated women remain within the home, were considered "liberated" in being able to work outside the home in the labor market. But once there, they found themselves at a disadvantage because of race and gender discrimination. Despite their English proficiency, educational background, and Western orientation, most experienced underemployment and found themselves locked into low-paying, dead-end jobs. One second-generation Chinese summed it up this way in the *Chinese Times:*

> So far as the occupational opportunities are concerned, the American-born Chinese is a most unfortunate group of human beings. . . . The Americans will not accept us as citizens. . . . We cannot get occupational status in the American community, not because we are not worthy, but because we have yellow skin over our faces. If we turn back to the Chinese community there are not many places which can employ us. . . . There is a barrier between us and the old Chinese who are hosts of the Chinese community. We cannot get occupational status there either. The Americans discriminate against us, and we cannot get along in the Chinese community very well; what opportunities do we have in the country?

Still, second-generation women, though forced to endure discrimination in the workplace, took advantage of whatever opportunities arose, tried to find meaning and purpose in their jobs, and worked doubly hard to prove themselves. . . .

Initially, second-generation women's occupations were not very different from those of their immigrant mothers. The 1900 and 1910 manuscript censuses indicate that Chinese women in San Francisco, whether immigrant or native-born, worked as either prostitutes or seamstresses. By 1920, however, as increased numbers of the second generation became better educated and more Americanized, their work pattern was taking a path distinctly different from that of their mothers. They began to branch into clerical and sales jobs. . . . As Rose Chew, a social worker and second-generation woman herself, observed in 1930, whereas immigrant mothers worked primarily in garment and shrimp factories, did hemstitching and embroidery work, and served as domestic day workers, daughters were working outside the community as waitresses, stock girls, and elevator operators. Within the community, a few were now employed as public school teachers, doctors, dentists, bank managers and tellers, nurses, and beauty parlor owners.

Although their work lives were an improvement relative to the drudgery and low wages of their parents, many of the second generation were disappointed by America's false promises of equal opportunity. They had studied hard in school, but despite their qualifications they were not given the same consideration in the job market as white Americans. College placement officers at both the University of California, Berkeley, and Stanford University, for example, found it almost impossible to place the few Chinese or Japanese American graduates there were in any positions, whether in engineering, manufacturing, or business. According to the personnel officer at Stanford,

> Many firms have general regulations against employing them; others object to them on the ground that the other men employed by the firms do not care to work with them. Just recently, a Chinese graduate of Stanford University, who was brought up on the Stanford campus with the children of the professors, who speaks English perfectly, and who is thoroughly Americanized, was refused consideration by a prominent California corporation because they do not employ Orientals in their offices.

Occupational opportunities for American-born Chinese women were further circumscribed by gender. Economic pressures at home often forced girls to curtail their education and enter the labor force, where they worked at the same menial, low-wage jobs as their immigrant mothers. Domestic work was one such option. Protestant missionaries particularly encouraged Chinese girls to pursue this line of work because it prepared them for their future role as homemakers. They also regarded domestic work as "honest toil," unlike service in tearooms, restaurants, and clubs that "leads to many serious dangers for young and attractive Oriental girls.". . . Although great care was taken to place Chinese women in "respectable" Christian homes, many were unhappy in these positions, complaining about the low pay, heavy workload, intrusive supervision, and rude condescension they experienced on the job. . . . Few Chinese women wanted to make a career out of domestic work.

Compared to second-generation European American women, who were finding upward mobility in office and factory work, Chinese American women were not doing as well. When they tried to compete for office jobs outside Chinatown, they were generally told, "We do not hire Orientals," or "Our white employees will object to working with you." In many cases white establishments that hired them did so only to exploit their "picturesque" appearance or their bilingual skills in Chinatown branch offices. According to the sociologist William Carlson Smith,

> Chinese or Japanese girls on the Coast have been employed in certain positions as "figure-heads," as they themselves termed it, where they were required to wear oriental costumes as "atmosphere.". . . A merchant on Market Street in San Francisco said of the Chinese girls: "They dress in native costumes, they attract attention, and they can meet the public. That is why many of them are working as elevator girls and

salesladies in big department stores, some as secretaries and others in clerical positions. One girl is a secretary in a radio station and she, too, wears Chinese dress."

Gladys Ng Gin and Rose Yuen Ow are examples of Chinese American women who were willing to work in teahouses, restaurants, stores, and nightclubs as "figure-heads." Their stories shed light on how second-generation women were able to use the stereotyped images of Chinese women in mainstream culture to their advantage. Although they recognized that they were being used as "exotic showpieces," young women like Gladys and Rose took the jobs because there were few positions open to them that paid as well. In most cases they were temporary jobs, because once the novelty wore off the women were usually let go.

Although American-born, Gladys was practically illiterate in English as well as Chinese, her education having been interrupted when she was taken to China as a young girl. She therefore considered herself "lucky" when she found work as an usher at a downtown theater upon her return from China in 1918. She was only fifteen and did not know how to speak English. It didn't matter, she said, because all they wanted her to do was read numbers and take people to their seats. The one requirement was that she wear Chinese dress. For six months she was quite happy, because despite the trouble of constantly having to wash and starch the white Chinese dress she had to wear, she was making good money. But gradually, she and the twelve other girls were laid off one after another. In 1926, after Gladys learned English, she got a job running an elevator at a department store downtown. Again she was required to wear Chinese dress, but the hours and wages were equally good, so she was willing to tolerate the inconvenience. "Worked nine to six, six days a week," she said. "Seventy-five dollars a month was very good then. I was considered lucky to have found such a *see mun* [genteel] job." This time she stayed on the job for over ten years.

Rose Yuen Ow, whose parents were quite open-minded (in spite of strong objections from relatives, her mother dressed her in Western clothes, refused to bind her feet, and allowed her to attend public school until she reached the eighth grade), was among the first in her generation to work outside the home in 1909. She recalled facing more discrimination in the Chinese community than in the outside labor market. "The first place I worked at in Chinatown was a movie house," she said. "I sat there and sold tickets. The cousins immediately told my father to get me home." She was about fourteen or fifteen years old then, and her father paid no attention to this meddling. In 1913, when she went to work at Tait's Cafe, a cabaret outside Chinatown, handing out biscuits and candy before and after dinner, "everyone talked about me and said I worked and roamed the streets." Men would even follow her to work from Chinatown to see where she was going. But despite what people in the community said about her, her father permitted her to continue working at the cabaret. Like Gladys, she was required to wear Chinese dress to provide atmosphere; otherwise, it was an easy job. And she was earning good money for the time—$50 a week.

Rosie later moved up the wage ladder by capitalizing on mainstream America's interest in Chinese novelty acts. Chinese performers who sang American ballads and danced the foxtrot or black bottom were popular nightclub acts in the 1920s and 1930s. Billed as "Chung and Rosie Moy," Rose and her husband, Joe, performed in the Ziegfield Follies and in big theaters across the country with stars such as Jack Benny, Will Rogers, and the Marx Brothers. While the interest lasted, Rose earned as much as $200 to $300 a week. She would never earn that much money again. With the exception of Anna May Wong, few Chinese American entertainers ever made it big in show business. Despite their many talents, racism prevented them from making a profitable career out of it.

The double bind of sexism within the Chinese community and racism in the larger society also made it difficult for women who tried to enter and succeed in the business and professional fields. When white firms did hire Chinese American women, it was usually for the purpose of attracting Chinese business to their branch offices in Chinatown. Such was the situation for Dolly Gee, who had to fight both race and sex discrimination in order to establish a career in banking. At a time when there were few business opportunities for women in Chinatown, Dolly was regarded by her contemporaries as an exceptionally successful career woman. With the help of her father, Charles Gee, a prominent banker, she got her first experience working at the French American Bank in 1914 at the young age of fifteen. As she told the story, her father was initially hesitant to recommend her for the job because she was female:

> Early in 1914 I heard him say that another bank, the French American, desired to expand its savings activities and that there was a need for such a service in Chinatown. He said it was a fine opportunity for a young man, and regretted he had no son ready to take it up and follow in his footsteps as a banker. I immediately pointed out that although he had no son old enough, he had an energetic and ambitious daughter. I could see no reason why I could not take on the job and bring credit to my house, and he could advance no reason against it that I would listen to.

When Dolly was introduced to the head of the bank, he raised objections to both her age and her gender. "I am surprised that you would consider allowing your daughter to go to work, like a common laborer," the bank manager said. "In two or three years she should be married, according to your custom." "It's true she is only fifteen years old," replied her father. "But you'd better take her on. I'll never hear the last of it if you don't. If she fails, it will be out of her head and no harm will be done." That challenge drove Dolly to prove herself. She canvassed Chinese households and refused to budge until she got an account or two from each family. She later recalled:

> Naturally I met opposition because of my sex and my youth. This was before the [Second] World War, remember, before even American girls had invaded the business world to any significant extent. But I did get accounts, even among horrified elders who shook their heads at me while shelling out. Second-generation Chinese, born in this country, were more amenable.

In 1923, when the French American Bank opened a branch in Chinatown, Dolly became the manager. And in 1929, when the bank merged with the Bank of America and the branch office moved to a new location, she was retained as manager. She hired an all-female staff of bank tellers to work under her and operated on the principles of trust and personal service to the Chinese community. As the first woman bank manager in the nation, Dolly Gee built "a brilliant record for herself in banking," according to one corporate publication. Despite her abilities to draw deposit accounts and run an efficient branch, however, she was never promoted to a higher position outside Chinatown.

Unable to find jobs except in Chinatown, many Chinese American women who were high school graduates and bilingual worked as clerks and salespersons in local gift shops and businesses. Although these jobs were better-paying and more prestigious than domestic work, they seldom compensated women for their education and skills or led to higher positions of responsibility. Women who worked at the Chinatown Telephone Exchange, for example, had to know not only English but also five Chinese dialects and subdialects, memorize 2,200 phone numbers, and handle an average of 13,000 calls a day. Until the 1906 earthquake led to the rebuilding of Chinatown, only male operators had been employed at the Chinatown Exchange. Because of the low pay and customer complaints about the men's gruff voices and curt manner, however, they were replaced by women, who had more pleasant voices and accommodating ways—and who, when dressed in Chinese clothing, also proved to be tourist attractions. In the 1920s, telephone operators, working eight hours a day, seven days a week, earned only $40 a month, compared to $50 a month earned by housekeepers and $60 a month by clerks and stock girls. Yet the limited number of jobs open to them and the family atmosphere of their work environment both still made employment as a telephone operator desirable for second-generation women. Indeed, Chinese telephone operators were grateful for their jobs and seldom complained about the dress code or the working conditions, which other female operators deemed unsatisfactory.

The few college graduates who had professional degrees also found themselves underemployed and confined to Chinatown because of racism in the larger labor market. Many an engineer and scientist ended up working in Chinese restaurants and laundries. As was true for black professionals, white employers would not hire them, and white clients would not use their services. When Jade Snow Wong went to the college placement office for help, she was bluntly told, "If you are smart, you will look for a job only among your Chinese firms. You cannot expect to get anywhere in American business houses. After all, I am sure you are conscious that racial prejudice on the Pacific Coast will be a great handicap to you." Later, frustrated by the limited role of a secretary, she sought advice from her boss about a career change and discovered that Chinese American women like her also had to contend with sexism. Her boss said,

> Don't you know by now that as long as you are a woman, you can't compete for an equal salary in a man's world? If I were running a business, of course, I would favor a man over a woman for most jobs. You're always taking a chance that a woman might marry or have a baby. That's just a biological fact of life. But you know that all things being equal, a man will stay with you, and you won't lose your investment in his training. Moreover, he's the one who has to support a wife and family, and you have to make allowance for that in the larger salary you give him. It's not a question of whether he's smarter than a woman or whether a woman is smarter than he. It's just plain economics!

Aware of both racial and sex discrimination in the job market, Jade Snow took the accommodating route by pursuing writing and ceramics, two fields in which she thought she would not have to compete with men or be judged by her race. These creative channels also allowed her to meld unique styles of expression that utilized both her Chinese and Western sensibilities. Her books, *Fifth Chinese Daughter* and *No Chinese Stranger,* addressed her experiences as a Chinese American woman; her pottery combined Chinese classic lines with Western functional forms. She also chose to set up shop in Chinatown, where she could attract the tourist trade. By making the best of her circumstances, she found an economic niche and became both a recognized writer and ceramicist.

Their experiences paralleling those of black professional women, Chinese American women who were the first to enter professions had trouble establishing careers for themselves, even in female-dominated occupations like teaching and nursing. When Alice Fong Yu appeared before the examination board of the San Francisco School District, they asked her pointed questions not usually asked of white candidates, such as "How [in what language] do you dream?" Although she was hired as a schoolteacher, she was deliberately kept out of the classroom and assigned the tasks of an assistant principal, but without due recognition or compensation. In addition, she was overworked and asked to perform duties beyond her classification. As the only Chinese-speaking teacher, Alice was called upon to counsel, translate, and act in the capacity of clerk, nurse, and social worker to the 100 percent Chinese student population at Commodore Stockton Elementary School.

Her sister Mickey Fong also faced difficulties in entering and advancing in the nursing profession. First, her application to the Stanford School of Nursing was rejected because at the time Asians were not permitted to enroll. Next, upon graduation from the San Francisco Hospital School of Nursing, she was discouraged from taking the public health nurses' examination: "they said I was Chinese and how would I get along with the white community." Then, a minimum height requirement of 5 feet 2 inches stopped Chinese women like her who were short from taking the examination for field nursing. Only after protests by both European and Chinese American doctors, the Chinese Six Companies, and Chinese American Citizens Alliance was the requirement waived for her and then stricken from all examinations. Finally, when it came time for Mickey to take the supervisor's examination, she had an equally hard time with the Civil Service Commission. "The Commission people were quite prejudiced," she recalled. "They didn't seem very friendly or encouraging. One of them said, 'How do you think that you could supervise American nurses!' in that tone of voice." With a great deal of pluck, Mickey retorted, "Well, if I'm qualified, and if I pass the examination, I don't see why not." Mickey did pass the examination, but chose to continue working as a public health nurse in Chinatown until she moved to Washington, D.C., with her husband in 1945.

Racial and gender barriers also made it difficult for the first Chinese American women who chose medicine as their profession. Considered "men's work," being a doctor was popular among Chinese Americans for status reasons and also because they could work as doctors in their own communities should their services not be welcome in the larger society. The few Chinese women who held medical degrees inevitably had to establish their practices in Chinatown, though even there they were not always accorded the same respect as male doctors. Dr. Bessie Jeong, for example, had to omit her first name in public listings in order to attract patients who might be prejudiced against female doctors. "If they see 'Bessie,' they hesitate, even women sometimes, to go to a woman doctor," she said. "So I put 'B. Jeong' and before they know it—it's kind of embarrassing to turn and run, you know—they sit down and I try to make them feel at home with me." Dr. Margaret Chung initially moved to San Francisco to escape discrimination in Los Angeles against single women, although she also wanted to serve the Chinese community. Being young, female, and non-Chinese-speaking, however, she found it difficult to gain the trust of Chinese patients there. Not until she proved her surgical skills and commitment to community service did Chinese patients begin coming to her Dr. Rose Goong, an obstetrician/gynecologist, had less trouble finding Chinese clients, largely because Chinese women were still reluctant to see male physicians. But she was also popular because she was known for being available around-the-clock to her patients and for providing free postnatal care to mothers and their babies. . . .

The work lives of second-generation women attest to the extent of racial and sex discrimination they faced in the labor market and the ways in which they were able to cope. Most accommodated by making the most of their limited circumstances; some went to China for better economic opportunities. Even though discrimination in the work world often stopped them from fulfilling their potential in their chosen occupational fields, Chinese American women managed to earn enough to support themselves and, more often than not, help out their families. At the same time, their work experiences drew them away from the influences of their cultural upbringing at home and further into the public arena, broadening their outlook in life and encouraging them in the direction of American consumerism and modern living.

 ## For Further Study

1. How were the traditional Chinese views of how girls should be treated different from the views that exist today in American society? How different were they from the views that prevailed at the time described in this selection?

2. What were the main strategies the author describes for dealing with the cultural strains that second-generation Chinese American women experienced? Briefly describe how each of the three individual lives the author portrays is an example of one of these strategies.

3. Chinese American women had to contend with many different forms of discrimination, both from the Chinese community and from the general society. Describe some of the ways they were discriminated against.

4. What were some of the adjustments Chinese American women had to make to cope with the problems they encountered in their work places?

For Further Reading

The literature on immigration and the lives of immigrants in the United States is massive. General accounts include Philip A. M. Taylor, *The Distant Magnet: European Emigration to the U.S.A.* (1971); three books by Oscar Handlin, *The Uprooted* (2nd ed., 1973), *Children of the Uprooted* (1966), and *Immigration as a Factor in American History* (1959); Alan M. Kraut, *The Huddled Masses: The Immigrant in American Society, 1820–1921* (1982); and Roger Daniels, *A History of Immigration and Ethnicity in American Life* (1990). General histories about Asian immigrants to the United States include Sucheng Chan, *Asian Americans: An Interpretive History* (1991), Roger Daniels, *Asian America: Chinese and Japanese in the United States since 1850* (1988), and Ronald Takaki, *Strangers from a Distant Shore: A History of Asian Americans* (1989). Yong Chen, *Chinese San Francisco, 1850–1943: A Trans-Pacific Community* (2000) is a detailed history of the oldest established Chinese community in the United States. Craig Storti, *Incident at Bitter Creek: The Story of the Rock Springs Chinese Massacre* (1991) deals with one explosively violent example of anti-Chinese prejudice in a mining town. Another autobriography of a Chinese American woman besides those mentioned in the selection is Maxine Hong Kingston, *The Woman Warrior: Memoirs of a Girlhood among Ghosts* (1989). The most complete treatment of anti-immigrant feelings in the United States is John Higham, *Strangers in the Land: Patterns of American Nativism* (1955).

Chapter 9

African American migrants making their way north.

African American Migration

Florette Henri

Throughout much of the twentieth century, African Americans abandoned the cotton fields and small towns of the South for the industrial cities of the North. In the last decade of the nineteenth century and in the first of the twentieth, 200,000 African Americans came North. Between 1910 and 1920, a half-million more came, and larger and larger numbers migrated North in succeeding decades. They came, as Florette Henri makes clear in the essay that follows, for a number of reasons: some came to sightsee and never returned South; some came to escape the violently racist attitudes of the South; some came to enjoy the economic opportunities the North afforded. African Americans who came to the North were motivated by the same search for opportunity that drew rural and small-town whites as well as the "new" immigrants to the cities—the millions of jobs for able-bodied men and women made available by a vibrant and ever expanding industrial economy. For many, a job even at the lowest of ranks in the factory provided an income higher than they could earn as sharecroppers or tenant farmers.

Many parallels can be found between the migration of African Americans from the South to the cities of the North and the "new" immigration to the United States by southern and eastern Europeans between 1880 and 1924. Both groups were abandoning a system of landholding where they were at once tied to the land and landless—African Americans as sharecroppers in a system of tenant farming and sharecropping, the Europeans as peasants in a feudal land system. There are other parallels as well: both groups settled, for the most part, in the big cities, not in the rural areas of the country; both were relegated to the unskilled levels of the industrial work force; and both created urban ghettoes as a shield from a strange, and even hostile, environment. But one important difference between these two groups of migrants remained: no white ethnic group had to overcome the barriers of color that confronted the African American.

[The] story of movement in the black population says clearly that many blacks did not sit quietly in one place waiting for things to change under them; that, in fact, they shared in the general American pattern of mobility. But early migrations were dwarfed by the surge of black people northward after 1900, and especially after 1910. According to various contemporaneous estimates, between 1890 and 1910 around 200,000 black Southerners fled to the North; and between 1910 and 1920 another 300,000 to 1,000,000 followed. . . .

What precipitated the mass migration of that period is succinctly expressed in this verse:

> Boll-weevil in de cotton
> Cut worm in de cotton,
> Debil in de white man,
> Wah's goin' on.

Drought, then heavy rains, and the boll weevils that flourish under wet conditions had ruined cotton crops in 1915 and 1916. Tenant farmers and croppers were desperate. Too, injustice, disfranchisement, and Jim Crow—"debil in de white man"—grew more severe and galling each year, until life in the South was intolerable for a black man. And at the same time, finally, there was a reasonable hope of escape from this suffering because of the Great War, as it approached and while it was going on. At precisely the time war production needed all the labor it could get, immigration was sharply curtailed, dropping from 1,218,480 in 1914 to 326,700 in 1915, to under 300,000 in 1916 and 1917, and finally to 110,618 in 1918—less than 10 percent of the 1914 figure. If immigration had continued at the 1914 rate, almost 5,000,000 more immigrants would have entered the United States by the end of the war, and war production could probably have employed almost all the workers among them. It seems reasonable to believe, therefore, that even if one accepts the top figure of 1,000,000 black migrants during that period, they and the immigrants who did manage to enter the country during the peak production years could not have filled the void. Such friction, then, as developed between black and white workers was probably not based on economic competition so much as on racism.

Woodson claims that even before the unskilled and semiskilled black laborers went North, there was a substantial movement in that direction by educated and professional-level black people—the group that [W. E. B.] DuBois named the Talented Tenth—who could no longer bear the violence, intimidation, and suppression that were part of everyday life in the South. The increasing callousness of the Republican administrations of Roosevelt and Taft badly shook their faith in the party of liberation. The Brownsville incident of 1906, when President Roosevelt and Secretary of War Taft arbitrarily punished 167 black soldiers, may have been final proof that blacks were deserted by the federal government and must look after themselves. These political facts may have motivated some of the poor, uneducated blacks also to leave the South, although by and large they clung to their faith in the party of emancipation. When Ray Stannard Baker asked a black man why he was leaving Atlanta (after a riot there in 1908) for Washington, D.C., the answer was: "Well, you see, I want to be as near the flag as I can."

According to several contemporaneous studies of the motives of migrants, most blacks left the South simply to be able to feed themselves and their families. George Edmund Haynes, one of the Urban League founders, reported in 1912 that of southern black migrants in New York City, 47.1 percent had come for better jobs. In a 1917 study made for the Secretary of Labor, again the economic motive came first. In the light of what has been said in previous pages about the condition of southern blacks, a rundown of all the reasons given in that study is interesting:

1. low wages: "The Negro . . . appears to be interested in having some experience with from four to six times as much pay as he has ever had before" even if, in buying power, 50¢ to $1 a day in the South should equal $2 to $4 a day in the North;
2. bad treatment by whites—all classes of Negroes are dissatisfied with their condition;
3. injustice and evils of tenant farming—difficulty of getting a planter to settle accounts, about which his word cannot be questioned; also, the high prices charged by planters and merchants for necessary supplies;
4. more dissatisfaction than formerly with these conditions, in the light of the world movement for democracy.

Poor pay was the leading reason for migration in a survey of 1917 in the *Crisis,* followed by bad treatment, bad schools, discrimination, and oppression. Abram L. Harris, an economist and informed student of Negro migrations, concluded that all the movements away from the rural South, from the Civil War on, were "fundamentally the result of the growth of machine industry, and of the lack of economic freedom and the non-assurance of a margin of subsistence under the one-crop share system of the agricultural South."

There were undoubtedly some migrants who moved about simply for adventure or to see new places. Out of the 400 interviewed by Epstein, 85 said they were just traveling to see the country. Gilbert Osofsky in his Harlem study speaks of some who were just wanderers, criminals, hoodlums, or adventurers. But most evidence shows, as Louise Venable Kennedy wrote in her study of Negro urbanization, that blacks move about for the same reasons as other American groups—for jobs, education, better conditions—and not because of a racial trait of rootlessness, as many believed. John Daniels in his 1914 book on black people of Boston spoke of the "excessive migratoriness which is inherent in the Negro character." He added, "Obstacles in the environment are not opposed by a quality of rootedness," explaining why almost 2,000 blacks left Boston between 1900 and 1910. But such an attack on character was hardly necessary to explain why numbers of blacks left Boston. Daniels himself mentions a notable decrease of interest and tolerance on the part of white Bostonians. Even more important was the scarcity of any but menial jobs in nonindustrial Boston. Howard Odum, also, spoke of migratoriness as a race characteristic of blacks, claiming that they have little attachment to home, siblings, or parents. Dillard, however, said that migration was motivated by an effort to improve their condition of living, and as such deserved "commendation not condemnation." And the Atlanta *Constitution* stated bluntly: "The Negro does not move North because he is of a restless disposition. He would prefer to stay in his old home if he could do so on a wage basis more equitable to his race."

The industrial cities were magnets. To farm workers in the South who made perhaps $.75 a day, to urban female domestics who might earn from $1.50 to $3.00 a week, the North during the war years beckoned with factory wages as high as $3.00 or $4.00 a day, and domestic pay of $2.50 a day. As the Dillard report pointed out, blacks longed to get more money into their hands, even if more went out of them; and though living was higher in the North, it was generally not 400 percent higher, as wages might be. A migrant who had gone to Cleveland wrote that he regularly earned $3.60 a day, and sometimes double that, and with the pay of his wife, son, and two oldest daughters, the family took in $103.60 every ten days; the only thing that cost them more than at home, he said, was the rent, $12 a month.

In Pittsburgh in 1918, black migrants were earning between $3.00 and $3.60 a day; only 4 percent of them had earned that much in the South. A 1919 study showed that only 5 percent of migrants in Pittsburgh earned less than $2.00 a day; 56 percent of them had earned less than $2.00 a day in the South. A migrant working in a Newark, New Jersey, dye plant made $2.75 a day plus a rent-free room, and the company had paid his fare North; back home he would have earned less than $1.00 for a long day's work on a farm. Tenant farmers in the Deep South often made less than $15 a month; in 1920, the average annual income of a rural Negro family in Georgia was $290. Even where there was some industry, as in the foundries around Birmingham, unskilled workers got a top of $2.50 for a nine-hour day, while the same sort of worker could make $4.50 a day in Illinois. In Haynes's survey of Negro migrants in New York City, the great majority reported earning from 50 to 100 percent more than they had in the South.

In the complex of motives active upon most migrants it is hard to assess the weight of better educational opportunities for their children. Letters of potential migrants to Emmett Scott and others often speak of this motive. One such letter, written by a representative of a group of 200 men in Mobile, said the men didn't care where they went "just so they cross the Mason and Dixie line" to "where a negro man can appreshate beaing a man" and give his children a good education. Southern politicians of the Vardaman stamp were constantly trying to reduce the little schooling black children got. As governor of Mississippi, Vardaman told the legislature in 1906: "It is your function to put a stop to the worse than wasting of half a million dollars annually"—the cost of black schools—"to the vain purpose of trying to make something of the negro which the Great Architect . . . failed to provide for in the original plan of creation." The black man had no vote, and without a vote he was not likely to enlist any politician in the cause of black education. When Powdermaker's study of Mississippi was made in the 1930s, black schooling was still brief and inadequate; she found fifth-grade children, in that grade because of automatic promotions, who could not read; and she found black parents, especially mothers, with a burning desire to give their children an education at whatever sacrifice to themselves.

Also, it is hard to assay a motive like wishing to appreciate being a man, or wanting to go "where a man's a man" or any place "where a man will Be anything Except a Ker . . . I don't care where so long as I go where a man is a man." The theme is repeated over and over again, and it is a difficult thing to say, a hurtful thing, much harder than simply saying one wants better pay. But it was possibly the overriding reason for leaving the South. W. T. B. Williams, the writer of the report of the Dillard team and its only black member, pointed out that although better pay was most frequently named as a reason for migrating, "the Negro really cares very little for money as such. Cupidity is hardly a Negro vice." He quoted a Florida woman as saying: "Negroes are not so greatly disturbed about wages. They are tired of being treated as children; they want to be men."

Southern blacks were tired of "bene dog as [if] I was a beast"; of never, never being addressed, as they must always address the white man, with a title of respect. Powdermaker says that in Mississippi whites will address a black grade school teacher as "doctor" or "professor" to avoid the Mr., Mrs., or Miss; the consistent withholding of those titles endowed what is a mere polite form with such symbolic force that blacks felt the values of the whole system were concentrated in that Mr. or Mrs. or Miss, and not to be called so meant to be outcast by the system. The sense of being outside the society was reinforced by the equally consistent practice of better-class whites of addressing even the meanest, most illiterate white laborer or loafer as Mr., a cheap way of flattering him into docility by giving him, through the magic of the title, assurance that he was a white man and that as such he shared the superiority of other white men to blacks. This was most damaging to the black man's sense of who he was; because if he, a respectable black, perhaps well educated and fairly prosperous, was not treated like even the dregs of white society, then perhaps he was a different species, not a man at all.

In the many bitter complaints of blacks that they were never Mr. in the South although the white man always was, and in the boast of a migrant writing home that in the North you didn't have to "sir" the white men you worked with—in these there is the cry of the dispossessed and disinherited, a summing up of all the reasons for the black migration. A black minister in Philadelphia put it this way to Ray Stannard Baker: "Well, they're treated more like men up here in the North, that's the secret of it. There's prejudice here, too, but the color line isn't drawn in their faces at every turn as it is in the South. It all gets back to a question of manhood."

Scott said that fear of mob violence and lynching were frequently alleged reasons for migrating, and Booker T. Washington had said that "for every lynching that takes place . . . a score of colored people leave . . . for the city." In the statements of migrants themselves, however, these reasons are not mentioned nearly so often as jobs, pay, justice, better living, and education. Charles Johnson came to the conclusion that persecution, and its ultimate expression in lynching, were not nearly such dominant stimuli to migration as the hope of economic betterment. He claimed that many black migrants—almost 43 percent of them—had gone not North but Southwest, mostly to Arkansas, Oklahoma, and Texas—where economic opportunities might be better but where mob violence was far from uncommon; and that Jasper County in Georgia, and Jefferson County in Alabama, both with fearsome lynching records, had increases rather than declines of black population during the migration period. Kennedy's findings indicated that insecurity of property and life was more likely a supporting cause of migration than a fundamental one, underlying the frequently named reasons of social and educational inequities, humiliations, and insults. In Dutcher's analysis of changes during the 1910–20 decade is the statement that "social grievances appear never to have been sufficient of themselves to produce any considerable movement of the Negro population," and that economic betterment had much greater force. It is amazing, if true, that fear of lynching should not have been a chief reason for flight, considering that ninety-three blacks were lynched in 1908, and fifty, sixty, seventy, or more each year (except 1917) from then until 1920; but the fear may have been too terrible to be given expression in so many words.

Also, there appears to have been a generation gap that made for different motives among older and younger blacks. Many of the older generation, although desperately in need of financial succor, were not so rebellious against "keeping their place." But their sons, who had some schooling, who could read, did not take kindly to the old customs. They were not going to endure being knocked about and beaten on the job "to an extent hardly believable," as the Labor Department reported, and hit with anything that came to the white man's hand, a tool or a piece of lumber. Particularly they resented abuse when their women were with them, and black women were so terrified of what their men might do and what might happen to them as a result, that often the women defended themselves rather than expose their husbands or male friends to danger. A young black said to his father, who was trying to persuade him not to migrate to Chicago: "When a young white man talks rough to me, I can't talk rough to him. You can stand that; I can't. I have some education, and inside I has the feelin's of a white man. I'm goin'.". . .

Those who had left early wrote home about freedom and jobs in the North. Labor agents came South recruiting for the big industrial companies, especially the railroads. The Chicago *Defender* carried northern help-wanted ads and detailed accounts of southern lynchings in its "national edition," widely read in the South, thus both pulling and pushing black people. The idea of "exodus" became surrounded with religious fervor. Many believed that God had opened a way for them to escape oppression. Scott described a group of 147 Mississippi blacks who, when they crossed the Ohio River to freedom, knelt, prayed, and sang hymns; they stopped their watches to symbolize the end of their old life. "Exodus" was a matter of excited secret discussion among southern blacks. Anyone who advised against going was suspected of being in the pay of whites. If a black businessman opposed migration, his customers began to vanish; a minister who preached against it from the pulpit was stabbed the next day. Rumors of jobs and of transportation to them increased unrest. Incautiously, many blacks sold or gave away their belongings and followed any crowd of migrants without an idea of their destination. Some rural areas emptied out so thoroughly that one old woman complained she hadn't enough friends left to give her a decent funeral.

"I should have been here twenty years ago," a man wrote back from the North. "I just begin to feel like a man. . . . My children are going to the same school with the whites and I don't have to humble to no one. I have registered. Will vote in the next election and there isn't any yes Sir and no Sir. It's all yes and no, Sam and Bill." A man wrote from Philadelphia telling of good pay, $75 a month, enough so he could carry insurance in case of illness, and added that there you "don't have to mister every little white boy comes along" and that he hadn't heard "a white man call a colored a nigger" since he'd been North; what was more, he could sit where he chose on the streetcars—not that he craved to sit with whites "but if I have to pay the same fare I have learn to want the same acomidation"; still, this far from rootless wanderer would always "love the good old South," he said. A Columbia, South Carolina, Negro paper reported that a migrant brother had come home for a visit with "more than one hundred dollars and plenty of nice clothes." All this was hallelujah news to the home folks. They could easily ignore the occasional cautionary letter, like one from a Cleveland migrant who warned of loafers, gamblers, and pickpockets and said the city streets weren't safe at night. An unnamed but allegedly widely respected black educator is reported to have said: "Uncle Sam is the most effective [labor] agent at this time. All who are away are writing for others to come on in, the water's fine."

Stimulating the urge to "vote with their feet," as the migration was sometimes called, were the solicitations of northern labor agents. In 1916, the first year of large-scale movement, most agents were representing railroads or the mines. Baker reported: "Trains were backed into several Southern cities and hundreds of Negroes were gathered up in a day, loaded into the cars, and whirled away to the North." For example, in February 1917 a special train was sent to carry 191 black migrants from Bessemer, Alabama, to Pittsburgh at a cost to a coal company of $3,391.95. So great was the excitement, Baker said, that Negroes "deserted their jobs and went to the trains without notifying their employers or even going home." Between 75,000 and 100,000 got to Pennsylvania that way, Baker said, many of them to work for the Pennsylvania and Erie railroads, and still more for the steel mills, munitions plants, and other heavy industries. As might be expected, men so hastily and haphazardly gathered up included a good share of shiftless characters, and in addition, the companies had not prepared for their sudden arrival the necessary housing or facilities; because of this combination of circumstances, many of the labor recruits drifted off the job before they had worked out the railroad fare the companies had advanced.

Some of the labor agents were salaried employees of large industrial companies, and these included some blacks. Others were independent employment agents who charged the migrants from $1.00 to $3.00 for placing them in jobs, and collected from the companies as well if they could get anything. Often the labor recruiters gained access to Negro quarters in the cities where they worked by disguising themselves as salesmen or insurance agents. There were probably some honest men among them, but others were flagrantly unscrupulous in their promises. An agency soliciting workers in the Birmingham and Bessemer areas advertised in such phrases as: "Let's go back north where there are no labor troubles, no strikes, no lockouts; Large coal, good wages, fair treatment; Two weeks pay; Good houses; We ship you and your household goods; All colored ministers can go free; Will advance you money if necessary; Scores of men have written us thanking us for sending them; Go now while you have the chance." Some of the "agents" were downright crooks who collected fees from men wanting to migrate and then failed to be at the depot where they were supposed to rendezvous with their clients. Such was the fate of 1,800 Louisiana blacks who paid $2.00 each to an agent who promised them jobs in Chicago but never made good on the promise. The hardship was greatest when men had quit their jobs in the expectation of leaving the South. Micheaux described one agent who, after collecting $3.00 from a man, sent him to several places in search of imaginary jobs; in the end, the agent refused to refund more than $1.00, although he had done nothing for his client. Another racket was to induce ignorant black girls to sign contracts they could not read that obligated them for the cost of their journey plus a placement fee; in many cases the agents were recruiting for brothels, although what they promised the girls was domestic service.

Alarm spread throughout the white South as farm laborers and city menial and domestic help drifted off in twos, twenties, and two hundreds. State laws and city ordinances were passed to oust or curb the agents who were taking most of the workers. In the light of complaints against the agents by a number of migrants, it seems believable that licensing laws for agents were meant at first to protect black workers as well as their white employers. In South Carolina, for example, an 1891 law requiring all labor agents to pay $500 for a license might simply have been aimed at assuring the reliability of the man promising work out of the state; but when in 1907 the fee was raised to $2,000 it was due simply to panic on the part of whites who saw their cheap labor force dwindling. According to Scott, a license cost $1,000 in Jacksonville, under penalty of a $600 fine and 60 days in jail; in Alabama the state, city, and county fees totaled from $1,000 to $1,250; in Macon, a license cost $25,000, and the applicant had to be vouched for by 10 local ministers and 35 local businessmen, which seems not so much regulatory as prohibitive, as the Atlanta *Constitution* called such licensing. In Montgomery, recruiting labor for out-of-state jobs was punishable by a $100 fine and 6 months at hard labor on a convict gang. Force was not infrequently used to prevent the taking of blacks North, Scott says. Labor agents were arrested. Trains carrying migrants were stopped, the blacks forced to return, and the agents beaten. Blacks might be terrorized or lynched on suspicion of trying to leave the state. "But they might as well have tried to stop by ordinance the migration of the bollweevil," Baker said; by ordinance, or by hitting them on the head, one by one.

Robert Abbott, editor and publisher of the Chicago *Defender* and himself a migrant from the "Negro town" of Yamacraw, was the loudest single voice calling for the northward flow of black labor, but not the only one. Many other Negro papers also encouraged migration, Baker reported. The Richmond *Reformer* spoke out against Jim Crow, segregation, and living conditions "like cattle, hogs or sheep, penned in" as evils that black people in the South must continue to endure "until they rise up in mass and oppose it openly"; self-respecting Negroes, said the

Timmonsville (South Carolina) *Watchman,* should take a hint from a recent lynching and "get away at the earliest possible moment." But it was Abbott who fleshed out the vision of escape, who gave it a definite and dramatic form—even a birthday: the Great Northern Drive of May 15, 1917. Carl Sandburg wrote in the Chicago *Daily News:* "The Defender more than any other one agency was the big cause of the 'Northern fever' and the big exodus from the South." A Georgia paper called the *Defender* "the greatest disturbing element that has yet entered Georgia." The U.S. Department of Labor said that in some sections the *Defender* was probably more effective in carrying off labor than all the agents put together: "It sums up the Negro's troubles and keeps them constantly before him, and it points out in terms he can understand the way of escape.". . .

Abbott put out a "national edition" of his weekly, aimed at southern blacks. It carried in red ink such headlines as: 100 NEGROES MURDERED WEEKLY IN UNITED STATES BY WHITE AMERICANS; LYNCHING—A NATIONAL DISGRACE; and WHITE GENTLEMAN RAPES COLORED GIRL. Accompanying a lynching story was a picture of the lynch victim's severed head, with the caption: NOT BELGIUM—AMERICA. Poems entitled *Land of Hope* and *Bound for the Promised Land* urged blacks to go North, and editorials boosted Chicago as the best place for them to go. Want ads offered jobs at attractive wages in and around Chicago. In news items, anecdotes, cartoons, and photos, the *Defender* crystallized the underlying economic and social causes of black suffering into immediate motives for flight. Repeated stories of those who were leaving the South or who were already in the North conveyed the excitement of a mass movement under way and created an atmosphere of religious hysteria; the *Defender* called the migration the "Flight out of Egypt" and the migrants sang "Going into Canaan." The more people who left, inspired by *Defender* propaganda, the more wanted to go, so the migration fed on itself until in some places it turned into a wild stampede. Even illiterate people bought the paper, as a status symbol. A black leader in Louisiana was quoted as saying, "My people grab it [the *Defender*] like a mule grabs a mouthful of fine fodder." Sandburg wrote that there was in Chicago "a publicity or propaganda machine that directs its appeals or carries on an agitation that every week reaches hundreds of thousands of people of the colored race in the southern states.". . .

Abbott enlisted the aid of two very mobile groups of black people, the railroad men and the entertainers. Chicago was the end of the North-South railroad lines, and a great junction. Hundreds of Pullman porters, dining-car waiters, and traveling stage people passed through it, some of them on their way to remote whistle-stops in the South. The *Defender* paid many of them to pick up bundles of the newspaper in Chicago and drop them along their routes at points where local distributors would meet the trains, get the bundles, and circulate them. In a town where the *Defender* was unknown, the porters would give copies away to any black person they saw. Stage people took bundles of papers and distributed them free in the theaters. The well-known concert singer Sissieretta Jones, who was called the "black Patti" in the patronizing style of the day, asked the ushers in theaters where she performed to give out free copies to all comers.

By such devices the circulation of the *Defender* soared to 283,571 by 1920, with about two-thirds of its readers outside Chicago. This was by far the largest circulation any black newspaper had ever achieved. If each copy reached five readers, a reasonable guess, about 1,500,000 blacks saw it.

Abbott's master stroke in materializing a migration that in 1916 was more rumored than real was the setting of a date, a specific month and day in 1917, for what the *Defender* called "the Great Northern Drive." The incendiary message spread that on May 15 railroad cars would back into the stations of southern towns prepared to carry North any who wanted to go, at a very low fare. The word struck southern blacks with messianic force. There was to be a second coming of freedom on May 15, and it behooved everyone to be ready. . . .

They went with whatever possessions they could carry, "wearing overalls and housedresses, a few walking barefoot.". . . Although it is hard to see how they took their goats, pigs, chickens, dogs, and cats along, as he claims, they certainly must have carried provisions for their long, long journeys, a thousand miles or more for many of them, days and nights of travel with no prospect of any creature comforts along the way. To Chicago from Savannah was 1,027 railroad miles; to New York from San Antonio, 1,916 miles; to Cincinnati from Jacksonville, 822 miles; to Newark from Vicksburg, 1,273 miles; to Detroit from New Orleans, 1,096 miles; to Cleveland from Mobile, 1,046 miles. Some stopped at Chicago for a time before going to their destinations, but most went straight through: from Florida and Georgia to Pennsylvania and New York; from Alabama, Mississippi, Tennessee, and Louisiana to Illinois and Michigan. Most of these people had probably never been more than 20 miles from their homes. . . .

One cheap way to travel was in a group. The *Defender* encouraged the formation of "clubs" of ten to fifty persons and arranged special fares and travel dates with the railroad companies. Many people wrote to the newspaper that they could bring "about 8 or 10 men" or "a family of (11) eleven more or less" or "15 or 20 good men" or "25 women and men," and so on up to "300 or 500 men and women" and finally "as many men as you want." Some of these correspondents sent stamped return envelopes and asked the paper not to publish their letters—"whatever you do, don't publish my name in your paper"—or asked that, if an answer was sent by wire, there should be no mention of the number of people because "if you say 15 or 20 mans they will put me in jail." "This is among us collerd," says one letter offering to bring 20 men and their families.

With so many concerned for secrecy, many must have been too frightened to write at all. They never revealed the presence among them of labor agents. Migrants described how they had to slip away from their homes at night, walk to some railroad station where they were not known, and there board a train for the North. If they were found to have tickets, the police confiscated them. If three or four blacks were discovered together it was assumed that they were "conspiring to go North" and they would be arrested on some trumped-up charge.

For migrants to New York from a coastal city in the South—and most of those who went to New York were from the South Atlantic states—the cheapest and most direct passage was by boat. Steerage fare from Virginia, from which most New York migrants came, was $5.50 or $6.00, including meals. The Old Dominion Line ran boats twice a week from Virginia to New York, and the Baltimore,

Chesapeake & Atlantic Railway ran steamers from Baltimore, Washington, and as far south as Florida. By train it would have cost at least $7.50 from Norfolk to New York City, without meals. So the boat was a good buy, although blacks might find themselves in a separate section of the vessel with the household pets of white travelers.

Toward the end of the peak migration period another category of southern blacks settled in northern cities: soldiers returning from France. Rudolph Fisher, a writer of the period, spoke in a short story of a family of Waxhaw, North Carolina, whose son "had gone to France in the draft and, returning, had never got any nearer home than Harlem." There were many such men whose fare, in a roundabout way, had been paid by Uncle Sam. "How're you gonna keep 'em down on the farm, / After they've seen Paree?" a popular song asked.

The rapid flow northward of black people, especially from 1916 when war production went into high gear, aroused much concern and discussion among whites and blacks, North and South. The word "exodus" was apparently so current that Octavus Roy Cohen used it as both noun and verb in his spurious Negro stories of the early twenties: "the merrymakers exodusted" from a party, he wrote; and, there was a "complete exodus from Decatur." Census figures show that in 1900 only 15.6 percent of black people (1,373,996) lived in a state other than that of their birth, whereas in 1910 the percentage born elsewhere had increased to 16.6 (1,616,608), and in 1920 to 19.9 (2,054,242). Of the 300,000 to 1,000,000 blacks estimated by contemporaries to have gone North, almost all went to urban centers. In 1900, 22.7 percent of Negroes lived in cities, North and South; in 1910 this had increased to 24.4 percent, and in 1920 to 34 percent, in numbers totaling more than 3,500,000. By 1920, almost 40 percent of the black population in the North was concentrated in the eight cities of Chicago, Detroit, New York, Cleveland, Cincinnati, Columbus, Philadelphia, and Pittsburgh, although those cities contained only 20 percent of the total northern population. The city with the most dramatic percentage increase in black population between 1910 and 1920 was Detroit, by an astounding 611.3 percent; Cleveland came next with a 307.8 percent increase; then Chicago, 148.2 percent; New York, 66.3 percent; Indianapolis, 59 percent; Cincinnati, 53.2 percent; and Pittsburgh, 47.2 percent. In numbers Chicago gained nearly 65,500 black residents, New York 61,400, and Detroit 36,240.

A question that immediately comes to mind is: what did these southern people know how to do that would earn them a living in the North? Since so much of the South was rural, it is amazing the number of occupations represented by the migrants whose letters are in the Scott collection. But indications are that about half the migrants came from towns, a Labor Department survey found. The largest number said they wanted work as laborers at unspecified common labor, with some longshoremen, stevedores, freight handlers, stokers, miners, packers, and warehousemen; many of these men had experience in southern industries such as lumbering, railroading, iron and steel foundries, sawmills, and turpentine stills. The next largest category was the semiskilled or skilled craftsman: plumbers and roofers, painters and plasterers, cleaners and pressers, hotel waiters, brickmakers and bricklayers, machinists and machinists' helpers, caulkers, carpenters, wood-workers, cabinetmakers, mailmen, auto workers, engineers, blacksmiths, glaziers, lumber graders and inspectors, foundry workers, and a large number of molders. The majority of women who wanted to migrate, and some of the men, sought menial or domestic jobs: cooks, laundresses, baby nurses, housemaids, butler-chauffeurs, janitors. Among the businesses represented by migrants were insurance man, barber, hairdresser, laundry owner, merchant, and packer and mover— memorably, the moving company owner who called himself "the Daddy of the Transfer business" of Rome, Georgia. In the much smaller class of professionals and white-collar workers the majority were teachers, including the Alcorn College graduate who was four feet, six inches tall and weighed 105 pounds—a woman, presumably, as were many of the teachers who wanted to leave the South. There were also a sixty-three-year-old graduate of Howard University Law School, an eighteen-year-old artist and actor, and a fifteen-year-old cartoonist; also printers, a college-educated bookkeeper, and a stenographer-typist. Many of the educated class expressed their willingness to do any kind of work, even common labor, if only they could get jobs in the North. Only a few who wrote of their wish to migrate described themselves as farmers, and two of these wanted to go to Nebraska and Dakota to farm. But probably many of those who were looking for laborers' jobs were tenant farmers, sharecroppers, and farm workers; and probably also many other rural people could not write or were afraid to, so we do not know about them—they simply disappeared off the farms and took their chances of finding work in northern cities. Baker says that whole tenant-farming areas of Georgia and Alabama were emptied of prime-age workers. A small number wound up in the tobacco fields of Connecticut, but the great majority must have gone to industrial cities. The black rural population of the South dropped by almost 250,000 between 1910 and 1920.

As the trains and boats pulled out week after week and month after month, the South began to hurt from a loss of the black labor force, especially the Deep South. For the first time in their history, Mississippi and Louisiana showed a decrease in Negro population between 1900 and 1910; and between 1910 and 1920 Mississippi suffered a loss of 129,600 blacks, Louisiana a loss of 180,800. In that decade the black population of the East North Central states increased by 71 percent, and that of the Middle Atlantic states by over 43 percent, although the national increase was only 6.5 percent.

Contemporary estimates by observers such as Baker and Epstein of a million or so migrants seem wildly out of line with the 500,000 figure to be calculated from 1920 census figures, which were not available to them, but it may be that their estimates were more nearly correct than figures arrived at from census returns. For one thing, it has been and remains a fact, substantiated by recent studies by the Census Bureau of its own operation, that black males are significantly under-counted. . . .

If there was finally a black Joshua it was Robert Abbott, blowing the trumpet call of jobs through a rolled-up *Defender;* his troops were the Pullman porters and road shows, with labor agents as mercenaries. Half a million blacks followed behind. Where the metaphor breaks down is that their Jericho was a dirty, crowded, sickly, dangerous city ghetto, which must often have seemed scarcely worth the trouble of getting to.

But the getting there was a tremendous feat of initiative, planning, courage, and perseverance—qualities never appearing in any catalogue of Negro traits drawn up by white people, yet here demonstrated incontestibly not by one or two "exceptional individuals," as blacks were called who did not fit the stereotype, but by at least five hundred thousand perfectly average southern Negroes. They were not passive reactors, waiting for something to happen to them; they made it happen.

For Further Study

1. Which African Americans, according to the author, tended to come North first—and why?

2. Outline the motives that brought about this mass migration and then find similarities and differences (from your text) between these motives and those of the immigrants from Europe.

3. Were there migratory patterns in the movement from the South to the North and, if so, what were they?

4. Offer a generalization about the following: (a) the attitudes of the African Americans toward the South and to the North once they arrived; (b) the means through which they earned their livelihood in the South and in the North; and (c) the temperament of those who came North.

5. And finally: What role did Robert Abbott play in the Great Migration—and with what motives?

For Further Reading

John Hope Franklin, *From Slavery to Freedom: A History of Negro Americans* (1978), is a basic general history. While some of his conclusions have been questioned, C. Vann Woodward's *The Strange Career of Jim Crow* (1974) remains a compelling account of the system of racial oppression that southern African Americans tried to escape by moving to the North. In addition to the book from which this selection is taken, Florette Henri, *Black Migration* (1975), a general history of the movement of African Americans to the North is provided by Carole Marks in *Farewell—We're Good and Gone: The Great Black Migration* (1989). The following books deal with what African Americans found in specific cities after they had arrived in the North: James Borchert, *Alley Life in Washington* (1980); James R. Grossman, *Land of Hope: Chicago, Black Southerners, and the Great Migration* (1989); Kenneth Kusmer, *A Ghetto Takes Shape* (1976); Gilbert Osofsky, *Harlem: The Making of a Ghetto* (1966); Allen H. Spear, *Black Chicago* (1967). Nicolas Lemann takes the story of the migration up to recent times in *The Promised Land: The Great Black Migration and How It Changed America* (1991).

Part III

The Tensions of Prosperity

A s the Republican candidate for the presidency in 1920, Warren Gamaliel Harding promised the American people "not nostrums but normalcy." Under his leadership and that of his Republican successors, the idealism of the Progressive era and the moralistic fervor evoked by Woodrow Wilson give way to a more prosaic and less exalted vision of American life.

But the 1920s, in retrospect, were neither prosaic nor exalted. The maturing of the American economy of mass production and mass consumption produced social changes and social divisions. Many of those committed to the values, social practices, and institutions of native, rural, nineteenth-century Protestant America began to wonder if "progress" was a virtue or a vice. Others—largely recent immigrants and middle-class city dwellers—saw little value in maintaining the older, agrarian, puritanical way of life, enjoyed the changes taking place, and looked forward to more.

The issues that polarized the nation were many and bitterly fought. In addition to the "Red Scare" of 1919 and the controversy that surrounded the Sacco-Vanzetti case, the nation debated immigration policy. Nativists wanted an end to unrestricted immigration and to make certain that most future immigrants to the United States would be Anglo-Saxons rather than southern or eastern Europeans or Asians. The Immigration Act of 1924 made both these demands law. Other controversies concerned the teaching of evolution in the public schools and the fitness of a Catholic for the office of President of the United States. John T. Scopes was sentenced to jail for teaching evolution to his students in Tennessee in 1925; and the defeat of Alfred E. Smith in the presidential campaign of 1928 can, in part, be attributed to the nation's distrust of Catholics.

The following selections offer a sense of the American experience of the 1920s. The first concerns the Ku Klux Klan, an organization that grew out of and exploited the racial, religious, ethnic, and political prejudices of the time. The second describes the lives of Mexican-Americans in the Southwest in the 1920s. The last shows how the increasing prevalence of the automobile changed American life and especially the lives of American women.

Chapter 10

Bettmann/CORBIS

A legacy of bigotry and violence–for today and tomorrow.

The Ku Klux Klan in Indiana

KATHLEEN M. BLEE

The 1920s were marked by strong social divisions and conflicts between various segments of the American people: between native-born Americans and immigrants, city dwellers and rural folk, African Americans and whites, religious fundamentalists and modernists, Protestants and members of other faiths. To these divisions can be added powerful antiradical feelings, disputes over the wisdom of Prohibition, and generational conflicts, particularly the concern of many parents that the moral code they had been brought up to believe in was being rejected by their children. These conflicts combined to create a widespread feeling that traditional American ways, institutions, and values were under threat and that action to protect them was urgently necessary.

These feelings found expression in a number of ways, one of them being the reappearance of the Ku Klux Klan. The Klan had been first organized at the end of the Civil War. Originally intended as a social club for ex-officers of the Confederate Army, it quickly became a secret terrorist organization devoted to maintaining white supremacy throughout the South by means of violence and intimidation directed toward African Americans and their white supporters. As an organization, the Klan largely disappeared in the 1870s, although Klan-like activities continued. The organization was revived in 1915, however, and by the early 1920s it had attained a large membership and, in some parts of the United States, considerable political influence.

The new KKK was similar to the original in some ways. Both were secret organizations, both restricted membership to white, native-born Americans, and both adhered to a philosophy of white supremacy. There were also differences. The old KKK had existed only in the South, while the new one found many if not most of its members in the North. (Its political impact was greatest in Indiana, Oregon, and Colorado, and the state with the largest Klan membership was probably Ohio.) The new Klan also added Catholics, Jews, and foreigners to its list of enemies. And its mode of operation was different. It was less secretive than the original Klan, and while it occasionally used violence, far more often it relied on political and economic pressure to secure its ends.

There was one other difference between the old and new Klans that the following selection makes clear: women were an important part of the new one. They had a separate organization of their own, the Women's Ku Klux Klan (WKKK), which worked alongside the KKK. Some of the most prominent Klan spokespersons were women, among them Helen Jackson and Daisy Barr, mentioned in the following selection. The stated goal of much of the KKK's social and political agenda was the protection of Protestant women from the supposed threats directed against them by foreigners, Catholics, African Americans, Jews, and even, on occasion, native-born Protestant men. All in all, women played a major role in many of the KKK's most important activities.

The KKK achieved the height of its power in the 1920s by posing as the defender of traditional American moral values at a time when they were supposedly under attack by a variety of alien forces. Thus, when it became known that some prominent leaders of the organization were guilty of a variety of economic and sexual misdeeds, the resulting scandal came as a crushing blow. Of course, the KKK did not disappear—it still exists—but never again did it achieve the breadth of support and influence that it had had in the early 1920s.

To many who enlisted in the fiery crusade of the 1920s Klan, racial, religious, and national antagonisms were *moral* issues. The Klan, its leaders and members insisted, did not preach hatred and intolerance of any group. It sought only to defend traditional moral standards against the seductive allurements of modern society. And thus the Klan battled those groups—primarily Jews, Catholics, and blacks—who it claimed promoted vice and immorality. . . .

Many white Protestant women heard the Klan's message about morality and embraced it readily. Klanswomen across the country marched under banners proclaiming We Stand for True Godliness, Purity, and Loyalty; We Are the Foe of Vice, the Friends of the Innocent; Love Thy Neighbor as Thyself but Leave His Wife Alone; and Wife Beaters Beware. Women's Klan chapters often described their mission in self-righteous terms, as safeguarding public virtue and as keeping "the moral standards of the community at a high plane." The underlying message of klannish morality was effective, too. Klanswomen and Klansmen across the country responded to the Klan's appeal and launched a frenzied assault upon "immoral" Jews, Catholics, and blacks.

From Kathleen M. Blee, *Women of the Klan.* Copyright © 1991. Reprinted by permission of the University of California Press.

The Klan's morality campaigns succeeded in normalizing fear and hatred of minorities. When the second Klan attacked racial, ethnic, and religious groups, it did so by portraying them—especially minority men—as ruthless beasts who operated outside the moral code that shaped civilized life. In this way, the Klan deepened an existing perception among white Protestants that nonwhites and non-Protestants were strange, alien, and inexplicable. Disguising a viciously racist, anti-Semitic, and anti-Catholic agenda as a moral crusade was particularly effective in homogeneous white Protestant communities in which racial and religious minorities posed no immediate economic or social competition to the majority population. It allowed the Klan to denounce Jews, Catholics, and blacks as evil, even as devils, and as a potent threat to white Protestant moral values. . . .

Indiana was a particularly fertile field for the bigoted appeal to morality used by . . . Klan spokespersons. That it was may seem odd, for Indiana in the 1920s was one of the most racially, culturally, and religiously homogeneous states. The history of racism and intolerance in Indiana, however, suggests that the Klan's appearance in the state simply made visible deep racist and bigoted attitudes that many of the state's white native-born Protestants had long held. Indiana's tradition of racism, anti-Catholicism, and moral vigilantism fit well into the Klan's political agenda. . . .

Morality crusades . . . were the Klan's entrée into many communities in Indiana. The 1920s Klan was extraordinarily successful in bringing a wide range of white Protestants who feared liquor or sexual promiscuity or gambling into an organized political force with common targets: nonwhites, immigrants, and non-Protestants. The call to morality fired political passions while obscuring white Protestants' real differences in sentiments toward sexuality, alcohol, and leisure time activities. A resident of Indianapolis recalled the excitement of joining the Klan's crusade: "It gave people a feeling that they were doing the right thing . . . really felt like they were doing the Christian duty."

Klan recruiters portrayed themselves as a movement of righteous Protestants beleaguered by forces of immorality. Thousands of cards were distributed on street corners and in churches and lodges by Klanswomen and Klansmen seeking new recruits for the crusade. Each small calling card bore the terrifying message:

> Remember, every criminal, every gambler, every thug, every libertine, every girl ruiner, every home wrecker, every wife beater, every dopepeddler, every shyster lawyer, every K of C [Knight of Columbus], every white slaver, every brothel madame, every Rome-controlled newspaper—is fighting the KKK.

The Klan's claims to support women's rights and its efforts to recruit women did not prevent it from directing its morality crusades in Indiana to Klansmen and urging them to fight on behalf of white Protestant women. It invoked women to justify nearly every action that the Klan took against vice and corruption. When the Klan fought against prostitution, gambling, "bawdy houses," pool halls, dog and horse racing, and slot machines, it did so in the name of women who faced financial ruin by wayward or erring husbands: in gambling houses, "men are robbed, by shrewd house men of their weekly payroll, and their poor wives and children must suffer hunger and real need in order to please these bands of thieves."

The Klan claimed to oppose liquor for the same reason: women were vulnerable to physical abuse and economic ruin at the hands of drunken husbands and fathers. Klan chapters threatened, raided, and assaulted bootleggers and moonshiners and condemned those (outside the Klan) who used alcohol. Some Indiana chapters even gathered evidence for the arrest of local druggists who sold alcohol-based preparations. Despite its self-portrayal as an antiliquor group, KKK klaverns often protected bootleggers and moonshiners, raiding only those who did not pay for the Klan's protection.

At least initially, campaigns against vice were popular. Across Indiana, Klan members were recruited by local elites who introduced the group as a community reform organization. The Klan placed ads in local papers announcing its "clean-up campaign" and warning officials of repercussions if they failed to take action against gambling houses and liquor. Too, the Klan's ability to define itself as the major barrier to vice appealed to Protestant clergy, who recruited for the Klan from among their congregations.

Klan chapters frequently threatened those it regarded as violators of the moral code through letter or visit. Physical attacks on offending persons were less common since the Klan's reputation for violence made threats extremely effective. A resident of rural Warren, Indiana, recalled that "in spite of no record of violence there was a general feeling of fear, mystery, and power associated with the Warren Klan. Young girls were warned never to get into a car with men—especially men wearing white hoods!" . . .

There were few standards for selecting Klan victims. Women and men who were hostile to the aims of the Klan or who were not native-born white Protestants were the most likely targets. Even Klan members, however, might be singled out by fellow Klansmen or Klanswomen for not living a proper klannish life. One such incident in Williamsburg, Indiana, involved a Klansman who was accused of spending money on illegal liquor in lieu of providing adequately for his wife and children. After an evening visit by his Klan brothers the man changed his ways. A former Klansman from west-central Indiana explained that the Klan was able to make use of powerful political connections to locate its victims. "They used to take men that would leave their wives and not provide for their wife. They would get a hold of that fellow and sometimes horsewhip him." Asked how the Klan got its information, he said, "Well, a lot of lawyers were members of the Klan and the judge and those people. They were members of the Klan."

Another aspect of the Klan's moral code concerned the chastity of white Protestant women themselves. Like its predecessor, the second Klan vowed to defend women's sexual purity. The impetus for this aspect of the Klan's moral crusade came primarily from the KKK, although the women's Klan was occasionally involved.

Young women were the particular objects of male Klan protectiveness. The KKK press roused intense public fear with suggestions of a vast sexual traffic in young white women, alleging that tens of thousands of girls were snatched into a sexual netherworld each year. The northern Indiana Klan attempted to stop a scheduled boxing match near Chicago on the grounds that Jack Johnson was a professed "negro white slaver." Making a similar appeal, a Klan pamphlet posed this chilling question to potential recruits: "Do you know that annually there are 50,000 girls, from approximately 50,000 American homes, whose virtue is sacrificed upon the altar of vice? [That] there are thousands of girls of foreign birth who were once sent to this country's shores and sold as slaves to the godless passions of men?"

Klansmen's vigilantism in defense of girls' virtue, though, often mixed with other concerns, such as fear of female sexuality and attention to the interests of local elites, as in this story related by a southern Indiana former Klansmember.

> The Klan asked a chap by the name of Neth who was a minister . . . to leave town and he did. . . . In addition to being a minister of the church, he taught two or three classes in high school. . . . But this high school girl, she decided she kind of liked Neth, and so she was always a'hanging around, and the real problem was the girl was just pretty much of a tramp, anyway you'd figure it. So, but . . . nevertheless her dad was a rather prominent businessman in town and so on, and they thought that Neth and this girl was a gettin' too thick and so they advised him to leave and he did.

Many Klan actions, in which both Klansmen and Klanswomen participated, were aimed at curbing the sexual temptations of young women and men. Two areas were of particular concern: dance halls and automobiles. Both allowed young people a measure of privacy away from the watchful eyes of parents and other adults. Both gave young people a chance to indulge in liquor and sex. Both, the Imperial Wizard warned, subjected the weak to unnecessary and dangerous "seductive allurement."

In town after town in Indiana the Klan tried to make a public issue of dance halls and other "vile places of amusement." In some areas the Klan appealed to local authorities to intervene for the sake of public morality and the protection of town youth from sexually suggestive dances. An Indianapolis Christian church minister, later a Klan lecturer, generated much publicity by condemning as "immoral" the mayor's support of public dancing. In Hammond, Indiana, the Klan announced that it would monitor all dance halls, pool halls, picture shows, and other places of amusement for the town youth in order that the "moral conditions" of such places (and presumably also of the youth who frequented them) be improved. In taking this action, the Hammond Klan claimed, it was responding to protest from an aroused citizenry, citing complaints from local women about "brazen male mashers" and impassioned "love grips" in the "cheaper movie houses" of the town. Similarly, in South Bend the Klan engineered a police raid on a local liquor establishment and claimed, in an article entitled "Klan Plays Part of Good Samaritan to Modern Magdalene," that three white teenaged girls were being held prisoner there.

In other Indiana towns the Klan acted more directly, destroying and burning buildings that permitted youth dancing. The Pittsburg, Kansas, chapters of the KKK and WKKK summed up the feelings of many Indiana Klansmen and Klanswomen when they demanded the closing of all public dance resorts since "most of the cases of assault between the sexes have followed dances where they got the inspiration for rash and immoral acts." Many times, the condemnation of dance halls only thinly veiled anti-Semitic attitudes. The Klan implied and sometimes openly declared that Jews benefited financially from places of amusement and thus were responsible for the "misuse of girls" and "promiscuous petting" that these places encouraged among the young.

Automobiles offered an even more direct threat to the moral standards of young persons. Often, the Klan's first public action in a community would be a campaign to "clear the highway of spooners." Parties of masked and hooded Klansmembers (presumably, but not certainly, men) patrolled highways and back roads in search of young couples in parked automobiles. In some communities Klan delegations simply reported to parents and police the names of those found parked at the sides of roadways. In other areas couples caught in an embrace faced a more immediate punishment, including threats and beatings by night-riding Klan posses. The Klan's fervor made people fearful of using the roadways in many areas. Indeed, the Klan's enthusiasm for breaking up "petting parties" by searching all cars on highways caused several motor clubs to blacklist the entire state.

The Klan reserved its greatest terror for nonwhite men who were "involved with" white women. To the Klan of the 1920s, dating and marriage across racial or ethnic lines evoked the same images of white female exploitation and usurpation of white men's privileges that fueled the Reconstruction-era Klan. Nonwhite, foreign-born, and non-Protestant men who were caught with white women faced fierce reprisals by the Klan, including whipping, beating, kidnapping, and even lynching. White women who consorted with Jewish, immigrant, or black men met similar fates. In Muncie, Indiana, a Klanswoman even accused blacks and Catholics of a conspiracy, claiming that Catholics had discovered a powder that would bleach the skins of black men so that they could marry white girls.

Although the Indiana Klan presented itself as an agency of moral reform, the Klan's real message was clearly different. At the same time as it proclaimed itself the force of morality and sexual purity, the Indiana Klan offered audiences graphic tales of female enslavement and sexual exploitation, usually by Catholic priests but also by black and Jewish men.

Typical of such stories was the Klan's attack on a photoplay picture it described as "coarse, degrading, and insulting to the white race." In fact, the Klan's fury over the play centered on its "tendency to create aspirations in the lives of negro people." As was true in much Klan propaganda, it referred to illicit sexual aspirations and to black men: "the revolting spectacle of a white woman clinging in the arms of a colored man is simply beyond words to express." To make the threat of black men's sexual aspirations more threatening, the Indiana Klan press charged that when the picture played in Texas, a bulletin board adjoining the theater bore the message, "White-skinned ladies will flirt with black-skinned men when their husbands are away."

Similarly, the Indiana Klan justified its anti-Semitic attitudes as a defense of Gentile womanhood against the avarice of Jewish men. Jewish businessmen, according to the Klan, were attempting to destroy the very foundations of Christianity by seducing and raping Protestant girls. A typical Klan publication argued that its anti-Semitic policies were simply giving voice to the disgruntlement of many Protestants who "are tired of the outrages inflicted upon innocent girls by Hebrew libertines."

The most common target of the Indiana Klan, however, was Catholics. Anti-Catholic lectures, stories, and books that proliferated in the 1910s were recycled with few changes by the Klan a decade later. The Klan circulated thousands of copies of an alleged Knights of Columbus initiation that was the secret blueprint for a Catholic takeover of the country. In the purported pledge, aspiring Knights of Columbus promised to "wage relentless war, secretly and openly, against all heretics, Protestants, and Masons." The document detailed the Catholic initiates' vow: "Burn, waste, boil, flay, strangle and bury alive these infamous heretics; rip open the stomachs and wombs of their women and crash their infants' heads against the walls in order to annihilate their execrable race [or] secretly use the poisonous cup, strangulation cord, the steel of the poiniard, or the leaden bullet."

The most powerful anti-Catholic allegations made by the Indiana Klan concerned sexual practices of priests and nuns. Klan publications and lecturers described an international network of convent prisons that enslaved young Protestant women, exacting forced labor and sexual favors from the girls and turning them into compliant Catholic adults. According to . . . the WKKK, Romanists prevailed upon innocent Protestant couples to sign over their children to the religious upbringing of Catholics. Occasionally, boys were the alleged target of Romanist avarice, as in the tale of fifty-two boys snatched from a Methodist Episcopal orphanage by a Catholic-incited police raid and placed in Catholic homes from which they fervently endeavored to escape. But it was mainly Protestant girls who were alleged to be ensnared by Catholic institutions, allowing the Klan to claim that it was safeguarding the virtue of 100 percent females.

Indiana Protestant preachers commonly adopted the klannish term for the Roman Catholic church and titled lectures on the Klan's battle with the Catholics "The Beast vs. the Invisible Empire." In Muncie, Indiana, the Lynds' *Middletown* reported that "local Klansmen vowed they would unmask 'when and not until the Catholics take the prison walls down from about their convents and nunneries.'" One of the Lynds' informants, indicating a copy of a common Klan periodical, declared, "Look at this picture of this poor girl—look at her hands! see, all those fingers gone—just stumps left! she was in a convent when it was considered sinful to wear jewelry, and the Sisters, when they found her wearing some rings, just burned them off her fingers!"

To make initial contact in a new territory, the Klan sent lecturers posing as former nuns and former priests to titillate audiences with details of Romanist sexual depravity and to prepare the way for the Klan's troupe of Protestant minister-lecturers. The tactic was so successful that the same "nun" and "priest" lecturers returned to areas over and over, drawing massive crowds. Lurid stories of Catholic depravity were rumored in public and discussed openly and in great detail in assemblies restricted to Klan members.

The Klan's genius at self-promotion was evident in its Indiana lecture tours. Publicly distributed Klan newspapers described the "torture and abuse of Protestant girls in the Roman Catholic hell holes" of Catholic convents that observers would relate since the girls themselves demurely declined to reveal intimate details of their abuse in a public forum. Memories of the sexual tales spread by the

Klan are still fresh in the minds of former Klansmembers and contemporaries of the 1920s Klan movement in Indiana.

> They were saying that the Catholic priests and nuns were having sexual relationships and they'd kill the babies. They'd have abortions. All that kind of stuff. They ripped the stomachs of the nuns open and would take the baby. All that kind of business. Just horrible things.
>
> They would never come out and say things but they would imply a lot of things. And, then you would draw your own conclusions about how the Catholics and priests and nuns behaved. In fact, you know, the convent at Huntington and the friary was right there. Of course, the friary didn't belong to the Catholics anymore. But, there actually was an underground passage between the two. And, of course, the whole community made a lot of that.
>
> Where the [convent] academy was, they had their own graveyard to bury their dead from the babies that was born to the girls there in that thing. . . . I was curious where the graveyard was [but] I didn't ask anybody.

One of the most successful Klan emissaries was Helen Jackson, billed as an "escaped nun." Jackson traveled across the country, regaling her sex-segregated audiences with tales of sexual horrors behind convent walls. She claimed to have firsthand knowledge of infanticides and abortions forced on nuns by the priests who fathered their babies. Displaying little leather bags, Jackson told her riveted audience that these were used to dispose of the convents' murdered newborns and aborted fetuses. In small towns of the West and Midwest, she regaled thousands of avid listeners with tales of Catholic sadomasochistic practices, including one incident in which a cross was burned on her own back. One informant recalled an anecdote of convent life from Helen Jackson's speech: "When they misbehaved, they were soaked in the bathtubs where, they didn't have kotex in those days, it was just cloth that was washed out in tubs and soaking with those pots. That was the most hideous thing, it just hit me."

Jackson's autobiography, *Convent Cruelties,* was sold at Klan rallies. . . . It also was advertised in Klan publications, with a suggestive cartoon of a girl being whipped by nuns. Provocatively subtitled—"A providential delivery from Rome's Convent Pens: a sensational experience"—the volume traced Jackson's alleged imprisonment by sadistic Catholic officials in a convent in Detroit, Michigan, and in a House of the Good Shepherd in Newport, Kentucky. Jackson maintained that she was constantly humiliated by other nuns, forbidden any contact with the outside world, subjected to torture by immersion in cold water, forced to drink vile substances, and ordered to work unceasingly at ironing and embroidery. She also claimed that she had witnessed the tortures and imprisonment of other girls, some of whom were Protestants abducted into the Romanist slave den. Appended to the volume were affidavits from other "escaped nuns" who provided their own tales of imprisonment and abuse in Catholic convents and homes.

Helen Jackson frequently traveled with L. J. King, who billed himself as an "ex-Romanist." King had made his living for years on the anti-Catholic lecture circuit, claiming to be a former priest. Like other anti-Catholic evangelist lecturers of the 1910s, King specialized in highly emotional harangues. With his audiences separated by sex, King regaled the crowd with horrid tales of Catholic sexual tortures dating from the European Inquisition. In modern times, King thundered, these same perversions continued, fostered by priests whose "unnatural" pledge of celibacy drove their sexual desires in depraved directions.

In the early 1920s L. J. King enlisted in the Klan and joined forces with Helen Jackson on the Klan lecture circuit. King's propaganda—on the implications of the unmarried clergy and the sexual exploits of the mysterious Catholic church— was ideal for the Klan's anti-Catholic agenda: "Every priest and nun connected with the [school] system is chained to a life of celibacy in defiance of nature and clad in a strange, unsanitary costume."

Jackson and King held revivals on behalf of the Klan in many small towns in Indiana, setting up headquarters in a local restaurant or hotel and meeting nightly for two or three weeks—as long as a month—drawing crowds of hundreds and even thousands. In a single visit the pair would deliver lectures with titles such as "My Visit to the Nunnery at St. Louis, Missouri," "See Bottle Convent Booze," "The Fruits of the Confessional," and "Priest Hans Smytt Murders Two Girls." On the Klan circuit, King expanded on Jackson's personal account, regaling audiences with highly detailed tales of imprisonment in convents and sexual debauchery between Catholic nuns and priests. He described convent dungeons with bolted doors, iron-barred windows, and high massive walls that imprisoned hapless girls, making suicide their only escape.

King and Jackson vividly described the grotesque tortures to which nuns were subjected for the sexual pleasure of priests, including tales of nuns confined in coffins filled with human excrement. A favorite legend recounted by the pair was the tale of Maria Monk and the nunnery of the Hôtel-Dieu in Montreal, a famous anti-Catholic diatribe dating to the early nineteenth century. Indeed, nearly all my respondents recalled owning a copy of Maria Monk's story, and most could recount its "awful disclosures" of convent life, including the murder of illicitly conceived infants.

> It was a horrible tale. My grandmother and I read it when we were in Florida one winter. And, she laughed about it. She thought it was horrible too, but she let me read it, and it was just like all these things they had in that messy newspaper [*Fiery Cross*]. You know, incredible things.

Jackson and King were expert at picturing even innocuous Catholic rituals as sordid and perverse. Their stump speech on the "abomination of secret auricular confession" is an example. King exclaimed that the secret confessional of the Catholic church was nothing more than "a school of licentiousness, seduction, and adultery." Priests encouraged innocent young girls to participate in confidential sexual fantasies in the confessional by means of suggestive questions whispered outside the hearing of male relatives or husbands. Secret confessions also provided the pretext for illicit love making between priest-confessors and nuns in convents, leading to abortion or infanticide.

King's lectures and his annual, *The Converted Catholic and Protestant Missionary*, included many stories of women victimized in Catholic rectories, homes, and convents. These ranged from innuendo of sexual torture and intrigue to case histories of girls condemned to a life of drudgery, deprivation, and cruelty in convent "prisons." Before her lectures, Jackson would read from letters by local Klan chapters that charted successes in liberating Protestant girls from "Rome's slave pens" and encouraged others to free girls imprisoned in their localities. The traffic in white women, King seethed, was increasing "to fill up the place of poisoned, deluded, outraged, starved, raped, and murdered victims of priestcraft in the nunnery, to feed the lust of the adulterous bachelor, overfed, drunken priesthood of the Romish fake."

The magnetism of King's and Jackson's oratory is evident in the account that the daughter of an active Indiana Klanswoman and Klansman gave of how her parents "practically broke out in tears about some of the things that were being taught to the children in the school . . . all these things that went on in the priest's home and the nun's home and all these babies that were buried underneath the mother's houses."

Even girls who avoided the terror of the convent life, the Klan suggested, were not safe. Jackson, King, and other Klan lecturers charged priests with attacking girls in school dormitories and in church sanctuaries; with being drunk, stupid, or intolerant; and with gambling and promoting law breaking. Sometimes the finger of blame pointed toward priests in general; at other times it accused particular priests or convent schools.

The Klan's success in bringing sexual morality into the political agenda gave it great public credibility (and an enormous following) among white Protestants who applauded the Klan's efforts to subvert the immoral intentions of Catholic clergy, Jewish businessmen, and black and immigrant men and to uphold morality within white Protestant families. Tales of sexual perversity also normalized hatred of the Klan's enemies. The Klan's accounts of sexual depravity among Catholic clergy and the wanton sexual exploitation of youngsters by priests and nuns led many white Protestants to view Catholics as far removed from accepted standards of moral and ethical behavior.

When the Klan had established Catholics as strange and inexplicable beings, few stories about them seemed implausible. And the Klan was expert at generating rumors for gullible audiences. In reaction to news that the 1917 U.S. dollar bill was covered with secret Catholic symbols, loyal Klan members dutifully tore off a corner of the bill where the pope's picture was said to be hidden. Indiana Klan members heard, and often believed, accusations against the Catholic church that ranged from plotting the assassination of President Abraham Lincoln, to fomenting World War I in order to strengthen the papacy, to leading the massacre of American Indians.

As befitting an organization built on xenophobia, Klan propaganda was hysterical on the topic of the Italian pope and Vatican City. The pope, known in Klan parlance as the "dago on the Tiber," was identified with the biblical Delilah, putting the Samson of the United States to sleep in order to carry out her evil plans. Many Klanswomen and Klansmen in Indiana firmly believed that the arrival of the pope as emperor of the United States was imminent. Rumors circulated that a palace was being built in Washington, D.C., to allow the pope to oversee his empire.

A major theme of the Klan's anti-Catholicism was that of a church under foreign leadership. Catholics in the United States—citizens as well as immigrants—were accused of being spies for the Vatican. The police forces of the major cities, the Klan asserted, were dominated by Catholics who owed their allegiance to the pope in Rome. The Klan's opposition to the World Court was based on a similar belief—that the Vatican would manipulate the World Court as a tool for "romanizing" America and forcing "papist aliens" into the United States. Ignoring its own hierarchical structure, the Klan argued that the strict lines of authority in the Catholic church were antithetical to democracy and individual freedom. Catholics, according to the Klan, came from the lower classes and criminal elements of Europe and were forced to do the bidding of the pope.

Typical of the way that many Protestants in 1920s Indiana regarded Catholics is the account given by a woman in Muncie when attempting to convince an interviewer for the Lynds' ethnographic work, *Middletown,* to join her in the local Klan. She insisted that the pope started the first Klan in order to divide and conquer Protestants, a convoluted logic meant to underscore the malevolent intentions of the Catholic empire.

> It's about time you joined the good people and did something about this Catholic situation. The Pope is trying to get control of this country, and in order to do it, he started the old Klan to stir up trouble among the Protestants, but instead of doing that he only opened their eyes to the situation, and now all the Protestants are getting together in the new Klan to overcome the Catholic menace.

The Catholic fraternal order, the Knights of Columbus, was a frequent target of Klan propaganda, which typically insisted that the Knights were the secret military arm of the pope. According to the Klan, the Knights planted Catholic girls in Protestant homes as maids and child helpers who then filed weekly reports with the Vatican on the activities and conversations of Protestant families.

Protestants in Indiana also commonly believed that Catholics were arming themselves for a massacre of non-Catholics, using guns and ammunition stockpiled in the basements of Catholic churches. Rumors circulated throughout the state that Catholics buried a rifle under the local church each time a Catholic boy was born, for his later use to defend the papal empire that would rule the United States by the time the child grew to manhood. A woman in central Indiana recalled that "stories floated here that the Catholic church, that the basement was really an armory, getting ready for a revolution . . . the Catholic church was getting ready for a civil war in this country, they were going to take over the government." . . .

Often a fine line separated the Klan's goodwill campaigns from its political terrorism. This was most obvious in the Klan's goodwill activities for hospitals and public schools. When the WKKK and KKK made philanthropic gestures toward public schools or raised money to build Protestant hospitals, they warned Protestants that Catholics and foreigners had invaded the most basic institutions of public life. The crusade of nearly every WKKK chapter to present flags and Bibles to the public schools of their county and to build Protestant-only hospitals in communities then dependent on Catholic hospitals roused images of Catholic teachers secretly indoctrinating Protestant youth or Catholic doctors and nurses insisting on religious conversion in exchange for hospital treatment.

WKKK chapters competed among one another to bring Protestant values to the public schools. When one WKKK klavern presented a Bible to every public school in the township, another donated a Bible to every school in the county, or a flag *and* a Bible to every school. Some schools received copies of *Stories of the Bible* together with their flags and Bibles. Others received multiple copies of new Bibles for the use of their students or placards with the Ten Commandments for every schoolroom.

The way schools received their Bibles, flags, and books was important. The favored manner of donation was a public ceremony of presentation and acceptance. The WKKK of Coal City succeeded in this endeavor: it presented its gifts to the school principal on stage during intermission of the school play. Less successful was the WKKK of Terre Haute whose presentation involving one hundred Klanswomen was marred by the school board's refusal to allow the Klanswomen to don robes for the ceremony.

Many Indiana Klan chapters received favorable publicity by announcing lavish fundraising drives to assist or build local Protestant hospitals. Although few, if any, such fundraising promises were fulfilled, the WKKK and KKK made lavish predictions that it would collect sums of $50,000 and more for hospitals and schools in Indiana's cities and towns. If nothing else, these fundraising drives replenished the treasuries of Klan locals and realms.

Another deft publicity tactic pioneered by the men of the Klan and then adopted in identical form by the women's Klan was the church visit. Within a three-month period thirteen WKKK chapters reported making church visits in small Indiana communities, involving between five and seventy women. In a church visit, robed and masked Klanswomen would interrupt a Protestant service, stride up the center aisle, and present the minister with a sum of money. Ostensibly the money was for church work, in keeping with the Klan's pledge of militant Protestantism, but money easily found its way to the minister's personal funds. The minister's role was to act surprised, if pleased, by the visit of the Klanswomen. Often the drama was prearranged with cooperating ministers who viewed the proffered purse as payment for espousing Klan doctrines from the pulpit.

While the school, hospital, and church campaigns of Indiana's WKKK and KKK chapters demonstrated the Klan's muscle, they delivered the message in indirect terms. Other political actions by Klanswomen more directly abused and harassed the enemies of the Klan. WKKK chapters in Indiana bombarded public schools with protests and calls to reform a school system that Klanswomen insisted was permeated with foreign, Catholic, and even Bolshevik influences. Klanswomen fought to remove Catholic encyclopedias from public school libraries, campaigned against the teaching of German (the language of the wartime enemy), and constantly pressured for a cabinet-level Department of Education to monitor and shore up the public school system and thereby undermine parochial education. Women of the Klan in many Indiana counties met with township trustees to urge compulsory Bible reading in public schools.

Klanswomen in Indiana also were active in the effort to "cleanse" public schools of the corrupting influence of non-Protestants. The innocent minds of Protestant children, Klanswomen insisted, were being filled with Romanist doctrines. A number of Indiana's WKKK klaverns worked to have Catholic teachers, even Catholic school superintendents, fired. The Anderson WKKK, for example, mounted an effort to get two Catholic teachers fired. After being bombarded with letters from the women's Klan demanding her resignation, one teacher left town. The other teacher resigned after "several other small incidents happened," but she refused to leave town. In Muncie the Klan worked to remove a Catholic teacher with thirty-seven years' experience but without success. . . .

Though the Klan could elect members and supporters in Indiana, its electoral efforts were less effective than another political tactic: the boycott. This technique drew on women's traditional role as manager of the family's consumption. A boycott brought even the act of shopping into the fight for racial and religious supremacy. It infused the ordinary tasks of Klanswomen's lives with political content. Acting individually but with a collective direction, Klanswomen could force Jews, Catholics, or blacks out of their communities or into financial bankruptcy. Indiana Klanswomen avidly took to the task.

Daisy Barr set the tone for the WKKK's crusade of selective shopping in weekly addresses to Indianapolis Klanswomen. At each meeting, attended by as many as fifteen hundred women, Barr read the roll of Indianapolis WKKK and KKK members who were engaged in local retail or service trade. These businesses and products had the WKKK seal of approval. These, and only these, were to be patronized by Klanswomen; all others were "Catholic or Jew" (or "alien") and should be rejected. Barr was particularly indignant about "Jew-owned" stores and claimed that "Jews had 75 percent of the money of the United States." This situation would change, however. "When the women should be as strongly organized as the men," she raged, "THEY WOULD HAVE THE POWER AND THEN GOD HELP BLOCK [Jewish businessman] AND HIS SLACKER SON. THERE WILL BE NO JEWISH BUSINESS LEFT IN INDIANAPOLIS."

Organizing Klanswomen as consumers had an immediate and phenomenal effect. Businesses with Jewish owners, ranging from large department stores to small shops and professional services, went bankrupt throughout Indiana. Jewish professionals and business owners fled communities in which they had lived for decades.

The consumption campaign of the WKKK gave many communities their first indication of the strength of women's klaverns and the extent of pro-Klan sentiment among local women. Shopping at one place over another allowed women to exercise considerable political clout without overstepping even the most conventional definition of their roles as mothers and wives. Moreover, the political content of the act was elusive. Women could act on racist, anti-Semitic, or anti-Catholic sentiments in a completely invisible fashion. It was not necessary to attend klaverns, become an official WKKK member, or even discuss the Klan to participate in the Klan's economic crusade. Shopping, after all, involves myriad subjective choices about quality, price, and convenience—any woman could justify her selections, if need be, without revealing sympathy with the goals of the Klan. For many women in Indiana who declined to join the WKKK because of fear of being identified with the Klan or because of reluctance to be involved with a political movement, the economic strategy of the WKKK was perfect.

The diffusion of information about approved and boycotted businesses operated through a shadowy network of Klanswomen and Klan sympathizers. Informal conversations among women—dismissed as insignificant gossip by contemporary men and Klan historians—fueled one of the Klan's most powerful weapons. Rumor did not spread randomly; the WKKK used tightly organized bands of Klanswomen to ensure its dispersal across the state. The impact of the "poison squad of whispering women" . . . was profound. Women's poison squads could spread stories to every corner of the state within twenty-four hours. Even when the story in its entirety was known to be false, doubts lingered, as a woman in central Indiana attested: "Many of the rumors possibly had a degree of truth in them so you could not deny it all but it was not the truth as it was told."

In its political efforts, the WKKK relied on the patterns of daily activities of Indiana women. Women visiting friends and relatives or stopping to chat with acquaintances at shops or schools and over the proverbial back fence passed information about who *owned* what and who *sympathized* with what. Women needed not identify their own sentiments to pass on information; the assumption that women's conversation was personal, not political, shielded women from accusations and attacks by anti-Klan forces. Some women heard the information and dismissed it as inconsequential. To receptive ears, however, the implications for action were clear.

Few rumors seemed too farfetched. In 1923 North Manchester was swept by a rumor that Negroes were coming north in great numbers, a rumor purportedly based on sighting one local man traveling in the South. Another rumor spread by the women's Klan in North Manchester proved embarrassing to the organization after it was made public. The incredible nature of this tale indicates not only the Klan's striking ability to disseminate rumors but also the immediacy of fears about a papal assault on Indiana:

> Some Klan leader said that the Pope was coming to take over the country, and he said he might be on the next train that went through North Manchester. You know, just trying to make it specific. So, about a thousand people went out to the train station and stopped the train. It only had one passenger train and one passenger on it. They took him off, and he finally convinced them that he wasn't the Pope. He was a carpet salesman. And so they put him on the next train and he went on to Chicago.

The organized gossip of Klanswomen spread poison about Jews, Catholics, and others opposed to the crusade of militant Protestantism. Tales about the personal life, merchandise, and political allegiances of the town's outsiders destroyed the Klan's enemies without a trace. Since gossip left no visible traces on the participants, it created no trail for those opposed to or victimized by the Klan. Indeed, the political power of gossip lay precisely in its apolitical character. There were no reports to seize, no meetings to invade, no publications to refute. One might guess at its existence from its consequences, but even those were hard to measure on the local level. Did a department store go out of business because of an invisible boycott or because of poor management or shoddy goods? Did a Jewish family leave town because of actual economic pressure or because of its exaggerated fear of such pressure? Did stores and businesses go bankrupt, or did they simply move to areas of greater financial potential? Only in retrospect did the pattern of business closures and out-migration by Jewish owners across Indiana communities become clear. Only in retrospect, and by looking closely at the lives of women, can we reveal the political character and the economic power of these networks of gossip. . . .

To victims, the Klan's power and tactics were confusing as well as destructive. Catholics and Jews who had been at least partially integrated into the social, cultural, and commercial life of the community now found themselves inexplicably labeled as outsiders and enemies. One woman gave an account of the Klan's boycott of her (Catholic) family's grocery store, made more ironic by the fact that the men's and women's Klans met in a room above the grocery.

> I blame the Klan indirectly for my father's death. . . . It just broke his heart to have people shun him, pass right in front of our door, our grocery store door and go upstairs and not look at him. Not look in our store, and he was never able to take that and he used to say, what did I do, and nothing changed on his part, he was the same person. . . . I don't think he minded losing the customers so badly . . . but the fact that he lost friends and he just was never able to accept that.

Although rumors and gossip were the most effective weapons, the Klan employed more visible mechanisms to direct the power of purchasing. The *Fiery Cross* published a "who's who" roster of Catholic businessmen, complete with names and addresses of their business establishments. No loyal Klanswoman need wonder what actions the list encouraged.

Klan members developed an organizational policy of "vocational klannishness" in which Klan members pledged to conduct "trading, dealing with, and patronizing Klansmen in preference to all others." The Klan planned to publish a National Service Directory that would list all businesses in the United States owned by Klansmembers who took out a $35 membership in the National Service Corporation. This project was never completed, but local klaverns issued their own directories and the Indiana Klan compiled a listing that covered all cities in the state. Shopkeepers supplemented these directories with advertising that broadcast the owner's political sympathies. Shopkeepers who joined the KKK or WKKK received placards for their store windows that read TWK—Trade With a Klansman. Those who belonged to the National Service Corporation received a round red, white, and blue sign to display in their businesses.

Klan papers as well as local non-Klan papers carried numerous ads openly proclaiming the klannish sympathies of local business owners. Rarely were these ads subtle. The *Franklin Evening Star* ran one such advertisement:

Every person in Johnson County is invited
to join the KKK Keystone Kleaning Kompany
"keep klothes klean" campaign

The Klan's claim to represent 100 percent Americans provided merchants with another advertising ploy. Evans's American Cafe in Kokomo promised the "best 100% 25-cent meals in state," Indianapolis barber shops declared their employees to be 100 percent American, underwriters in Logansport promised insurance that was 100 percent safe, a Haughville company guaranteed 100 percent service in delivering ice, coal, and wood, and an Indianapolis jeweler urged Klan couples to examine its 100 percent workmanship before purchasing a wedding ring, adding that it would give a 10 percent discount to any 100 percent American. The *Fiery*

Cross even published its own business directory in every issue, with ads for Klan-owned companies, professional services, and evangelical preachers. The issue for June 1, 1923, for example, contained notices for hotels, furniture stores, realtors, seed stores, and many other businesses:

> Columbus, Indiana, Hunter Repair Shop—Everything for a Ford, 100% shop operated by 100% man with 100% workmen. We want 100% American business.

> Marion, Indiana, Chiropractor—Dr. O. G. McKeever, for 100% service.

The tactic of vocational klannishness affected workers as well as merchants and professionals. Employers sympathetic to the Klan, or fearing Klan reprisals, advertised for 100 percent American employees and refused to hire Catholics, Jews, blacks, new immigrants, or people of "poor character." For its own members, the Klan served as a quasi–employment service. The state headquarters sent directives to all field officers of the KKK and WKKK in Indiana, indicating employment situations for 100 percent women and men. The *Fiery Cross,* like commercial newspapers, listed notices of "Situation Wanted" or "Employees Wanted" separately for women and men.

Workers who were Catholic, Jewish, or suspected of anti-Klan leanings often discovered vocational klannishness by being suddenly fired from their jobs. A county extension agent who refused to join the Klan found himself out of work. The treasurer of Marion County, who owed his position to the Klan, received a threatening letter forbidding him to hire Catholics. The *Muncie Post-Democrat* maintained that the courthouse matron in Muncie was fired when it was discovered that her daughter attended parochial school, even though she denied that her family was Catholic.

The Klan even used its economic power to try to drive anti-Klan newspapers out of business. The most famous episode involved the *South Bend Tribune,* which the WKKK and KKK klaverns in South Bend identified as adverse to the interests of the Klan. A Klansman later provided insights into the boycotting methods of the Indiana Klan when he testified that Klanswomen and Klansmen decided to "use all their influence possible . . . call up the *South Bend Tribune* by 'phone and not take their paper, and also to talk it over the streets . . . refuse to buy any articles advertised in the *South Bend Tribune* . . . refuse to buy of those merchants who advertised in that paper." The South Bend WKKK provided leadership for this campaign.

The Klan in Indiana exerted its power through physical violence and terrorism, actions more often practiced by Klansmen than Klanswomen, and through threats and intimidation, actions of both men and women. But in Indiana and most other places incidents of physical violence by the 1920s Klan were scattered and sporadic. Although the 1920s Klan practiced kidnapping, beating, and even lynching, these were not the typical practice of WKKK klaverns or the daily practice of KKK chapters. Rather, the more subtle destructive fury of the 1920s Klan lay in its use of rumor, gossip, and demonstrations of political strength. In these tactics—political tactics typically overlooked in scholarship on the Klan movement—Klanswomen were key actors.

For Further Study

1. What were some of the specific ideas and practices that the KKK targeted in its morality crusades?

2. Describe the nature of the KKK's attack on the Catholic Church. Why do you suppose KKK spokespersons chose to emphasize such things in their attempts to attract support for their cause? Why do you suppose that Catholics rather than African Americans or Jews seem to have been a more frequent target for the Klan in Indiana?

3. KKK restricted its membership to native-born white Protestants, but most native-born white Protestants did not become members. What factors led some to join the Klan while others did not?

4. It is sometimes said that the KKK's appeal in the 1920s was rooted in the distress felt by many people because America was becoming modern and up-to-date and losing touch with older values and traditions. What evidence do you see in the selection that would support the conclusion that the KKK was trying to cling to the past? What evidence do you see that might contradict such a view?

5. Compare the Klan revival of the 1920s with some of the other conservative social movements of the period such as the movement for Prohibition, the anti-immigrant crusade, and the widespread anti-union feelings that existed. What connections do you see among them?

For Further Reading

Frederick Lewis Allen, *Only Yesterday: An Informal History of the 1920s* (1921); William Leuchtenberg, *The Perils of Prosperity, 1914–1932* (1958); Geoffrey Perrett, *America in the Twenties* (1982); and Arthur M. Schlesinger, Jr., *The Crisis of the Old Order* (1957) are general histories of the 1920s. On the Klan in the 1920s see David M. Chalmers, *Hooded Americanism: The First Century of the Ku Klux Klan* (1965); Kenneth Jackson, *The Ku Klux Klan in the City, 1915–1930;* and Arnold S. Rice, *The Ku Klux Klan in American Politics* (1962). The book from which this selection was taken, Kathleen M. Blee, *Women of the Klan: Racism and Gender in the 1920s* (1991) focuses on the role women played in the KKK. Nancy MacLean also has a great deal to say on this subject in *Behind the Mask of Chivalry: The Making of the Second Ku Klux Klan* (1994). A deeper understanding of the Klan's growth and influence may be obtained by considering some other social phenomena of the 1920s. On religious fundamentalism see Norman Furniss, *The Fundamentalist Controversy, 1918–1933* (1954); Ray Ginger, *Six Days or Forever? Tennessee v. John Scopes* (1958); and George Marsden, *Fundamentalism and American Culture* (1980). On prohibition see Joseph Gusfeld, *Symbolic Crusade* (1963) and Andrew Sinclair, *Prohibition: The Era of Excess* (1962). Don Kirschner, *City and Country: Rural Responses to Urbanization in the 1920s* (1970) discusses the rural-urban conflict that was also an important root of the Klan's upsurge.

Chapter 11

Courtesy, Colorado Historical Society

*Mexican Americans celebrating Mexican independence day in Sedgwick, Colorado,
preserving their ties to their native land.*

Mexican Americans in the Southwest

Sarah Deutsch

There is a tendency for English-speaking Americans to think of non-English speakers as immigrants and aliens. In fact, in the southwestern United States, it was the English speakers, the Anglos, who were the latecomers. Native Americans had lived there for thousands of years and Spanish-speaking people for hundreds when the Anglos began to arrive in Texas and other parts of the Southwest in the 1820s. But when the entire area became part of the United States after the Mexican War, Anglo political control was quickly extended to include economic, social, and cultural dominance as well.

Anglos tended to view those of Mexican ancestry living in the area as an alien minority. But some also saw them as a valuable source of cheap labor for the area's farms and mines. The demand for such labor was met not only by the current residents but also by increased immigration from Mexico, continuing through the late 1800s and into the twentieth century. Like other ethnic minorities, Chicanos (people of Mexican ancestry living in the United States) tended to live in compact communities of their own, partly out of preference and partly because prevailing prejudices forced them to. Like other ethnic minorities, too, they had to face the issue of whether and how to preserve their own culture in the face of the dominant culture's disrespect for it.

The following selection deals with Chicanos living in northern New Mexico and southern Colorado. Initially their communities consisted mostly of an interlocked network of small, rural villages, but economic pressures forced them into increased contact with and dependence on the economic and social institutions of the larger society. In the process they encountered economic, social, and cultural dilemmas little different from those faced by Chicanos in other parts of the United States. Like others, they tended to be confined to hard, unskilled, and low-paying jobs, to suffer from serious health problems, and to lack educational opportunities. The picture was complicated by the tendency of Anglos to lump together all Chicanos, whether immigrants or American citizens, and to regard them all with prejudice.

It was early spring when they began to arrive. In the lingering chill twenty thousand Chicanos settled over the beetfields, five here, ten there. To house them, farmers rousted the hens from the chicken coops and took the last of the grain out of the storage shacks. Most of the shacks had only one or two rooms to shelter the large families—families had to be large to make a living working beets—and throughout the twenties, most shacks provided "utterly inadequate" shelter at that. Investigators continually testified that they found shacks located "with no attention to adequate sanitation, toilet facilities, sleeping room, or water supply." Without shade, the shacks became hotter than the fields; often they had no screens. The surroundings were dirty barnyards and corrals.

If they worked on the western edge of the South Platte Valley, due north of Denver, Spanish Americans could look up from the five miles of rows they tended per acre (each averaged ten acres per season) and, looking across the plain, be soothed by the sun setting over the mountains, a reminder of home. But if they worked in the long stretch of the valley to the east, there was nothing to relieve the eye from the endless rows and level terrain; they were alone on the plain, alone in the Anglo north, with nothing to remind them of the mountains, the villages, the relatives, the gardens, and the churches of home. This frontier demanded from them a new life, a new way of living. To understand their life as it evolved in the 1920s, it is necessary first to set it in the context of the regional community, then to examine the factors that conspired to make the creation of a stable community in the north difficult—including the impact of the migration on Chicanas, the community builders—and finally to analyze new strategies as they emerged in the north.

With spiraling intensity, old and new factors combined in northern New Mexico to deprive Hispanics of land and livelihood, to drive them into increased dependency on the networks and settlements, and the success, of the regional community. Each new disaster of the 1920s, natural or man-made, meant reduced resources to meet the next. Hispanic vigilante groups like the Manos Negras continued to cut fences that blocked access to traditionally communal pasture and to burn barns of Rio Arriba County's Anglo and Hispanic commercial farmers, but such efforts to resist the trend had little impact. There also continued a depressed cattle market; limited access to Anglo-controlled credit; equal division of dwin-

---

dling holdings among heirs, which left each with smaller and smaller parcels of land; and an average crop failure in some parts of northern New Mexico reaching 59 percent. In addition to these older factors, a 1924 Pueblo Lands Act resulted in the eviction of nearly three thousand Hispanics and Anglos. At the same time, Texans and Oklahomans with enough capital to stake a homestead invaded the region. They disrupted the Hispanic villages and demanded services such as moving a high school from a Hispanic settlement to their own settlement or building expensive irrigation projects that would increase the tax burden on the financially strapped Hispanics just when a 1926 state tax law made land that had been tax-delinquent for three years subject to foreclosure and sale for back taxes.

These events ensured that a rapidly escalating proportion of Hispanic village families increased their reliance on wage labor or, like farm folk all over the country, left the villages altogether. Many headed for such larger towns of New Mexico as Grants and Albuquerque. Others departed for the state's coal-mining areas, Gallup and Raton, and for railroad shops and Colorado's coal mines. But the largest contingent set out for the beetfields, where push and pull came together.

Colorado's sugar-beet industry provided approximately 20,000 jobs each season, while the state's railroads employed only about 5000 Chicanos for maintenance of way, and its coal mines just over 3000. Moreover, to ensure an ample labor supply, Great Western Sugar Company, Colorado's largest, spent lavishly on recruitment campaigns throughout the decade, as much as ninety dollars per family recruited, or $250,000 in a single year. The company focused with particular intensity on the already vulnerable areas of southern Colorado and New Mexico, until the two states' share of the recruited Chicano labor rose from approximately 65 percent in 1923 to approximately 85 percent in 1927.

According to one ex-villager, recruiters claimed "you'd rake in the money," and they distributed brochures that led Hispanics to expect a garden plot for each family, decent housing, a water supply, and a friendly employer who might provide milk and eggs at cost. While it is true that a few of the Chicano beet-labor houses, more of them toward the end of the decade, were sturdy and weatherproof, that some farm owners and tenants had houses and sanitation little better than their labor did, and that farm labor conditions in other parts of the nation, notably in the South, were little if any better than those in Colorado, nonetheless, for the majority of Chicanos in the 1920s, life in Colorado's beetfields did not fulfill recruiters' promises. A simple description of conditions and attitudes there reads like a harangue against the agricultural system of the time.

Most of the farmers seemed to agree with Americanization teacher Alfred White, that "the peon has always lived like a pig and he will continue to do so." National Child Labor Committee investigator Charles Gibbons found that "the local people . . . feel they are giving the Mexican all he deserves; in fact one frequently finds the opinion that they (residents) are performing an act of charity in allowing the Mexican to work for them, and therefore any kind of a house will do for them to live in." Most growers and even investigators were convinced that whatever the conditions in Colorado, they represented an improvement over Hispanic and Mexican villages.

Most Chicanos, on the other hand, saw little if any improvement. They had come north, to the margins of the Hispanic regional community, to better their condition. Though often bitterly disappointed in what they found, many could not afford to turn back. An exasperated Chicana living in a one-room shack with her family of twelve demanded, "How can you expect folks to live decently when given a place like that?" The Chicanas tried desperately to turn these shacks into homes, despite their long hours in the fields and the meager furnishings they could bring with them. The migrants used boxes as tables and cupboards, and often slept on the floor. Mary Vela remembered that her mother stayed up all night to clean when they moved. Another mother made her own paste and pasted a two-room shack with newspapers for decoration and warmth; her daughter remembered, "[W]e would lay there and read all the news there was in the newspapers."

As to the work itself, there were some Anglo school children and a few Anglo women who, not needing to provide their entire support from the beets, contracted small acreages, an amount easily managed in workdays of reasonable length. A local lawyer assured investigators that "children are in much better conditions in the open fields and the open air than they would be in their homes. In general," he asserted, "this summer outing is looked upon by the children as a frolic." But Mary Vela recalled beetwork as "backbreaking and heavy. During the harvest we'd work 18-hours days." At least one Spanish-speaking woman lost two sons to a kidney disease exacerbated by long hours of stooping over the fields. Thinning the beets in the early summer required crawling, and topping them during the harvest required stooping, and it was all, according to investigator Paul Taylor, "disagreeable . . . dirty . . . monotonous and repetitive." Even C. V. Maddux, labor commissioner at Great Western Sugar Company in the 1920s, warned that "a man who is highly-strung could never work beets, because there are five miles of row to every acre. . . . He could not see the end."

Great Western Sugar remained the recruiter and not the direct employer of beet labor, but it taught its agricultural fieldmen Spanish, retained files on each of the laborers it recruited, and mediated in grower-labor disputes. As the roving villagers created new and reinforced old paths connecting the village economy to the large one, Great Western Sugar, by centralizing and expanding its recruiting and labor services, increased its control over the labor and the labor market on the Anglo-Chicano frontier, and so its power in the regional community.

The sugar companies together with the growers set the wages of beet labor, a crucial factor not only for Hispanic life in the north but for the possibilities of the regional community. Yet the laborers' cost of living did not enter into the companies' calculations. They simply promised to procure beet labor at the farmers' agreed rate per acre. Under the set rates, a Chicano beetworker earned only about $250 each season. Meanwhile, the cost of living in Denver for a family, according to the Colorado Industrial Commission, was $1,197.78 per year at minimum comfort. For Chicanos wintering in rural areas, the cost may have been slightly less, but not 75 percent less. Chicanos quickly came to see in the family system of labor not the promise of vastly increased wealth, but simply survival.

And even survival was questionable. "Families" under this system sometimes included distant cousins, neighbors from the home village, or even subcontractors. With more than six working members, at least four of them adult men, such a family could contract as many as 60 to 80 acres and make between $1500 and $2100 per season. But there were few such families, fewer, in fact, than 5 percent of the whole. Investigating the South Platte area in 1924, Sara Brown found earnings from beets for over half the contract families with children amounted to less than $900. Forty percent of Brown's families earned less than $700 for the season. In other beet-producing areas of Colorado, beet-labor families earned even less. Having promised to provide cheap labor to the growers, sugar companies had indeed fostered a family system where, according to one pair of investigators, "instead of paying one laborer a bare subsistence wage, the labor of father and several children is secured at this rate." But family earnings of seven hundred dollars did not provide even subsistence, except, perhaps, during the months of labor.

Clearly such low wages demanded some kind of supplement, and it was here that the village strategy of migration and the beet industry's labor strategy intersected. Credit, relief, or the beet laborer's own farm in southern Colorado, New Mexico, or Mexico could supplement beet wages in the absence of winter work. Each of these alternatives informally subsidized the beet industry by making the low wages possible, but in some ways, perpetual migration seemed the most desirable to all parties. . . . Having at the end of the beet season an average of approximately $150, "plenty to get them out of the country," as one farmer observed, and spending approximately two-thirds of it on returning to the village, a beet-labor family would have fifty dollars to pay taxes on the farm and supply cash needs throughout the winter. In turn, the farm that could not support the family year round might provide the missing six months' subsistence. This semi-autonomous cultural retreat fit the mythological image of the vanishing "Mexican" whose "homing instinct" saved the Southwest from "the terrible mistakes which have been made in the southern states . . . a civilization of masters and servants." In Colorado, growers sent the "servants" home when they were not wanted, in an extended echo of a day work system rather than live-in help. This migratory pattern permitted members of each culture to deny their membership in and responsibility for the other, and allowed farmers to keep the doors to Mexican reserve labor open.

The number of Chicanos who either lacked the farm to which to return or lacked the means to get there belied the comforting myth. Mexican nationals in particular, unlike most Spanish Americans tended to come from landless families. But both groups settled in the north in greater numbers than during the war. The resident Chicano population of northeastern Colorado more than doubled relative to the total population and more than tripled in absolute numbers between 1920 and 1927 alone. Approximately one-third wintered in the open fields and the rest in towns. In Denver their number grew from approximately two thousand to over eight thousand. Expanding earlier settlements in Denver, Spanish Americans clustered west of the city center, in the vicinity of West Colfax between the Platte River and Cherry Creek, and also to the north along the east coast of the river. To the northeast of this latter area were the Mexicans, perhaps a fifth of the total Chicano population in the city. These were poor parts of the city, multiethnic, with rooming houses, the unemployed, and the transient. Among these last, Denver's Chicanos fit well. Over three-quarters of the families from each section left Denver each spring for seasonal labor. By 1929, such Chicano clusters, however transient, made it clear that the "Mexicans" disappearing from the fields after harvest had not moved very far. . . .

Hispanics found the traditional agricultural ladder to ownership full of broken rungs. Landowners hesitated to lease farms to Hispanics. One who did complained, "People around here blame me for leasing to Mexicans and so displacing the whites." But even a lease proved at best a rickety, inadequate vehicle. Few Chicanos would follow their predecessors, the German-Russian immigrants, to farm ownership. Chicanos arrived with smaller families than the German-Russians, and with an unwillingness to keep the women and children in the fields for the same long hours. Moreover, they came at a time when land values had escalated while beet-labor wages had not and when the move to ownership had generally dwindled. It was, in fact, only the lack of movement between tenancy and ownership that reconciled Anglos to Chicano lessees at all. As one farmer's wife explained, "There is no danger from the Mexicans. They won't save enough to buy land." Without land ownership it would be difficult for Hispanics to convert the periphery of one Chicano regional community, the outermost edge of the network system, into the center of another, the node of a new set of networks.

What year-round residences Chicanos could buy consisted of town lots and even these were not easily acquired. "Dealers in real estate," Paul Taylor revealed, "carry out the policy of separating Mexicans in northeastern Colorado." And even a modest $250 mortgage on a lot in a Chicano enclave, with the family paying only twelve dollars a year, outran beetworker resources. One former beetworker remembered an Anglo realtor in Greeley in the late 1920s who "was working the Spanish real good, he *lived* off the Spanish," providing loans and repossessing partially paid-up houses. A reluctant Anglo host society joined with the dynamics of the beet industry to keep most Chicanos transient and hovering on the margins of society.

Nor did the Great Western Sugar Company's compromise of company-financed colonies impinge markedly on this system. Faced with increasing recruiting costs, the company, unlike the farmers, wanted a larger resident population. In colonies they provided land lots Chicanos could buy as house sites. While the colonies did allow a number of Chicano families to winter in the north each year, the high turnover and lapsed payments proved them not much more affordable for Chicanos than noncompany housing. In addition, the company colonies themselves emblemized the system which kept the Chicanos safely (for the Anglos) marginal and had as its aim the preservation in Chicanos of a perpetual and distinct laboring force. Their one- or two-room distinctive adobe structures stood on lots devoid of shade or farmland, a mile or two outside of Anglo towns or literally across the tracks.

For those Chicanos who did succeed in purchasing such a home, it offered a measure of stability and avoided a winter in the often leaky, overcrowded, and unsanitary farm buildings and Denver shacks. But it offered scant if any aid to gaining subsistence or even acceptance into Anglo society. It had little in common with owning land in the village. For Chicanos, ownership of a home on the periphery of an Anglo community and unaccompanied by ownership of productive land could mark not upward mobility, but confinement to a seasonal laboring class.

When these Chicano colonists and settlers no longer disappeared each winter below some imaginary border, the Anglo townspeople erected their own borders. They used the burning crosses of the Ku Klux Klan, so popular elsewhere in Colorado in the 1920s, to mark the edges of the adobe colonies, and used signs in restaurants, barbershops, and movie theaters bearing such inscriptions as "White Trade Only" and "No Mexican Trade Wanted," which made it impossible for Hispanics in towns like Greeley and Brighton to buy so much as a hamburger. The rhetoric of a "Mexican invasion" continued virtually unabated both in the national popular press and in Colorado. And Hispanic colonists remembered vividly nearly sixty years later the indignity of having an Anglo doctor arrive unannounced to take blood samples for Wasserman tests to detect syphilis. "That's how bad they wanted to get rid of us," recalled one. Spanish Americans had difficulty registering to vote, and local Anglos continued to "wish the Mexicans were not there."

It was ironic that the local growers simultaneously protested the invasion of their neighborhoods by "Mexicans" and petitioned Congress to retain unrestricted Mexican immigration. It was ironic, also, that at the same time Great Western Sugar was erecting its colonies, its representative vigorously contended that "the Mexican eventually returns south of the Rio Grande," having "ebbed and flowed into agriculture and industry as needed for the past fifteen years, with good results to all interests concerned." Colorado's Congressman, Charles Timberlake, even denied that the company had built any houses for Mexican labor. The public and the private face of the industry, its social and its economic needs, had become increasingly disparate under the strain of reinforcing the myths which perpetuated the labor system.

Local Anglos and sugar company officials came up with new myths, or applied old ones, to justify the developments. Although the local Anglos gave the colonies unattractive names—the one in Eaton was called "Ragtown"—the vice president of Holly Sugar Company informed a Senate committee that "Mexicans" were "content to conduct their own community life apart from other races," and Robert McLean claimed that segregation was "due quite as much to the clannishness of the Mexican, as to the opposition of the American." Mexican segregation, it was implied, was by their own choice. When the Fort Collins hospital relegated its Hispanics to the basement, "there were always some real good reasons why they did it," remembered Arthur Maes, "'more at home' . . . 'we can serve them better' . . . 'they can talk to each other in the same language.'"

Many Chicanos—not consumers of the myths—resented the implications of such segregation. Some Hispanics remembered that people were considered "better" if they lived outside the colony, and that the colonies' lack of modern sanitary facilities helped give some colonists the attitude of "If I ever get a chance, I'll move out of this place." But the isolation from Anglo life, the Anglo prejudices, and the low wages reinforced each other and created, as one investigating team expressed it, "a vicious circle." "From this circle," they concluded, "few can escape through their own efforts."

For during winter it was not only the housing situation that created an unstable life for Hispanics. As a rule, the majority of beetwork families who wintered in the north found no work at all between beet seasons. And those whose family members did find jobs, including mothers who did laundry and domestic service, averaged less than $300 in earnings for the winter. Most earned less than $200. The sugar company itself admitted that in northern Colorado "the growers, generally speaking, have been less inclined with the Mexican than with the German-Russian to afford opportunities for extra work." As with those reluctant to lease land to Chicanos, these growers hesitated to displace regular Anglo winter farm labor. In the area's small industrial sector, too, it seemed to some Chicanos that unless jobs were so temporary or so bad that Anglos did not want them, Hispanics could not get them. The Mexican Welfare Committee of the Colorado State Council of the Knights of Columbus concurred, reporting in 1928 that only about 150 of the 7,000 men in northern Colorado employed in industry outside the mines and railroads were "Mexicans," and these, the Committee revealed, "were on rockpiles and at work no other laborer [would] do." Some Chicanos left their families in the north and migrated for winter work, becoming sheepherders in Colorado or Wyoming or going to coal mines or to Pueblo's steel mill. But in this way, they were not replicating the migrant patterns and village systems as much as extending them, since their life in the north centered not on a stable village core, but on a transient migrant settlement, marginal to both Anglo and Hispanic worlds.

Even the number of summer field-labor jobs fluctuated, offering no security for the resident laborer. The beet acreage harvested in a single sugar factory district could go up or down by as much as 75 percent from one year to the next. The beetgrower a Chicano family had worked for one summer may not have been in beets the next. And even if the grower stayed in beets, he might choose newly recruited labor over resident labor, or Mexican over Spanish American. Mexican immigration provided only one-quarter of beetfield labor, but it provided the valve which allowed sporadic large increases in beet acreage, and thus in demand for labor without commensurately increased wages.

The use of Mexican labor affected Hispanic community-building in the north even beyond the lowered wage rates. According to Taylor, the sugar company often brought the labor north a month early to avoid the increasingly strident competition among recruiters as summer approached, and tried to place the recruits on spring railroad work to allow them to support themselves until beetwork began. This employment service brought the two groups, resident and migrant Chicanos, into direct competition even before the beet season. With Mexicans posing the most immediate and visible threat to the Spanish Americans, the latter did all in their power to dissociate themselves from the former and to assert their prior claims to services and employment as citizens and particularly as veterans. One Spanish American told investigator B. F. Coen that Mexicans "aren't any good. You'll only find one out of every 100 that's a 'sitter' [citizen] and I don't think it's right." Spanish Americans also blamed the Mexicans for the new restrictions posted in barber and other shops. Living under the same conditions, Spanish Americans and Mexicans usually resided in separate colonies, rejected each other's company, and fought when mixed. Enrique Lopez recalled of his youth in Denver, "the bitterest 'race riots' I have ever witnessed—and engaged in—were between the look-alike, talk-alike *surumatos* [Mexicans] and *manitos* [Spanish Americans]."

Even a few Anglos made distinctions between the two groups, endowing Mexicans with a character more docile and less educated, and allowing Spanish Americans "more fiery blood in their veins" and more Anglo habits which made them "less passive in their attitudes toward social and civil rights." On the whole, those who made such distinctions placed the Spanish Americans above the Mexicans, and the Spanish Americans certainly placed themselves there. Some of the children of Mexican immigrants began to adopt the term "Spanish American" to describe themselves as well, but most of them heartily resented the condescending attitude of the Spanish-speaking from Colorado and New Mexico and labeled them "comprado," or "bought," for having remained in the United States after 1848 instead of leaving for Mexico. They taunted them with Anglo discriminations, calling them people without a country.

Infuriatingly, most Anglos continued in daily practice to make no distinction among them at all. "During the war," complained one citizen of Anglo attitudes, "we were Spanish Americans; now we are just Mexicans." Anglos referred to the "Mexican, or his cousin the Spanish-American" as people "who easily merge" on United States soil, and in one area officials expressed their chagrin that not one of the local "Mexicans" had showed up at citizenship classes, apparently unaware that the majority of local Hispanic residents were already citizens, by birth. To most Anglos, as one investigation team discovered, both groups "are called 'Mexes' or 'Greasers' and are regarded as foreigners." This amalgamation continued the trend begun at least during World War I of excluding Chicanos from the United States polity both as foreigners and as a separate "race." . . .

As for immigrant groups and minorities elsewhere, education was supposed to provide the compensating factor. The Great Western Sugar Company touted educational benefits as lending "a humanitarian impulse" to their proposals that beetworkers remain over the winter. Even economist Paul Taylor believed that "despite interrupted attendance, as good or better education advantages are offered in the beet area than in the places from which the workers came." Certainly public education in Hispanic northern New Mexico continued in the 1920s to be plagued by lack of funds, short school terms, and underqualified teachers. Of the Spanish American parents who moved north, approximately one-quarter were illiterate in any language, one-half in English, and one-third had had no schooling. For their children, they wanted more. They kept fewer of their school-age children in the fields than the German-Russians did, though it meant they made less money, and when Hispanic mothers worked beets it was often so children could attend school. "They want me to go to school so that I won't have to work beets," explained a Spanish American boy, and one girl's parents promised her a better job if she went to college.

Hispanic children, however, often remained skeptical of their future possibilities, "because," as the college-bound girl put it, "the Americans won't give me a chance." They had some reason for doubt. Teachers who said, "Oh, why don't you go back to the god-damned beet fields," did not instill confidence. A more sympathetic teacher reported that the Anglo children, also, "feel as hostile to the Mexican children on the playground as they do toward Negros in Gary, Indiana." And so did their parents. A school superintendent of Weld County insisted that "the respectable white people of Weld County do not want their children to sit alongside of dirty, filthy, disease-infested Mexicans in schools." Chicano school children found that, indeed, Anglos would not sit next to them, taunted them with phrases like "dirty Mexicans" and "greaser, greaser, sitting on an ice-cream freezer," "wouldn't want us ever to touch them," and made fun of their food until the Hispanic children hid away to eat. The state's constitution, written within recent memory of the Civil War, forbade segregation, but de facto segregation, particularly with the erection of company colonies at some distance from town and with the mid-term entrance and departure of beetworking children, was relatively easily achieved. Northern schools may have been better equipped than those in Hispanic villages, but the atmosphere was definitely more hostile, and the degree to which Hispanics would benefit remained in doubt.

Even when schools welcomed Chicano children, or were at least neutral, the necessity of family labor kept many children from attending. The work of children under sixteen, according to one 1925 study, contributed nearly one-third of the total contract labor's seasonal beet earnings. Most children working in beets were between ten and fourteen years old, but even six-year-olds sometimes spent their days thinning beets. Schooling for these children represented a substantial and sometimes impossible sacrifice for the whole family. A few Hispanic children managed to get through grammar school by asking for advance work each March and doing extra work all winter, but even for these children, high school, which demanded a set number of credits, was impossible. Almost universally, parents cared about education, but sometimes the alternative to child labor was starvation; Margarita Garcia remembered of her parents, "There was not much they could do. I guess we were so close to them, we didn't insist."

Missing approximately one-third of each school year, though regular in attendance once they enrolled, four-fifths of the Chicano children fell behind in school, almost two-thirds of them, by 1925, three years behind. Often they had lost interest in school activities and had little in common with their classmates. As a result, Chicanos in the north stayed in school little longer than those who remained in Hispanic villages. Most left school before sixth grade, and while the number of more advanced students rose in the 1920s, still only a handful enrolled in high school.

Faced with economic pressures and hostile neighbors, many Chicano families simply did not enroll their children in school. To many Anglos, this seemed the best solution to the educational dilemma, better than segregated schools or special classes. A former school board member asserted. "They're needed in the fields and the school don't do them any good anyway." Officials in the South Platte Valley granted illegal school exemptions to Chicano beetworking children and tended to turn a blind eye to those not applying. One confessed, "[W]e never try to enforce the compulsory attendance laws on the Mexicans. We just wink at the law." And Great Western Sugar, despite its claims for education, perpetrated myths that justified this denial of duty. The company claimed that "while beet children may be absent for several weeks each year from their classes in geography and spelling," they learned not only "industry and thrift," but "the craft of their fathers," a blessing for "people whose social and intellectual state may be below the standards of our ideals."

Underneath the justification ran other concerns. "If every child has a high school education," sugar company representatives demanded, "who will labor?" If the Anglo farmer was to keep his own children in school, he had to hire someone else to do the work. "[I]t is believed that a cheap labor supply is necessary for this industry," reported investigators in the Arkansas Valley, "and that the Spanish-American or Mexican is the one to furnish it. Too regular school attendance would not be compatible with this." The marginalization of Chicanos was no haphazard social development. Great Western Sugar's C. V. Maddux explained, "We no longer want settlers to occupy vacant land. . . . What we want is workers to work for the settlers who came before." Fred Cummings, a beetgrower from Fort Collins, elucidated, "[N]o man can accumulate anything in this world until by some means or device he is enabled to enjoy the benefit of some other man's labor." That Anglo farmers well understood the developing situation was revealed even further by one South Platte school official who feared, "[W]e are building up a caste system that inside of two generations will be worse than India ever dreamed of." Far from liberating the next generation of Chicanos from their backbreaking toil, the educational system of the north, better endowed than that of the Hispanic villages, seemed for the majority geared only to perpetuate the Chicanos as marginal agricultural labor. . . .

With Chicanas unable to recreate the stable village core that sustained social harmony in the villages, and with Chicanos marginal economically and socially to the Anglo community, it was unclear what sort of community Hispanics could create on the northern Colorado frontier. Indeed, Anglos tended to be pessimistic about the ability of Chicanos to adjust to life in northern Colorado at all. Inheriting a legacy of disdain for seasonal workers and migrant laborers, which labeled their relationship to farm labor as "excrescences upon its fair face," Anglos were disposed to agree with a Weld County sheriff that "a Mexican is a 'natural born liar, thief, and gambler.'" Visions of lawless and irresponsible hordes, visions unanchored by statistics, floated in the public imagination. The colonies were seen as potential dens of iniquity, where "the dancing girl and the wine-cup are star attractions." Their inhabitants appeared in local papers almost solely in criminal context, with their ethnicity prominently featured.

Chicanos did commit some crimes. Most involved petty theft—stealing from coal bins—or revolved around prohibition: moonshining and drinking and selling liquor, activities popular among Chicanos in both New Mexico and Colorado, but hardly peculiar to them. Anglos, however, even those with the most direct contact with Hispanics, consistently and greatly distorted the scale of lawbreaking. The official line held that prosecution of Chicanos accounted for three-quarters of Weld County court cases. An investigation in 1924 revealed instead that even including appearances as plaintiffs, Chicanos accounted for only 6 percent of the total county court cases and 10 percent of the justice of the peace cases, a figure not disproportionate to their number in the county's population. Conspicuous in their "otherness" and their poverty, Chicanos found themselves subject to these myths and to arrest, according to contemporary investigators, "without a clearly defined case or cause against them." Where a fee system ruled, constables and other officers whose income depended on fines and costs advised their victims to plead guilty.

In terms of relief and family stability, fears had also exaggerated the reality. Hispanic divorces in Weld County occurred at a lower rate than either Anglo divorces in that county or Hispanic divorces in southern Colorado or New Mexico. Few Hispanic children spent time in either the state home for dependent children or the state Industrial School for Girls. And the proportion of relief accounted for by Hispanics, while slightly greater than their proportion of the population at large, remained well under 20 percent, less than the proportion of Hispanics among the lowest-income groups. On the whole, concluded one investigator, impoverished Anglos in northern Colorado "indicated a much poorer social adjustment proportionately than did the Spanish-speaking group." It is possible that, after northern trauma, divorcées, single and deserted mothers, and delinquent children all fled back to the Hispanic homeland. It seems more consistent with the evidence, however, that despite frequent migration, low income, and severe discrimination, solidarity and not disorganization characterized Chicano families in the Anglo north. These families proved stronger than the forces which buffeted them on the edge of the regional community. . . .

As the Hispanic presence became more established, the coal camps, the Hispanic section of Denver, and the beet colonies all became foci of Chicano communities whose inhabitants' social needs were met from within rather than from the villages of the regional community. Of these, the Chicano enclaves in Denver, growing in size and becoming more stable during the 1920s, were among the largest and most articulated. When Arthur Maes's father died in 1927, the second winter after the family had come from New Mexico to northern Colorado to work beets, his mother was unable to survive in Fort Lupton. She took the family to Denver where they had spent the previous winter, as she "knew the community in the Bottoms," and it was the only place she had any friends. Whereas other towns in the area had at most one Hispanic realtor or cleaner to represent the community in the business world, Denver had tamale shops, some family stores, and the occasional scion of an upper-class New Mexican, southern Colorado, or Mexican family. Yet even Denver hardly compared in the scale of its Hispanic community to Trinidad, and the majority of its Hispanic residents were seasonal laborers.

Like many of the coal camps, the Chicano sections of Denver were distinctly unlovely. Robert McLean and Charles Thomson described one in 1924 as "a district which looks as if both God and Denver had forgotten it . . . the mongrel offspring of a deserted village and a city slum" with "no paving, sidewalks, no sewers." Nevertheless, the concentration of Chicanos made possible some early attempts at organization on ethnic lines, including not only the Anglo sponsored missions such as Jerome Park Mission and the First Spanish Methodist Church, but the Sociedad Protectora, a mutualista [mutual aid society] in the Lawrence Street area originating in 1921, the Cruz Azul for Mexicans, the Spanish-American Club—a cultural association whose president was a former Mexican consul—and the Spanish-American Citizens Association, the latest of these organizations and one which in 1931 intended to organize the estimated 15,000 Spanish American citizens in Denver and the vicinity for industrial, political, and social justice in all public affairs.

Denver was not unique. Larger than other enclaves, its Hispanic communities garnered more elites and Anglo attention, but they shared many of the same strategies and problems as the colonies and barrios across northeastern Colorado. The nascent Chicano community in the north was not yet entirely centered on a single site, despite the hostility of the environs. And while many Hispanics in northern Colorado wintered in Denver, more lived outside it, and many moved from winter to winter among the towns, the company colonies, and the city and had, by the late 1920s, relatives scattered across the area.

First erected in 1924, the Great Western Sugar Company's beet-labor colonies soon became not only the more stable clusters the company desired, but, like Denver, centers of Hispanic community organizing. Unlike Colorado Fuel and Iron, the sugar company allowed its control to lie loosely on these colonies. It retained the right to dispossess undesirables as long as it held the leases, and it contributed to church and community buildings, but the colonies were not closed camps, not located at the workplace, and not polyglot. Within them, colonists bought not just houses, but the land on which they stood. And ironically, their very isolation from Anglo society helped foster their development as something more than transient labor camps.

As with racial and immigrant enclaves elsewhere, the colonies' homogeneity relieved some of the pressure to assimilate. Residents had, as one investigator found, "their own favorite dishes," and no one encouraged them "to abandon their native language for American." Though economically dependent on the Anglo world, they retained, as had the villages, some social and cultural autonomy. Here, perhaps, those who did remain year after year could re-create the regional community in truncated and more vulnerable form. The barrio could be a new core.

By the late 1920s, some colonies increasingly resembled the interrelated villages. Chicano couples met and courted there, among the "meticulously tended lawns, and the watered and swept earthen patios," that one colonist remembered. They held dances and even fiestas in the colonies. The women, recalled one early settler, "had their own clubs," and sewing, cooking, mutual aid, and church groups, and in January 1930, it was their efforts, in part, which culminated in a new Pentecostal Assembly of God Church built by colonists in the Greeley colony.

From this more cohesive base, colonists and other settlers began to shift to more aggressive strategies in intercultural matters. The regional community, with its migrant patterns, was in some sense a strategy of retreat, as was the high turnover that embodied Chicano protest at conditions in beetwork. In the same vein, Mexicans consciously decided against citizenship, rejecting the second-class status they believed it would bring. A Mexican in the South Platte Valley declared, "To hell with the United States. We don't have to be slaves in Mexico." But as retreat to the villages became increasingly impracticable and more stable communities evolved, direct protests occurred. At least one Chicano in Weld County filed a civil rights case in 1927 against Greeley restaurant proprietors who ejected him on the grounds that he was a Mexican. World War I veterans among the colonists also early asserted the colonists' rights in the community at large in regard to voting and discrimination. Their membership in local American Legion branches provided virtually the only organized non-charitable social link between ethnic groups and bolstered their legitimacy as spokesmen in each.

As the sense of neighborhood in the colonies grew, resistance began to take more collective forms. Chicano boycotts in Greeley and Johnstown led to the removal of discriminatory signs from the shop windows, at least temporarily, in 1927. Though less successful, a committee of Chicanos also protested the establishment of separate school rooms for Chicano children. By the end of the decade, like Denver, the colonies and mining towns had their own Hispanic groups and mutualistas. Some accepted both Mexican and Spanish Americans, others only one or the other. Some of the colonies even organized into self-governing bodies under commissioners of their own choosing. In 1928 the Greeley colony, for example, drew up "articles of association for the management of colony affairs," including police and sanitary regulations, and filed them with the county police. This was, perhaps, the ultimate declaration of an autonomous community on the Anglo-Hispanic frontier. These Hispanics created room for themselves and committed themselves to permanent residence without committing themselves to assimilation.

 ## For Further Study

1. The author of the selection uses different terms in referring to people of Mexican ancestry living in the United States. From the context, determine the precise definitions of "Chicano," "Chicana," "Hispanic," and "Mexican" as the author uses them. Check newspapers, television, and other sources to see whether she uses

these terms in the same way as others do. Although Deutsch does not use the term "Latino" or "Latina," try also to find out what these terms mean.

2. Describe the strategies Chicanos employed to enable them to live on the low wages provided by the sugar-beet companies.

3. Compare the Chicano communities in western cities like Denver to those of immigrants described in earlier selections. What are the main similarities and differences with regard to employment, housing, education, the attitudes of the dominant population, and attempts to foster or resist assimilation into the dominant culture?

For Further Reading

Rodolfo Acuña, *Occupied America: A History of Chicanos* (1981), is a general history of people of Mexican ancestry in the United States. Albert Camarillo, *Chicanos in a Changing Society* (1979), and Mario T. Garcia, *Desert Immigrants: The Mexicans of El Paso, 1880–1920* (1981), deal with particular cities, Santa Barbara, California, and El Paso, Texas, respectively. Carey McWilliams, *Factories in the Field: The Story of Migratory Farm Labor in California* (1939), and *Ill Fares the Land: Migrants and Migratory Labor in the United States* (1942), are early and still illuminating examinations of migrant labor. Jacqueline Jones, *The Dispossessed: America's Underclass from the Civil War to the Present* (1992), also has much to say about migrant labor in general. Mark Reisler, *By the Sweat of Their Brow: Mexican Immigrant Labor in the United States, 1900–1940* (1976), tells part of the story of Mexican immigration to the United States. James D. Cockcroft, *Outlaws in the Promised Land: Mexican Immigrant Workers and America's Future* (1986), discusses the same subject in more recent years. David Reimers, *Still the Golden Door: The Third World Comes to America* (1985), covers recent immigration from Mexico along with that from other lands.

Chapter 12

Bettmann/CORBIS

In the early years of the automobile, driving presented women with many challenges.

Women Take to the Road

Virginia Scharff

Except for a sharp but short-lived economic downturn early in the decade, the 1920s were quite prosperous. Productivity and real wages—that is, the amount of goods and services that a person could buy with an hour's labor—both rose. New industries such as radio and aviation became prominent and profitable. Older industries such as the movies and advertising enjoyed rapid growth. People spoke about "The New Era" in the nation's economic life, in which mass production was linked to mass consumption in such a way as to generate uninterrupted growth and general prosperity and ensure that depressions would become relics of the past. That optimism was proved false when the stock market crash of 1929 signaled the start of the worst depression the nation had ever endured.

Still, the prosperity of the 1920s, temporary as it may have been, had permanent effects on the way Americans lived, in large part because the primary engine driving the decade's economic growth was spending on consumer goods. The introduction and widespread use of installment-plan buying, time-purchase plans, and other forms of consumer credit permitted millions of Americans to acquire the profusion of goods that a flourishing mass-production economy was turning out for their delight.

Of all these goods, the automobile had the greatest impact on the way Americans lived. Automobiles tended to be toys for the rich until Henry Ford revolutionized auto production with the introduction of the assembly line at his plant in Highland Park, Michigan in 1914. The new system of mass production lowered costs and brought the Model T within the economic reach of millions of Americans. Other car makers quickly adopted the new innovations, and by the 1920s the car was becoming a standard possession for most middle class American families and many in the working class as well.

As cars became more and more common over the course of time, they changed many aspects of Americans' lives—the way they shopped, worked, and spent their leisure time, for instance—and they also profoundly altered the landscape of America's cities. At the time they first became widespread in the 1920s, cars also had a significant relationship to the challenges to traditional gender roles that were being mounted. The feminist upsurge of the first decades of the twentieth century that finally led to the adoption of the constitutional amendment granting women's suffrage in 1920 continued into the 20s.

The tendency to divide car buyers' preferences by gender grew particularly acute in discussion of the most significant automotive design innovation of the 1920s, the closed car. In 1919, less than ten percent of all cars produced in the United States were enclosed models. By 1929, closed cars comprised eighty-seven percent of all passenger automobiles produced in the United States and Canada. Even the Model T, which Alfred Sloan described as "pre-eminently an open car design" because its light chassis was ill adapted to the heavy closed body, would sprout a roof; nearly forty percent of 1924 Model Ts were closed cars.

The industry-wide decision to manufacture cars with fixed roofs was frequently depicted as a concession to female vanity and frailty. Women were said to prefer sedans and coupes because they wanted to ride in opulent comfort without messing up their hair and clothing. Advertisements and trade features on various makes of closed autos employed a vocabulary reflecting the industry's common assumptions about feminine preferences, noting the model's "refinements," "conservative lines," "comfort," "smartness," "ease," "grace," and "beauty."

Whatever its decorative advantages, the sedan or coupe had numerous practical advantages over the open touring car or roadster for motorists regardless of sex. Those who rode with a roof over their heads stayed dry in wet weather, cooler on hot sunny days, and warmer during the cold weather. The closed car was a year-round means of transportation, while the open cars that dominated the market before World War I had to be stored during the winter and overhauled in the spring. As early as 1920, the Anchor Auto Top manufacturer pointed out such benefits in an advertisement rare for its message that "the whole family wants the open car made a closed car for winter." The ad featured samples of testimony from a typical family, the father noting the advantages of driving "to and from the office in snug warmth no matter how hard it snows or blows," the children citing transportation for grandparents and trips to and from school, the mother declaring the closed car superior for visiting, theater-going, comfort, and style. . . .

Had manufacturers recognized the benefits of providing mobile shelter from the beginning of the automotive era, the private auto might have made a more rapid transition from "pleasure car" to practical means of daily transportation for middle-class workers, both those employed outside the home and those who pursued a domestic vocation. Why, then, was the closed model an automotive after-

---

thought? And if woman's influence was responsible for the innovation, as so many assumed, "why didn't she make her voice felt in the matter much sooner?"

Price was certainly an important factor in delaying the coming of the closed car. Closed models before 1920 cost hundreds of dollars more than open versions of the same vehicles; a 1922 editorial claimed that "the sedan of any given make costs at retail anywhere from $500 to $1,500 more than the touring model of the same make." Price differences, however, did not completely explain the belated trend toward closed vehicles, since a number of manufacturers offered inexpensive tops for low-priced cars. As early as 1916, the Anchor Buggy Company had advertised a sedan top for the Ford touring car selling for $77.50, and a coupe top for the Ford roadster at $62.50. Moreover, the price of automobiles was not simply a function of the amount of metal or cloth or labor required for the machine itself, since wages were set in the context of ideological considerations and conflict over the labor process, and automobile manufacturers' costs included substantial fixed investment in assembly lines, tools, skills, and materials geared to existing designs.

Once manufacturers realized that there was a market for closed vehicles they quickly narrowed the price gap. Roy D. Chapin of the Hudson Motor Company pioneered in the effort to bring down closed car costs. In 1920, Hudson offered an Essex sedan priced at $2,450, with a comparable touring model at a cost of $1,595. The following year, the Essex coach sold for $1,495, only $300 more than the touring model. By 1925, the Essex coach, priced at $895, cost $5 *less* than the touring car. Scientists and engineers had to work out technological problems concerning metallurgy, steel processing, machine tools, and spot welding before the closed all-steel body that Dodge introduced in 1924 could be made at a reasonable cost. Still, these material and intellectual barriers were rapidly surmounted in the wake of the success of the Essex closed model. Closed cars rapidly came to dominate the low-priced market. In 1922, manufacturers in the United States and Canada produced 1,338,000 open vehicles and 436,000 closed cars in the "under $1,000" price category. By 1929, in the same price category, 592,000 open cars and 3,328,000 closed cars were produced.

"For some reason or other," wrote Alfred Sloan, "it took us a long time to realize that the way to keep dry in a motorcar was to keep the weather out of the car." Car makers' assumptions about gender blinded them to the potential market for enclosed vehicles, thus delaying the industry's effort to meet the technological challenges of producing closed cars, and contributing to their tardiness in bringing America's motoring families in out of the rain. Given a tendency to identify women's activities and perceived preferences as at best supplementary, and at worst harmful, to men's interests, manufacturers' identification of enclosed automobiles with women and with home may have done as much to perpetuate price differences between open and closed cars (with the concomitant early market predominance of touring cars and runabouts) as more material factors.

When American family men bought closed cars, they defied expectations that rugged masculinity governed their automotive taste. They, and the industry that hoped to sell ever more automobiles, asserted manhood by attributing the change to "feminine influence." A Colorado man said that his next car would be a closed model, but explained: "The reason for this preference (for the closed body) is my wife. I personally prefer an open model, as I drive a lot in the mountains." A Californian insisted that he would buy an open model "because it is a *man's* car, not a society car."

As the sedan and coupe gained popularity, definitions of male and female automotive taste shifted, though many remained inclined to contrast simple masculine practicality with complicated feminine subjectivity. "To father," *Motor* columnist John C. Long wrote, "the automobile means transportation. It will take him around on his business trips and it will get him out in the open air in the evenings. Similarly, he regards his house as a place for keeping the heat in and the rain out." If men dispassionately regarded cars and houses as tools, women, Long believed, expected both the auto and the home to serve as vehicles for domestic cultural missions: "Mother sees the car, like the home, as a means for holding the family together, for raising the standard of living, for providing recreation and social advantages for the children."

Throughout the decade, commentators would describe roofed vehicles in domestic terms, calling the closed car a "delightful living room on wheels," "a drawing room on wheels," or "a boudoir on wheels," or suggesting that cars could be accessorized to provide "all the comforts of home." Couched in such terms, the car roof appeared as a prelude to interior decoration rather than a utility feature. But there was no necessary contradiction between men's and women's interests when it came to choosing a family car; the closed car offered advantages to both. It makes sense to see the adoption of this consumer good as the product of familial agreement, rather than as the result of male-female conflict resolved by the triumph of women's vanity or physical timidity over men's better judgment, particularly given the husband's power as titleholder and the practical advantages the closed car offered to individuals regardless of sex.

The tendency to confuse preferences believed to be masculine or feminine with men and women led many to see woman's influence at work where there was no evidence to support such a conclusion. Those on the supply side of the auto sales equation assembled relatively little data on what women consumers of automobiles *said* they wanted. The powerful assumption that women would invariably act feminine seemed to need no proof, and it offered a reassuring explanation for men's changing consumption patterns. According to trade logic, male buyers' taste had not altered; husbands had simply decided to start humoring their wives, and manufacturers ought gallantly to follow suit. When a survey of 20,000 auto owners revealed that sixty percent planned to purchase a closed car, John C. Long deduced, with circular logic, that "the reasons given for the preference, such as appearance, cleanliness, and comfort, indicate the influence of the woman in the home, directly or indirectly." Despite the reported preference of some women for open cars and the endorsement of closed cars by many men, Long and others continued to insist that sex governed the preference for open or closed cars.

Fragments of personal testimony suggest that industry strategists and publicists oversimplified and distorted women's (and men's) wishes. To be sure, in some instances women consumers confirmed stereotypes. Lucile Lady Duff-Gordon, owner of several cars, claimed that color, graceful lines, and "little accessories

which . . . make all the difference in the world" were women's paramount considerations. Comparing autos to sedan chairs, Lady Duff-Gordon insisted that the
auto ought to be a work of art, a romantic setting, and a symbol of luxury. She believed that "if one could afford to have an automobile decorated for each mood
or occasion, it would be ideal." Although such views were clearly in harmony with
assumptions about female extravagance, Lady Duff-Gordon insisted that her ideas
did not "apply to women alone. A man ought to have at least two or three cars
decorated according to his needs."

While this fashion expert urged both sexes toward the ornamental, car buyer
Edith M. Garfield described her experience visiting several automobile dealers,
suggesting that manufacturers, advertising agents, and sales personnel were acting
according to conventional beliefs about feminine frivolity rather than paying attention to women consumers' stated preferences. Her ideas about what she wanted in
a car spanned conventional notions of the businesslike masculine and the hedonistic feminine. She explained that she had narrowed her search to "eight or ten automobiles, all in the same price and performance class." After making this pragmatic
judgment, she "wanted to be convinced that the car I finally signed on the dotted
line for was absolutely the smartest, most comfortable, smoothest and hill-climbiest
one of the lot." Some salesmen ignored her and some bowled her over with hard-
sell tactics, but none treated her as a serious and informed consumer. One dealer
"greeted me with an amused smile much like the one I use on my collie when he's
trying to pick up a stick several sizes too big for him. Somehow that smile made me
feel that I should be home playing with paper dolls, leaving such matters as buying
an automobile to a *man*." When the dealer persisted in disregarding her questions
about power, while rhapsodizing about "delicate little touches that *make* a car," she
fumed that "he had me down as a dumbbell! But dumbbell is a compliment compared with what I thought of him." . . .

Had women motorists acted in the fatuous manner so many industry commentators alleged, we might well see them as too stupid to decide how to spend their
money. The woman who could be satisfied entirely by plush upholstery and the
aptly named vanity case, paying no attention to the question of whether the car
would get her where she wanted to go, would not pose a profound threat to yesterday's order of things. Neither would she need to get into an automobile; she
might as well stay at home and buy new slipcovers. To imagine so passive and nar-
cissistic a person pursuing her own interests—even knowing what she wanted or
needed—is difficult to say the least. At the same time, attributing all demand for
automotive amenities to women reassured men that when they chose a car that offered comfort and aesthetic appeal, they were doing something nice for the little
lady, not getting soft themselves. . . .

In the 1920s as never before, auto manufacturers occupied themselves with the
business of selling, as well as making, cars. Industry commentators' solicitude for
the feminine consumer betrayed an embarrassment about male consumption patterns tantamount to anxiety about the preservation of masculine identity.
Uncertain and defensive, auto makers and their marketing people both won-

dered what women (and men) wanted, and tried to assure themselves that indeed, they already knew.

For good or ill, the public received the industry's marketing message with enthusiasm. Budget-conscious and hard-pressed American families of the twenties often determined to sacrifice other services and goods to purchase automobiles. While car manufacturers and their army of promoters contemplated the relevance of masculinity and feminity to auto marketing, some observers, notably those who sold other consumer goods, treated the act of buying a car as a threat to women's spending priorities. Textile and shoe manufacturers and retailers were said to be particularly concerned about the auto's inroads in the family budget. The *New York Daily News Record,* an organ of the textile trade, declared, "It seems impossible to overlook the fact that people are buying too many automobiles and not enough washing machines."

It remains to be proven that women opposed car buying, or that they should have done so. A *Ladies' Home Journal* writer, pointing out the advantages of her "conservation car," said driving her children to school saved the family money on clothing and shoe leather. A Muncie, Indiana housewife told Robert and Helen Lynd that her family "would rather do without clothes than give up the car," while another explained that "I'll go without food before I'll see us give up the car."

Why would women say such things? What benefits did they believe the family car brought them? Automobility meant much more to women than a chance to recline in sumptuous surroundings, just as it meant more to men than a chance to feel the wind in their hair. Buying and driving a car, not simply an end in itself, was a means of acting on personal choices, which were sometimes individualistic, but were in most instances shaped by family negotiations, responsibilities and loyalties. Acting on behalf of such values, women drivers would play a critical role in the transformation of the American way of life in the twentieth century. . . .

By 1920, the modern woman made her appearance on the American road. Sleek and streamlined, she had slipped the ponderous drapery of Victorian clothing. The hem of her dress no longer trailed on the ground. Often enough, now, it swung free at knee level. Some youthful female motorists, sporting the bobbed hair and daring demeanor of the flapper, even abandoned dresses altogether in favor of suits with knickers. The cumbersome picture hats and veils of the early motoring period had given way to snug-fitting cloches, and tailored motoring coats replaced heavy dusters. Whether a sedate housewife or a high-spirited jazz baby, the woman motorist of the twenties announced with her very clothing that she took mobility for granted.

The automobile, more than any of the other consumer goods Americans adopted so enthusiastically in the 1920s, offered women new possibilities for excitement, for leisure and for sociability. During the twenties, many would travel further and further from home, from woman's vaunted place, in pursuit of pleasure. Social critics of the period worried that women would be so beguiled by the era's new entertainments, motoring not least among them, that they would neglect home, family, and morality. As much fun as they had with motorcars, however, women generally did not abandon hearth and duty in favor of the road, which posed perils of its own. Instead, they reconciled mobility and domesticity, using the automobile to fulfill their family roles as well as to enjoy themselves. . . .

Amid the multitudes of automobile tourists who took off on cross-country vacations in the 1920s, adventurous American women carried on the legacy of the emancipated women drivers of earlier years. "Dilettantes, debutantes, and even dowagers are falling under the spell of western touring," wrote motorist Laura B. McClintock. "Mothers with their children are seen as frequently as college girls out for a lark, and schoolteachers and business women in increasing numbers are seeking this form of relaxation."

Some female tourists, traveling alone or with women friends, saw themselves as modern pioneers. Winifred Hawkridge Dixon embarked from Boston in 1921 with her friend Katherine Thaxter, bound to see the American West, to "follow the old trails, immigrant trails, cattle trails, traders' routes." Determined to prove that they could cope with the rigors of the journey without male companionship, they "mutually divided the labor as our tastes and talents dictated." Dixon claimed plenty of experience as a mechanic, declaring that "I love to tinker!" and proclaimed her friend Thaxter a wizard at tire changing: "The jack holds no mysteries for her, and tire rims click into place at the sound of her voice." Like their emigrant forerunners, faced with oozing mud and roadbed craters, Dixon and Thaxter sometimes relied on the good will of benevolent strangers. They had to ask a man with a mule team to extricate the car from sticky Texas gumbo, and were sometimes reduced to trying to attract aid by "fix[ing] smiles fairly dripping with saccharine on our faces." Yet they were less embarrassed at needing on occasion to ask for help than at the fact that wherever they went, men remarked that they were "a long way from home, ain't you?"

Far from home as they were, these two self-described "ladies from Boston" fended for themselves to a remarkable degree. They gloried in fixing their ignition fifty miles from the nearest garage, and were thrilled when a Montana cowboy observed. "They ain't helpless." They clearly regarded their Western motoring adventure as a journey to personal liberation. As they approached the Rocky Mountains, Dixon observed, "for the first time in my life. I felt I had all the room I wanted." Navigating rugged mountain and desert roads strengthened her fingers and made her wrists "like iron." Confronting the rawness and vastness of the western landscape, they rejoiced at their newfound confidence and vision: "We had a sense of courage toward life new to us all." Returning home, they lamented leaving "the great, free West, 'where a man can be a man and a woman can be a woman.'"

For many other American women, cross-country auto touring was less a personal quest than a family undertaking. Employing a fantastic array of camping equipment, from elaborate "homes on wheels" to pup tents and bedrolls mounted on running boards, "gasoline gypsies" by the thousands spent summer vacations on the road. Motorists had enjoyed picnics and other outdoor entertainments since the beginning of the automobile era, but such outings became both more commonplace and more ambitious in the twenties, as western towns and cities welcomed tourists to municipal auto camps. Twenties tourists celebrated the democracy of the camp, a place where strangers mingled companionably, exchanging information on road conditions and scenic attractions, borrowing supplies, and helping one another with repairs.

For men, autocamping was a way to "get away from it all," to commune with nature and leave the workaday world behind. Women also enjoyed the chance to see the country, and to dress for comfort rather than fashion, but putting the family on wheels did not necessarily mean getting away from housework. Domestic routines, transferred to the road, could still be elaborate, and jobs that had been performed with familiar equipment in customary surroundings could become problems requiring extra energy and creativity. Buying food and keeping it from spoiling, doing laundry, and keeping passengers and gear clean and dry taxed women's ingenuity and their patience. Men might lend a hand with cooking, but other traditionally female tasks, from dishwashing to laundry to child care, remained women's work. As writer Mary Roberts Rinehart observed, "The difference between the men I have camped with and myself, generally speaking, has been this: they have called it sport; I have known it was work."

If women found motor camping a form of fun well mixed with labor, surely not all automotive entertainments entailed drudgery. There was such a thing as joy riding, a fancy supposed to be particularly appealing to that most visible and boldest symbol of American womanhood in the 1920s, the flapper. Her appetite for self-display, for pretty objects, and for reckless fun made her seem a perfect customer for the "pleasure car."

To be sure, some social critics, contemplating the flapper, worried that the attractions and diversions of modern life would seduce young women away from home and duty. Dr. French Oliver of the Los Angeles Bible Institute referred to the auto, the movies, and the dance hall as a "triumvirate of hell" for American youth. Like ragtime, jazz, and motion pictures, and the new public spaces associated with popular entertainments, the auto seemed to embody an attractive and dangerous modern "freedom in manners and morals" for those previously socially constrained. The pleasures of motoring ranged, after all, from a few minutes away from mundane responsibilities, to a stolen kiss away from prying eyes, to the utter abandonment of family and reputation in the name of love or adventure. The seemingly innocent Sunday drive might erode a family's attendance at church: how much more threatening the spectre of Saturday night roadhouse escapades, far from community censure. Would motor-mad men throw over their jobs in wild pursuit of distance and velocity? Would women drive so far and fast that they would forget to come home? Would children appropriate the family car only to wreck it and the familial future?

No idea seemed more alarming or more irresistible to observers than the notion that, instruments of hedonism that they were, motorcars would make people more sexually demonstrative. From the earliest days of the car culture, automobiles had been expected to provide a new space for courtship and sex. Magazine covers, stories, jokes, and popular songs linked cars with romance, and experts ranging from sociologists to ministers offered varied opinions of the auto's effect on Americans' sex lives.

Some women doubtless took advantage of the motorcar as a means to sexual ends. F. Scott Fitzgerald's picture of the flapper as a girl who considered the automobile an ideal place to pet had its basis in fact, and such activities were not limited to the wellborn or the young or the unmarried. Magazine writer Eleanor Wembridge reported:

> Every evening in the city, "gas hawks" or roving young men in automobiles, pick up the young girls as they come out from work, and "pet" them even in the streets. They have done it outside my window with an enthusiasm which even two large paper bags filled with water and hurled against their windshield by an interested spectator failed to cool.

Some also viewed the motorcar as a threat to marital fidelity. An aggrieved husband, suing for divorce, told a Los Angeles judge that he had followed his wife and another man to a lonely spot, then hidden in a ditch and watched as "his wife and the man climbed into the back seat."

Yet if sexually adventuresome women made use of the auto for their own purposes, the Jazz Age was also the era of enforcement of the Mann Act of 1910. That law, intended to combat "white slavery," was designed to safeguard female purity by prohibiting men from transporting women across state lines "for immoral purposes." Such protective legislation, predicated on the notion of woman as passenger rather than pilot, at once denied women the right to, and the responsibility for, control over both sexuality and transportation technology, regardless of women's own wishes or capacities.

Where women sought openly to seize sensual or mobile pleasure, they risked placing themselves outside the protection of public opinion, if not the law. Parents cautioned their daughters not to get in cars with boys, and the newspapers rushed to point out the dire consequences when such warnings were ignored. In Los Angeles, some members of the California Congress of Mothers and PTAs insisted that "school boys' and girls' promiscuous use of the auto is one of the greatest menaces of the age." Girls who gave in to the temptation to take a joyride received little sympathy when things turned out badly.

There was, of course, truth in the notion that men in cars endangered women. Women who sought sexual pleasure risked loss of reputation and unwanted pregnancy, whereas men's participation in sex, if discovered, generally enhanced their peer standing. Getting into a car added a dimension to men's relative power in sexual encounters, since more men than women drove, more men than women owned cars, and even where both were qualified, men usually took the wheel. When, in 1920, Los Angeles police cracked down on "mashers" (men who made unwelcome sexual overtures to women), a member of the police "Purity Squad" commented, "We seem to have men in this town who have no sense of decency and will brazenly stop a woman anywhere on the streets." Frightening on foot, such men became even scarier when they drove automobiles. The *Los Angeles Record* noted that "girls complained these men have lurked around with autos inviting them to 'come and have a good time,'" and that "parents of two little girls claim [an] old man has tried to lure little girls into his car with offers of chocolate."

While in many areas the police made a concentrated effort to prevent male drivers from harming female pedestrians, sometimes even making arrests without asking women to testify against those accused, drivers' numbers grew faster than did police capacity to prevent abuses. In Los Angeles, at New Year's 1919–1920, one Mary

Gelso, described by the *Los Angeles Record* as "a beautiful girl living at the Continental Hotel," had felt "lonely last night and dressed up to go to a dance somewhere." Accosted by a "gentlemanly, very well-dressed stranger" in downtown L.A., she agreed to take a short ride down Broadway "to see the New Year crowd." Another man was at the wheel of the automobile. "Before she realized it," the *Record* reported, they were speeding to Vernon, a remote suburb. When they reached a lonely point on the road, the man who had originally engaged her in conversation sexually assaulted her and beat her severely, finally hurling her out of the car.

While the police declared their outrage at "this detestable mashing nuisance," and promised to arrest any man caught "ogling, or winking, or [making] obscene remarks," the inclusion of details about the victim in the story cast doubt on her character, depicting Gelso as a loose woman who only got what she deserved. Mary Gelso's ordeal, and the implicit criticism of her behavior, offered a typical moral lesson to young American women of the 1920s. Hedonistic flappers might find temporary pleasures, but danger lurked too. The wise girl would temper her behavior in the interest of personal safety, and discard wild ways upon assuming the responsibilities of marriage. The motorcar could provide young women with almost unlimited potential for entertainment, but America's daughters knew they went joyriding at their own risk.

Presented thus with the manifold fascinations and hazards of motoring, American women were urged to accept a compromise. If they had to forsake the fiery delights of youthful adventure for the soberer satisfactions of adult womanhood, the auto, they learned, might enable them to salvage some fun, to claim pleasure as well as security, mobility as well as domesticity. Few contemporary observers doubted that household pursuits would (and should) define women's days and identities. Ideas such as female responsibility for domestic activities (including child rearing, cooking, housekeeping, and managing consumption) so pervaded American thinking that they remained powerful in the face of even so potent a technological force as the automobile. These vital concepts would shape women's car travel, distorting and widening woman's sphere without exploding it.

Auto manufacturers, advertising in such publications as *The Ladies' Home Journal* and *Good Housekeeping*, depicted the motorcar as the key to reconciling women's household business and personal pleasure. The ads featured smiling groups of well-dressed women enjoying each other's company in Cadillacs and Chevrolets and Overland Sixes, and frequently set the dry comfort of the closed car against a backdrop of rainy weather outside. Ford Motor Company, in its first ever large-scale advertising campaign, promised readers of *The Ladies' Home Journal* that a Ford would be "An 'Open Door' to Wider Contacts," asserting that "By owning a Ford car a woman can with ease widen her sphere of interests without extra time or effort. She can accomplish more daily, yet easily keep pace with her usual schedule of domestic pursuits." Ford ads showed women in a variety of situations—vacationing, going shopping, visiting, and even conducting business—but always emphasized the social aspect of the product. No woman need feel lonesome, Ford implied, because "the car is so easy to drive that it constantly suggests thoughtful services to her friends. She can call for them without effort and share pleasantly their companionship."

Auto advertisements that made driving appear perfectly effortless and enjoyable claimed far more for their products than they could deliver. Cars were not always reliable; road conditions left much to be desired; the noise, congestion, and dirt of traffic was on the rise in many places. Yet for at least one group of women, the motorcar offered the noteworthy benefit of diminished social isolation. Rural Americans of the 1920s, experiencing the enormity of the American landscape to a far greater degree than their urban compatriots, regarded the automobile as a solution to the problem of distance from community life.

In 1919, U.S. Department of Agriculture home demonstration agents conducted a survey of over 10,000 women in rural homes to determine farm women's attitudes toward their situation. The survey suggested that "the farm woman feels her isolation from neighbors as well as from libraries and other means of keeping in touch with outside life." Given an average distance from the farm of 5.9 miles to the nearest high school, 2.9 miles to the nearest church, and 4.8 miles to the nearest market,

> country people are far enough from the centers of trade, social, and religious activities to tempt the spirit of individualism and to put their neighborliness and piety to the test. . . . The automobile contributes materially to community life by reducing the distance factor.

Not surprisingly, farm families had taken to the motorcar with relish. Sixty-two percent of farms in the USDA study reported owning cars, with the highest percentage in the Midwest (seventy-three percent), next highest in the West (sixty-two percent), and lowest in the East (forty-eight percent). An article in the *Rural New Yorker* based on 1920 Commerce Department records indicated that more than 166,000 farms (or eight percent of all farms in the country) might have had more than one car. . . .

If they brought more visitors to the farmstead, automobiles also enabled rural women to participate in town life much more frequently than they had in the days of horse and foot transportation, to more easily combine household duties with sociability. They used cars to attend meetings, visit friends, shop for items formerly produced at home, and generally to relieve the monotony of the household routine. One farm woman expressed her preference for the auto over other modern conveniences quite simply, telling an interviewer, "You can't go to town in a bathtub." Many rural housewives expressed great satisfaction in attending homemakers' extension clubs, organizations intended not only to introduce them to new consumer goods and techniques, but also to enhance both social life and domesticity. A Montana woman told an oral history interviewer, "We looked forward to the meetings—the information they gave there, and the sociability that was involved. It was really the social life of the community." Getting there might nevertheless require both creativity and cooperation. Just having a car did not guarantee the access to the consumer goods and social resources which farm women saw as the chief benefit of automobility. Mechanical difficulties, lack of driving ability or experience, and wretched roads sometimes barred the door to wider contacts.

Country women devised ingenious solutions to their transportation problems. Posey County, Indiana farm woman Vernell Saltzman recalled a meeting at which extension agents taught club members how to preserve food by the coldpacking method:

> I drove a horse and buggy halfway, and I met up with Carlena Cowan Ramsey. She had a car. I could drive a car straight forward, but I could not back one. So I picked her up and Lena Thompson Holler up and Lena had one of those newfangled coldpackers, and I drove the car up to Farmersville School, and we worked all day canning.
>
> When we got ready to go home, Carlena couldn't drive that car straight, but she could back it, so she backs it up, and we loaded Lena in with her precious cold-packer, and I drove the car home, and got my horse and buggy and come on home.

Vernell Saltzman's anecdote reveals not only that farm wives sometimes used technology with remarkable imagination, but also that country women, in any case, did not necessarily regard domesticity and sociability as contradictory, even when the two endeavors were spatially segregated.

Paradoxically, the notion that women needed to stay at home to meet the demands of domestic work persisted as a cultural fiction. A 1916 article in *Motor Age* accused rural women of gadding about in autos and neglecting their laying hens. Woman's place, if still defined by domesticity, was less than ever strictly confined to the household, but not everyone was happy about the fact. As housewives used the auto to change the way they made use of time and space, they inadvertently fueled long-standing confusion about whether American women were doing their familial duty.

As deeply as Americans believed in women's domestic mission, they had a hard time visualizing what women did in the home as real work. The homemaker's vocation had changed radically since preindustrial times. Where housewives had once had to make much of what their families used, occupying themselves with spinning and weaving and sewing, butchering and rendering and cooking, their modern counterparts could go to a department store and buy ready-to-wear clothes, then stop off at a grocery and purchase whatever they needed for the evening's meal. Social scientists of the time referred to this change as the departure of "economic functions" from the home, and they tended to cast a disapproving eye on the modern homemaker, celebrating earlier commodity production as "real" work and at least implicitly denigrating the contemporary woman's activities as profligate idleness.

Certainly the modern middle-class housewife produced fewer commodities than had her preindustrial predecessor. Instead, she invested her energies and time in emotionally intense child rearing and husband nurturing, in purchasing the things her family needed, and in providing the services that made goods usable and family members productive—cooking complicated meals, keeping up with rising standards of cleanliness for household and clothing. Such changes in the domestic vocation reflected a wider transition in the United States, from a country grown wealthy by producing commodities, to a nation investing more and more of its resources in providing services. They also meant that domestic work tended more and more to be self-erasing. Shopping, cooking, cleaning, accommodating husbands, and cuddling and disciplining children could be emotionally and physically taxing, but those activities were seldom considered as labor, especially since the most successful practitioners were those who called least attention to their efforts. Groceries purchased were consumed. The process of shopping, cooking, and washing dishes was designed to create an impression that no meal had ever been served. Cleaning meant eradicating messes before anyone perceived disorder. The job of delivering children to school and husbands to commuter trains reversed itself when housewives returned to pick up family members and bring them home. The woman who worked hardest, who succeeded most brilliantly in creating a relaxing "haven in a heartless world," labored mightily to obscure her own exertions. No wonder she could be accused of indulging herself with bonbons and trashy novels while others toiled. In a cultural climate where women's domestic work achieved fruition only when it reached the vanishing point, the distinction between labor and leisure was far from obvious.

The job of driving embodied the difficulty of distinguishing between women's work and play. As American cities grew, and millions of families bought automobiles, women found themselves increasingly responsible for producing transportation. By the middle of the twentieth century, as historian Ruth Schwartz Cowan noted, "the time that housewives had once spent in preserving strawberries and stitching petticoats was being spent in driving to stores, shopping, and waiting in lines. The automobile had become . . . the vehicle through which she did her most significant work." Homemaking included the responsibility for negotiating the temporal, spatial, and emotional conflicts and distances between private and public life. Being a successful wife and mother meant not only attending to one's family, but connecting the household with the community.

Given the division of labor between most adult female workers (who stayed at home and did not earn money) and most male workers (who left the household in order to secure paychecks), it seemed reasonable that women and men might use cars for different purposes—men generally to travel to work, women generally to shop and chauffeur other family members—though both would use the car for family outings and personal leisure. The automobile, particularly the closed car, would prove to be a useful tool for homemakers, but it would not render driving visible as work. The privacy of the family car would have been notably appropriate for that 21.3 percent of the American population described in the census of 1930 as "housewives not gainfully occupied," women whose very vocation implied private solutions to social problems, but it would seclude and obscure their activities. Moreover, the cultural legacy of the years when the motorcar had been designed and priced for leisure meant that even when activities like cooking and cleaning were recognized as labor, shopping or taking the children for a drive were treated as entertainment. In 1917, a husband blithely told a *Ladies' Home Journal* writer, "My wife tucked away in the car the two children every dry day last summer and scooted here and there all over the country around us." Columnist Mildred Maddocks Bentley, in an article titled "The Housekeeper and Her Car," urged women, "Away, away from the kitchen stove/ And drive the car to the picnic grove." Advertisers also often contrasted automobility and leisure with domesticity and work. A Westinghouse electric range ad in the October, 1920 issue of *Sunset* depicted two smiling women out for a drive, one apparently declaring, "I go anytime—I've an *Automatic* Cook." Below, the company asked, "Wouldn't *you* rather be motoring . . . or doing any one of a hundred things than standing over a hot stove in a hot kitchen?" The American Laundry Machinery Company promoted public laundries in a 1926 *Ladies' Home Journal* spread with the assertion that sending the family laundry out would "lead to motor trips and matinees, to golf links and club meetings—to all the things that keep a woman young." This advertisement featured a testimonial from a Corvallis, Oregon housewife who declared, "Since I have been sending my washing to the laundry, I am better able to do other household duties, look after my family, and get out in the car during the late afternoon hours to enjoy our beautiful Oregon scenery, or to visit with my friends."

Such statements contributed to the mystification of middle-class women's work. No matter how much women enjoyed the company of their offspring, the combination of children and automobiles contributed to the increased time and effort devoted to shopping and driving. A New York woman wrote the *Woman's Home Companion* describing a money-making scheme in which she offered to chauffeur "tired out mothers with small children" on country picnics, portraying the outings as "a day of loafing for the parents." At the same time, she advised her customers to "get a big lunch ready," and mentioned the fact that once the right spot was found, "out go the blankets, cushions, and lunch baskets," all of which the housewife would have to clear up, wash, and put away upon returning home. In offering advice on what to pack when taking the children for a motor outing, Mildred Bentley unwittingly provided a glimpse of the work involved in pursuing leisure. She suggested that housewives prepare sandwiches and pack drinks in thermos bottles, "since children do not take kindly to a strange water or a strange milk," taking along "plenty" of white enameled dishes and cups and silverware, all in carefully labeled customized containers. She also outlined the new disciplinary strategies mothers would have to learn in order to teach their children to "ride acceptably":

> At the first sign of restless moving or noise, draw to the side of the road and stop. Turn around and assure the small offenders that the car will not start again until they are all quiet. . . . It takes but a few similar stops before they develop good riding manners, provided the discipline is begun early enough.

Bentley went on to note the perils of leaving children in a parked car while mothers went about their business. "It is a nuisance, I know, to let the children out at every stop, but actually it is the only safe procedure." The danger that curious children might play at driving, injuring themselves or damaging the car, was compounded by the possibility of other drivers' carelessness. Bentley explained that she had herself returned from shopping one morning to find that a truck had bashed in the back end of her car, and pointed out that "any child if left in the car would have been badly frightened, if not thrown about and bruised." Insuring child safety was unquestionably part of a mother's job, but most Americans would have classed such activity as caretaking rather than employment.

Conventional language helped to obscure women's work as family chauffeurs. A Los Angeles auto dealer advertised a National coupe as "the ideal woman's car," referring to a seating arrangement designed for child safety and compartments to store large and small parcels as "conveniences" for mothers and shoppers, rather than as engineering innovations designed to make the tasks of mothering and purchasing more efficient. We might describe an object or plan intended to minimize waste of time and energy as either "convenient" or "efficient," but these terms came to have gendered meanings as the sites of domestic life and paid labor diverged. Outside the home, in increasingly centralized and specialized workplaces, the advocates of scientific management had begun to refine the process of translating time and motion into money. Although professional promoters of domestic science sought to apply the principles of economics and engineering to the home, most Americans tended increasingly to define work as activity performed for cash remuneration. Since "efficiency" was presumed to promote money-saving by improving wage workers' productivity, that which was seen as efficient was regarded as worth promoting. The housewife's activities, not compensated in cash, were often considered valueless. Whatever saved her time and energy was trivialized as optional and somehow frivolous "convenience," rather than celebrated as "efficiency."

 ## For Further Study

1. What specific advantages did access to automobiles offer women? What were the drawbacks of such access, according to the author?

2. In what ways did the automobile change women's domestic duties?

3. From what you have read about the auto industry's sales strategies, what seem to have been the main elements in prevailing definitions of femininity and masculinity?

4. Consider the city landscapes you are familiar with. How would they be different if Americans were not as dependent on the automobile as they are? How do you suppose American city landscapes were different in the years before cars became widely prevalent?

For Further Reading

Frederick Lewis Allen's nearly contemporary account of the 1920s, *Only Yesterday* (1931) remains lively and informative. William E. Leuchtenberg, *The Perils of Prosperity, 1914–1932* (1958) and Ellis W. Hawley, *The Great War and the Search for a Modern Order, A History of the American People and Their Institutions, 1917–1933* (1979) are more scholarly. George Soule, *Prosperity Decade: From War to Depression, 1917–1929* (1947) is the standard economic history of the decade. For how ordinary Americans were living, see two books by Robert S. Lynd and Helen Merrill Lynd, *Middletown* (1929) and *Middletown in Transition* (1937), detailed studies of life in Muncie, Indiana. The lives of women in the 20s are discussed in Dorothy M. Brown, *Setting a Course: American Women in the 1920s* (1987) and J. Stanley Lemons, *The Woman Citizen: Social Feminism in the 1920s* (1973). Ruth Schwartz Cowan, *More Work for Mother: The Ironies of Household Technology from the Open Hearth to the Microwave* (1984) has an interesting section on the ways in which the new consumer goods of the 1920s, including the automobile, affected the lives of American women. For a general history of the American automobile see John B. Rae, *The American Automobile: A Brief History* (1965). Jane Holtz Kay, *Asphalt Nation: How the Automobile Took Over America and How We Can Take It Back* (1997) is a highly critical look at the impact of the automobile on American life. James J. Flink, *The Car Culture* (1975) is an earlier treatment of the same subject.

Part IV

Depression and War

The stock market crash of 1929 signalled the beginning of the end of the prosperity of the 1920s. For the next three years the economy declined steadily until, during the winter of 1932–33, the United States was at the low point of the worst depression it had ever suffered. With the benefit of hindsight it is possible to see that the causes of the Great Depression of the 1930s are to be found in some of the economic conditions and practices of the 1920s, including the tendency to use business profits for speculation rather than reinvestment, declining prices for agricultural goods and declining income for farmers, and a maldistribution of income that sent too much money flowing into too few pockets producing a steady erosion of purchasing power. The stock market crash and declining demand generated a crisis of confidence among American businessmen, and they responded by cutting back production and laying off workers. Naturally, this resulted in further declines in purchasing power, still lower demand levels, further cutbacks in production, more layoffs, and on and on in an ever-downward spiral. The nation's problems were further complicated by the continuing dominance of a political philosophy that severely limited the role of government in reacting to the nation's needs because it saw such action as contrary to the Constitution and American traditions.

The situation began to change with the election of Franklin Roosevelt to the presidency in 1932. Roosevelt brought a new activist approach to Washington, inaugurating the New Deal, a massive array of government programs that tried to alleviate the suffering the Depression was causing and generate economic recovery. In the meantime, however, the problems remained acute: an unemployment rate that ranged as high as 25% according to conservative estimates, continuing business failures, thousands upon thousands of mortgage foreclosures on homes and farms, widespread homelessness, and so forth. The first selection in this section describes the impact the Great Depression had on the lives of ordinary Americans, and the second focuses on some of the relief programs the New Deal created in its attempts to combat the Depression.

The anti-Depression programs of the New Deal won the wholehearted support of a considerable majority of the American people, but the fact remains that these programs were only marginally successful in bringing the country out of the Depression. Conditions in 1939 were better than they had been in 1932 but not as good as they had been in 1929. It was the start of World War II that provided the economic stimulus that finally ended the Depression once and for all. Suddenly, unemployment vanished, to be followed almost immediately by a serious labor *shortage* as the United States entered a war that everyone was convinced would be won in our factories even more than on battlefields. The noneconomic effects of the war were equally great. The third selection in this section deals with some of the social consequences of the war. The last takes a close look at one particular policy that resulted from the war, the so-called GI Bill of Rights.

In the short span of roughly fifteen years, the United States lived through two of the greatest crises in its entire national existence: the worst depression it had ever endured and the largest foreign war it had ever fought. Each had permanent effects in changing and remaking the nation. Together, their influence was massive.

Chapter 13

Chicago Historical Society, (ICHi-05601)

Carrying a sandwich sign in the hope of putting food on the family table, 1934.

The Nation Confronts the Great Depression

Caroline Bird

Karl Mannheim, one of Europe's greatest sociologists, has stressed the importance of trying to understand human behavior as a response to an experience shared by members of a particular generation. Several historical examples of an experience that served to influence the outlook of an entire generation can be cited: the bitterness and anger experienced by southern whites as a consequence of their defeat at the hands of the North in the Civil War and the humiliation of the Radical Reconstruction that followed; the disillusionment of the generation that went to war in Europe trying to fulfill Woodrow Wilson's promise to "make the world safe for democracy"; and the susceptibility of the German people to the glorious future offered them by Adolph Hitler and his Nazi regime after their defeat in World War I and their postwar social and economic agonies. The Great Depression of the 1930s was a similarly traumatic experience for millions of Americans left without jobs and, in some instances, without food or shelter. These Americans shared a common generational experience: hunger and want, an unemployed father, no money for recreation or schooling, and a constant fear of what their economic future might be.

The pervasiveness and the duration of the Great Depression are unparalleled in the history of the American people. The stock market crash of 1929—which wiped out the hopes and the savings of all but a few—only served as the first act of a drama that was to last for more than a decade. By the early thirties, hundreds of banks were failing, tens of thousands of businesses were going bankrupt, and millions of Americans were being added to the unemployment rolls each month. Industrial production by 1933 fell to pre–World War I levels, farm prices plummeted to unprecedented lows, and foreclosures were common experiences as the farmer lost his land and the city dweller his home.

While the pursuit of material wealth has always been central to the American ethos, one may find a causal relationship between the deprivations suffered by the generation of Americans who grew up in the 1930s and their frenzied postwar pursuit of material comforts—new suburban homes, annual editions of chrome-decorated automobiles, and credit cards for every occasion. The Great Depression, as this selection by Caroline Bird makes amply clear, created an "invisible scar"—and a lasting one.

You could feel the Depression deepen, but you could not look out of the window and see it. Men who lost their jobs dropped out of sight. They were quiet, and you had to know just when and where to find them: at night, for instance, on the edge of town huddling for warmth around a bonfire, or even the municipal incinerator; at dawn, picking over the garbage dump for scraps of food or salvageable clothing.

In Oakland, California, they lived in sewer pipes the manufacturer could not sell. In Connellsville, Pennsylvania, unemployed steelworkers kept warm in the big ovens they had formerly coked. Outside Washington, D.C., one Bonus Marcher slept in a barrel filled with grass, another in a piano box, a third in a coffin set on trestles. Every big city had a "Hooverville" camp of dispossessed men living like this.

It took a knowing eye—or the eye of poverty itself—to understand or even to observe some of the action. When oranges fell off a truck, it wasn't always an accident; sometimes they were the truck driver's contribution to slum kids. A woman burning newspapers in a vacant lot might be trying to warm a baby's bottle. The ragged men standing silent as cattle, in a flatrack truck parked on a lonely public road, might be getting the bum's rush out of town. In the Southwest, freight trains were black with human bodies headed for warm weather. Railroad dicks shooed them off at stations. Deming, New Mexico, hired a special constable to keep them out of town. When the Southern Pacific police ordered the men off the train, the special constable ordered them back on again.

Everyone knew of someone engaged in a desperate struggle, although most of the agony went on behind closed doors. The stories were whispered. There was something indecent about them. A well-to-do man living on the income from rental property could not collect his rents. His mortgages were foreclosed, and his houses sold for less than the debt. To make up the difference, he sold his own home. He moved himself and his wife into a nearby basement and did odd jobs for the people upstairs in exchange for a room for some of his six children. He

---

mowed lawns, graded yards, and did whatever common labor he could find in or-der to pay for groceries, until his health broke down under the unaccustomed work. The doctor told him that he needed an operation and would have to rest for a year afterward.

A 72-year-old factory worker was told that he could no longer be employed be-cause he was too old. He went home and turned on the gas. His 56-year-old widow, who had worked as a proofreader before developing heart trouble, sat alone star-ing at their few sticks of furniture for three days after her husband's death. Then she too turned on the gas. The neighbors smelled it in time and saved her life.

Neither the property owner nor the widow was an uncommon case. They merely were lucky enough to be among the Hundred Neediest Cases chosen by *The New York Times* for 1932. Unlike the hardship cases of the 1960s, who are often urgently in need of psychiatric help, these people were in trouble only because they were physically sick and had no money. By the charitable standards of the rich at that time, they were regarded as the "deserving poor," as distinguished from the undeserving poor, who were thought to be unwilling to work or to save.

If the "deserving poor" had been few, charitable help might have sufficed. But there were too many, and more all the time. In December 1929, three million people were out of work. The next winter, four to five million. The winter of 1931–1932, eight million. The following year, no one knew exactly how many, but all authorities agreed that additional millions were unemployed. In 1965, unem-ployment is a "problem" when one in twenty is idle. In the fall of 1932, *Fortune* thought that 34 million men, women, and children—better than a fourth of the nation—were members of families that had no regular full-time breadwinner. Estimates differed, but none included farmers unable to make both ends meet, in spite of the blessing of seven-day, sunup-to-sundown employment, or factory hands who were making out on two or three days' work a week.

There were too many in want to hide. There were too many in want to blame. And even if the poor were shiftless, a Christian country would not let them starve. "Everyone is getting along somehow," people said to each other. "After all, no one has starved." But they worried even as they spoke.

A few were ashamed to eat. The Elks in Mt. Kisco, New York, and Princeton University eating clubs were among the organizations that sent leftovers from their tables to the unemployed. A reporter on *The Brooklyn Eagle* suggested a cen-tral warehouse where families could send their leftovers for distribution to the needy. John B. Nichlos, of the Oklahoma Gas Utilities Company, worked out a leftover system in detail and urged it on Hoover's Cabinet. It provided:

> Sanitary containers of five (5) gallons each should be secured in a large number so that four (4) will always be left in large kitchens where the restaurants are serving a volume business. The containers should be labeled "MEAT, BEANS, POTATOES, BREAD, AND OTHER ITEMS." Someone from the Salvation Army with a truck should pick up the loaded containers every morning and leave empty ones. The civic clubs, restaurants, the proprietors and the workers should be asked to cooperate in order to take care of all surplus food in as sanitary a way as possible. In other words, when a man finishes his meal he should not (after lighting his cigarette or cigar) leave the ashes on the food which he was unable to consume.

Many more fortunate people turned away from the unemployed, but some tried to help in the traditional neighborly way. A Brooklyn convent put sandwiches outside its door where the needy could get them without knocking. St. Louis society women distributed unsold food from restaurants. Someone put baskets in New York City railroad stations so that commuters could donate vegetables from their gardens. In New York, Bernard Macfadden served six-cent lunches to the unemployed and claimed he was making money. In San Francisco, the hotel and restaurant workers' union arranged for unemployed chefs and waiters to serve elegant if simple meals to the unemployed.

But there was more talk than help. A great many people spent a great deal of energy urging each other to give, to share, to hire. President Hoover led a national publicity campaign to urge people to give locally and to make jobs. At the suggestion of public-relations counsel Edward L. Bernays, the first President's Emergency Committee was named "for Employment" (PECE) to accentuate the positive. In 1931 it was reorganized more realistically as the President's Organization for Unemployment Relief (POUR). Both undertook to inspire confidence by the issuing of optimistic statements; POUR chairman Walter Gifford told a Senate committee offhandedly that he did not know how many were unemployed and did not think it was the committee's job to find out.

Local groups responded by pressing campaigns of their own to "Give-A-Job" or "Share-A-Meal" until people grew deaf to them. Carl Byoir, founder of one of the country's biggest public-relations firms, declared a "War against Depression" that proposed to wipe it out in six months by getting one million employers to make one new job each.

Results of such appeals were disappointing. Corporation executives answered the pleas of PECE and POUR by saying that they had no right to spend stockholders' money hiring men they did not need. Even in New York City, where the able and well-supported Community Service Society pioneered work relief, there were enough hungry men without money to keep 82 badly managed breadlines going, and men were selling apples on every street corner. Newspapers discovered and photographed an apple seller who was formerly a near-millionaire.

The well of private charity ran dry. A Westchester woman is said to have fired all her servants in order to have money to contribute to the unemployed. "Voluntary conscription" of wages helped steelworkers weather the first round of layoffs in little Conshohocken, Pennsylvania, but the plan broke down as there were more mouths to feed and fewer pay envelopes to conscript. Local charities everywhere were overwhelmed by 1931, and the worst was yet to come.

Kentucky coal miners suffered perhaps the most. In Harlan County there were whole towns whose people had not a cent of income. They lived on dandelions and blackberries. The women washed clothes in soapweed suds. Dysentery bloated the stomachs of starving babies. Children were reported so famished they were chewing up their own hands. Miners tried to plant vegetables, but they were often so hungry that they ate them before they were ripe. On her first trip to the mountains, Eleanor Roosevelt saw a little boy trying to hide his pet rabbit. "He thinks we are not going to eat it," his sister told her, "but we are." In West Virginia, miners mobbed company stores demanding food. Mountain people, with no means to leave their homes, sometimes had to burn their last chairs and tables to keep warm. Local charity could not help in a place where everyone was destitute. . . .

A Quaker himself, Hoover went to the American Friends Service Committee. The Philadelphia Meeting developed a "concern" for the miners. Swarthmore and Haverford students ventured into the hollows, winning the confidence of suspicious miners. They systematically weighed the children, so they could feed those in greatest need first. Hoover gave them $2,500 out of his own pocket, but most of the contributions seem to have come from the Rockefellers.

"No one has starved," Hoover boasted. To prove it, he announced a decline in the death rate. It was heartening, but puzzling, too. Even the social workers could not see how the unemployed kept body and soul together, and the more they studied, the more the wonder grew. Savings, if any, went first. Then insurance was cashed. Then people borrowed from family and friends. They stopped paying rent. When evicted, they moved in with relatives. They ran up bills. It was surprising how much credit could be wangled. In 1932, about 400 families on relief in Philadelphia had managed to contract an average debt of $160, a tribute to the hearts if not the business heads of landlords and merchants. But in the end they had to eat "tight."

Every serious dieter knows how little food it takes to keep alive. One woman borrowed 50¢, bought stale bread at $3\frac{1}{2}$¢ a loaf, and kept her family alive on it for 11 days. Every serious dieter knows how hunger induces total concentration on food. When eating tight, the poor thought of nothing but food, just food. They hunted food like alley cats, and in some of the same places. They haunted docks where spoiled vegetables might be thrown out and brought them home to cook up in a stew from which every member of the family would eat as little as possible, and only when very hungry. Neighbors would ask a child in for a meal or give him scraps—stale bread, bones with a bit of good meat still on them, raw potato peelings. Children would hang around grocery stores, begging a little food, running errands, or watching carts in exchange for a piece of fruit. Sometimes a member of the family would go to another part of town and beg. Anyone on the block who got hold of something big might call the neighbors in to share it. Then everyone would gorge like savages at a killing, to make up for the lean days. Enough people discovered that a five-cent candy bar can make a lunch to boom sales during the generally slow year of 1931. You get used to hunger. After the first few days it doesn't even hurt; you just get weak. When work opened up, at one point, in the Pittsburgh steel mills, men who were called back were not strong enough to do it.

Those who were still prosperous hated to think of such things and frequently succeeded in avoiding them. But professional people could not always escape. A doctor would order medicine for a charity case and then realize that there was no money to pay for it. A school doctor in Philadelphia gave a listless child a tonic to stimulate her appetite and later found that her family did not have enough to eat at home.

A reporter on *The Detroit Free Press* helped the police bring a missing boy back to a bare home on Christmas Day, 1934. He and his friends on the paper got a drugstore to open up so they could bring the boy some toys. *The Detroit Free Press* has supplied Christmas gifts for needy children every year since.

A teacher in a mountain school told a little girl who looked sick but said she was hungry to go home and eat something. "I can't," the youngster said. "It's my sister's turn to eat." In Chicago, teachers were ordered to ask what a child had had to eat before punishing him. Many of them were getting nothing but potatoes, a diet that kept their weight up, but left them listless, crotchety, and sleepy.

The police saw more than anyone else. They had to cope with the homeless men sleeping in doorways or breaking into empty buildings. They had to find help for people who fell sick in the streets or tried to commit suicide. And it was to a cop that city people went when they were at the end of their rope and did not know what else to do. In New York City, the police kept a list of the charities to which they could direct the helpless. In 1930 they took a census of needy families, and city employees started contributing one percent of their salaries to a fund for the police to use to buy food for people they found actually starving. It was the first public confession of official responsibility for plain poverty, and it came not from the top, but from the lowest-paid civil servants, who worked down where the poor people were.

Teachers worried about the children who came to school to get warm. They organized help for youngsters who needed food and clothing before they could learn. Sometimes Boards of Education diverted school funds to feed them. Often the teachers did it on their own. In 1932, New York City schoolteachers contributed $260,000 out of their salaries in one month. Chicago teachers fed 11,000 pupils out of their own pockets in 1931, although they had not themselves been paid for months. "For God's sake, help us feed these children during the summer," Chicago's superintendent of schools begged the governor in June. . . .

Men of old-fashioned principles really believed that the less said about the unemployed, the faster they would get jobs. They really believed that public relief was bad for the poor because it discouraged them from looking for work or from taking it at wages that would tempt business to start up again. According to their theory, permanent mass unemployment was impossible, because there was work at some wage for every able-bodied man, if he would only find and do it. Charity was necessary, of course, for those who were really disabled through no fault of their own, but there could never be very many of these, and they should be screened carefully and given help of a kind and in a way that would keep them from asking for it as long as possible. . . .

The view persists. In 1961, the mayor of Newburgh, New York, cut off relief to make the unemployed find jobs. In 1965, it was thought that raising the minimum wage would hurt the poor by pricing them out of jobs.

Thirty years earlier, respectable folk worried about the idea of public relief, even though accepting the need for it. On opinion polls they agreed with the general proposition that public relief should be temporary, hard to get and less than the lowest wage offered by any employer. In the North as well as in the South, relief stations were closed at harvesttime to force the unemployed to work at getting in the crops, for whatever wages farmers offered.

It was a scandal when a relief client drove an old jalopy up to the commissary to lug his groceries home. In some places, a client had to surrender his license plates in order to get relief, even if the old car meant a chance to earn small sums to pay for necessities not covered by relief. Phones went, too, even when they were a relief client's only lifeline to odd jobs. It was considered an outrage if a woman on relief had a smart-looking winter coat, or a ring, or a burial-insurance policy, or a piano. She was made to sell them for groceries before relief would help her. The search for hidden assets was thorough. One thrifty family in New York was denied relief "because it does not seem possible for this family to have managed without some other kind of assistance."

When a woman on relief had triplets, newspapers pointed out that for every 100 children born to self-supporting parents, relief parents produced 160. It was hard even for the social workers to see that big families were more apt to need relief. Almost everybody thought relief caused the poor to become irresponsible and to have children they could not support—if, in fact, they did not have babies deliberately in order to qualify. . . . During the Depression, if some way could have been found to prevent married couples on relief from indulging in sexual intercourse, there would have been those who would have demanded it.

People who took public relief were denied civil rights. Some state constitutions disqualified relief clients from voting, and as late as 1938 an opinion poll showed that one out of every three Republicans thought this was right. In some places, village taxpayers' organizations tried to keep the children of tax delinquents out of the local schools. People suspected of taking public relief were even turned away from churches.

During the first and worst years of the Depression, the only public relief was improvised by cities. Appropriations were deliberately low. If funds ran out every few months, so much the better. The poor would have to make another effort to find work. Every program was "temporary." In most cases, this was sheer necessity. Cities could not afford otherwise. Their tax bases were too narrow. Some of them had lost tax money when banks folded. Detroit could not collect property taxes because landlords could not collect the rent from their unemployed tenants. Bankrupt Chicago was living on tax anticipation warrants doled out by bankers. Some well-heeled citizens refused to pay their taxes at all. Cities cut their own employees, stopped buying library books, and shot zoo animals to divert money to relief. . . .

Cities had to ration relief. In 1932, family allowances in New York City fell to $2.39 a week, and only half of the families who could qualify were getting it. Things were worse elsewhere. In little Hamtramck, Michigan, welfare officials had to cut off all families with fewer than three children. In Detroit, allowances fell to 15¢ a day per person before running out entirely. Across the country, only about a fourth of the unemployed were able to get help, and fewer than that in many cities. Almost everywhere, aid was confined to food and fuel. Relief workers connived with clients to put off landlords. Medical care, clothing, shoes, chairs, beds, safety pins—everything else had to be scrounged or bought by doing without food. Those on relief were little better off than those who couldn't get it. Private help dwindled to six percent of the money spent on the unemployed.

Still, Hoover kept insisting, no one starved. In May 1932, Hoover's Secretary of the Interior, Dr. Ray Lyman Wilbur, reassured the National Conference of Social Workers meeting in Philadelphia. "We must set up the neglect of prosperity against the care of adversity," he philosophized. "With prosperity many parents unload the responsibilities for their children onto others. With adversity the home takes its normal place. The interest of thousands of keen and well-trained people throughout the whole country in seeing that our children are properly fed and cared for has given many of them better and more suitable food than in past good times."

Social workers were indignant. "Have you ever seen the uncontrolled trembling of parents who have starved themselves for weeks so that their children might not go hungry?" social worker Lillian Wald demanded. Others told how fathers and even older brothers and sisters hung around the street corners while the younger children were being fed, for fear they would be tempted to eat more than their share. The social workers knew the facts. They also knew newspaper reporters. In 1932, the public began to listen.

"Mrs. Green left her five small children alone one morning while she went to have her grocery order filled," one social worker reported. "While she was away the constable arrived and padlocked her house with the children inside. When she came back she heard the six-weeks-old baby crying. She did not dare touch the padlock for fear of being arrested, but she found a window open and climbed in and nursed the baby and then climbed out and appealed to the police to let her children out."

Eviction was so common that children in a Philadelphia day-care center made a game of it. They would pile all the doll furniture up first in one corner and then in another. "We ain't got no money for the rent, so we's moved into a new house," a tot explained to the teacher. "Then we got the constable on us, so we's movin' again." Philadelphia relief paid an evicted family's rent for one month in the new house. Then they were on their own. Public opinion favored the tenant. An eviction could bring on a neighborhood riot.

Landlords often let the rent go. Some of them needed relief as much as their tenants, and had a harder time qualifying for it. In Philadelphia a little girl whose father was on relief could not get milk at school, under a program for needy children, because her father "owned property." Investigators found some unemployed tenants sharing food orders with their landlords. In the country, where poor farmers had been accustomed to paying their taxes in work on the roads, tenants who could not pay their rent sometimes did the landlord's road work for him.

It was not true that "no one starved." People starved to death, and not only in Harlan County, Kentucky. The New York City Welfare Council counted 29 deaths from starvation in 1933. More than 50 other people were treated for starvation in hospitals. An additional 110, most of them children, died of malnutrition.

A father who had been turned away by a New York City welfare agency was afraid to apply for help after public relief had been set up. Social workers found one of his children dead; another, too weak to move, lay in bed with the mother; the rest huddled, shivering and hungry, around the desperate father.

A New York dentist and his wife died rather than accept charity. They left a note, and then took gas together. "The entire blame for this tragedy rests with the City of New York or whoever it is that allows free dental work in the hospital," the note read. "We want to get out of the way before we are forced to accept relief money. The City of New York is not to touch our bodies. We have a horror of charity burial. We have put the last of our money in the hands of a friend who will turn it over to my brother."

Health surveys were made to pound home the fact that poor people are sicker than the well-to-do. Doctors, nurses, teachers, and social workers warned that privation was ruining the nation's health. In 1933, the Children's Bureau reported that one in five American children was not getting enough of the right things to eat. Lower vitality, greater susceptibility to infections, slower recovery, stunting, more organic disease, a reversal of gains against tuberculosis—all were freely predicted. Medical care for the poor was sketchy. Doctors were hard hit financially, and they did not always live up to the Oath of Hippocrates. Frequently, the poor were afraid to call a doctor because they did not have money. New York City surgeons sometimes demanded cash in advance or delayed operations until the family could get money together.

Middle-class people put off the doctor and the dentist. "Illness frightens us," John Dos Passos writes of his Depression days at Pacific Grove, California. "You have to have money to be sick—or did then. Any dentistry also was out of the question, with the result that my teeth went badly to pieces. Without dough you couldn't have a tooth filled." Hospitals could never fill the private rooms that helped to pay for their charity cases, with the result that they had fewer patients than they do now, but sicker ones. They learned to be tough in admitting people who could not pay.

The harder the middle class looked, the more critical poverty seemed. It did not seem possible that people could stand lack of regular food, unstable homes, medical neglect. The Depression would leave its mark in the future. "If we put the children in these families under a period of malnutrition such as they are going through today, what sort of people are we going to have twenty years from now?" Karl de Schweinitz of the Philadelphia Community Council asked a Senate committee in 1932. "What will we say at that time about them?" . . .

. . . The Depression did not depress the conditions of the poor. It merely publicized them. The poor had been poor all along. It was just that nobody had looked at them. The children of Depression grew up to be bigger and healthier than their parents, who had enjoyed the advantages of a prosperous childhood. World War II recruits were more fit in every way than doughboys drafted in World War I. The death rate did not rise in the Depression. It kept going down. The health record of the Depression parallels that of rapidly industrializing societies everywhere: infectious diseases dropped, but mental illness, suicide, and the degenerative diseases of an aging population rose. . . .

. . . The poor survived because they knew how to be poor. The Milbank Foundation found more sickness among the poor than among the well off, but they also found that the newly poor were sicker more often than those who always had been poor. In the 1960s, social work provided steady jobs for people who often were close to poverty themselves. In the 1930s, charity was work for middle- and upper-class volunteers, who were charmed and awed by the techniques for survival that they discovered.

A family eating tight would stay in bed a lot. That way they would save fuel, as well as the extra food calories needed in cold weather. The experienced poor, particularly the Negroes, knew about eating the parts of the animal normally rejected. And the poor generally did not spend as much money on food as their middle-class advisers thought they should be spending.

The poor worked at keeping warm. A family with no money for the gas company would economize by cooking once a week. When it was cut off, they would cook in the furnace. They gathered scrap wood to keep the furnace going. They saved by heating only the kitchen. When fuel was low, the experienced poor would sneak into a movie house. Even if they had to spend ten cents to get in, they could sometimes keep out of the cold for two double features. When the electricity was turned off, some men found ways to steal current by tapping a neighbor's wire.

Shoes were a problem. The poor took them off when they got home, to save them. Do-it-yourself shoe-repair kits were popular with the middle class, but if you could not afford the dimestore item you could resole a pair of shoes with rubber cut from an old tire, or wear rubbers over a wornout sole. Clothes were swapped among the family. One mother and daughter managed to get together an outfit both could wear. They took turns going to church.

The poor whose lives were laid bare by the Depression lived in the same world of poverty that Michael Harrington has recently described in *The Other America,* and Oscar Lewis in his studies of the working classes in Mexico. They lived for the present without much thought for their own past or future. They ate literally from hand to mouth. Even when they had a little money, they did not lay in stocks of food. They paid high interest rates on what they bought or borrowed, and seldom got their money's worth. Their world was small, limited to the people they saw every day, and they did not venture out of it. A trip to the relief office was a daring undertaking. They had few friends. They did not read. Without outside contacts, they could not organize or revolt or escape.

A year after his defeat by Roosevelt, Hoover—who had repeated so many times that no one was starving—went on a fishing trip with cartoonist "Ding" Darling in the Rocky Mountains. One morning a local man came into their camp, found Hoover awake, and led him to a shack where one child lay dead and seven others were in the last stages of starvation. Hoover took the children to a hospital, made a few phone calls, and raised a fund of $3,030 for them. . . .

The Depression gave the middle classes a double vision of the poor. They did not give up the notions that the poor should have saved or that they did not want to work, or that their poverty was their own fault. These were concepts hard to change. While firmly holding to these ideas, however, they saw contradictory facts before their eyes. When the Depression forced them to scrutinize the condition of the working people, they could see that wages were too low and employment too intermittent for most wageworkers to save enough money to see them through emergencies, or old age, even if banks had not failed. A favorite cartoon of the times pictured a squirrel asking an old man sitting on a park bench why he had not saved for a rainy day.

"I did," said the old man.

For Further Study

1. What would you consider the major socioeconomic differences (for example, in employment) between the 1930s as described by Caroline Bird and the 1990s? Are there segments of American society today experiencing the conditions described by Bird? Who? Where?

2. What services, institutions, and agencies has our nation established—during and since the Depression—to prevent the kind of suffering described by the author? Could this nation enter another depression similar to the one of the 1930s? Why or why not?

3. What impression do you get of the frame of mind of the millions of poor and the unemployed? How does the author account for the divergent responses to the Depression by various socioeconomic segments of American society?

4. Explain how each of the following institutions and groups responded to the plight of the American people during the Depression: (a) newspapers; (b) industrialists; (c) social agencies; (d) landlords; and (e) political leaders.

5. Some historians have suggested that many Americans may have accepted the sufferings of the Depression out of a feeling of guilt—an acceptance of the notion that their unemployment and their inability to provide the basic necessities for their family were consequences of their own deficiencies rather than the results of defects in the economic system of the nation. Does this idea—the passivity of the nation in the face of joblessness and hunger—seem to be borne out by this essay? Or do the American people appear to have been hostile or angry or rebellious during the Depression? If so, at whom? If not, why not?

For Further Reading

The Great Depression of the 1930s started with the stock market crash of 1929. John Kenneth Galbraith's *The Great Crash* (2nd ed., 1989) is a readable account of what happened, why, and what its consequences were. David Burner, *Herbert Hoover* (1979); Donald J. Lisio, *The President and Protest: Hoover, Conspiracy, and the Bonus Riot* (1974); and Albert Romasco, *The Poverty of Abundance: Hoover, the Nation, the Depression* (1965), all deal with the Hoover administration. Frederick Lewis Allen, *Since Yesterday* (1939), and Robert S. McElvaine, *The Great Depression: America, 1929–1941* (1984), are general histories of the decade. Charles Jellison, *Tomatoes Were Cheaper: Tales from the Thirties* (1977), and many of the essays in Isabel Leighton, ed., *The Aspirin Age: 1919–1941*, talk about aspects of life during the period that conventional history books often ignore. Studs Terkel, *Hard Times: An Oral History of the Great Depression* (1970), is a collection of recollections of the Depression. Robert S. McElvaine, ed., *Down and Out in the Great Depression: Letters from the Forgotten Man* (1983), uses letters to government agencies to provide insights into the hardships people faced.

Chapter 14

National Archives

One of hundreds of murals painted by artists working for the WPA. Its focus on how ordinary working people built America is characteristic of American art in the 1930s.

Work Relief in the Great Depression

Edward Robb Ellis

The social and economic crisis that gripped the American nation in 1933, the year Franklin D. Roosevelt came to office, was, in many ways, more serious than any other crisis since 1861, when Abraham Lincoln came into the White House on the eve of the Civil War. By 1933, the stock market crash had turned into a full-fledged depression: World War I veterans marched on Washington and were dispersed by federal troops; one-quarter of the work force was unemployed; farmers were halting foreclosures on their land by threats of armed violence; and in the cities, a rising tide of radical protest appeared to be equally imminent. Only within this context of economic deprivation and social tension can one understand the depth and breadth of the legislation of the New Deal—and the contribution made by that singular figure in the history of the American nation in the twentieth century, Franklin Delano Roosevelt.

The New Deal program of social and economic reform, launched by Roosevelt in 1933, endured until 1939, when World War II broke out in Europe. This program massively reformed our country's institutions and way of life to a far greater degree than had the unrealized reforms demanded by the Greenbackers and Populists in the late nineteenth century or those enacted into law by the Progressives in the early twentieth. In addition to New Deal efforts to promote recovery and reform of the nation's economic institutions, the reformers of the 1930s launched an unprecedented program of relief for the poor and the unemployed. In contrast to the sociopolitical philosophy of Herbert Hoover, whose "rugged individualism" consigned relief programs to private philanthropy, Franklin Roosevelt accepted the notion that ultimately—if all else proved inadequate—clothing, housing, and feeding the nation's poor was the responsibility of the federal government.

The relief programs funded by the federal government can be divided into two basic categories: *direct relief,* funded by the federal government and administered by the states and the cities, and *work relief,* funded by the federal government and administered out of Washington. As the next selection makes clear, work relief was both a controversial and significant element of the New Deal. By the end of the decade, however, millions of Americans had found succor through one of the relief programs sponsored by the New Deal: the multifaceted Works Progress Administration (WPA), the conservation-oriented Civil Conservation Corps (CCC), and the National Youth Administration (NYA), a program for high school and college students.

Harry Hopkins loped into the federal security building in Washington, D.C., twisting his scrawny neck from side to side and barking orders at the assistants trying to keep up with him.

The previous day, May 22, 1933, President Roosevelt had named him the administrator of the Federal Emergency Relief Administration. His lips taut, his movements jerky, Hopkins scurried down a hall, saw a desk that had not yet been moved into the room that was to become his office, flopped down into the chair behind it. Oblivious to the confusion swirling about him and raising his voice to be heard over the clatter of heels in the corridor, the former social worker began dictating telegrams to the governors of all forty-eight states. . . .

Harry Lloyd Hopkins was born in Sioux City, Iowa, on August 17, 1890, the fourth of David and Anna Hopkins' five children. His father was a harness maker; his mother taught school. After Harry became the most influential man in the United States government, next to Roosevelt himself, he continued to boast about his humble origins—sometimes to the annoyance of his friends. Frances Perkins thought this a sign of insecurity—that he always felt inferior to others despite what she considered to be his superior mind and character.

When Harry was two years old, his family moved to Nebraska. By the time he was eleven the Hopkins' had settled in Grinnell, Iowa, a folksy town with a strong Methodist flavor. From his mother, a zealous Methodist, he got his strong sense of righteousness, while from his father he inherited geniality and wit. As a boy Harry scrubbed floors, beat carpets, milked cows and toiled on nearby farms like other underprivileged young people. In 1908 he entered Grinnell College, a small institution with a high reputation for scholarship. He made only average grades, seldom revealing the probing intelligence which later caused Winston Churchill to dub him Lord Root of the Matter. . . .

In 1912, after graduation, he headed for the East Coast. One of his professors, who was connected with a Manhattan settlement house named Christodora House, had won his appointment as head of a summer camp for boys across the Hudson River in New Jersey. When camp was over, he began working in Christodora House itself, located on Manhattan's Lower East Side, and there the naïve youth from the Corn Belt met Jewish boys for the first time in his life. He was amazed to see gangsters stroll into settlement dances and street bullies fighting with broken bottles.

Over the next few years Hopkins developed into a social worker and an executive of social agencies, slaving sixteen hours a day, organizing boys' clubs, plodding up tenement stairs, listening to the laments of the underprivileged, making pioneer surveys of unemployment. Humble and sincere, he was able to get along with all kinds of people. With the stench of the slums constantly in his nostrils, he made a slight turn to the political left and seemingly was registered for a while as a Socialist—a matter of some concern after he entered the federal government. And after his divorce he suffered so much personal strain that he had himself psychoanalyzed. . . .

"Dole" had become an emotionally charged word ever since the advent of the Depression. Throughout the Thirties people criticized the dole or praised the dole, often in a slipshod way since they did not bother to define the term and applied it to a variety of conditions and plans. Their arguments frequently ended in semantics—a debate over the meaning of meaning. . . .

Franklin D. Roosevelt, for his part, tried to balance idealism with practicality. As governor of New York he had said that "to these unfortunate citizens aid must be extended by government, not as a matter of charity, but as a matter of social duty." Nonetheless, while still governor, he had also said: "The dole method of relief for unemployment is not only repugnant to all sound principles of social economics, but is contrary to every principle of American citizenship and of sound government. American labor seeks no charity, but only a chance to work for its living."

Harry Hopkins agreed with Roosevelt. He detested direct relief. Work relief, said Hopkins, "preserves a man's morale. It saves his skill. It gives him a chance to do something socially useful." Both the President and his key relief administrator were keenly aware that the Federal Emergency Relief Administration was a quick thrust at a massive problem calling for greater leverage. On November 27, 1934, Roosevelt wrote to a friend: "What I am seeking is the abolition of relief altogether. I cannot say so out loud yet but I hope to substitute work for relief. . . ."

The heavily Democratic Seventy-fourth Congress opened its first session on January 3, 1935, and one day later the President delivered his annual message. After reporting that more than $2 billion had been spent in direct relief, he went on to say: "The federal government must and shall quit this business of relief. I am not willing that the vitality of our people be further sapped by the giving of cash, of market baskets. . . ."

Roosevelt then announced that he intended to establish a new relief system. . . . This new program, the President added, would be guided by the following principles:

1. All work to be as useful and permanent as possible.
2. Relief wages to be higher than those paid under the FERA and CWA, but not so high as to discourage men from taking jobs in private industry.
3. More money to be spent on wages than on materials. . . .

On April 5, 1935, the Senate and House passed a joint resolution giving the President the relief money he had sought—$4 billion in new funds and

$880,000,000 unused from previous appropriations. This $4.8 billion was the largest peacetime appropriation in American history. One day later the bill was signed by the Vice President and the Speaker of the House and put on a plane bound for Jacksonville, Florida. Roosevelt, who had been fishing off the coast, came back to port, boarded a north-bound train and on April 8 signed the measure to the contrapuntal clickety clack of train wheels. . . .

On May 6, 1935, the President issued an executive order establishing the Works Progress Administration. As of that date no one could foretell that, with one change of name, it would continue in existence until June 30, 1943—eight years and two months.

The WPA was designed as the key agency in the government's entire works program, which came to include a total of forty federal agencies. It withdrew the federal government from the field of direct relief, leaving that responsibility to the various states and cities. Roosevelt flatly said that the principal purpose of the WPA was to provide work.

Hopkins began this new job with his usual demonic energy. At one of the first WPA staff meetings he raised the question of whether women should be paid the same wages as men. Everyone said no. Everyone, that is, except Hopkins' assistant administrator, Aubrey Williams, who said he thought women should be paid equal wages with men.

"Oh, you do?" Hopkins barked. "What makes you think you could get away with it?"

Williams said he did not care whether he could get away with it or not.

"Do you know who disagrees with you?" Hopkins persisted. "The secretary of labor—a woman!"

"Pay 'em the same!" Williams said doggedly.

Hopkins, who was testing his assistant, baited him further until Williams became silent and glum.

Then Hopkins ended the session with the words: "Well, fellows, thank you very much. Aubrey's right about this, and that's what we'll do."

As the others walked out, Hopkins turned to Williams, smiled a lopsided smile and asked: "What's wrong with those other fellows?"

The WPA paid wages slightly higher than the grants for direct relief but lower than wages prevailing in private industry. There were exceptions, however, for the WPA refused to lower its rates to meet the substandard ones prevailing in certain districts, notably in the South. For wage-fixing purposes the country was divided into four regions. Monthly rates of pay in each region varied according to the character of the work and to the population. Unskilled work paid as little as $19 a month while professional and technical jobs paid up to $94 a month—and sometimes slightly higher.

The nerve center of the WPA—and thus of the nation's entire works program—was located in the Walker-Johnson Building in Washington at 1734 New York Avenue, NW, a few blocks from the White House. It was a dirty, shabby old place with a blind newsdealer on its front steps. Upon entering it one smelled antiseptic odors and then rode in an elevator so rickety it was frightening. But Hopkins, who detested elegance, felt this was what a relief office should be like. . . .

In the aggregate the WPA did spend a great deal of money, but, as has been indicated, individual wages were hardly lavish. In December 1935, WPA workers averaged $41.57 a month. Between 60 and 70 percent of those on the rolls were unskilled workers.

But among the skilled workers were accountants, architects, bricklayers, biologists, carpenters, chemists, dentists, draftsmen, dieticians, electricians, engravers, foresters, firemen, geologists, gardeners, hoisting engineers, housekeepers, instrument men, ironworkers, jackhammer operators, janitors, kettlemen, kitchen maids, librarians, linotypers, locksmiths, lumbermen, millwrights, machinists, musicians, nurses, nutritionists, oilers, painters, plasterers, plumbers, patternmakers, photographers, printers, physicians, quarry men, quilters, riveters, roofers, roadmakers, riggers, sculptors, seamstresses, stonemasons, stenographers, statisticians, teamsters, truck drivers, teachers, tabulators, upholsterers, veterinarians, welders, woodchoppers, waiters, watchmen, X-ray technicians—and others.

During its more than eight years of existence, the WPA employed 8,500,000 different people in more than 3,000 counties and spent in excess of $11 billion on a total of 1,410,000 projects. It was by far the biggest employer and spender of all the New Deal agencies. WPA workers built 651,087 miles of highways, roads and streets; constructed, repaired or improved 124,031 bridges; erected 125,110 public buildings; created 8,192 public parks; built or improved 853 airports. Besides its immediate importance to the people who worked on this massive program, Americans were using and enjoying some of these facilities one-third of a century later. More than anything else, however, the WPA was an escape hatch from the trap of the Depression.

Early in the program Roosevelt had warned: "It must be recognized that when an enterprise of this character is extended over more than three thousand counties throughout the nation, there may be occasional instances of inefficiency, bad management, or misuse of funds." Cases of this kind did, of course, occur. A few Senators, Congressmen, governors, state WPA directors and small-time politicians tried to enrich themselves and enhance their power by means of the WPA.

Harry Hopkins was incorruptible and, for a man who liked to spend money, strangely economy-minded in some ways. Loathing organizational charts and fossilized bureaucratic procedures, he ran the national organization with the smallest possible staff and the smallest possible overhead. He got help to the people as directly and quickly as possible. "Hunger is not debatable," he liked to say. "People don't eat in the long run—they eat every day.". . .

The New Deal did more to promote culture than any previous administration in the history of this nation. . . .

The WPA's arts division consisted of four separate programs. As overall supervisor of them Harry Hopkins chose Jacob Baker, liberal in his tastes and a believer in experimentation. The music program was headed by Nikolai Sokoloff, conductor of the Cleveland Orchestra and a frequent guest conductor of many other symphony orchestras throughout the nation. The art program was directed by Holger Cahill, an art critic, authority on folk art and an outstanding museum technician. The theater project was headed by Hallie Flanagan. The writers' program was headed by Henry Alsberg, an editorial writer for the New York *Evening Post* and a foreign correspondent for liberal magazines.

Alsberg told Hopkins that the WPA could make a lasting cultural contribution to the nation if the men and women employed by the writers' project were put to work preparing a series of guidebooks about the states, one for each state. He pointed out that the latest issue of Baedeker's guide to America had been issued in 1909—so outdated that it advised Europeans planning to visit this land to bring along matches, buttons, and dress gloves. Agreeing, Hopkins gave Alsberg the word to launch the American Guide Series. . . .

Alsberg began hiring unemployed writers and editors, librarians and photographers, until at last he had 7,500 people at work. A director was named for each of the forty-eight states, and they, in turn, received the help of local reporters, historians, genealogists, librarians and businessmen. Each did his part in the massive chore of researching, writing, editing and publishing the state guidebooks, and soon copy was pouring into the Washington headquarters at the rate of 50,000 words a day. . . .

One of the greatest accomplishments of the writers' project was its historical records survey, instituted in 1936. Relief workers took inventories of local public records stored in city hall cellars, library lofts and courthouse garrets. They indexed old newspaper files. They made abstracts of court cases containing nuggets of local history. They examined business archives, looked through church records, studied tombstones to verify vital statistics. The perfection of microfilm had made it possible for them to photograph, and thus to preserve, millions of pages crumbling into decay. They measured, sketched, diagrammed and photographed 2,300 historic buildings.

In 1937 the American Guide Series became a reality with publication of the first of the set, a book about Idaho. By the end of its life the project produced 378 books and pamphlets—a volume for each of the forty-eight states, 30 about our major cities, others about historic waterways and highways, such as *The Oregon Trail*. Various commercial and university publishers issued these works, with royalties either paying for everything except labor costs or going into the federal treasury.

In a *New Republic* article Robert Cantwell said of the writers' project: "The least publicized of the art projects, it may emerge as the most influential and valuable of them all." Nearly one-third of a century later the American Guide Series continued to be a prime source of information for every serious writer of American history.

Musicians were suffering even before the beginning of the Depression. The popularity of radio, the advent of talking movies and the death of vaudeville had thrown 50,000 musical performers out of work. After the Crash there were few Americans who could afford music lessons for their children, so music teachers lost their pupils or had to cut their fees for the few who remained. Music publishers, recording companies and manufacturers of musical instruments earned less or suffered heavy losses. To most of these people the federal music project, under Nikolai Sokoloff, came as salvation.

Established in July, 1935, the music program put musicians to work in orchestras and bands, in chamber music and choral and operatic groups throughout the nation. Forty-five cities obtained their own WPA symphony orchestra, while 110 other cities got orchestras with more than thirty-five players. Just before the start of a concert by a WPA orchestra in Florida, a violinist apologized to the audience on behalf of his colleagues and himself for the quality of their concert. He explained that their fingers were stiff because of their previous relief job—working on a road gang.

When the music project was at its peak it supported 15,000 people. They gave a total of 150,000 programs heard by more than 100,000,000 people, many of whom had been unfamiliar with anything but popular songs. Each month more than 500,000 pupils attended free music classes. WPA musical groups relieved the boredom of hospital patients. Project workers dug out and recorded American folk music—the Cajun songs of Louisiana, the Indian-flavored songs of early Oklahoma, the British-born ballads of Kentucky mountaineers, the African-inspired songs of Mississippi bayous.

Although the program was designed to help performers more than composers, since the former outnumbered the latter, it established a composers' forum-laboratory. Before the project was terminated, 1,400 native composers produced 4,915 original compositions—some bad, many mediocre, a few hailed by music critics as "distinguished." One prominent critic, Deems Taylor, wrote in 1935: "It is safe to say that during the past two years the WPA orchestras alone have probably performed more American music than our other symphony orchestras, combined, during the past ten."

Thanks to this project, music became democratized in this country. In about the year 1915 there had been only 17 symphony orchestras in the United States; by 1939 there were more than 270. Europe's leadership in the musical world, together with its snobbish aloofness, had been shattered.

The WPA art project was set up by Holger Cahill on "the principle that it is not the solitary genius but a sound general movement which maintains art as a vital, functioning part of any cultural scheme."

All a person had to do to get on the art project was to obtain proof from local authorities that he needed relief and that he had once had some connection, however tenuous, with the world of art. As a result, of the more than 5,000 people ultimately hired, fewer than half ever painted a picture, sculpted a statue or decorated a building with a mural. This does not mean that the art program was a boondoggle. While creativity flowered among the great artists—Jackson Pollock, Aaron Bohrod, Ben Shahn, Willem de Kooning, Concetta Scaravaglione, Anna Walinska and the like—those with limited talent taught free art classes, photographed historic houses, painted posters and designed stage sets for the federal theater project. Others maintained sixty-six community art centers which attracted a total of 6,000,000 visitors.

In addition to the invaluable and enduring artworks produced by the most gifted relief workers, the art project left all of us a monumental *Index of American Design*. This part of the program was directed by Constance Rourke and gave employment to about 1,000 artists. Wishing to find and preserve specimens of early American arts and crafts, they ransacked New England farmhouses, museums, antique shops, historical societies, Shaker barns, and California missions. They photographed or painted every treasure they discovered—embroidered seat covers, oil paintings, watercolors, carved figureheads, antique quilts and samplers, weather vanes and such. Collectively, these artists produced 7,000 illustrations of every variety of native American art.

On May 16, 1935, the phone rang in the Poughkeepsie, New York, home of a small, red-headed middle-aged woman named Hallie Flanagan. When she answered it, she heard Jacob Baker, the head of the WPA's four arts program, saying that he was calling from Washington. "Mr. Hopkins wants you to come to Washington to talk about unemployed actors," Baker said. Miss Flanagan was in charge of Vassar College's Experimental Theatre. She knew Hopkins, for they had grown up together in Grinnell, Iowa, and attended the same college. . . .

Actors, as Miss Flanagan knew, were suffering severe hardships. Like musicians, many had lost their jobs with the death of vaudeville and the birth of the talkies. No one knew for sure just how many performers were out of work. Actors Equity said there were 5,000 unemployed actors in New York City alone, while WPA officials put the nationwide total at 20,000 to 30,000 people. In Harlem black entertainers were kissing the Tree of Hope, a local talisman, for luck.

In 1931 two-thirds of Manhattan's playhouses were shut. During the 1932–33 season eight out of every ten new plays failed. The Shuberts had plunged into receivership. In 1932 no less than 22,000 people registered with Hollywood casting bureaus. *Variety* had reduced its price from 25 to 15 cents. . . .

On July 27, 1935, Miss Flanagan was sworn in as administrator of the new federal theater project. The ceremony was held in a Washington playhouse called the old Auditorium, a vast hulk of a building now abuzz with rushing people, whirring electric fans, riveting machines and cement-slapping plasterers. She sat down in a new cubicle and conferred with her staff of four about the possibility of getting at least 10,000 theater people back to work within a short time.

Since Broadway was the heart of the American theater, Miss Flanagan wanted an especially able man to direct the New York City unit of her project, and her choice was Elmer Rice. The forty-three-year-old Rice had proved himself as a playwright, stage director and novelist. With the deepening of the Depression, his plays had shifted from realistic reporting to social and political themes. Rice already had sent Hopkins a letter outlining a plan for the establishment of a national theater, but he hesitated about accepting Miss Flanagan's offer because he was about to begin writing another novel.

"What could we do with all the actors?" he asked her. "Even if we had twenty plays in rehearsal at once, with thirty in a cast, that would keep only a fraction of them busy."

Badly wanting Rice, she grabbed at a straw and impulsively said: "We wouldn't use them all in plays. We could do *Living Newspapers*. We could dramatize the news with living actors, light, music, movement."

This idea appealed to Rice, who cried: "Yes. And I can get the Newspaper Guild to back it!". . .

Elmer Rice was paid $260 a month on the theory that he worked thirteen days at $20 a day, but actually he worked from early morning until late at night every day of the month, including Sundays. It amused him to get nasty letters accusing him of making a fortune on a soft government job. Sometimes he opened press conferences by saying to reporters: "Well, what do you vultures want to swoop down on now?"

At first jobs were limited to entertainers on home relief rolls, but this excluded many who had been too proud to ask for help. Miss Flanagan and Rice managed to get this rule modified. She watched in horror as a man applying for work went mad and beat his head against a wall. A famous clown was taken on the WPA rolls, became so excited at the chance to work again that on the opening night of the show he suffered a stroke from which he never recovered. . . .

Into the project flocked young men and women who later became celebrated actors—Joseph Cotton, Orson Welles, Arthur Kennedy, Burt Lancaster, Arlene Francis, Ed Gardner, Rex Ingram, Canada Lee, Howard da Silva, William Bendix, Bil Baird. Another employed by the WPA, but not on the theater project, was Robert Ryan, who worked as a paving supervisor.

At its peak the program gave work to 12,700 theater people in twenty-nine states. Besides the actors themselves, there were producers, directors, playwrights, stagehands, electricians, propmen—all the crafts found in stage work. Hopkins had told Miss Flanagan: "We're for labor—first, last and all the time. WPA is labor—don't forget that." He insisted that $9 of every $10 be spent on wages, leaving only about $1 to meet operating costs. Nine out of every 10 people hired had to come from relief rolls. Wages averaged $83 a month, although some actors were paid up to $103.40 a month for performing in New York City. According to the place and circumstance, admission to WPA shows was free, or cost 10 cents, 25 cents, 50 cents, and in rare instances as much as $1.

The federal theater project presented many different kinds of shows—Negro drama, dance drama, children's theater, puppet and marionette shows, a documentary about syphilis, classical drama, modern drama, foreign language drama, musicals, Living Newspapers, pageants, vaudeville, circus, religious drama, spectacles, opera, and radio programs. . . .

George Bernard Shaw let the WPA stage his plays at $50 a week, writing to Miss Flanagan: "As long as you stick to your fifty-cents maximum for admission . . . you can play anything of mine you like unless you hear from me to the contrary. . . . Any author of serious plays who does not follow my example does not know what is good for him. I am not making a public-spirited sacrifice; I am jumping at an unprecedentedly good offer."

Eugene O'Neill released his own plays on similar terms, telling reporters: "The WPA units can present important plays before audiences that never before have seen an actual stage production. The possibilities in this respect are thrilling. . . . These units are translating into action the fact that the government has an obligation to give a reasonable amount of encouragement and assistance to cultural undertakings."

Sinclair Lewis had been offered a lot of money by commercial theater producers to make a play out of his novel *It Can't Happen Here*. Instead, he offered it to WPA. The red-headed writer told reporters: "I prefer to give it to the federal theater for two reasons: first, because of my tremendous enthusiasm for its work and, second, because I know I can depend on the federal theater for a non-partisan point of view."

Lewis and his collaborators began their rewrite work in the Essex House on Manhattan's Central Park South—but not at government expense. Much newspaper space was given to the fact that this famous author was working on a play for the WPA. Some editorial writers and readers felt that his study of the rise of an American dictator was Communist-inspired, or the result of Fascism, or a plot to reelect Roosevelt, or a scheme to defeat him. Huey Long had been dead only about a year, so New Orleans officials would not book this show into a city where the late dictator still had many friends. *It Can't Happen Here* became so controversial that before it premiered, the nation's newspapers printed 78,000 lines of pro and con comment about the production.

On October 27, 1936, the play opened simultaneously in twenty-one theaters in seventeen states—the most multiple and extensive first night in the history of the American theater. From Bridgeport and Cleveland, Miami and Birmingham, Detroit and Indianapolis—from each of the several cities came reports that audiences had received the play with wild enthusiasm. In its first few weeks it drew more than a quarter million spectators.

In the *New York Times* Brooks Atkinson wrote: "Mr. Lewis has a story to tell that is calculated to make the blood of a liberal run pretty cold. . . . *It Can't Happen Here* ought to scare the daylights out of the heedless Americans who believe, as this column does, that it can't happen here as long as Mr. Lewis keeps his health."

A smash hit, the play was presented here and there across the country for a total of 260 weeks. . . .

The federal theater project was sponsored and patronized by unions and schools, colleges and universities, Catholics and Jews, Protestants and civic groups, industrial and philanthropic organizations. It brought the living theater to youths who never before had seen flesh-and-blood actors. In the *Federal Theater Magazine* a writer described this huge audience in these words: "We're a hundred thousand kids who never saw a play before. We're students in colleges, housewives in the Bronx, lumberjacks in Oregon, sharecroppers in Georgia. We're rich and poor, old and young, sick and well. We're America and this is our theatre.". . .

Earlier, while the government was setting up the Civilian Conservation Corps, Eleanor Roosevelt lamented that it did nothing for girls. She wanted single, jobless women brought together in urban clubs somewhat similar to CCC camps, but got nowhere. Trying to go it alone, she held a series of meetings in her Manhattan home with a group of about thirty underprivileged young people.

Ensnared in the Depression, few young men and women could afford to attend college, while at the same time they found it increasingly difficult to get jobs. Between 1920 and 1930 college attendance had more than doubled, but from 1932 to 1934 college enrollment fell by 10 percent. High schools, colleges and universities slashed their budgets and cut the salaries of teachers, many of whom went for months without getting a paycheck. By the spring of 1935 a total of 3,000,000 people between the ages of sixteen and twenty-five were on relief—an average of 1 in 7. Even more distressing was the fact that many youths became transients; on a single day in May, 1935, the WPA's transient service counted 54,000 of them registered at its camps and shelters.

Besides the intrinsic misery of this situation, it was also politically dangerous. One confused young man said: "If someone came along with a line of stuff in which I could really believe, I'd follow him pretty nearly anywhere." In Germany and Italy millions of youths had harkened to the evil music of those corrupt pipers, Hitler and Mussolini.

Here in America the President's wife felt it would be wise to create a kind of junior CCC or WPA to help young people and give them a sense of direction. Perhaps such a program could be set up as a subdivision of the WPA. She explained her plan to Harry Hopkins and his assistant, Aubrey Williams, who liked it so much that they expanded on it and outlined what became the National Youth Administration. However, they hesitated about presenting the idea to the President. Hopkins told Mrs. Roosevelt: "There may be many people against the establishment of such an agency in the government, and there may be bad political repercussions. We do not know that the country will accept it. We do not even like to ask the President, because we do not think he should be put in a position where he has to say officially 'yes' or 'no' now."

One night Eleanor Roosevelt entered her husband's bedroom as he was about to go to sleep. When he saw the expression on her face, he smiled and said: "Well, well—what new program is hanging fire?"

She described the idea for the National Youth Administration, frankly adding that Hopkins was unsure of the wisdom of pushing it.

The President asked: "Do you think it is right to do this?"

"It will be a great help to the young people, Franklin. But I don't want you to forget that Harry Hopkins thinks it may be unwise politically. Some people might say it's like the way Hitler is regimenting German youths."

This, as Mrs. Roosevelt may have intended, was a challenge to the President.

"If it is the right thing to do for the young people," he said, looking up at her, "then it should be done. I guess we can stand the criticism, and I doubt if our youth can be regimented in this way or in any other way."

On June 26, 1935, President Roosevelt issued an executive order creating the National Youth Administration. Its purpose was to administer a relief and unemployment program for young women between the ages of sixteen and twenty-five, for young men of this age who were physically unsuited for CCC labor, for the children of rural families, for those no longer attending school regularly and for needy students who wanted to finish their educations but lacked the means. The NYA was set up as a part of the WPA. As executive director of this new agency the President appointed Aubrey Williams. . . .

Now he [Williams] faced an enormous task. The first fiscal year Williams had $41.2 million to spend, and in 1936 he got $68 million more. Because the president wanted the NYA to be as decentralized as possible, separate administrations were set up in each of the forty-eight states and a special one in New York City, owing to its size. These forty-nine administrations were supplemented by district and local directors, together with advisory committees throughout the nation.

Just about the time of the creation of the NYA, a twenty-six-year-old Texan by the name of Lyndon B. Johnson suffered a shock. For nearly three years he had worked in Washington as secretary to Representative Richard M. Kleberg of

Texas. Johnson, an aggressive young man, pretty much dominated his boss, and when Mrs. Kleberg told her husband that the boy was planning to run against him in the next election, the enraged Congressman fired his secretary. Johnson scurried to Representative Maury Maverick of Texas with the sad news that he was just out of a job. Maverick, who liked Johnson, knew that President Roosevelt was about to name forty-eight state NYA directors.

On easy terms with Roosevelt, Maverick went to him to say he knew just the man to direct the Texas NYA—Lyndon Johnson. The President was agreeable until he learned that Johnson was only twenty-six years old. He scoffed that he would not give such an important position to a child, but the Texas Congressman persisted. "After all," said Maverick, "you need someone who's honestly interested in helping his own generation work their way through high school and college and improve themselves, rather than sit around unemployed." In July, 1935, President Roosevelt named Lyndon Baines Johnson the head of the NYA in Texas.

Johnson, who hero-worshiped Roosevelt then and thereafter, flew from Washington to Texas and opened state headquarters of the NYA on the sixth floor of the shabby Littlefield Building in Austin. Then he flew back to the national capital to attend the first nationwide meeting of state NYA directors, called into session by Aubrey Williams on August 20, 1935. Johnson was not shy about telling reporters that he was the youngest of all the state directors and was delighted when this news item was published in newspapers from coast to coast. Also making a good impression on Williams, he obtained more funds for Texas than had originally been allocated to it. . . .

During the twenty months that Lyndon B. Johnson served as state director of the NYA in Texas, he helped 18,000 students by giving them money to go to school and by arranging part-time work in colleges at 35 cents an hour. He also aided 12,000 out-of-school youngsters, seeing that they learned trades and did useful work on public projects. Since Texas was the biggest state in the union, Johnson spent much of his time traveling, and the contacts he made were of use to him in furthering his political career.

In the spring of 1937 he decided to run for Congress. When the news reached Aubrey Williams in the national capital, Williams called the White House and spoke on the phone with Presidential aide Tommy Corcoran.

"Tommy," said Williams, "you've got to get the President to make this guy Johnson lay off running for the Congressional seat down in Austin. He's my whole youth program in Texas, and if he quits, I have no program down there."

Corcoran spoke to Roosevelt, who gave him orders to make sure that Johnson stuck to his NYA job and forgot about running for Congress. But before Corcoran could locate Johnson to relay this word from on high, LBJ had quit his NYA post and filed for Congress.

Richard M. Nixon, who succeeded Johnson as President in 1969, also benefited from the New Deal. In September, 1934, Nixon arrived in Durham, North Carolina, to enter Duke University's new law school. Having been graduated second in his class from Whittier College in California, the twenty-one-year-old student had been given a $200 tuition grant; to keep it he had to maintain a B average at Duke. Because of the Depression, his family was able to send him only $35 a month. To supplement this grant and allowance, Nixon accepted aid from the National Youth Administration, earning thirty-five cents an hour for doing research in the law library. . . .

With three other students he rented a room in a ramshackle farmhouse a mile from the campus and set in the midst of tall pines. They shared two double beds in a big room heated by an old iron potbellied stove. Their quarters lacked any lights, so Nixon studied in the law library. It was also without water, so he showered in the university gym. He used his trunk for a closet, could afford only secondhand books and paid twenty-five cents a meal in a boardinghouse.

Helen Gahagan Douglas, with whom Nixon later feuded politically, was a member of the California state committee of the NYA. Eric F. Goldman, who developed into a noted historian and educator, got through Johns Hopkins University at Baltimore with NYA help. Raymond Clapper was another who had reason to be grateful to the NYA. After Clapper became a famous columnist, he wrote that "some of our leading citizens who are so violently opposed to institutions like the National Youth Administration are not so opposed to subsidizing college students for football teams."

Arthur Miller, who subsequently won renown as a dramatist, got NYA aid while attending the University of Michigan. Of those days he later wrote:

> I loved the idea of being separated from the nation, because the spirit of the nation, like its soil, was being blown by crazy winds. Friends of mine in New York, one of them a *cum laude* from Columbia, were aspiring to the city firemen's exam; but in Ann Arbor I saw that if it came to the worst a man could live on nothing for a long time.
>
> I earned $15 a month for feeding a building full of mice—the National Youth Administration footing the bill—and out of it I paid $1.75 a week for my room and squeezed the rest for my Granger tobacco (two packs for thirteen cents), my books, laundry and movies. For my meals I washed dishes in the co-op cafeteria. My eyeglasses were supplied by the Health Service, and my teeth were fixed for the cost of materials. The girls paid for themselves including the one I married.

While still in college, Miller wrote several plays. In the spring of 1938 he was graduated, and two months later he was on relief. Then he returned to his hometown, New York City, where he joined the federal theater project. Before the project could present his first play, though, its activities were ended.

A sampling of 150 NYA work projects for out-of-school youths showed that the young men and women employed on them engaged in 169 types of work. Among other things, they installed floodlights in airports, built athletic courts, beautified parks, made brooms, canned vegetables and fruits, took care of infants, cleaned bricks for reuse, cleaned lagoons, cleared land, clipped newspapers in libraries, cooked for lunchrooms, excavated for artifacts, made furniture, worked as nurses, laid pipes, planted grass and so on.

In Fort Morgan, Colorado, fifty-two NYA boys converted a dump into a public recreation ground with 40 acres of grass, shrubs, trees and a new 5-acre swimming pool. At Gloucester, Massachusetts, rubber-booted NYA youths took eggs from lobsters to restock a federal fish hatchery. On the Onondaga Indian reservation in New York State some Indian boys working for the NYA chopped down trees, shaped logs and built a summer camp for children. At the Fort Valley Normal and Industrial School in Georgia a group of Negro boys and girls, few of whom had finished grade school, were paid by the NYA as they were trained in farming, homemaking, and various trades. In the Flint-Goodridge Hospital in New Orleans black NYA girls helped regular staff members in every department of the hospital.

Under NYA rules the youths were to work no more than eight hours a day, forty hours a week or seventy hours a month. They earned from $10 to $25 a month, depending on prevailing local wage standards. What did they do with these meager earnings? First they helped their families. Then they bought themselves new clothes, since they had worn nothing but hand-me-down clothing for years. Telling what the NYA meant to him, one boy said: "Maybe you don't know what it's like to come home and have everyone looking at you, and you know what they're thinking, even if they don't say it, 'He didn't find a job.' It gets terrible. You just don't want to come home. . . . But a guy's gotta eat some place and you gotta sleep some place. . . . I tell you, the first time I walked in the front door with my paycheck, I was somebody!". . .

However, to some Americans who ate three square meals a day without the help of the government, the overall program of the Works Progress Administration seemed less than noble. One of the popular pastimes was telling WPA jokes like the following:

"A farmer asked a druggist for 'some of that WPA poison. It won't kill squirrels, but it will make them so lazy I can just stomp them to death.'"

"A WPA worker sued the government because he hurt himself when the shovel he was leaning on broke."

"Why is a WPA worker like King Solomon? . . . Because he takes his pick and goes to bed."

"I hear Harry Hopkins is planning to equip all of his WPA workers with rubber-handled shovels."

"Don't shoot our still life—it may be a WPA worker at work."

"There's a new cure for cancer, but they can't get any of it. It's sweat from a WPA worker."

Some of these jokes were thought up by professional comedians, but at last the American Federation of Actors ordered all its members to stop poking fun at the WPA. . . .

As has been said, the WPA employed 8,500,000 people in 1,410,000 projects in more than 3,000 counties at a cost of more than $11 billion. Naturally, in a program of such magnitude there were bound to be inequities and injustice, scandals and corruption. Campaigning by WPA staff members in Pennsylvania, Kentucky and Tennessee in the 1938 Congressional elections led to adverse comment and passage of the Hatch Act of July, 1939, curbing "pernicious political activities" by federal appointees. President Roosevelt discharged at least one state WPA director and began keeping a closer eye on the others.

Harry Hopkins was loved and hated by relief workers and politicians according to how well the WPA treated them. While he certainly had personal preferences in which he indulged, he was totally honest and therefore beyond the reach of provable scandal. Except for betting on the horses and lifting a glass of champagne with rich friends, he maintained his modest way of life. None of that $11 billion ever found its way into his pockets. . . .

In 1939 the Works Progress Administration had its name changed to the Works Projects Administration, and it continued in existence until June 30, 1943.

This vast, long-lived agency created enduring public works, helped the United States prepare for the approaching war, increased purchasing power and left grateful memories among millions of Americans who, without it, might have lost their lives, their hope of salvation, their faith in their country.

For Further Study

1. What impression do you get of Franklin Delano Roosevelt in the following areas as a result of reading this essay: his temperament, his social outlook, and his accomplishments?

2. What was the reasoning behind the establishment of these cultural programs by the New Deal? On what grounds were these programs criticized—and which ones came in for the greatest criticism? Do you feel these criticisms were justified? If so, why; if not, why not?

3. What was the total cost of the WPA program, and how many Americans benefited from it? Do you consider this cost excessive? If so, why; if not, why not?

4. Given a depression similar to that of the 1930s, would there be a controversy *today* over the need for work relief for the unemployed? If so, why; if not, why not?

For Further Reading

The amount of historical literature on Franklin Roosevelt and the New Deal is staggering. A good general introduction is William E. Leuchtenberg, *Franklin D. Roosevelt and the New Deal* (1963). The last two volumes of Arthur Schlesinger, Jr.'s three-volume work *The Age of Roosevelt* (1957–1960) are more detailed. Paul Conkin has written a brief, thought-provoking criticism of the New Deal in *The New Deal* (1967). Joseph Lash, *Dealers and Dreamers: A New Look at the New Deal* (1988), is more sympathetic. Geoffrey Ward has written two biographical works on FDR, *Before the Trumpet: Young Franklin Roosevelt* (1985) and *A First Class Temperament: The Emergence of Franklin Roosevelt* (1989). Kenneth S. Davis has also produced a two-book account in *FDR: The New Deal Years, 1933–1937* (1986) and *FDR: Into the Storm, 1937–1940* (1993). Some of the books dealing with workers in the Depression are Irving Bernstein, *A Caring Society: The New Deal, the Worker, and the Great Depression* (1985), and *Turbulent Years: A History of the American Worker, 1933–1941* (1969); and Lizabeth Cohen, *Making a New Deal: Industrial Workers in Chicago, 1919–1939* (1991). On the WPA see Jerre Mangione, *The Dream and the Deal: The Federal Writers' Project, 1935–1943* (1972), and Karal A. Marling, *Wall-to-Wall America: A Cultural History of Post-Office Murals in the Great Depression* (1982), which shed much light on the socioartistic aspects of the New Deal era.

Chapter 15

Culver Pictures, Inc.

A military wedding, 1944. Family allotments and full employment made early marriage possible for millions.

The Home Front During World War II

RICHARD R. LINGEMAN

In a number of ways, World War II was an ideal war for the American people. The United States suffered none of the devastation that was visited on other warring nations, and American casualties were relatively light compared to those incurred by Britain, Russia, Germany, Japan, or China. There was less internal dissent about the wisdom or morality of the war than for any other conflict in American history. Increased spending for defense purposes brought the country out of the depression of the 1930s and restored prosperity. There were jobs for all and even a labor shortage. It is true that some consumer goods like automobiles and large appliances were unavailable because the factories that used to produce them were converted to war production. It is also true that other goods were rationed and that wage and price controls were imposed for the duration of the war. But the vast majority of Americans put up with wartime restrictions and shortages with good humor, accepting them as part of the price of victory. The general feeling was that we were engaged in an eminently worthwhile crusade on behalf of values that all Americans believed in, a crusade, in fact, in defense of civilization itself against German Nazism and Japanese militarism, forces that could readily be defined as truly evil.

While the war was going on, the United States was transformed in fundamental ways, not all of them by design. Full employment produced a substantial redistribution of income and a degree of economic security for middle-class Americans that became the foundation of postwar prosperity. Employment opportunities for women expanded enormously under the pressures created by the scarcity of labor. The same was true for African Americans, and the increased economic security and political clout that they achieved during the war years were important factors in the postwar civil rights movement. The war also saw a trend toward marriage at a younger age and an increase in the birth rate that was to persist into the postwar years and become known as the baby boom. Finally, World War II saw the first development and use of nuclear energy, holding out great hopes for a variety of peaceful uses, but also chilling prospects about what might happen if it were ever used again as a weapon. The following selection by Richard R. Lingeman shows how the war overseas affected many aspects of life within the United States for both good and ill.

The end of Hard Times was a motley caravan observed on Route 66, near Albuquerque, New Mexico, a road that was both *via doloroso* and passage of hope in John Steinbeck's *Grapes of Wrath.* Now, by the same route, in early 1942 the Okies were returning home. They came in old battered sedans and wheezing trucks and Model T's, sometimes twelve in a car, with all their possessions strapped on the tops and sides—rockers, buckets, shovels, stoves, bedding and springs. A few of the migrants were fleeing what they regarded as the imminent invasion of California by the Japanese, but the attitude of most was summed up by the man who said: "We ain't war-scared or anything like that, but a lot of others were pulling up and clearing out—not all of 'em understand—and Ma and I figured that if we was going back, now was the time. And, besides, Ed Lou is pretty big now and there ought to be a job for him in the oil fields and maybe for me too."

There were still more than 3,600,000 men unemployed. So the migration had momentum to gain as hillbillies from Appalachia, po' whites and Negroes from the South, farmers from the Midwest, garment workers from New York City picked up stakes and swarmed to the centers of war production.

The factories were rising up out of the raw, graded earth. The year 1942 was a year of frantic construction—more than $12 billion worth of it financed by the federal government, most of that on military camps, factories and installation of heavy machinery.

Near the little town of Starke, Florida, Camp Blanding had been erected in six months of feverish building. The workers turned the little town upside down. "Why, people were sleeping in the streets, in the churches, in the trees," one resident recalled. The local grocer reminisced: "I had two stores and I sold groceries to the construction gangs. Two stores and I couldn't get any help. I worked 18 to 20 hours a day. My weekend profits were unbelievable, but I wouldn't want to go through it again. These fellows from the construction jobs—these carpenters and plumbers—were getting more money than they'd ever had in their lives and they had no place to spend it except in Starke. They were always hungry and they were always buying. It went for five or six months. We all got rich.". . .

To millions who had suffered the Depression years on relief, with occasional spells of odd jobs, this meant a time of opportunity, a time to pick up stakes and head to the war production centers, where there were steady jobs and good money to be had. In times of depression people tend to crawl into their holes and lick their wounds: in good times they head for the money. Estimates of the number of Americans who left their homes to seek work elsewhere—in a different county, a different state or even a different region—ranged as high as 20,000,000. Probably the true number will never be known, but the Census Bureau attempted to capture the figures as best it could, before the time was irretrievably gone. Based on a sample of 30,000 persons, the bureau took a demographic snapshot of the nation in March, 1945, and compared it with the prewar period. The Bureau estimated that by 1945, 15,300,000 persons were living in counties different from those in which they lived at Pearl Harbor; 7,700,000 of these migrants were living in a different state and 3,600,000 in a different part of the country. . . .

A major source of this migration was the farm, where, most agrarian economists agreed, there were about 2,000,000 too many people in 1940. Between Pearl Harbor and March, 1945, nearly 5,500,000 people left the farms to live and work in the city (another 1,500,000 went into the armed forces). So effectively did the war siphon off the surplus that there were severe labor shortages on the farms, and in 1943–44, farm deferments were drastically increased by Selective Service. Women, city teen-agers, Axis war prisoners, interned Japanese-Americans and even GI's were pressed into service to help out with the harvest (a time when an additional 3,000,000 laborers are needed). The grip of the agriculture depression, which had held since the early twenties, was at last broken, and farmers' profits soared to record highs. With all this farm prosperity, a reverse migration trend was also operative, for some 2,500,000 people moved from nonfarm to farm areas, presumably to take up farmwork. Still, the farm population suffered a net loss of nearly 17 percent, not counting those in the armed forces. . . .

The greatest percentage of the immigrants settled in the immediate environs of the city or cities, rather than inside the cities. This was reflected in the mushrooming growth of war worker towns and federal housing projects laid out where there were only rural fields before or, even worse, the ubiquitous "New Hoovervilles"—trailer camps, tent settlements, shanty towns, "foxhole houses" and all other temporary conglomerations of people which sprang up over the countryside, often as satellites of the new war plants which had been erected on unused land. What this further meant was that these settlements were often located outside the service ambit of city and township governments. They were in a jurisdictional limbo, and there was no local government unit to take responsibility for them: further, many of the small towns to which they were often closest, hence most directly affected, lacked the resources with which to help them, even if they had wished to. Most of the migrants were nonvoting, nontaxpaying, nonhomeowning—in effect, political pariahs.

The geographical flow of the migration was strikingly skewed. Between April, 1940, and November, 1943, thirty-five states showed a net *loss* in total civilian population. The thirteen states that gained did so in numbers varying from California's 1,020,000 to Delaware's 7,240, but the geographical pattern was clear: By far the largest gainer was the Far West—the three coast states of California, Washington and Oregon, in that order, and to a much smaller degree, Arizona, Utah and Nevada. Next to the Pacific coast states, were three South Atlantic states: Maryland, Florida and Virginia. (In a class by itself was the District of Columbia, which gained 162,469 people; the federal government was also a booming war industry.)

The people went to the Far West because the opportunity was there, and the opportunity was there because the war money went West: California alone, with 6.2 percent of the population had by 1944 received war contracts totaling $15.8 billion, or 9.7 percent of the total for the nation. More than half the wartime ship-building took place in the three Pacific coast states, and nearly half the airplane manufacture. Because of its location on the sea and the existence of a prewar air-craft industry, California logically helped itself to a large chunk of this produc-tion. When the war ended, an estimated 1,000,000 war workers would be out of work, but till then California was truly the Golden State. All told its population in-creased by almost 2,000,000 between 1940 and 1945. Per capita income rose apace, reaching $1,740 annually, the highest in the nation. Here was the real gold rush in California's colorful history.

In sum the general pattern of the great national migration seemed to be this: Deep South po' whites to the shipyards around the Gulf crescent and in the Hampton Roads—Newport News—Norfolk complex and, farther North, to the Michigan manufacturing complexes.

Southern Negro sharecroppers and tenant farmers to the shipyards and facto-ries of the West Coast; up the East Coast and to the factories of the Middle West.

Arkies, Okies, Tennessee, Kentucky and West-by-God-Virginia hillbillies to Illinois and Indiana and Michigan or to the southern oilfields and shipyards.

Kansas, Nebraska, Iowa, North and South Dakota plowboys to the great aircraft factories of the West Coast.

New York and other urban small-manufacturing workers to the Mid and Far West.

They came in cars, driving their rubber down to the rims and then paying ex-orbitant prices for used tires or retreads en route; or, more likely, they sat up or stood in the aisles for days and nights on crowded trains; or they packed their few working clothes into cardboard suitcases, made dust down the red dirt roads of the backwoods South to the crossroads store, and there waited for the bus to take them on the long trip to Pascagoula or Mobile or New Orleans. . . .

Everyone, on the move. Young wives with colicky babies, making the long jour-ney to join their husbands at this new war job. Lone men, creased and weathered by work, and pink-cheeked young farm boys, migrating West because they heard there was plenty of work out there, sitting in the dark loneliness of the bus at night, only the glow of the orange spark of their cigarettes for company, their thoughts set free to range back and forth in time and space from regret to hope, over the vast American landscape of shadowy, empty hills and somber forests and little towns, their dark windows staring like empty-skulled eye sockets. In the next seat might be another man, he too sitting staring out at the landscape at night, he too coming from somewhere but off to somewhere else. The low voices hummed in talk of "where-are-you-going?" and "what's-it-like down there?"....

Men were picking up stakes and moving on. Some left signs on the doors of closed businesses, letting their customers and friends and the whole world (and maybe even God) know that they had vamoosed, flown the coop, skedaddled, made tracks, hit the road, up and went. Signs that read like the one on the door of Joe's Country Lunch in Alabama:

> Maybe you don't know there's a war on. Have gone to see what it's all about.
> Meanwhile good luck and best wishes until we all come home. (Signed) Joe.

Or that of Lem Ah Toy, Chinese laundryman of Seattle:

> Go to war. Closed duration. Will clean shirts after clean Axis. Thank you....

Signs, signs. Cocky, patriotic signs. The whole country, it seemed, was bursting out in a springtime of patriotism.... On bar mirrors in small dusty roadside taverns were soap-scrawled fighting slogans, like:

SLAP THE JAPS OFF THE MAP!
TO HELL WITH THE JAPS!
REMEMBER PEARL HARBOR!!! ...

Young girls sitting in soda fountains adorned themselves with the unit patches of their boyfriends, sergeant's stripes or lieutenant's bars; the soda fountain they were lounging in purveyed such patriotic combinations as: Blackout Sundae, Commando Sundae (War Workers, Get Your Vitamins the Delicious Way), Flying Fortress Sundae, Morale Builder and Paratroops Sundae (Goes Down Easy). In more and more windows hung service flags: red border, surrounding a white rectangle in which were one or more blue stars. Gold ones were making their appearance too. ("THE WAR DEPARTMENT REGRETS TO INFORM YOU THAT YOUR SON...." The papers printed names on casualty lists, but never gave total killed and wounded until mid-1942.) Along with the service flags in homes and places of business, small towns had erected Honor Roll signs, with lengthening lists of names and branches of service of their local boys....

At last the journey would near its end, and the migrant would catch a glimpse of the city of his destination: "snowy plains where great manufacturing plants jut up among their parking lots like mesas in the desert . . . mills that smear the sky with brown smoke out of tall cylindrical chimneys. . . ."

In green, gently rolling farmland, long, low dull-red brick factories rose up where bulldozers had scraped the land bare. Walter Wiard owned a farm and orchard in an area near Ypsilanti, Michigan, known as Willow Run after a stream that meandered through it on its way to the Huron River. In early 1941, Walter Wiard's land lay next to the site the Ford people had chosen for their new bomber plant, and the Ford people came to him and offered him a nice price for the land. Then Wiard watched as the giant groundbreaking machines went to work. Later he remarked: "It took me twenty-nine years to plant, cultivate and make that fine orchard. It took those tractors and bulldozers just twenty-nine minutes to tear it all down.". . .

So the workers arrived at the towns and cities where the war plants had risen and got off their crowded buses and walked the streets looking for a job, which was easy to find, and a bed, which was not. They might have landed in LA or San Francisco or Detroit or Pascagoula or Buffalo or Mobile. . . .

San Diego, once a quiet coastal town, was inundated with a lusty gang of workers and servicemen. For a new dry dock the Navy dug a hole that seemed as deep as the Grand Canyon, and one old resident described it as "a hole that you could have dumped most of this town [into] when I first saw it 70 years ago." Another graybeard, shaking his head in wonderment, recalled, "We used to go to bed by ten, or anyway, by eleven. Now some theaters and cafes never close! I remember it was like that in the Klondike. Now when boatloads of sailors hurry ashore, and all those soldiers from Fort Rosecrans and Camp Callan swarm in on payday, this town goes crazy. In one day they eat 50,000 hot dogs! Even shoe shine boys get the jitters. Sherman's Cafe has ten bars, and a dance floor so big that 5,000 of 'em can dance at once." Ten years before, exactly 6 men worked in San Diego's one aircraft factory; now there were 50,000. Any innocent tourist who decided to sit for a moment on a park bench would find himself approached by a series of people wanting to hire him to do some kind of job. . . .

Consider the town of Beaumont, Texas, which needed an incinerator. Next door to the Pennsylvania Shipyards stood a giant garbage dump which exhaled a miasma that could be smelled miles away when the wind was right. With the nauseating smells came flies. An official of the shipyards described what the flies were like: "The flies we get from the dump in the executive offices are so thick that it is almost impossible to concentrate on our duties. Twice a day the rooms are sprayed and the dead swept out with a broom. As soon as it gets warm we have to send people around the yard to spray the men on the job, or they would be eaten up by mosquitoes and flies."

The incinerator had been approved by the Federal Works Administration, and work had been begun. Then the WPB [War Production Board] refused the town a priority on a needed bit of equipment worth about $14,000. And so work stopped, and a half-finished incinerator stood in the midst of the stench and rotting garbage, a monument to government shortsightedness, while the stink grew and the danger of typhoid increased apace. . . .

Housing was an immediate and frequently insoluble problem for the migrant war workers. The government and private builders, largely with federally insured mortgage money, built a total of $7 billion of new housing, much of it temporary—barracks, trailers, demountable homes, dormitories, and the like. The NHA [National Housing Agency] calculated that it had to provide new or existing housing for 9,000,000 migratory workers and their families. To do this, it built and it scoured up existing vacant rooms and houses with the assistance of local community groups. Existing housing took care of 600,000 workers and their families. Over and above this, private companies built something more than 1,000,000 new units and the federal government 832,000 for a total of 1,800,000 units or housing for about 5,000,000 people: housing for at best 7,000,000 out of 9,000,000 migrants was provided; the remaining 2,000,000 presumably had to scour up their own shelter.

These bare statistics do not of course reflect the flesh and blood of the housing situation—the thousands who had to live in trailers, converted garages, tents, shacks, overpriced rooms, "hot beds," even their own cars during the early part of the war; the rent gouging that went on, even though rents were regulated by the Office of Price Administration; and the difficulties people with children had, especially the wives of servicemen who followed them to their training camps.

Landlord hostility to the newcomers was endemic in this sellers' market. An ad in a Fort Worth, Texas, newspaper revealed it: "Fur. Apt., no streetwalkers, home wreckers, drunks wanted; couple must present marriage certificate." On the West Coast, which had had an influx of more than 2,000,000 newcomers, it was chaotic. In San Francisco people lived in tents, basements, refrigerator lockers and automobiles. A city official reported in 1943: "Families are sleeping in garages, with mattresses right on cement floors and three, four, five to one bed." In Richmond, where the Kaiser shipyards were located, people were living under conditions that were worse than the Hoovervilles of the Depression. A trailer camp in San Pablo was crowded with people in trailers, tents and shacks; there was no sewage, and children waded about in a stagnant pond. A family of four adults and seven children lived in an 8-by-10-foot shack with two cots and one full-sized bed. A war housing project at Sausalito offered good living conditions for 4,500 people with self-government, low rentals and health insurance; but when a 90-mile-an-hour gale hit the area in January, 1943, all the tarpaper roofs of the temporary housing blew off. . . .

The philosophy underlying the governmental housing program was that "the government doesn't belong in the housing business," which meant that private housing interests were deferred to. In San Francisco, for example, which had a population increase of 200,000, local realtors had initially opposed war housing, saying there were 10,000 vacancies in the area. They were fearful of the competition, of course, but then, when the housing situation reached crisis proportions, they did a turnabout and blamed the federal government for not building enough war housing. And though they had relented on allowing government housing, they were adamant in their demands that only temporary housing, which could be torn down after the war, be built, lest property values suffer. This insistence that war workers be given only temporary or demountable housing was widespread and reflected not only the real estate man's pocketbook talking but also fear that the outsiders would stay after the war. As a result (and also because of the shortage of building materials), much government housing was jerry-built—instant slums, they might be called. . . .

One of the better federal housing projects was that erected near the Willow Run bomber plant. Because of opposition on the part of the townspeople in nearby Ypsilanti and the Ford Motor Company to a planned permanent residential area known as Bomber City . . . and material shortages, construction of alternate, temporary units was proposed and finally got under way in 1943. The first units—a dormitory for single workers called Willow Lodge—were open for occupancy by February, 1943. There followed trailer homes and prefabricated units for families, which were completed in August 1943. In all there was housing for about 14,000 workers—or one-third the number working at Willow Run plant at peak production.

By wartime housing standards these units were luxury housing, although they were not much to look at, being row upon row of gray, monotonous, flat-roofed buildings. The residents often had difficulty locating their own quarters. One lady always marked her house by a bedspring leaning against the adjoining unit. So much did she come to rely on the bedspring that she forgot the number of her own dwelling, and so one day, when inevitably, the bedspring was removed, she spent hours searching for her place. . . .

Most of the married workers with families overcame these minor hardships at Willow Run and turned it into a stable community. Still there were problems that could have been predicted among such a large and fluid population, many of them unmarried immigrants from the South. One reporter was critical of the "lack of wholesome recreational facilities and the generally drab social environment of Willow Run" which "stimulated private-party types of entertainment, featured by heavy drinking and promiscuous sex relations among fun-starved workers."

The center of the "promiscuous sex" was, not surprisingly, the Willow Lodge dormitory, which the FPHA [Federal Public Housing Agency] had opened to unmarried workers of both sexes. The result: "Professional gamblers and fast women quickly moved in for a clean-up." The co-ed policy was quickly dropped, however, and tenant policing, in cooperation with the FPHA, cleaned up the budding Gomorrah. . . .

Roving youngsters with nowhere to go were widespread. In Mobile, there were more than 2,000 children who didn't go to school at all, and one high school with an enrollment of 3,650 had a total of 8,217 absences during a single month. One movie theater owner joked with the local lady truant officer: "Miss Bessie, why don't you bring your teachers down here? My place is always full of children.". . .

Some towns, even without federal assistance, made an effort to set up day-care centers and nursery schools in a variety of ways, and the unions and war industries made an even greater contribution, the latter prodded by the labor shortage and the need to attract women workers, the former by a doctrine of demanding work rights. On the other hand, there was a distinct strain of prejudice against working mothers, who were regarded as selfishly materialistic; forgotten was the desperate need for them in the plants, the fact that many were servicemen's wives who needed to supplement their allotments, and the desire of others to take advantage of an opportunity to save up some money for the future. One of the leaders in the opposition to women working was the Catholic Church, which in many areas opposed nursery schools and day-care centers. . . .

Not unrelated to the shortage of day care, the overcrowded schools, the entry of youngsters into industry, and the lack of parental supervision was an increase in the incidence of crimes committed by teenagers (a term that came into wide currency during the war, along with juvenile delinquency). Juvenile arrests increased 20 percent in 1943; in some cities it was even higher—San Diego, for example, reported an increase of 55 percent among boys and 355 percent among girls. This was not a reflection of a nationwide crime wave, for crime on the whole—at least according to FBI figures—dropped during the war, with the exception of assault and rape. This was because the young men, who committed the largest percentage of crimes, were off in service. One of the heaviest areas of increase was among girls under seventeen who were arrested not only for various forms of "sex delinquency" such as prostitution, but also for violent crimes. In 1943 alone, the number of girls arrested for prostitution increased by 68 percent over the previous year.

Among the boys, it was largely theft and a striking incidence of acts of vandalism, destruction and violence. Some of these acts seemed a kind of acting-out of war fantasies—such as the thirteen-year-old "thrill saboteur" who put a stick of dynamite under a railroad track, lit the fuse and ran. The dynamite did not go off because he had attached no cap. He explained his action by saying he was attempting to close off all roads into the town and set himself up as "dictator."

With the girls, delinquency took the form of an aggressive promiscuity, and the lure was the glamor of a uniform. These "khaki-whacky" teenagers—some barely thirteen—were known as V-(for Victory) girls. They hung around bus depots, train stations, drugstores or wherever soldiers and sailors on leave might congregate, flirted with the boys, and propositioned them for dates. They were amateurs for the most part, the price of their favors being a movie, a dance, a Coke or some stronger drink. (A joke of the time ran: Sailor: "I'm going to Walgreen's to meet a girl." "What's her name?" "How should I know?")

The V-girls were easily recognizable in their Sloppy Joe sweaters, hair ribbons, anklets or bobby sox and saddle shoes, trying to look older with heavily made-up faces and blood-red lipstick. In Detroit the Navy had to build a fence around its armory, located in the city, to keep out not the enemy, but the bobby-soxers. In Chicago, sailors said it was worth one's life to try to walk from the Navy Pier to State Street, where the V-girls swarmed like flies. In Mobile, the girls themselves bought contraceptives for their dates, and when one druggist refused to sell them to a group of girls, he was jeered at and called an old fuddy-duddy.

The V-girls had their similarities all over the country. Some of them followed their lovers when they were transferred to another post, but many were left stranded when the boyfriend left. These often ended up working as waitresses or as barmaids in servicemen's hangouts, passing from one uniform to another.

There had always been teen-age girls who "did it," of course; war made them more visible, more independent, more mobile. One estimate had it that the V-girls represented at most only one in 1,700 out of their age group. More conservative girls, caught up in the transitoriness of wartime meetings and the glamor of a uniform, might also "do it," but they were more discreet and less promiscuous and conducted their assignations in more privacy.

The V-girl was next door to being a prostitute, yet there was about her at least a certain refreshing lack of cold professionalism. She offered a lonely GI transitory fun and excitement, devoid of the professional's matter-of-fact indifference. She could also, of course, offer him VD, for there was a higher incidence among the amateurs than among the professionals. In 1941, Congress, worried about the mother's vote, had passed the May Act, which forbade houses of prostitution near military bases. The result was that a lot of establishments were closed down and their inmates put out to walk the streets. These and their amateur competitors were found to inflict VD at a much higher rate than the house-based girls. . . .

The guardians of morality—whose view on the subject had been expressed in a 1942 *Reader's Digest* article by Gene Tunney entitled "The Bright Shield of Continence"—of course were against any kind of sex by soldiers with women other than their wives (if that) and would be shocked at the idea of brothels near Army camps where innocent young selectees would be exposed to unholy, irresistible temptation leading to inevitable corruption. (There was a similar logic running through the efforts of temperance groups to ban the distribution of beer to combat troops or its sale at PX's.)

As for the servicemen themselves, the Army traditionally liked to say that 15 percent "won't," 15 percent "will" and the remainder occasionally would succumb to temptation if the serpent insinuated itself (these figures derived from World War I). For that wavering 70 percent, the problems of finding "nice girls" in the camp towns, whether their intent was to deflower them or take them to the Sunday night meeting of the Epworth League, were often insuperable. . . .

Still, if the number of marriages and families formed is any sort of index to the degree of adherence to the American fundamental belief in marriage, the war period could be looked upon as fostering a salubrious moral climate. Beginning in 1940, as prosperity began to take hold and the Depression receded, the marriage rate began to rise abruptly—one is tempted to say alarmingly. . . .

The rush to wed was impelled as much by prosperity as it was by the war. A justice of the peace in Yuma, Arizona, a marriage town just over the California border, explained the sudden upswing in business in 1941. Not love but "aircraft did it for us," he said. "The figures began going up as soon as those boys were given employment in those plants at San Diego and Los Angeles and were taken off W.P.A. [Works Progress Administration]." Aircraft workers had been issued 90 percent of the licenses since the summer of 1941. "You see, when they were on the dole they had girls but no money. Once off the dole and once getting good money they began sending for the girls back home—girls in the Middle Western states, a great many of them. The girls wouldn't waste any time in coming in and then on weekends—we get the great rush on weekends—they'd all come hustling over to Yuma." It was the same story in Cincinnati, where weddings involving defense workers increased 51 percent; in Baltimore, where they were up 47 percent; and in Youngstown and Akron (up 17 percent) and Detroit (up 12 percent).

Of course, at that time a wife would also qualify as a dependent and men with dependents were deferred, until Congress discouraged this by establishing an allotment system in 1942. Under it, a man's wife would receive a minimum of $50 a month, $22 of which was deducted from his pay and $28 contributed by the government. To preserve family life and also perhaps to encourage a population increase to offset anticipated manpower losses in the war, the Selective Service Act deferred fathers until 1943, when manpower needs were so pressing that so-called pre–Pearl Harbor fathers were drafted.

Whether the Selective Service Act's policy was responsible or not (and we must give the parents some credit for initiative), the birthrate did go up during the war in a preview of the postwar baby boom when returning GI's set about forming families as fast as they could. Since the 1920s the birthrate, like the marriage rate, had been declining, but in 1943, it rose to 22 per 1,000—the highest in two decades. Most of these babies were "good-bye babies," conceived before the husband shipped out. Since the wife's allotment check would be increased upon the child's arrival, finances were no longer a major worry. In addition, there were compelling emotional reasons: The father, faced with the possibility of being killed in battle, was depositing a small guarantor to posterity, an assurance that someone would carry on his name, while the wife was given something to hold onto, a living, breathing symbol of their marriage. . . .

So they were married, this courageous young couple; perhaps they did know each other well and were in love, or perhaps they had met on a weekend pass and married in haste. Or perhaps the woman had eyed covetously the allotment check and looked forward to a life of some ease (and if he was killed, there was always the $10,000 to the widow from his life insurance). A $50-a-month allotment was of course not princely, but a GI overseas, with nothing else to spend it on, would usually send part of his regular pay home.

With the going rate only $50 per month per husband, a really ambitious girl might decide she needed four, five, six or more husbands to support her in any kind of style. Inevitably there developed the wartime racket of bigamous marriage for allotment checks. The girls who engaged in it came to be known as Allotment Annies. They posted themselves in bars around military bases and struck up acquaintances with lonely servicemen, otherwise known as shooting fish in a barrel. The men, desirous of the certainty that when they went off to battle, there would be a girl back home waiting for them, writing them V-mail letters, could often be had. So they married, the hero went off to war, and Annie stayed home and collected a lot of those pale blue-green checks from the U.S. Treasury Department.

A representative Allotment Annie was a hustling seventeen-year-old named Elvira Tayloe, who operated out of Norfolk, Virginia, and specialized in sailors shipping out from the large naval base there. Working as a hostess in a nightclub, she managed to snare six live ones and was working on her seventh when caught. This came about because a couple of sailors on liberty had met in an English pub, and as servicemen are wont, as the warm beer flowed, took out wallets and exchanged pictures of their gorgeous wives. Both were surprised, to put it mildly, when their pictures turned out to be identical, both of Elvira. A fight ensued over whose wife was being adulterous with whom. After the shore patrol had cooled them off, the boys joined forces, Elvira was traced and her career of cupidity brought to an end. . . .

Wartime marriage was hard, and the real miracle was that so many survived it. What the husband did overseas during off-duty hours is beyond our scope, but the girls back here were, largely, brave—and true. Not heroic; but they got by. Some, it is true, cracked up, or fell into dalliance with a representative of the local supply of 4-F's and joyriding war workers.

Life gave another portrait of the typical Army wife. Her husband is a lieutenant in India and her $180-a-month allotment makes her atypical right there, yet she adds some less dramatic hues to the portrait. She lives in a $3\frac{1}{2}$-room apartment, rent $65 a month; she spends $45 a month on food for her herself and the baby; she doesn't go out on dates, goes to parties unescorted and doesn't have a great deal of fun ("There's always some woman who thinks you're trying to take their man away"); sometimes at night she gets the blues and cries, but her baby son cheers her up a lot; she writes her husband a letter every day; she spends her evenings listening to the radio a lot (Guy Lombardo's is her favorite orchestra); when she hears "Soon"—"their song" in 1935, when they were married—she becomes sad. . . .

Dr. Jacob Sergi Kasanin, chief psychiatrist at Mount Zion Hospital in San Francisco, went so far as to identify a neurotic syndrome characteristic of servicemen's wives in 1945. Like many men who went overseas and cracked up before they reached combat (there were estimates that as high as one-half of the combat-trained troops avoided battle by "psyching out," getting a dishonorable discharge and the like), the wives had their own form of crackup. The physical symptoms included depression, colitis, heart palpitations, diarrhea, frequent headaches. Hardest hit were the recently married who had no children. They often developed "pathological reactions" in the form of resentment against their husband or even inability to recall what he looked like. (This was true even among fairly normal wives. One such wife decided to knit a sweater for her husband. As the months of separation drew on, her idea of her tall husband grew accordingly. He sent a picture of himself in the new sweater: it reached halfway down to his knees.) These women often had followed their husbands to his embarkation point; then in symbolic identity with him, they stayed there, and some couldn't take the loneliness, away from home, and began going to the bars, meeting other servicemen in transit. (The ratio of female alcoholics—defined as those who got into trouble with the police—to male alcoholics in Chicago was one to two, compared to one in five in 1931.)

For the more mature marriages, the ones in which the couple would pick up the pieces of their life and put them back together after long separation, there were still changes to be faced. A Navy doctor took a look at himself in the mirror one day and saw that he had grown bald and fat. He wrote about this to his wife, and she wrote back, sadly, "You will find that three years have done quite a bit to me, too."

The war, then, upset the social topography as it did the physical landscape; people met new places, new situations, new jobs, new living conditions, new ways of life, new temptations, new opportunities. There were social ills aplenty, but for all their novelty, they were perhaps the familiar ones; war simply exaggerated them and made them more visible. A sociologist writing on juvenile delinquency in *Federal Probation Officer* expressed a view that most diagnosticians of society would share:

> . . . many mothers of school-age boys and girls work in normal times; families are "broken" either physically or psychologically in normal times; children are exploited in normal times; some young people have always earned good wages and spent them unwisely; families always have moved from one neighborhood or community to another; some recreational facilities of an undesirable nature can be found in most communities in normal times. . . . Actually war does not create new problems with which we are unfamiliar. It accentuates old problems and in so doing the number of boys and girls affected is increased greatly.

One can only add that, in view of the familiarity of the problems and their increased magnitude, the governmental agencies might have done more to alleviate them. But of course, to Congress, stepped-up programs of social welfare would have smacked of "New Deal social experiments," and besides—don't you know there's a war on?

The citizenry out in the provinces who thought they had problems could take a measure of malicious satisfaction, if they wanted to, over the fact that their nation's capital was perhaps the most mixed-up, down-at-the-heels war town of them all. Its traditional industry was mainly government, of course, but everybody in the provinces knew that Washington's "bit" was doing the war's desk work—paper shuffling, tabulating, enumerating, filing. What people in Washington did was concoct complicated forms and schedules, issue directives, create agencies and, when they had some spare time, which was often, sit around and lobby, trade favors, peddle influence, gossip, boondoggle and, above all, take part in colorful feuds for the delectation of newspaper readers everywhere.

An exaggeration of course, but Washington was easy to poke fun at. It was a sort of sitting lame duck for conservative writers who gleefully pointed to whopping inefficiencies, pullulating paper work, labyrinthine bureaucracies, overlapping jurisdictions and a steady stream of executive directives. (FDR issued more executive orders during his Presidency than all previous Presidents combined.) "Washington Wonderland," they called it; "A red-tape-snarled, swarming, sweating metropolis"; "an insane asylum run by the inmates"; or in the words of a taxi driver: "the greatest goddamn insane asylum of the universe."

Overcrowding was Washington's most obvious physical symptom. Since 1940, more than 280,000 government job seekers had poured into town to hold down jobs as clerks and typists in the burgeoning wartime bureaucracy. Most of them were girls; most came from small towns all across the nation. They were drawn by the lure of higher wages—a girl could make $1,600 a year as a typist—and though they reveled in their newfound affluence, they could never get over the high prices, at which they clucked and shook their heads like tourists.

They were set down into a sort of Dogpatch with monuments, plagued by an acute housing shortage, overburdened and capricious public transportation, a cost of living that gobbled up their salaries (that government typist making $1,600 was lucky if she saved $25 in a year) and temporary office buildings that were as homey to work in as a railroad station.

Washington's housing shortage became an overused comic premise in movies and plays about the city, but to the people who lived there it was not always so funny. People paid $24 or $35 or more a month for glorified cubicles or jammed into shabby boardinghouses. They jostled for bathroom access with a herd of fellow boarders and were lucky if they could get a bath once every ten days. Landladies discouraged women tenants because they were wont to do their own laundry, request kitchen privileges and entertain gentlemen callers in the parlor. "Men, on the other hand," observed one concierge, "don't wash anything but themselves and eat all their meals out."

Hotels limited guests to a three-day stay. Hospitals had reverted to something out of Dickens; it was the practice to induce childbirth, for otherwise a room might not be available at the right time. . . .

For a family—especially a family with children—it was nearly impossible to find a place. Pathetic want ads appeared in the newspapers: "Won't someone help a refined enlisted Navy man and wife, employed, no children, to obtain an unfurnished room or two with kitchen?" Houses for sale were flagrantly overpriced, and people in Georgetown bought up old, run-down houses for $3,000, renovated them and sold them for five times what they had paid. Renting a house was dearer yet: tiny Georgetown houses rented for a minimum of $250 a month, and some larger houses in other neighborhoods that were by no means mansions were going for $1,000 a month. After President Roosevelt's death, the thought quickly occurred to a lot of people at the same time that the new President would soon be moving out of his two-bedroom, $120-a-month, rent-controlled apartment. The switchboard at Mr. Truman's building was jammed with calls; the operator told each caller that the president had already promised the apartment to at least three people. . . .

Uniforms were everywhere, representing a rainbow of international military pageantry. At night American soldiers and sailors crowded into the little nightclubs, and Washington night life boomed as it never had before or since. As part of its hospitality to servicemen, Washington offered, in addition to man-starved G-girls ("Washington is the loneliest town," one of them said), the highest VD-contraction rate among servicemen of any city in the country. . . .

Like housing, office space was in short supply, even with the ugly new temporary buildings. The government resorted to pressuring businesses and private residents to move out, and the President spoke darkly of "parasites"—useless people occupying vitally needed space. About the only solution to the office shortage was for the government to move out of town. This it did, in part, setting up branch offices in Richmond, New York, Chicago, St. Louis, Cincinnati, Kansas City, Philadelphia and Baltimore. More than 35,000 government employees moved out, too. . . .

In 1942 the world's largest office building was completed across the Potomac near Arlington. Called the Pentagon, its labyrinthine corridors and offices housed 35,000 office workers. When people wondered what in the world the War Department would do with such an enormous building in peacetime, the President explained that it would be used to store government records and quartermaster supplies, which seemed to satisfy everybody.

 ## For Further Study

1. World War II brought an end to the widespread unemployment of the Great Depression. Is there any hint in the author's narrative of a regret on the part of the nation that it took a war—and a massive one at that—to pull the country out of the Depression?

2. What impression do you get of the spirit of the nation in its newly found prosperity and employment: a sense of dedication to the war effort? gratitude to the government for a job and a weekly income? sadness that a war was going on?

3. How did the federal government respond to the *social* needs of war workers? Was housing for workers planned as well or as extensively by the government as, for example, munitions plants or airplane factories? Support your answer with evidence from the essay.

4. Compare what Lingeman says about the behavior of teenagers during the war years with the way they behave today. What differences, if any, do you see?

5. World War II, at least as it affected the United States, is sometimes referred to as "the good war." To what extent and in what ways does this label make sense to you? In what ways does it seem wrong?

For Further Reading

The volume from which this selection was taken—Richard R. Lingeman, *Don't You Know There's a War On?: The American Home Front, 1941–1945* (1970)—is an entertaining account of life during World War II. It may be supplemented with the following general accounts: Richard Polenberg, *War and Society: The United States, 1941–1945* (1972); Geoffrey Perrett, *Days of Sadness, Years of Triumph: The American People, 1939–1945* (1973); and John Morton Blum, *V Was for Victory: Politics and American Culture During World War II* (1976). The lives of American women during the war are the focus of D'Ann Campbell, *Women at War with America* (1984); Sherna Berger Gluck, *Rosie the Riveter Revisited* (1987); and Susan M. Hartmann, *The Home Front and Beyond* (1982). Clayton R. Koppes and Gregory D. Black provide an interesting account of how American movies became a part of the war effort in *Hollywood Goes to War* (1987).

Chapter 16

Wisconsin Historical Society (3338)

Taking advantage of the educational benefits of the GI Bill of Rights created problems, as well as opportunities, for the veterans and the colleges they attended.

The GI Bill of Rights

MICHAEL J. BENNETT

Even before World War II ended in 1945, the nation was making plans for the future. One special area of concern was how to treat the people who would be released from military service when hostilities ended. There were concerns that the veterans might have difficulty readjusting to civilian life. Even more worrisome was the question of how to find jobs for all of them. Most Americans were aware that the economic stimulus of the war had finally pulled the nation out of the Depression of the 1930s, and they feared that the end of wartime spending might see a return of hard times, especially when there would be literally millions of new job-seekers flooding the labor market. In 1944 Congress passed and President Roosevelt signed into law the Serviceman's Readjustment Act, better known as the GI Bill of Rights, in an attempt to deal with or forestall some of these problems as well as to express the nation's gratitude to the veterans for a job well done.

The law extended a variety of benefits to veterans. For example, they were entitled to unemployment compensation in the amount of $20 per week for a period not to exceed 52 weeks, so that they would have something to live on while looking for a job. (It was possible to live on $20 a week at the time, although certainly not lavishly.) They received a preference—usually a certain number of points automatically added to their actual score—when they took exams for civil service jobs. They had re-employment rights, meaning that the employers for whom they had been working when they entered military service were required to give them their old jobs back if they asked for them. They were eligible for low-interest, government-guaranteed loans to buy homes or start businesses.

But the Act's most famous provision, and the one that probably had the greatest impact on the future, was the one that made it possible for veterans to begin or complete educations at schools of their choice with all the costs, including tuition, fees, and books, borne by the government, with a small stipend for living expenses thrown in so that veterans would be able to devote full time to their studies. The consequences were enormous. Not only were the lives of the veterans changed, so was the nation as a whole. Tens of thousands to whom a college education would have been nothing but a distant dream now were able to attend the best universities in the land. In doing so they were able to acquire the degrees and the skills that helped to make the United States into the world leader in research and technology in the postwar period. American higher education was transformed, too. Previously, with some limited exceptions, it had been regarded as something available only to the economic and social elite, but the GI Bill of Rights democratized it. Not only was college now within the economic grasp of all veterans, regardless of their social origin, it was becoming a target for the aspirations of others to whom the idea of going to college simply would not have occurred previously. The nation's experience with the GI Bill of Rights was a major step toward the idea that higher education ought somehow be available to all those who were educationally qualified, regardless of their economic circumstances.

An enormous price had been paid for peace, but, for the survivors, there were great rewards. Never before had so many people been so free economically, educationally, and socially. Astonishing numbers of people were entering and leaving the workforce. Military enrollment plunged from 11.4 million in 1945 to 3.4 million in 1946. Another nearly 2 million were discharged between 1946 and 1947, bringing military strength down to 1.5 million in 1947. At the same time, civilian employment climbed from 53.8 million in 1945 to 57.5 million in 1946, and to 60.8 million in 1947. In other words, while 10 million were discharged from military service, civilian employment increased by 7 million. In the jargon of statisticians, the labor market was "churning." Amid all those zigzagging figures, in theory as many as 7 million to 8 million were out of work at all times during those two years. Indeed, almost 9 million veterans drew 52-20 benefits between 1944 and 1949, but presumably because they were counted as part of the civilian labor force, the unemployment rate was unaffected. On the other hand, they did so for an average of only seventeen weeks—less than a third of the fifty-two weeks they were entitled to.

Where were those people who were out of work but not apparently looking for jobs? A great many were in school. About 7.8 million World War II veterans, in all, enrolled in some sort of educational or training program under the GI Bill. Total college and university enrollment leaped from 1,676,856 in 1945, with 88,000 veterans attending, to 2,078,095 in 1946 with veterans accounting for 1,013,000, or 48.7 percent of the total. In 1947, veteran enrollment peaked at 2,338,226 with 1,150,000 veterans, or 49.2 percent, among them. . . .

Reality is conveyed better in individual terms, in stories about a few of the many millions whose lives were transformed during those years. One such story was that of Les Faulk of Turtle Creek, Pennsylvania. Faulk graduated from high school in May 1944 and celebrated the death of Hitler and the overthrow of the Nazi regime a year later as a Seventh Army infantryman in Germany. When Faulk had left Turtle Creek, he had a pretty clear notion of what his life would be like after the war—assuming he survived. He'd come back to the small town wrapped in industrial haze and get his old jobs back—if he was lucky—caddying at the local golf course and racking balls at Kindler's poolroom. In time, he could expect to get a "good" job stoking an open-hearth steel mill or winding copper armatures in the Westinghouse generator plant.

Faulk was one of twelve Turtle Creek High School graduates that Edwin Keister, Jr. interviewed for an article in *Smithsonian Magazine* in 1994, a class that was a microcosm of hundreds of thousands of others. The young man who left high school in 1944 expecting to become no more than a steel mill stoker or an armature winder instead spent thirty-eight years as a teacher and an elementary school principal. Les Faulk had not only gone to college, he also had acquired both a bachelor's and a master's degree and several credits toward his doctorate, even though the name on his high school diploma was "Falcocchio." That name—and his decision to change it—was significant. In those days, being the son of an Italian immigrant family with a "foreign" name could be almost as much a barrier to getting into college as a black skin. "College," as Faulk recalled fifty years later, "was for teachers' kids and the preacher's kids. For the rest of us, with names like Tarantini and Trkula, it was a distant dream."

Faulk and his classmates in Mrs. Whittum's American history class had been urged to believe that that dream, no matter how distant, could come true for them. But the hopes held out in school didn't stand up very well to the living and working conditions Faulk and his classmates grew up in. Turtle Creek was a factory town where half the male students dropped out of high school. Only 5 percent went on to any kind of postsecondary education, even barber or secretarial school, the latter being one of the few avenues to white-collar work then pursued by men as well as women. The war and the GI Bill changed everything. Faulk, like millions of other young Americans sent off to war, grew up fast in a foxhole. That alone might have made it difficult to accept what Turtle Creek had to offer when he came back home, even with a job awaiting him as an apprentice bricklayer, a job arranged by his father. That wasn't the reason he quit after one day, though, throwing away an opportunity for a skilled, well-paid, and prestigious job at the time. He had heard of the GI Bill, and he had made a decision. "I went to the poolroom and told my old boss, 'I'm going to college.' He said, 'I read that only one vet in 20 who enters college will finish.' I said, 'I'm going to be that one.'"

The government had turned him into a soldier who had helped beat the best the German army had to offer; now the same government thought he had the makings of a college graduate. Who was he to argue?

Faulk wasn't alone. Among the eleven other graduates of Turtle Creek High School who joined him at the fiftieth reunion of the Class of '44 were an aerospace engineer, a federal judge, a microchip engineer, a professor of law who is also a research scientist, and an engineer specializing in military survival techniques. . . .

Chesterfield Smith signed up for prelaw at the University of Florida back in 1935, but as his wife, Vivian Parker, recalled years later, "He was just a poker-playing, crap-shooting boy who couldn't settle down." By his own account, Smith "chose the easy life in college. I'd go to school a semester and then drop out for a semester to earn enough money to return"—in style. "I'd rather drop out and work than skimp in school." He worked as a clerk in the Florida legislature, a soda jerk, a debt collector, and a candy and tobacco vendor. By the time he was drafted in 1940, though, he had managed to complete three and a half years of college. Commissioned in the National Guard, he was assigned to a field artillery unit in France beginning "about D day plus 45" and served through the Battle of the Bulge before returning to the University of Florida in 1946.

By the standards of the day, Smith had done well financially, saving $5,000 from his pay and winning another $3,000 in craps on the long voyage home. But the man who had married Vivian in 1944 before shipping out for Europe had changed when he came back in 1945. She recalled, "He was a serious man when he returned." Smith didn't give up the good life entirely; he found time to golf five days a week through law school. Financially, his carefully budgeted savings and a teaching job obtained in his second year at law school meant the couple "had more than most." But he also budgeted his time as carefully as his money. "I didn't go drink coffee or sit out on the bench and bull it all the time. I never missed a day of class. I kept a work schedule just like I had a job. If I had a paper due in three weeks, I started it right away and finished a week early. Hell, here I was, almost thirty years of age—I wanted to get that law license and get into practice and make myself some money. The idea of playing around a university for unnecessary months or years had no appeal to me whatsoever."

Twenty years later, Smith was the president of the American Bar Association and the principal partner in a Tampa-Orlando law firm. "The way I was going before the war," Smith said, "I don't think I would ever have made it through law school. But after the war, I felt I had something invested in my country—five years of my life. I said to myself, 'Boy, you've got to settle down and make something of yourself, otherwise you ain't going to 'mount to nothing.' My classmates in the '40s, after the war, we wanted to get on with our lives. We were men, not kids, and we had the maturity to recognize that we had to go get what we wanted, and not just wait for things to happen to us." . . .

. . . social change on a seismic scale was happening and nowhere more so than at Harvard. Harvard was the oldest elite institution traditionally preparing the sons of America's WASP families to take their places as the economic and social leaders of the country. Yet it helped pioneer the new meritocratic society that . . . the GI Bill made possible. Harvard had taken the lead a generation before under President A. Lawrence Lowell in restricting the percentage of Jewish students. But under President Conant after the war, the university began vigorously recruiting students from every ethnic and religious background and section of the country, often to the discomfort of alumni who assumed admission of their sons into Harvard Yard was part of the family patrimony. For the veterans who were unexpectedly within the walls of the Yard, it was both a disconcerting and liberating experience.

Frank O'Hara, for example, who was to become a leading literary and art figure of New York in the 1950s and 1960s, wasn't even sure the GI Bill of Rights was a good idea. He had been an enlisted man working as a sonar operator in San Pedro, California, in 1946 when a conversation with a bunkmate, Douglas "Diddy" Starr, turned to the GI Bill. O'Hara, unlike most of his fellow sailors who were singularly pleased with the windfall, was wary, according to his biographer, Brad Gooch. O'Hara had read and been impressed with an article by President Hutchins of the University of Chicago in *Collier's* arguing the bill would turn the nation's colleges into "educational hobo jungles." He was also suspicious of a bandwagon mood that assumed education was the answer to all problems. Nonetheless, O'Hara, whose father graduated from the College of the Holy Cross in Worcester, Massachusetts, applied for and was accepted at Harvard—and so far as living arrangements were concerned, might as well have been back in the Navy. "In 1946, you might as well have been living in an American Legion post as in one of the Houses," a graduating senior reminisced in the 1950 *Harvard Yearbook*. Four thousand veterans were among the record 5,435 students enrolled at Harvard in 1946, filing through registration points in Memorial Hall at the rate of 3 a minute. The spectacle of seventeen-year-old beardless youths in white buck shoes, unloading Vuitton bags from their convertibles outside the "Gold Coast" houses along the Charles River was overshadowed by the sea of older faces surging into the red brick dormitories reserved for veterans on the north side of the Yard. Double-deck bunk beds had to be moved into some dorms, and cots were set up in the Indoor Athletic Building's basketball court to accommodate latecomers.

The words "invasion" and "siege" were predictably and incessantly used by *The Harvard Crimson* as lines formed everywhere—to register, eat, get books, cash checks. The more popular lecturers spoke in classrooms where students arrived early to claim seats on windowsills. The old rules still applied. Jackets and ties were required in the Union, the dining hall, but manufacturers had stopped making blazers and white shirts during the war, and veterans couldn't afford them even if they were available at the Coop, the university's cooperative store. So military coats were cut to hip length, service-issue trousers given a quick press, and insignia cut off old khaki shirts.

O'Hara found it amazing that he was at Harvard at all, Gooch wrote. A mere three months before he had been an enlisted man on the U.S.S. *Nicholas* who, without the GI Bill, would never have been able to afford Harvard's stiff fees. Yet not all of the nuances of Harvard pleased him. He couldn't help feel the pressure of elitism, and he wasn't sure if being at Harvard meant anything to anybody except snobs. He also felt pigeonholed by being Irish even though Irish-Catholics had been the first minority admitted to Harvard back in the 1870s. There had always been a subtle rivalry between Protestants and Catholics, Gooch wrote, although it usually didn't take any more serious form than drinking contests. O'Hara was also unlike relatively sophisticated big-city and wealthy Irish-Catholics like the Kennedys. He was from a small Massachusetts farm town, Grafton near Athol, and a graduate of a parochial high school. Almost another twenty years would pass before graduates of public and parochial high schools outnumbered the products of select private schools among the undergraduates of Harvard. One acquaintance described O'Hara at the time as looking "potato Irish, lower class, with pasty skin." He was often kidded as coming from "Asshole" and told a boyhood friend from Grafton, Phil Charron, "I'm going to Harvard; they say it's the death knell of all Catholics." O'Hara reacted to the social fencing, Gooch wrote, as did many others, by developing a personal style of speech using "arch Angloisms" to both blend in and subtly mock the accents and manners of WASP culture.

Arch Angloisms weren't any part of the style of another member of the class of 1950, although his potato face did go well with the Germanic accent he has retained. Henry Kissinger [later to become Secretary of State], before being drafted into the army, had enrolled as a college student in what was often called the Jewish Harvard, CCNY. The German-Jewish immigrant had planned on becoming an accountant, like this father. "My horizons were never that great when I was in City College," Kissinger said, according to his biographer, Walter Isaacson. Kissinger, who had fled Nazi persecution in Germany with his parents, became an American citizen in the army. The naturalization ceremony at dusty Camp Croft in South Carolina had been just another event in the daily process of, as Kissinger wrote to his brother, "being pushed around and inoculated, counted and stood to attention." The erstwhile accountant returned to Germany, Isaacson wrote, as part of a

> vast democratizing force, one that transformed how Americans lived. Soldiers from small towns in South Carolina and Louisiana for the first time saw places like Paris and Berlin, turning all-American boys with hardscrabble heritages into cosmopolitan conquerors. And, on a smaller scale, the army took young refugees from Nuremberg and Furth, put them into places such as Camp Croft and Camp Claiborne, then marched them off to war in melting pot platoons, thus turning cosmopolitan allies into acculturated American citizens. For immigrant boys, such as Kissinger, serving in the war made citizenship more than a gift merely bestowed; it was an honor they had earned. Having defended the United States, they now had as much claim as any Winthrop or Lowell to feel it was their nation, their country, their home. They were outsiders no more.

Lowells and Cabots mingled quite freely with O'Haras and Kissingers and the other provincial young men tossed up on the banks of the Charles River by the GI Bill. The war, after all, had given all of them the same veneer. Kissinger himself liked to say later that his experience with "the real middle American boys" in his regiment from Wisconsin, Illinois, and Indiana "made me feel like an American."

He quoted Helmet Sonnenfeld, a national security adviser, as observing, "The Army made the melting pot melt faster." Indeed, the melting-pot experience young men had undergone in the military was much more readily replicated on college campuses than in established multigenerational and ethnically dominated cities such as Boston, where veterans were sometimes suspected of getting above themselves. That was particularly true of Harvard in comparison to the Boston-Cambridge community where racial, ethnic, and religious tensions would plague the community long after they had subsided on the Harvard campus. Boston, in the late '40s, wasn't quite the city made famous by the doggerel toast of an Irish-Catholic alumnus of Boston College at the turn of the century: "Here's to Boston, the home of the bean and the cod, where the Lowells speak only to the Cabots and the Cabots speak only to God." Nevertheless, it was still a community in which the Yankees spoke rarely to the Irish; the Irish avoided conversation with their fellow Catholics, the Italians; and Jews talked with the Yankees, Irish, and Italians only on business. At the time, in fact, the Cabots were, according to a widely circulated story, suing a Jewish family named Cabotsky. The Cabotskys had changed their name so they could advertise their pharmacy as "Cabot's Drugs." Presumably the old toast had been changed to: "Here's to the home of the bean and the cod, where the Lowells speak to no one, for the Cabots speak Yiddish, by God!"

Kissinger's Germanic accent no doubt stood him in good stead on the Harvard campus and unquestionably helped him in his determination to avoid assimilation into democratic anonymity. His Teutonic tonalities served the same purpose as O'Hara's arch Angloisms. The difference was intriguing and enticing for insiders who not only accepted, but thought more highly of them for being outsiders. Kissinger had listened carefully to his first mentor, Fritz Gustave Anton Kraemer, a German refugee of Prussian background, who was his boss in the American military government of Germany. Kraemer advised him: "Go to a fine college. A gentleman does not go to the College of the City of New York." Kissinger was admitted to Harvard, however, only because the college was willing to take students whose papers were filed late, unlike Princeton and Columbia where he also applied. Isaacson attributed that to the fact that Conant, whom he incorrectly described as a driving force behind the GI Bill, had appointed an outreach counselor to make sure veterans had access to his university.

Once the bill was passed, Conant added his own support to the bill's influence in breaking down the ethnic, religious, and especially anti-Semitic prejudices on campus, although Jews entering Harvard in 1947 were usually assigned other Jews as roommates. The college administration did caution residential housemasters not to take more Jews "than the traffic will allow," for several years after the war, but the practice was discontinued by the end of the decade. So, too, was the custom of designating the names of Jews on college records with asterisks. Actual enrollment of Jews in the late '40s was about 17 percent, slightly lower than the level in the 1920s when President Lowell imposed quotas. The difference wasn't in the numbers so much as the degree of acceptance. "Harvard welcomed us with open arms," remembered Henry Rosovsky, who served with Kissinger in Germany and later became an economics professor, dean of the faculty, and the first Jewish member of the Harvard Corporation. Discrimination was a reality in some departments of the university, Isaacson observed, but it was least evident in government where Louis Hartz, a Jew, was professor of political theory and onetime chairman. . . .

Blacks especially came back from the war walking—and feeling—like free men. They took advantage of the GI Bill in the same way whites did, as individuals, not as members of a group except insofar as membership in the American Legion, the VFW, or the DAV might be helpful in negotiating red tape. Of course, blacks weren't free in the same way whites were, and it seems probable they didn't take advantage of the education benefits in the same percentages as whites. No authoritative numerical estimates of black beneficiaries are available other than an assertion, without documentation, in the *Encyclopedia of the Second World War* that 250,000 blacks were given the opportunity to go college for the first time under the GI Bill. The percentage of those who wouldn't otherwise have gone to college was certainly much higher than whites, according to Reginald Wilson, senior scholar at the American Council on Education, citing a study that "approximately 20 percent of veterans could not have gone to college without the GI Bill. I would conjecture the figure was much higher for African-American veterans. Besides, having come from families that were disproportionately poorer, most had been subjected to underfunded, segregated schools. However, when special accommodations were made and relatively open admissions policies were put in place, black veterans flocked to the colleges and universities and did well academically." At his own alma mater, Wayne State University in Detroit, Wilson recalled, "it is estimated that nearly a third of the veterans enrolled between 1946 and 1950 were African-Americans, and during those years, veterans were almost a majority of the school's students."

The northern and western colleges many blacks attended didn't keep racial census figures, at least not in any systematic fashion. Statistics for black colleges are the best indices for determining the numbers of Negroes who took advantage of the bill. In 1940, enrollment in black colleges was 1.08 percent of the U.S. college enrollment. By 1950, in a greatly expanded student population, it had almost tripled, to 3.6 percent. Overall enrollment in the Negro Land-Grant colleges after the war was 50 percent higher than before. More significantly, the number of veterans in the black colleges was double the entire 1937–38 enrollment. Partially because black colleges had been traditionally shortchanged in funding for building purposes, another federal bill, the Lanham Act of 1946, actually made proportionately more money available for construction and repair at black institutions. Acting under the law, the officers of the Commission of Education recognized the relatively large need of the Negro institutions, according to Wilson. Consequently, funds were distributed to institutions on the assumption that 33.4 square feet of construction was needed for veterans in black colleges as compared with 17.4 square feet in white schools. Nevertheless, despite the additional money for construction, black colleges had to turn away twenty thousand veterans for lack of space.

The shortage of seats was more than made up by colleges and universities in the North and West. "Black veterans with vouchers in hand, paid for by the federal government, were an attractive commodity to many institutions in the North that would not have welcomed them in vast numbers (nor could many have afforded to go before the war)," Wilson wrote. "The white colleges welcomed them and made special provisions to accommodate all of the veterans; they were given additional points on admission tests; in some instances, admission requirements were waived; they were given credit for special training received in the military; tutors were provided in recognition of the veterans being three to five years out of school; and, despite sometimes mediocre high school records, they were welcomed."

The special provisions, it should be noted, applied to many white veterans, not just blacks. As early as February 9, 1942, for example, the University of Wisconsin approved granting ten elective college credits to former enlisted men and fifteen to ex-officers. Wisconsin made other concessions, too. In March 1944, a veteran could even apply four special war credits to the sixteen high school credits needed for admission. If that wasn't enough to meet the admission requirements, a veteran could take an oral or written examination proving he was capable of college work. Credit was also given for college-level work completed in service schools and military training schools, and veterans were exempted from taking the physical education courses compulsory for other students. Wisconsin's medical school lowered admission requirements from three to two years of premed training. Refresher courses were offered in mathematics and English; a full-semester summer school was created; the engineering college operated on a trimester schedule with classes starting in March, July, and November.

The innovations and accommodations pleased some veteran students and didn't appeal to others. A navy officer, responding to a survey sent to former students by Columbia University, had mixed feelings about accelerated courses. "Education is too important to me to be rushed through," he wrote. "I want to have the feeling of leisure to do an honest job with the most valuable time of my life." A year-round trimester program would turn college into a factory, he thought. But a P-51 fighter pilot had a different attitude: "I remember how we used to think that a full year would be a tough grind, but it was probably laziness that prompted that feeling."

Robert A. Eubanks was a black veteran who wasn't the least bothered about going to college full time; he thrived on it. He was bright enough to have graduated in 1942 from high school at the age of fifteen. But he couldn't get a job because he was black and couldn't take advantage of a tuition-only scholarship to Howard University in Washington, D.C., because he didn't have enough money to live on. So he joined the army, and he heard about the GI Bill through word-of-mouth— as most veterans did—when he mustered out in 1946. Eubanks got into a year-round program at the Illinois Institute of Technology (ITT) and earned a degree in theoretical and applied mechanical engineering in 1950. Once again, his job-hunting forays ran up against whites-only hiring policies, so he stayed on at ITT, earning a master's and then a doctoral degree in 1953, all on the GI Bill. With the changing social climate after the *Brown* decision, he was able to get high-paying work in industry. Later, he was lured back to academia, first as a visiting professor at the University of Illinois. After six months, he was offered a tenured full professorship and stayed on until retirement in 1986, teaching and conducting research. "It's very hard to explain now how things were during the 1940s," Eubanks said in reflecting on this life. "The restrictions on blacks then were rough. The GI Bill gave me my start on being a professional instead of a stock clerk." . . .

As a matter of reality, with the great exception of the GI Bill of Rights, government programs to help people haven't directly given people the resources to help themselves. That was the GI Bill's greatest characteristic and accomplishment. It didn't have to appeal to shared human values and social goals by persuading people that institutions knew what was best for them. It gave the individuals the power to decide for themselves what was best for themselves and, at the same time, freed educational institutions to do what they did best, teach. It caused a silent revolution, not by the force of the state, but by using the resources of the state to encourage what George Mason spelled out in the Virginia Declaration much more explicitly than Thomas Jefferson did in the Declaration of Independence: the means of acquiring and possessing property for pursuing and obtaining happiness and safety. The GI Bill gave people the economic resources to train their minds, their most important property, and they went out and used it to pursue happiness and safety.

 ## For Further Study

1. In what specific ways did the GI Bill of Rights make higher education in America more democratic?

2. The essay suggests that some people believed that the effects of the GI Bill on American education would be unfortunate. What specific ill-effects do you suppose they were concerned about?

3. Name some of the problems that the presence of large numbers of veterans created for American colleges and universities and what adjustments these institutions made to accommodate these new students. Can you think of other problems that might have existed besides those mentioned in the selection?

4. In what ways were veterans different from their nonveteran fellow students? What special problems do you suppose they faced? Can you think of any advantages they may have had over their fellow students in their attempt to complete a college education successfully?

5. It has been said that the GI Bill of Rights may be the most successful piece of government-sponsored social policy ever enacted. Consider whether this is true in relation to other such policies as Social Security, Medicare, civil rights laws, and so forth. Can you see any negative features in the GI Bill of Rights?

For Further Reading

The books by Blum, Lingeman, Perrett, and Polenberg suggested for the previous selection all provide information about the hopes, worries, and expectations of GIs and the nation as a whole about their return to civilian life. Joseph C. Goulden, *The Best Years, 1945–1950* (1976) is an entertaining general account of the immediate postwar period. David R. B. Ross, *Preparing for Ulysses: Politics and Veterans During World War II* and the book from which this selection is taken, Michael J. Bennett, *When Dreams Came True: The GI Bill and the Making of Modern America* (1996) deal extensively with the political background of the GI Bill. Keith W. Olson, *The G. I. Bill, the Veterans, and the Colleges* (1974) is a detailed look at the impact of the Bill's educational benefits. Raymond Moley, Jr., *The American Legion Story* (1966) is a history of the nation's most influential veterans' organization, which played a crucial role in securing the passage of the GI Bill. Richard Severo and Lewis Milford, *The Wages of War: When America's Soldiers Came Home: From Valley Forge to Vietnam* (1989) compares the way the nation has treated the veterans of its major wars.

Part V

Affluence and Its Discontents

The material well-being of the American people in the decades since the end of World War II contrasts sharply with their poverty in the Great Depression of the 1930s. While not all Americans shared equally in the postwar prosperity, most enjoyed a standard of living far higher than that of previous generations. Furthermore, American influence abroad also reached its zenith following the end of World War II.

But the postwar decades were also marked by internal insecurities and divisions and external wars that belied the facade of confidence and contentment. In the Truman-Eisenhower years, from 1945 to 1960, the second Red Scare and the Korean War disturbed and divided the nation. Three assassinations in the 1960s, of John F. Kennedy, Robert Kennedy, and Martin Luther King, Jr., provided further proof that social and political stability did not necessarily go hand in hand with material prosperity and national power. Despite Lyndon B. Johnson's announcement of the "Great Society" and Richard Nixon's promise "to bring the American people together," developments from the mid-1960s to the late 1970s showed clearly that neither vision was being fulfilled. Instead, conflict and crisis seemed to rule. The 60s saw protest movements and bitter disagreements over the Vietnam War; the 70s, the energy crisis, and the Iranian hostage crisis. Public opinion polls showed that Americans were increasingly disillusioned with their society, particularly with their political institutions and leaders, as they showed by staying away from voting booths in increasing numbers in the 70s and 80s. On the other hand, there were indications that Americans were becoming increasingly interested in grassroots social and political movements that addressed immediate concerns close to home.

The essays in this section reflect the widely varying experiences of our nation since the end of World War II. The first describes conditions of life in urban neighborhoods in the years just after the war. The second deals with the impact of rock 'n' roll and especially the controversies it generated. Two essays are concerned with significant attacks on the status quo in the 1960s. One is on the civil rights movement, the other on the counterculture. The next essay examines the experiences of the soldiers who fought the Vietnam War. The last offers a detailed look at one example of a local campaign by the so-called religious right, a combination of political conservatism and evangelical or fundamentalist religion that emerged as a powerful political force in the 1970s and 1980s.

Chapter 17

Courtesy of the Worcester Historical Society

Downtown Worcester, Massachusetts, early 1950s. A typical commercial street of the period.

Urban Neighborhoods in Postwar America

Michael Johns

Apopular television program of the 1970s was set in the 1950s. The title, *Happy Days,* reflects not only nostalgia for a previous, presumably happier era but also the feelings of many Americans at the time. To be sure, the Cold War was an ever-present fact of life, and the prospect of nuclear destruction was terrifyingly real. Unresolved racial tensions gripped the nation, McCarthyism revealed the excesses that a fear of political dissent might lead to, and many commentators were disturbed by what they saw as a trend toward an all-encompassing and deadening conformity. Yet life for most Americans was quite pleasant when compared with what they had recently gone through. Americans of the 1950s had endured the worst depression and the largest foreign war that the nation had ever experienced and felt, understandably, that they were due for a little enjoyment. And they were able to afford it. During World War II there had been an unintentional and unforeseen redistribution of income that significantly improved the economic condition of the middle class. This became the foundation for an extended period of nearly uninterrupted prosperity. More Americans had more disposable income than ever before in the nation's history, and this affluence affected nearly all aspects of American life in the postwar period.

One important long-term consequence of the prosperity of the time was that many Americans, especially younger ones beginning their married lives, moved to the rapidly growing suburbs that ringed America's larger urban centers, and most accounts of American life in the postwar era place a heavy—and deserved—emphasis on this movement. Because the development of suburbia proved to have such profound consequences for many features of American life in the following decades, it is often forgotten that most Americans did not move to the suburbs—at least not right away—and that American cities retained much of the character that they had had prior to World War II and for some

time before that. In order to see the extent of the changes that suburban-
ization brought to the nation, it is essential to have a benchmark to measure from, and the following selection on American cities in the postwar period provides it.

"So complete is each neighborhood," observed E. B. White, "and so strong the
sense of neighborhood, that many a New Yorker spends a lifetime within the con-
fines of an area smaller than a country village." Writer Marya Mannes detected a
"structure" to the neighborhoods: "basically triangular" and consisting of "the relation of side street to avenue, of residence to commerce, of privacy to common
experience." To live in that structure, she felt, "is to be part of an intimate complex of people and services that form, as time goes on, a close familiar whole in
the midst of the great fragmentation which is the city." A recent memoir shows the
old neighborhood lending "a constancy, a consistency, a dependable texture to
everyday life."

Such images pervade memoirs about the 1950s, as well as books and magazines
written at the time. Neighborhood stores, after all, were small and were owned by
those who worked in them. Mothers stayed at home with their children. Sisters
and uncles lived a block over or a few streets away. Households were connected to
local schools, churches, union halls, and retail streets. One's neighborhood, in
other words, was basically the same thing as one's community. It was typically a
prosperous community, too, for the wages of both blue- and white-collar workers
rose steadily between the late '40s and the early '60s. . . .

Small stores, most of them run by their owners, drew people from the neighborhood's residential streets toward its main avenue, thereby creating a commercial focus for the area. Those stores supplied just about all of the area's everyday
needs, created a stable and personal world for shoppers and merchants, and
made local retail streets, or clusters of corner stores, the centers of neighborhood
social life. The commercial scene alone made the typical neighborhood of the
'50s a very different world from today's.

Most big cities had at least one residential district made up of tall apartment
buildings. Corner stores dominated every intersection. In some places, nearly
every block was lined with shops, stores, restaurants, and bars. These were "virtually self-sufficient" commercial worlds, writes E. B. White:

> A man starts for work in the morning and before he has gone two hundred yards he
> has completed half a dozen missions: bought a paper, left a pair of shoes to be soled,
> picked up a pack of cigarettes, ordered a bottle of whiskey to be dispatched in the
> opposite direction against his home-coming, written a message to the unseen forces

---

From Michael Johns, *Moment of Grace.*

of the wood cellar [where you placed your order for ice, coal, and wood on a pad outside], and notified the dry cleaner that a pair of trousers awaits call. Homeward bound eight hours later, he buys a bunch of pussy willows, a Mazda bulb, a drink, a shine—all between the corner where he steps off the bus and his apartment.

A more common type of neighborhood was made up of three-, four-, and five-story apartment buildings. Residents walked no more than five or six blocks to a major shopping street. In the Bronx, for example, East Tremont Avenue ran right through the center of the Tremont section of the borough. The avenue was "a bright, bustling mile" of butchers, bakers, delicatessens, laundries, coffee shops, and drug, grocery, clothing, and hardware stores. Until the 1950s, Brooklyn's Pitkin Avenue had "crowds of shoppers and strollers, day and evening." With its "banks, Woolworth's, classy shops, loan companies, Loew's Pitkin, the Yiddish theater, the Little Oriental restaurant," wrote Alfred Kazin in 1951, "it might be Main Street in any moderately large town." A man remembered Pitkin Avenue, after it had become the run-down commercial street of a slum, as "the best shopping street you could go to in the whole world. It was be-eee-you-ti-ful!" On Tremont and Pitkin, and on thousands of other commercial streets just like them, you bought your daily groceries, made an occasional purchase of furniture or clothing, met friends for coffee or lunch, went to the drug or hardware store, watched a movie, or had a drink.

The retail street gave focus to lower-density districts as well, like those comprised of row houses, bungalows, Victorian two-flats, or detached "triple-deckers." San Francisco's Richmond district was full of abutting houses and small apartment buildings on street corners. "Clement is the street," observed a journalist, "that unites them as a community. It is a street so warm, so *gemutlich,* so pleasant to shop, that first-time visitors often feel they have made a private discovery." The same could have been said of the commercial street that united St. Nick's parish in Chicago, a neighborhood of small, closely spaced, brick bungalows. The life of St. Nick's centered on Sixty-third Street, a retail strip that was especially dense and lively toward either end of the neighborhood. The street had a Walgreen's and a Kresge's, which were chain stores, but also a bank, a movie theater, a men's store, a shoe store, a candy store, a sporting-goods store, and a grocery store, all independently owned by local businessmen. Shoppers walked to these commercial clusters. Women wheeled shopping carts in the mornings, kids made late afternoon runs for fresh dinner bread, and couples and entire families took strolls on Monday and Thursday evenings, the weekday shopping nights. Such streets were open for at least one and often two nights a week in almost every big city during the '50s. Staying open at night was a way for neighborhood stores to compete with downtown nightclubs, department stores, and movie theaters, as well as with new shopping centers in suburbs.

Some of the neighborhoods made up of closely spaced single-family houses did not have a retail street and were served, instead, by an "oasis of local shops" on certain street corners. "Our neighborhood life," recalls Doris Kearns Goodwin, "converged on a cluster of stores at the corner of our residential area: the drugstore and butcher shop; the soda shop, which sold papers, magazines, and comics; the delicatessen; and the combination barber shop and beauty parlor." Bert Kemp's memoir *EB* describes a retail corner in Brooklyn that had, on one side, McDade's Saloon, Joe's Barber Shop, and Pease's candy store; across the street was Dubin's Drug Store, the Ideal Meat Market, Vick's Grocery, Wenn's Deli, and Gray's Real Estate: "Booze, beer, companionship, cigarettes, egg creams, ham sandwiches, pain relievers, and a shave and a haircut . . . what more could you ask? A man could live his entire life on that corner. And some men damn near did."

Not all neighborhood shopping districts were prosperous, pleasant, or safe. Plenty of poor whites lived near docks and rail lines, among warehouses and small factories, and in tenement districts that had housed several waves of immigrants. Such places had their share of decrepit buildings and littered sidewalks. Along the retail streets, writes novelist Irving Shulman, "blowzy housewives in soiled Hoover aprons and pajamas, over which they wore old coats frayed at the cuffs and hems, plodded to the bakeries, butcher shops, vegetable stands and groceries." Many of those old coats came from stores that sold "second-hand clothes, faded blouses and torn sweaters, uncalled-for laundry, yarns, threads, buttons, candles, penny hardware items, and old hats, coats, and ties." Some merchants allowed criminals the use of their bars, lunch counters, and pool rooms to run numbers or launder money. But mafiosi tended to be discreet, one man remembered, "and we weren't too aware of them." If hoodlums generally kept to themselves, they didn't think twice about roughing up a bookie who wasn't paying off, as in this scene from Shulman's novel *Cry Tough!*:

> The proprietor of the candy store, a balding man in a soiled apron, was placing packs of cigarettes in the racks on the wall behind the counter when the three of them entered. At the end of the counter, alone, hunched over the racing page of the next morning's *Daily Mirror,* sat a man who needed a shave. He wore a stained gabardine suit, with soiled jacket elbows, a blue sport shirt open at the throat, a light woven hat pushed back on his head, cheap white rayon hose with brown clocks, and brightly polished slip-on moccasins. The bookie's lips were blue in the neon light and his sharp nose appeared to be ferreting information out of the paper. . . . Larry's right fist, clenched around the roll of pennies, piled into the back of the bookie's head.

Despite differences in neighborhood size, wealth, or density, the commercial scenes in most neighborhood shared certain characteristics. One common trait that lasted throughout the '50s was the European flavor of many shops. Small bakeries featured the specialties of the neighborhood's dominant ethnic group: bagels, baklava, strudels, ryes, or rolls. Bars served the beer and hard liquor of the old country. Signs in German, Scandinavian, Polish, or Italian announced the restaurant's lunch specials. Plate-glass windows were lettered with the proprietor's name and shaded by a big canvas awning that said "delicatessen." Jewish delis had no ham or shrimp salad, of course. Instead, they grilled frankfurters and knishes in the window and filled their glass cases with rows of smoked meats, trays of garnishes, and bottles of soda and beer.

The commercial life of neighborhood stores was more direct and tactile than it would be in later years. The butcher cut your meat and the deli prepared its own dishes. The grocer sliced, measured, and weighed your order. He then took a thick-leaded pencil from behind his ear to

> tally the prices on the side of a brown paper bag plucked from the stack under the counter—he almost always knew the right size for the "order." Once the addition was done (and rechecked by adding *up* the column) he would lift his fingers like a concert pianist's and press down a group of keys, ringing up the total on his ornate, manually operated, cast-iron-and-bronze National Cash Register. . . . *Gzing*-GZING went the register, up into its glass-faced top went the numerical total . . . and out popped the wood-slatted cash drawer.

The butcher, deli owner, and grocer, as well as the hardware man and candy-store proprietor, knew more about their products than most store employees do today. So did the neighborhood's shoe-repair man, tailor or seamstress, and fixer of watches, clocks, radios, or television sets. Many proprietors hung a neon sign to announce the owner's name and the store's function—Jack's Men's Shop, Hank's Jewelry and Watch Repair, Goursau Meats, Brownie's Hardware, MacMinnis Stationery, Ratner Paints, Frank's Shoe Repair, Dino's Delicatessen, Ictor's Coffee Shop. The store owner, his daughter, or an artist who lived in the neighborhood painted window signs that advertised daily or weekly specials. Store-keepers naturally arranged their goods in some fashion, but without the extreme uniformity typical of today's chain stores. Many shoppers, according to a book about New York City, liked "to handle the profusion of merchandise" that was often "swinging overhead or stacked on every available inch of space."

Because so many stores were run by their owners, relations between customers and shopkeepers often became what a New Yorker at the time described as "friendship as well as habit." That is also how Doris Kearns Goodwin remembered it forty years later. The druggist, deli owner, and grocery man, she wrote, were "as much a part of my daily life as the families who lived on my street." Nearly everyone remembers the neighborhood stores as integral parts of their lives. Take Pease's candy store, described in Kemp's memoir *EB*. On your left as you entered Pease's was the cigar and cigarette counter; on your right were the comic book and magazine stands. Farther in on the left was the soda fountain, with its swivel-topped chairs, marble counter, and steel spouts. On the right side ran the penny and five-cent candy counters. Then came the back tables. The owner was Malcolm Pease. He was, according to one of the patrons,

> a benevolent dictator. He was a nice man who truly liked and enjoyed the kids, but he, like anyone else, had his limits. He would clear the place out when on a whim (or more likely a realization that his store was very crowded but he was not making very much money). AWRIGHT! EVERYBODY OUT. . . . Fifteen or twenty kids would dutifully spill out of Pease's candy store onto the sidewalk and congregate in small groups, talking and waiting. . . . Pretty soon the place was just as crowded as before.

Barbers, butchers, and grocers, like the owners of candy stores, drugstores, and delicatessens, watched the children grow up.

If merchants smiled at much of what they saw, they also shook their heads at some of it. Customers got on their nerves. A few teenagers shoplifted. A husband liked to insult his wife at the checkout counter. The heavy drinkers wanted more booze on credit. Plenty of shoppers, by the same token, disliked particular store owners. Some of them fell into foul moods, now and again yelling at a kid flipping through a comic book: "Hey, ya gonna read or ya gonna buy?" Others poked fun at certain customers, sometimes cruelly. A few were too burdened by life to care. Mrs. Sanew, for example, worked behind her candy-store counter seven days a week, from seven in the morning until ten at night. Writer Pete Hamill remembers her "pinched sour mouth" that knew no laughter. Every neighborhood also had its "empty-handed barber, the clerk in the antique store nobody ever comes into, the idle insurance salesman, the failing haberdasher— all of those," observed John Cheever, "who stand at the windows of the city and watch the afternoon go down."

In spite of a failing business, some rude merchants, and a few shoppers who shunned routine chit-chat, the commercial scene in the neighborhoods of the 1950s was overwhelmingly one of small shops run by owners who valued personal relationships with customers and of shoppers who valued their familiarity with merchants. Most women, like this one in Seattle, stuck to their local retail streets:

> I like to shop here in our neighborhood. . . . I try to buy at little places I know— where they will make things good for you and they won't be snotty. I may pay more sometimes by not looking for bargains, but the stores I know are good and if anything goes wrong they will take it back. I get personal attention and service because they know me. For example, I buy meat from a butcher I know—the meat isn't any cheaper there, but he always gives me choice cuts. Whenever I'm buying furniture I go to this one store in the neighborhood. I got my chest of drawers there a while back because the salesfellow was so darn nice.

Working-class women were especially tied to their local merchants. As a whole, they were less likely than middle- and upper-income women to classify themselves as "regular shoppers" in the downtown or as frequenters of new shopping centers in suburbs. A working-class woman who did like to shop downtown avoided "any of those small type shops" where the salesladies "try to make you feel that you can't walk out without buying something. They make you feel awful if you say you don't like something they have told you is nice. And they would certainly think it was terrible if you told them that you didn't have enough money to buy something."

The "salesfellow" who was "so darn nice," mentioned in the quote above, may have been unctuous. He may have turned to his partner, after a certain shopper left his store, and said, "Man, what a pain in the ass she is." But he, like she, lived in a commercial world where shopkeepers sold on credit, steady customers got better goods, and buyer and seller developed some trust. They talked about the merchandise, the weather, the new baby. The talk was superficial, but it was a predictable and genuine kind of superficiality. Even banks wanted close relations with customers. On Friday evenings or Saturday mornings, for example, neighborhood kids went to the local bank to fill their savings accounts with whatever remained from allowances, paper routes, and baby-sitting. Adults in one Chicago neighborhood went to the bank on every twelfth Friday to have quarterly dividends stamped in their books. There was no need to do this—dividends were automatically credited—but the bank encouraged the ritual to tighten its links with the community. Many shoppers valued familiarity with merchants because it gave them a feeling of trust, turned shopping into a minor social occasion, and made some of them think they were getting a good deal. Merchants, as they still do today, valued friendly relations with customers because they were good for business.

Itinerant peddlers, such as knife sharpeners and old-clothes buyers, added another dimension to this personal world of neighborhood commerce. They made weekly or monthly rounds along the side streets of many working-class districts. The clothes buyer, according to a magazine piece, yelled out, "I buy! Cash clothes!" He worked neighborhoods where the "housewives know him. When they hear his familiar cry, and they have clothes to sell, they lean from apartment windows and call, 'Hey, mister!' " A few customers, one buyer said, "look down on you. They show they don't like to deal with a peddler." Some bargained relentlessly and sent him away if they couldn't get their price. Others settled on a price easily and offered a chair and a cold drink on a hot day. The old-clothes buyer had to be friendly with the local tailor, druggist, or shoe-repair man, with whom he left his heavy package of clothes when he got to a neighborhood. After making the rounds, he returned to collect his stuff and took the trolley downtown, where he sold his goods to second-hand clothes dealers.

The local bar was as much of a neighborhood fixture as the deli, laundry, barber shop, produce stand, hardware store, funeral parlor, and pharmacy. The bartender knew most of the customers, bought a few of them a drink now and then, and went occasionally to a ball game with a couple of regulars. The porter was often a neighborhood hanger-on who cleaned up after the bar closed. If there was food, it was served by a local woman who cooked spaghetti and meatballs and maybe some roast chicken. Many bars participated in community activities. A Chicago cab driver, who in 1963 ended his career as a "neighborhood tavern keeper," talked about his former bar not only as a watering hole, but as a supporter of Little League baseball and a sponsor of a local softball team: "Every Sunday we'd have a game with a team from another neighborhood. We'd play for a half-barrel of beer. Then, after the game, they'd come over to my tavern and drink it." Other bars participated in less benign activities. The heyday of the saloon-keeper politician was long gone by the 1950s, but many tavern owners still had enough clout to obtain illegal building permits, fix parking tickets, get a Christmas turkey for a poor family, and procure jobs for a few of the locals as revenue clerks or park workers. Bar owners did such favors through "petty dictators" who were known to "run the show" in many working-class precincts. The recipient of a favor paid for it with his own vote and with those of his friends and relatives. Some neighborhood bars participated in even shadier exchanges, like peddling stolen property or engaging in payoff schemes with local cops, teamsters, and the association of jukebox operators.

Most neighborhood bars served men only. Some men stopped in each day for a couple of beers on their way home from work. A few spent Friday nights swapping war stories and watching the local fights on television. Others spent Saturday and Sunday afternoons watching baseball teams whose starting lineups, like the patrons of the bar, varied little from one year to the next. Adolescents became men in neighborhood bars by drinking with their buddies or by taking a girl to the one bar on the main street that had a little "class," thanks to its quiet back room or private booths. Every bar had its problem drinkers who routinely made their wives and kids nervous when they were late arriving home from work. On paydays, especially, many a young son was sent to the corner bar to fetch his dad. One of those boys later recalled how "it embarrassed his father to see his little son edge his way into that smelly saloon, hesitant, tentative, a little frightened, but determined to stick it out. And it didn't hurt any that the other men urged him to go home with his son." The scene in the bar was not always pleasant, but like nearly every other aspect of neighborhood commerce, it was always personal.

Writer Pete Hamill remembers trips downtown, to the beach, and to the other side of the city. "But it was to the Neighborhood that we always returned. Other neighborhoods were not simply strange; they were probably unknowable. I was like everybody else. In the Neighborhood I always knew where I was; it provided my center of gravity." The neighborhood provided residents their center of gravity because it was like a city in miniature. "In every neighborhood," remembered Chicago's Mike Royko,

> could be found all the ingredients of the small town: the local tavern, the funeral parlor, the bakery, the vegetable store, the butcher shop, the drugstore, the neighborhood drunk, the neighborhood trollop, the neighborhood idiot, the neighborhood war hero, the neighborhood police station, the neighborhood team, the neighborhood sports star, the ball field, the barber shop, the pool hall, the clubs, and the main street. . . . So, for a variety of reasons, ranging from convenience to fear to economics, people stayed in their own neighborhoods, loving it, enjoying the closeness, the friendliness, the familiarity, and trying to save enough money to move out.

The neighborhood was a bigger place back then because it offered almost everything residents needed and so included more of their lives than it does today. It was a smaller place, too, because it was so enclosed, even isolated, and therefore somewhat provincial and confining. Retail streets, full of owners who ran their own small businesses, certainly tied residents to their neighborhoods and helped create a sense of belonging and self-sufficiency. But it took more than commerce to consolidate the tightly knit communities of the late '40s, '50s, and early '60s. It also required (among other things) mothers at home, residents keeping company on stoops and porches, and teenagers at ease in an adult world.

A lot of social life took place on stoops. In a Chicago neighborhood, for example, a dozen people would sit in front of a house conducting several conversations at once or just watching the street. "You could have gone down the alley," a resident remembered of summertime, "and walked in the back door of every house and robbed people blind. Everybody was out on the front porch." More than 80 percent of the houses in another Chicago neighborhood had benches or couches on their porches in the late 1950s. So it was in other cities. "Everyone had a well-used stoop," a New Yorker remembers, where people talked, drank, bad-mouthed certain neighbors, watched the small children, encouraged stickball batters, and teased teenagers as they left for dates. Former residents of Philadelphia and Baltimore recall row-house porches full of women and kids during parts of the day. In San Francisco, neighbors chatted on the steep wooden steps of Victorians, while along Brooklyn's Eastern Parkway "men and women sat on benches and collapsible chairs, and caught up with the gossip."

Most residents sat outside to watch their kids play, see who walked by, or just wind down with the fading light. Some took to steps and porches because their houses and apartments were cramped or stuffy. Others did so because their dwellings were closed to outsiders: it is impossible, wrote an observer of a working-class neighborhood,

> to conceive of [many homes] as something other than a "woman's world." The curtains are of lace, the bedspreads are chenille, the furniture elaborate with design and doilies, the colors are light and delicate. Here, there is simply no place for a male with his dirty hands, informality, and coarse manners. . . . Ultimately, the home is a kind of ceremonial center used only at those rare moments when visitors are permitted to look into family life.

For all those reasons, neighborhood residents made good use of their stoops, porches, and sidewalks until at least the middle of the '50s. By then, most households had a television set, and "on summer nights," remembers Pete Hamill, "the streets were emptier, as each apartment lit up with a pale blue glow."

If many houses and apartments were a "woman's world," so too, in many ways, was the entire neighborhood. The vast majority of women did not earn wages. During the day, most women were either at home, shopping on the nearby retail strip, or visiting somewhere on the block. A woman describes life in her middle-class apartment building:

> The fathers went to their paid jobs early each morning, while we mothers organized days of housekeeping, child care, and plans for the evening, when the bread-winners would return. Mothers met in the lobby in the morning to take kids to the park, ending up eating lunch together. Once or twice a week a play group met in someone's apartment, mothers taking their turns overseeing the kids one week in order to free a couple of afternoons the next week.

The stoop, the block, the park, the retail street, the apartment building—these were the public places of women's lives in the neighborhood. A typical working-class mother, for example, met her longtime girlfriend on Thursdays at the local coffee shop and visited regularly with neighbors, a nearby in-law, or her sister or parents who lived a few streets away. One in four working-class women belonged to a local association of some sort. Mothers with school-age children tended to join the PTA. Some wives belonged to groups related to their husbands' work, like "fire ladies" or "policemen's pals." Many others lent time to their churches and synagogues. They went to weekly services, of course, and they (and some of their husbands) joined the church bowling team, volunteered to chaperone dances for teenagers, and helped organize summer trips for the children. In Catholic neighborhoods, especially, the parish—which offered weekly masses, parochial school, community-service groups, and links with the city's political machine—was nearly the same thing as the community. Like working-class women, middle-class women also met friends on the retail strip, volunteered at their church or school, and visited with neighbors and relatives. But they were more likely than women in the working class to go out of the neighborhood for a class or a reading group, volunteer at a museum, join the Rotary-Anns or Ki-wanitias, or meet friends downtown for lunch and shopping.

Mothers at home meant order in the household. The evening meal, for example, was a critical part of family life. The man came home from work, the kids assembled, the food was served. The meal meant continuity, a family routine, control over the children. It did not always mean happiness. Plenty of tyrannical fathers cowed their children, just as countless meals were eaten in anxious silence, broken only by the scraping of knives and forks and the occasional command to sit up straight or chew before swallowing. Whether pleasant, boring, or painful, the evening meal was rarely missed. Nor did the average family dine out often. There were fewer neighborhood restaurants back then, and fast-food franchises had yet to change the way Americans eat.

Mothers imposed order on public life as well. They constituted, along with the local merchants, the neighborhood's informal police. Youngsters knew that the neighborhood mothers, as well as the merchants who knew those mothers, watched almost everything they did on the block, at corner stores, and along the retail street. There was plenty to watch. High birth rates after the war resulted in a lot of kids in the late '40s and '50s. Those children participated in fewer organized activities than they do today, and so had more friends in the neighborhood and made regular use of stoops, alleys, sidewalks, and side streets as play areas. A kid's world, it was said, had two parts: the "block," where every stoop and alley had been explored and every neighbor and shopkeeper were known, and the alluring yet unknown "beyond," which was everywhere and everyone else. . . .

Continuity . . . was a dominant theme in most white neighborhoods during the late '40s and '50s. In Pittsburgh's Italian and Polish districts, for example, about a quarter of all houses in 1960 had a resident who had been living there for at least thirty years. Many houses without such long-standing inhabitants were occupied by the former owner's son or daughter, who was usually a young parent. We tend to think that every young couple moved to suburbs during the '50s. But in Pittsburgh, at least, the number taking over their parents' city houses exceeded those moving to suburbs. And of those who left their childhood houses but stayed in the city, nearly half continued to live in the neighborhood. "The pull of the ethnic neighborhood and the services it provided," concluded the authors of a study about Pittsburgh, "obviously remained strong. Even the so-called attractions of the suburbs and the threat of a black incursion that supposedly caused many to flee the city in the 1950s failed to lure the second-generation immigrant from his neighborhood."

That analysis agrees with casual comments, like this one, made in magazines at the time: "The neighborhood, in North Philadelphia, is lower middle-class economically, but most of the families own their own homes. Most of the men work at skilled trades and most of the women stay home and take care of their houses. Many of them grew up in the neighborhood." Even those who moved to suburbs kept ties, for a while at least, to the old neighborhood. Young couples visited their parents or siblings on weekends. Churches and synagogues were crowded with former residents during holidays. Some suburbanites still shopped on the old retail street for ethnic foods or because they knew the shopkeepers. Local clubs had dues-paying members who no longer lived in the neighborhood of their youth.

Most neighborhoods were quite settled down in the '50s. Merchants and customers got to know and sometimes trust each other. If most neighbors were not friends, they had grown accustomed to one another over the years. Bonds were strengthened by parents' embellishments on the neighborhood tales they passed to their children. A grocer could playfully remind a young mother, who struggled with her willful toddler in his store, what a little brat she had been twenty years earlier. Most of the neighborhoods had settled down ethnically as well. That is not to say cities lost their ethnic flavor. Many, in fact, were still accretions of little ethnic nations. Detroit, for example, was described in a 1956 magazine article as "a city of pockets" with "a variety of nationalities and races." The "old identifications" and the "pressure of old prejudices" still bound people to their neighborhoods. "Go that way, past the viaduct," Mike Royko wrote of white Chicago in the 1950s, "and the wops will jump you, or chase you into Jew town. Go the other way, beyond the park, and the Polacks would stomp on you. Cross those streetcar tracks, and the Micks will shower you with Irish confetti from the brickyards. And who can tell what the niggers might do?"

But ethnic identities and territorial loyalties slackened after the war. "No one can say that all is love and kisses in this grand mixture," wrote Jacques Barzun in 1954:

> there are two sides of the railroad track and on one side the poorer group, very likely ethnic in character, is discriminated against. But at what a rate these distinctions disappear! In Europe a thousand years of war, pogroms and massacres settle nothing. Here two generations of common schooling, intermarriage, ward politics, and labor unions create social peace.

The grand mixture in American cities had always meant the amalgamation and eventual blanching of incoming strains of European cultures. But that mix, as Barzun implies, had become a nearly uniform blend by the 1950s. Only five million foreigners entered the United States between 1926 and 1960. Five million came between 1850 and 1870, another five million came in the 1880s alone, and one million came each year between 1906 and 1915. The percentage of foreign-born residents in a typical city was halved between 1920 and 1950. The percentage fell further in the '50s, when most of the foreign-born were in later stages of their lives. The slowing of immigration starved ethnic culture. The number of ethnic theaters and musical organizations decreased after the Second World War. Social halls entertained only the older people. Ethnic newspapers folded; although a few survivors still provided information on the old country, the local churches, and the social affairs of the particular group in question, the proliferating English-language weeklies reported on their retail districts, displayed ads for downtown stores, and supplied information about educational opportunities and social-service agencies.

While the lack of fresh immigrants weakened the cohesion of what a writer called the "nationality groups," the neighborhoods gained a new kind of coherence during the '40s and '50s. Fewer arrivals and departures allowed people and cultural patterns to settle into place. Neighborhoods also became more tightly bound to the rest of the city. Every home, block, and retail street, in other words, was becoming like the others, as English became more widespread, ties to the old country frayed, and more people adhered to the rules, norms, and culture of American society. The gathering uniformity was a regular topic of books and magazine pieces. It was quickened by a federal government that expanded its role in the lives of city people, by the experiences of millions of second-generation boys in World War II, and by a postwar economy that featured a huge manufacturing sector, a big union movement, and an expanding mass market.

Alfred Kazin was part of this finer blending of what Barzun called the "grand mixture." Kazin grew up in a Jewish neighborhood in the 1920s and 1930s. "We were of the city," he wrote, "but not somehow in it. Whenever I went off on my favorite walk to Highland Park in the 'American' district to the north, on the border of Queens, and climbed the hill to the old reservoir from which I could look straight across to the skyscrapers of Manhattan, I saw New York as a foreign city." As a boy, he could not know that Manhattan and his Brooklyn neighborhood were, as he later put it, "joined" in him. But by the '40s he was not only "of the city" but also fully "in it," and so could write *On Native Grounds*, a now-classic account of the history of American literature. Kazin wrote not about Jews or the immigrant experience, but about the greatest of American writers. In so doing he went from being an ethnic outsider living in a Brooklyn neighborhood to being an insider living in Manhattan and writing about American literature. In 1951, Kazin wrote about his childhood community as the distant past. He did so, in part, because many of the Jews had left and taken with them much of the Jewishness of the place. He did so, as well, because the old neighborhood's people and culture were being folded into the blended American life that he personified.

Kazin's story resembles that of millions of second-generation immigrants who came of age in cities during the '30s, '40s, and '50s. They had ties to Europe through their parents, grandparents, and aunts and uncles, but they were home-grown. They grew up in American cities that for the first time were not significantly influenced by recent newcomers from Europe. They had fought a monumental war across two oceans. So even if, as a writer put it in 1955, the "nationality groups remain well organized around a persistent, intense sense of identification that spans the gulf between generations," the ethnic "ghettos" of American cities had clearly "shrunk" since the war.

They shrank in population: many older immigrants retired or died in the '50s, and second- and third-generation Americans took their places. They shrank culturally, too. The folk songs of the old country, for example, were losing out to Bing Crosby, Frank Sinatra, Ella Fitzgerald, and the big bands. What was left of ethnic theater had little chance against *Dragnet, The Honeymooners,* and *I Love Lucy.* Foreign-language newspapers lost their audiences to *Life* and *Reader's Digest.* Everyone who grew up in America during the '30s, '40s, and '50s grew up on baseball and the movies. Even though delicatessens sold ethnic dishes and some mothers cooked meals from the old country, more and more people ate chops and meatloaf, drank orange juice that had been frozen, and prepared their food from cans and boxes. So while some stores and eateries retained "the flavor of their homeland," it was observed that "many others strive to become modern and meet the demands of a new generation." Even the churches lost some of their cultural identity. Most were built between the late 1800s and early 1900s and were still fixtures in the neighborhoods. Some had even grown larger and richer after the war. But the inveterate sectarianism of most Protestant denominations blended into a larger brand of Protestantism. The patron saint and national origin of a Catholic parish meant little to native-born Americans. Fewer services were conducted in Greek, Polish, German, Latin, or Hebrew.

American culture has been built on the assimilation of newcomers. But assimilation quickened and deepened in the 1940s and 1950s, when city neighborhoods became more settled and cohesive than ever. When in the city, remembers Newark native Philip Roth, you might have thought of yourself as a Newark Jew, a Newark Pole, or a Newark Italian, because those designations still meant something in the neighborhoods. But once outside the neighborhood, and certainly once outside the city, you were just an American. Saul Bellow caught the mood, in 1949, with his opening line in *The Adventures of Augie March:* "I am an American, Chicago born." . . .

In many ways, those neighborhoods were fine arrangements for living. The stoop, the block, and the retail street, along with the church, school, and union hall, made an intimate and nearly complete little world that had a certain stability about it. But if residents were often kind and generous, they could just as easily spread gossip, resent a neighbor's success, believe women belonged in the house, mistrust those who dressed differently, suspect an honest Jewish merchant of cheating them, despise the upstairs couple for fighting on Saturday nights, and hector the black family across the street. All that familiarity, in other words, bred as much contempt as it generated respect. The sense of belonging, which so many people remember so fondly, also meant knowing your place—or paying a price.

Despite its faults, the typical neighborhood did provide its residents with security, familiarity, and stability. A second-generation Irish Catholic, whose father was a mailman, wrote the following about a part of San Francisco's Mission district:

> We were dominated completely by family and church and we were absolutely secure. Every one of our relatives from both sets of grandparents to each of our many cousins lived within walking distance of each other's houses. . . . Our neighborhood was our world. Although there were occasions when we took the J Streetcar or the 26 or 14 bus downtown, we rarely visited other districts of The City. . . . Our church and school were only a few blocks away and nearby Mission Street offered complete shopping and entertainment. Charley, the grocer on the corner of 26th and San Jose Avenue who gave us end pieces of bologna and salami before he shooed us out the door, had been on the same corner when my father was a boy. There was an overpowering sense of continuity. We were "Wishie's kids" or "Florence's girls" without need for further identification.

Such images of neighborhood life explain why 125 people who grew up in a residential district in Buffalo attended a *neighborhood* reunion in 1984—some twenty-five years after they had moved out.

For Further Study

1. Compare the picture of urban neighborhoods in this selection with the one drawn in the earlier selection by Nasaw. What is similar and different in the urban conditions that the authors describe? Compare the picture to the situation that currently exists. What are the similarities and differences? How do the neighborhoods described by the author of this selection resemble or differ from the neighborhood you live in?

2. One of the forces that helped to undermine the sorts of neighborhoods the author describes was the movement of large numbers of people out of central cities to the suburbs. What do you suppose the people who moved were looking for that they could not find in the neighborhoods they left behind? And what do you suppose they might have missed about the old neighborhoods after they left them?

3. What forces does the author mention as being responsible for the decrease in the distinctive ethnic flavoring of many of America's neighborhoods?

4. Consider what the author says about the role women played in the neighborhoods. What does this imply about the gender roles of that time?

For Further Reading

The following are general works on postwar America: Charles C. Alexander, *Holding the Line: The Eisenhower Era, 1952–1959* (1975); John Patrick Diggins, *The Proud Decades*

(1988); Eric F. Goldman, *The Crucial Decade—and After: America, 1945–1960* (1960); David Halberstam, *The Fifties* (1993); Marty Jezer, *The Dark Ages* (1982); William L. O'Neill, *American High: The Years of Confidence, 1945–1960* (1986). Jon Teaford, *The Twentieth-Century American City* (1986) is a general urban history. Jan Morris, *Manhattan '45* (1987), Doris Kearns Goodwin, *Wait till Next Year* (1997), and William Graebner, *Coming of Age in Buffalo* (1992) are accounts of what American city life was like in the postwar period based in part on the personal experiences of the authors. Jane Jacobs, *The Death and Life of Great American Cities* (1989) offers fascinating descriptions and analyses of urban life. St Clair Drake and Horace Cayton, *Black Metropolis* (1945, reprinted, 1993) tells the story of African Americans in the city. The book from which this selection is taken, Michael Johns, *Moment of Grace: The American City in the 1950s* (2003), besides talking about neighborhoods, also describes downtowns and many features of suburbia.

Chapter 18

Bettman/CORBIS

Fans gather in New York City to see Elvis Presley, "the king of rock 'n' roll", in his movie debut.

That Old Time Rock 'n' Roll

GLENN C. ALTSCHULER

The story goes that in the 1950s American popular music was stagnating in the worn-out banalities of the past until one day, down in Memphis, Tennessee, record entrepreneur Sam Phillips decreed, "Let there be Elvis!" and, lo, American music and American culture were forever changed. Rock 'n' roll was here. To stay?

Many contemporaries certainly hoped not. Their attitude is captured in the overheated language of Jack Lait and Lee Mortimer: "Teenagers speak their own mystic tongue, unintelligible to adults but understood by kids throughout the country. Their cells are in juke-box joints, soda dispensaries, and hot record shops. . . . Like a heathen religion, it is all tied up with tom-toms and hot jive and ritualistic orgies of erotic dancing, weed-smoking and mass mania, with African jungle background." Teenagers had become a focus of concern during World War II, when the growth of defense industry boom-towns had swamped the ability of many local school districts to provide adequate schooling and when the absence of men in the Armed Forces and of women at work had deprived many American children of the adult supervision they normally received. So juvenile delinquency became an issue, and people began to look at adolescents with a wary eye, expecting them to be a problem. The pattern continued into the postwar period, where youth gangs, sexual misbehavior among teenagers, and other departures from behavior that was thought to be normal and respectable became, often literally, front-page news.

Postwar affluence was also involved. It trickled down to teenagers, and some of those who had goods and services to sell suddenly realized that teens might constitute a large and potentially very profitable market. But mostly those interested in the teen market turned to music. Rock 'n' roll became the music of teenage America and an important social issue in itself, as parents and other social critics and commentators professed to be amazed, bewildered, and most of all mortified by this new and unprecedented phenomenon.

White southern conservatives were especially likely to find sinister significance in the unmistakable connection between rock 'n' roll and black rhythm and blues. In their eyes, it was proof positive that rock 'n' roll was a Communist plot to promote race mixing—just like the emerging civil rights movement. Others decried what seemed to them to be its complete lack of musical merit, either in its tunes or its lyrics, and saw it as a debasement of American culture in the name of commerce and corporate profits. Some saw it as an example of teenagers' rebellion linked to their willful disregard of and disdain for the standards and tastes of their parents.

But the feature that drew the most attention and caused the greatest concern was the perceived sexuality of rock 'n' roll. The lyrics of some rock 'n' roll songs were more obviously suggestive than those of mainstream popular music and the on-stage antics of some performers—most notably Elvis Presley—struck many observers as much too overtly erotic for the impressionable eyes of the teens in the audience. The fear was, of course, that continued exposure to such influences would awaken or strengthen teenagers' sexual impulses and make it even more difficult for them to control their raging hormones in a proper way. The following selection discusses the concerns that rock 'n' roll created and the attempted solutions to the problems that many saw in it. NOTE: *Billboard* and *Cash Box*, referred to in the following selection, are both magazines that deal with the entertainment industry.

In the '50s, rock 'n' roll became the focal point for anxiety that cultural life in the United States had become sexualized and teenagers addicted to the pleasures of the body. An ideology of abstinence, strenuously and sometimes stridently asserted, and the banishing of bedrooms from television underscored the depth and pervasiveness of that concern. Many adults feared that the weakening of traditional morality, diminished authority of parents, clergymen, and teachers, and availability of condoms and penicillin were making promiscuity safe, accepted, and universal to the post-World War II generation. Over the course of the decade, for example, all but two states dropped laws prohibiting the dissemination of contraceptive information or devices. At the same time, rock 'n' roll was demonstrating the power of the libido, as the music pulsated, the guitarist fondled his instrument, and the singer undulated sensuously. Rock 'n' roll seemed to be an anti-inhibitor, provoking erotic vandalism.

In several ways, '50s rock 'n' roll was less than its critics feared. The music rarely endorsed sex outside of established relationships. Rock 'n' roll was also quite traditional with respect to the sexual roles of males and females. While weighing in against sexual repression and prudery, rock 'n' roll set sexuality in a context of love and marriage. Thus . . . rock 'n' roll operated as a form of sexual control as well as a form of sexual expression. Nonetheless, parents made no mistake in identifying the subversive sexual charge in the music. Although it was criticized, softened, and censored in the service of the status quo, rock 'n' roll was pivotal in a reassessment of sexual attitudes and behavior that only seemed to spring out of nowhere in the 1960s. . . .

To many Americans, rhythm and blues was . . . a manifesto in the movement to repeal sexual reticence. Before R&B, popular songs used clichés and euphemisms to hint at sexual passion. Occasionally commented on but rarely criticized, the approach was similar to that employed by film directors when they showed a couple kissing, then faded out to a scene of the surf pounding on some rocks near the shore. The musical equivalent, "If I Knew You Were Coming I'd've Baked a Cake," Eileen Barton's hit in 1951, may or may not have reminded listeners of more than Sara Lee. That year, Rosemary Clooney was probably not thinking of a Hershey bar when she invited her boyfriend to "Come on-a my house/I'm gonna give you candy."

R&B lyrics, as we have seen, left rather less to the imagination. As long as the music was confined to the "black specialty market," latenight spots, and "out and out barrel houses," objections were few and far between, but as R&B entered the pop culture mainstream, a campaign against crudity was launched. Several songs were singled out. Recorded in 1951, "Sixty Minute Man," by the Dominoes, reached number 1 on the R&B charts and remained a best-seller for thirty weeks. Lead singer Clyde McPhatter made clear how the protagonist of the song spent his time: "If your man ain't treatin' you right, / Come up and see your Dan / I rock 'em, roll 'em all night long; / I'm a sixty minute man." In a provocative bass voice, Bill Brown added the chorus: "There'll be fifteen minutes of kissin' / Then you'll holler, please don't stop / There'll be fifteen minutes of teasin', / And fifteen minutes of squeezin' / And fifteen minutes of blowin' my top." In the background, as Brown sang, McPhatter sighed, more than once, "Don't stop."

Equally provocative were three hits by lead singer and songwriter Hank Ballard and the Midnighters in 1954. The group had scored modestly with a recording of Johnny Otis's "Every Beat of My Heart" and the erotic "Get It" in 1953. Drawing on the latter in a song tentatively titled "Sock it To Me, Mary," Ballard got a new idea when Annie Smith, the pregnant wife of the Midnighters' sound engineer, visited the studio. "Work with Me, Annie" leaped to number 1 on the R&B charts. In a high-pitched tenor voice, somewhat reminiscent of Clyde McPhatter, Ballard delivered the raunchy lyric: "Annie, please don't cheat, / Gimme all my meat, / Oo-oo-wee, so good to me; / Work with me, Annie." The group followed with "Sexy Ways": "Wiggle, wiggle, wiggle, wiggle / I just love your sexy ways; / Upside down, all around, / Any old way, just pound, pound, pound." Then, exploiting the success of "Work with Me, Annie," the Midnighters put an exclamation point on an extraordinary year with another R&B number I, "Annie Had a Baby." According to Syd Nathan, president of King Records, the distributor of "Annie Had a Baby," the response to the song was so great, sixteen presses worked twelve hours a day for weeks to produce platters.

With evidence that the "Annies" and other "smutty" songs were "being listened to and purchased by impressionable teen-agers almost exclusively," a campaign to "clean up filth wax" swept the country in 1954 and 1955. The crusaders focused most of their attention on distributors, record stores, and radio stations. They asked voluntary compliance with a ban on producing, selling, or playing dirty records. The initial response was mixed. A group of disc jockeys in the East, *Billboard* reported with evident approval, formed a club pledged to keep filthy records off the air, thereby signaling the independents and the major record companies not to manufacture more of them. Spokesmen for the group singled out records in which "rock," "roll," or "ride" did not "deal with the rhythmic meter of the tune." Although the club was "not an association in any formal sense," *Billboard* expected it "to have considerable influence in the R&B field." On the other hand, *Billboard* editors acknowledged that many in the industry "wondered what all the fuss is about" and declined to take any action.

The would-be censors did not trust the market. Recognizing that the very publication of the Top Ten gave a boost to every song on it, regardless of content, *Billboard* defended as a service to the industry its practice of showing what records were selling and what records were played in jukeboxes. But, the editors cautioned, "records on the chart should be listened to before they are played on the air, and if any of them are offensive, they should not be used." Any song denied airtime, they predicted, "will soon be a thing of the past."

The editors of *Cash Box* pondered the perils of popularity as well. "Naturally you can market smut," they agreed. "No one denies that." For this reason, R&B record companies, which "had claimed repugnance at the thought of dirty records, disclaimed any intention of ever releasing such filth, and shedding tears at the hurt and degradation it causes the Negro people, now vie for the 'filth' market." And jukebox operators, "without full consideration and study," were placing discs, "some of which feature double entendre lyrics," in locations frequented by teenagers. Although R&B records were gaining popularity throughout the nation, *Cash Box* warned, "every word in them is being carefully scrutinized, every phrase searched for subtle meanings." These were ominous signs for the long-term profitability of rhythm and blues.

Cash Box promised dire consequences if the industry continued to turn out dirty records to make "the quick buck." Negroes would be the first and worst casualties. After decades, rhythm and blues was making inroads into pop music so that the "buyer of 1954 recognizes and desires its beat, melody and artists. But this is only the beginning. Complete acceptance is not here yet." In fact, several jukebox operators were now refusing to place R&B tunes in their machines, while others warned that they would close down establishments transformed into "instruments of an immoral character by smutty recordings." Because of the onus attached to it, "the entire Rhythm and Blues field" faced ruin.

Ruin might come in many forms, and *Cash Box* counted the ways. As complaints from parents poured in, amidst almost "universal condemnation by schools, churches and crusading newspapers," pressure was building for the industry to censor itself as comic book manufacturers recently had, with a "hurriedly appointed czar at a huge salary," or, even worse, for each state to set up its own censorship board. Either approach would burst the bubble of prosperity the industry currently enjoyed. *Cash Box* also invoked "a sociological problem," juvenile delinquency. Until recently, the editors claimed, the music business had fought delinquency by gathering kids in wholesome places and letting them have fun under the proper supervision: "What a disaster it would be if suddenly the idea were implanted in the minds of educators and parents that records, instead of ameliorating delinquency conditions, were actually contributing to them."

Fortunately, a solution was at hand. While dirty records ultimately killed off the market for themselves and all R&B music, "R&B records can be hits without being dirty—as a majority of them have shown." As they achieved widespread acceptance among pop audiences, clean records would regain respect throughout American society for the industry as a whole.

Organized by groups as diverse as the National Piano Tuners Association, the National Ballroom Operators Association, and the Catholic Church, the censorship movement picked up steam. In the Midwest, Catholic high schools organized a "Crusade for Decent Disks," bombarding radio stations with tens of thousands of letters listing objectionable rhythm and blues songs. Chicago's WGN responded by establishing a board to review the lyrics of every song before permitting a DJ to play it. In New England, representatives from six radio stations formed a record censorship board, inviting religious leaders and journalists to join it. A Crime Prevention Committee in Somerville, Massachusetts, supervised by the police department, banned several R&B tunes, including the "Annie" discs, from jukeboxes. Radio stations in the South responded in a similar way to complaints about "off-color songs." WDIA in Memphis prepared a tape for callers requesting songs that had been banned: "WDIA, your goodwill station, in the interest of good citizenship, for the protection of morals and the American way of life, does not consider this record fit for broadcast. . . ."

The U.S. Senate and House of Representatives got into the act as well. Senator Pat McCarren, Democrat of Nevada, and Representative Ruth Thompson, Republican of Michigan, drafted bills forbidding the transportation or mailing in interstate commerce of any "obscene, lewd, lascivious, or filthy publication, picture, disc, transcription or other article capable of producing sound." Violators were subject to a fine of as much as $5,000, a prison term of up to five years, or both.

The bills did not become law, but the furor over "smutty songs" had a significant impact on popular music. Although critics continued to complain, often vociferously, about "leerics," 1954 marked the end, at least for a time, of sexually explicit R&B songs. "Annie," Arnold Shaw quipped, got a makeover and lessons in deportment. While the Midnighters's "Annie's Aunt Fannie" flopped, Georgia

Gibbs's "Dance with Me, Henry," a desexualized white cover of "Work with Me, Annie," became a Top Ten hit of 1955. The Midnighters tried again, this time with "Henry's Got Flat Feet," a tame, lame response to "Dance with Me, Henry." Neither critics nor fans noticed or cared.

Determined to be safe rather than sorry, record companies commissioned new lyrics for dozens of R&B songs. The transformation of "Shake, Rattle, and Roll" illustrates their thoroughness. Written by Charles Calhoun and originally recorded by Joe Turner, the song was sexually suggestive: "Well, you wear low dresses, / The sun comes shinin' through / I can't believe my eyes, / That all of this belongs to you." The version released by Decca in 1954 was dramatically different, as Bill Haley explained: "We take a lot of care with lyrics because we don't want to offend anybody. The music is the main thing, and it's just as easy to write acceptable words." Apparently concluding, as had the producers of TV sitcoms in the '50s, that if you can't stand the heat, you should get out of the bedroom, Decca scrubbed the song until it was squeaky clean: "You wear those dresses, / Your hair done up so nice / You look so warm, / But your heart is cold as ice." Omitted entirely was the steamy refrain: "I said over the hill, / And way down underneath / You make me roll my eyes, / And then you make me grit my teeth."

By early 1955, *Billboard* was reporting that "most of the R&B discs are comparatively dirt free." *Cash Box* changed its tune as well, expressing consternation at the continuing castigation of rhythm and blues and rock 'n' roll by "sensation-seeking" newspapers uninterested in the fact that "rhythm and blues tunes are just another form of music and no more off color than a lot of pop tunes." Dismayed by efforts in Boston and Chicago to intimidate disc jockeys through organized letter-writing campaigns, *Cash Box* editors pleaded with station managers not to "knuckle down and take the easy way out" because they feared a loss of prestige, listening audience, and advertisers.

The about-face of industry insiders was due, to a great extent, to the sanitizing of songs, but it was a response as well to the emergence of rock 'n' roll as a mass culture phenomenon. Whiter than R&B, rock 'n' roll could also be marketed as more wholesome. *Cash Box* took its name for a reason. "What the record industry needs," its editors claimed, with dollar signs dancing in their eyes, "is a change of attitude to coincide with its change of stature. . . . The point is, let's stop being unfair to ourselves. Let's stop knocking the products we create. An Elvis Presley, whether you like his style or don't, is a great thing for the record industry. Let's devote the energy we would spend in hating the guy to trying to develop several more who will sell records at the pace that he does." During the second half of the '50s, publicists labored to do just that, by "discarding improper material immediately" and associating performers and performances with good, clean fun. Examples abound. To combat the negative connotations associated with rock 'n' roll, Mercury Records sent the Platters on tour under the banner "Buck Ram Presents Happy Music" with a "Happy Beat for Happy Feet." Several disc jockeys invited listeners to phone in "Negative Requests," promising not to play any of the records they vetoed. To win over adults concerned that rock 'n' roll encouraged

sexual liaisons, the owners of radio stations and record companies helped organize, fund, and supply performers for "canteens" for teenagers who might otherwise meet "on the corner in the light of a dim street lamp," a place that "lends itself to brooding. To dangerous thoughts. To sudden, sorrowful acts." These rock
'n' roll canteens allowed youths to vent their "energies, enthusiasms, emotions,"
providing places for dancing, under appropriate supervision, sipping cool soft
drinks, and talking and laughing with other boys and girls.

Efforts to gain acceptance for rock 'n' roll among adults reached into the style
and content of the music itself. There were at least two streams of rock 'n' roll.
Some performers encouraged an association between rock 'n' roll, foreplay, and
intercourse. This stream did not disappear. But rock 'n' roll aimed a second,
more mainstream musical fare at young teens who were, presumably, less interested in earthy, graphic, coital connections. "Work with Me, Annie" and "Shake,
Rattle, and Roll" to the contrary notwithstanding, Bruce Pollock has recalled, at
most Friday night school dances the boys stood on one side of the gym, staring at
their shoelaces, while the girls peeked across the hall, then kicked off their shoes
and danced with each other. These thirteen- and fourteen-year-olds, experiencing
for the first time a crush, an awkward approach, a betrayal, or a breakup, were fascinated by music that spoke to their feelings. Smitten with the idea of eternal love,
as they experienced impermanent, even fleeting relationships, young teens encountered immortality, bliss, and loss in songs with the titles "Earth Angel," "Teen
Angel," "Altar of Love," "The Book of Love," "The Chapel of Love," and "Heaven
and Paradise."

Although he was a bit too old to be a rock 'n' roll pinup, Chuck Berry found in
"Sweet Little Sixteen" (1958) an apt and funny way to describe these boys and
girls, impatient to be adults: "Sweet little sixteen, she's got the grown-up blues /
Tight dresses and lipstick, she's sportin' high-heeled shoes. / Oh, but tomorrow
morning she'll have to change her trend / And be sweet sixteen and back in class
again." Tommy Sands had the looks as well as the lyrics. Along with Pat Boone, he
became the paradigmatic idol of wholesome young teens. "As uncomplicated as
most of the songs he sings," according to *Time* magazine, Sands did not smoke or
drink, lived with his mother in a four-room apartment, and confessed, with "his
brown eyes watering," that in his opinion "all religions are the greatest." Recorded
for Capitol Records, Sands's "Teenage Crush" climbed to number 3 in 1957, when
the singer was twenty years old. Like its sequel, "Goin' Steady," released that same
year, "Teenage Crush" captured the uncertainty, fragility, and demand for autonomy of youngsters uninitiated in the ways of love: "They call it a teenage crush, /
They don't know how I feel. . . . They've forgotten when they were young, / And
the way they tried to be free."

Much to the dismay of performers and industry executives, this tender, teeny-
bopper music did not escape scrutiny and censorship. Anxious about challenges
to their authority and suspicious that their own children might be ticking sexual
time bombs, many adults in the '50s found *all* rock 'n' roll music dangerous. In
1958, the Catholic Youth Center in Minneapolis demanded that DJs stop playing

Elvis's "Wear My Ring Around Your Neck" and Jimmie Rodgers's "Secretly." The lyrics, CYC officials pointed out, sanctioned going steady without parental approval. As these songs reached twelve- and thirteen-year-olds, they might accelerate the process of establishing permanent relationships between boys and girls who were not emotionally or physically prepared for them.

The same concerns motivated Bostonians to ban "Wake Up, Little Susie." Featuring a soft, harmonic country rock, the Everly Brothers song reached the top of the charts in 1957. It concerned Susie and her boyfriend, who fall asleep as they watch a dull movie in a neighborhood theater and then awake to realize that Susie has stayed out well past her curfew. What should she say to her irate parents, who will not be inclined to believe the innocent truth? In "Wake Up, Little Susie," as in "Bye Bye Love," Don and Phil Everly's other smash hit in '57, parents heard the narcissism and even petulance of teenagers. They also heard themselves stigmatized as suspicious and unreasonable, their rules undermined. When boyfriends woke up their little Susies, parents believed, sexual innocence was at risk.

To blunt these attacks, marquee rock 'n' rollers took to the offensive. Pat Boone became the principal spokesman for the music as wholesome entertainment. Clean-shaven, dressed in white sweaters and white bucks, a family man and a Christian, Boone came out of central casting as the model teenager. One look at him, and no parent could read sex into his songs. Onstage and in his films, fan magazines revealed, Boone refused to kiss any woman other than his wife, Shirley. No wonder one magazine called him "the first teen-age idol that grandma can dig too." With considerably more acid, Frank Sinatra made the same point. "I'd like my son to be like Pat," Sinatra quipped, "until he was three years old."

If not for the "vanilla versions" of R&B songs that he and others recorded, Boone would assert, "rock 'n' roll, as we think of it, never would have happened." In the dozens of songs he covered, Boone excised even the most mildly offensive lyrics. His version of T-Bone Walker's "Stormy Monday" dropped "drinkin' wine" and added "drinkin' Coca-Cola." When covering Little Richard's "Tutti Frutti," Boone "had to change some words, because they seemed too raw for me." So "Boys, you don't know what she do to me" became "Pretty little Susie is the girl for me."

Although he claimed to be a catalyst, "unwittingly and unintentionally," for rock 'n' roll's acceptance, Boone worked hard to associate himself and his music with middle-class values. *The Pat Boone Press Guide* enumerated the guideposts to maturity he thought most important: the Bible, the Golden Rule, the maxim "cleanliness is next to godliness," and sound financial practices. In his 1959 book, *'Twixt Twelve and Twenty,* Boone shared his philosophy of life with the baby boomer generation.

A nonfiction best-seller, *'Twixt Twelve and Twenty* was an advice manual for teenagers that was a godsend to their parents. . . . Boone sought in this book to bridge the generation gap. In doing so, he commented extensively on courtship, marriage, and sexuality. Boone began by associating himself with his teenage readers: "I know what we feel like sometimes. We feel that we're set apart, shooed off together, accused as a group until we get on the defensive." Teenagers must recognize that they are insecure, restless, inconsistent, and indecisive. "If we just let these symptoms run riot," the singer observed, "we will find we are out of balance." Again and again, Boone suggested that teenagers not be seduced by the advice of the White Queen to Alice—"The rule is jam tomorrow and jam yesterday." Instead of trying to act or be treated like adults, teenagers should enjoy the security and relative innocence of adolescence. Apparently unaware of the multiple meanings behind his call to teenagers to "jam today," Boone predicted that the "tomorrow habit" ruined the lives of girls and sent boys to juvenile court.

Boone's message to teenagers about sex was simple: go slowly, very, very slowly. To control youngsters' bodies, so that their minds were ready to follow what was being said, he endorsed the administration of discipline by adults, including spanking. Noting that it "worked wonders in my case," Boone confessed that until he was seventeen his mother had hit him with a sewing-machine belt as he leaned over the bathtub. With or without corporal punishment, of course, the bodies of boys and girls would begin speaking to them when they reached their teens. Boone told them not to listen, and certainly not to give in to physical impulse. "We all know that indiscriminate kissing, dancing in the dark, hanging around in cars, late dates at this early stage can lead to trouble," he wrote. "Kissing for fun is like playing with a beautiful candle in a room full of dynamite! . . . I really think it's better to amuse ourselves in some other way." Adolescents would really enjoy themselves, the singer suggested, if they joined "the nicer play-by-the-rules crowd." To guarantee a better tomorrow, "I say go bowling or to a basketball game, or watch a good TV program (like the 'Pat Boone Chevy Show'!), at least for a while."

Twixt Twelve and Twenty was silent about when, if at all, a teenager might kiss, discriminately or indiscriminately. Nor did Boone provide advice about dating, going steady, getting engaged, or any activities between the time spent with "the nicer play-by-the-rules crowd" and a wedding day. Like many adults, Boone seemed to sense how easily the elaborate courtship rituals of the '50s could proceed to promiscuity. When he was nineteen, Boone admitted (without connecting his behavior to the strict discipline of his parents), he eloped with Shirley. His readers, he hoped, would learn from his mistakes. The elopement "shocked, disappointed, and hurt" Mr. and Mrs. Boone. On these grounds alone, Pat and Shirley should not have done it. Equally important, teenage marriage "is a time-money problem." Newlyweds 'twixt twelve and twenty, Boone told his readers, rarely have the education, the maturity, or the financial wherewithal to make a go of it.

Having, in essence, skipped the teenage years, Boone concluded his discussion of love and marriage with reflections on the division of labor and authority within the household. The husband, he believed, should have the final say. Because she was a "normal female," Shirley enjoyed her role as "vice president in charge of housekeeping." She wanted Pat to "take care of her and our family. All right, she has to let me do it."

Pat Boone was enormously popular in the 1950s. In a survey of high school students in the pseudonymous "Elmtown, U.S.A.," sociologist James Coleman found that 45.2 percent of the girls and 43.5 percent of the boys named him their favorite singer. The comparable figures for Elvis Presley were 17.5 percent and 21.5 percent, while Tommy Sands was a distant third at 10.7 percent and 7.8 percent. Elites at the high school were much less inclined than other students to swoon over Elvis, whose appeal was greatest in "the rough crowd," most of whom smoked or drank and wore "rock 'n' roll jackets" as symbols of good times and a lack of concern with their academic work. Teenagers with high aspirations and achievements gravitated to Boone, Coleman concluded, because he "dispenses rock and roll without the implicit deviance and rebellion in Presley's image." Since 48.1 percent of high school females and 51.6 percent of males enjoyed rock 'n' roll more than any other kind of music, far more than any other popular genre, Coleman implied, parents were fortunate that Boone had made rock 'n' roll safe for tender ears, hearts, and other organs.

Dick Clark was even more influential than Pat Boone in the struggle over the cultural content of rock 'n' roll. Like Boone, Clark was squeaky-clean-cut, with not a hair out of place, a Dentyne smile, and a calm, detached demeanor. An aggressive entrepreneur, Clark had little personal enthusiasm for the music of teenagers and did not have an extensive record collection of his own. To build a multimedia empire, he promoted rock 'n' roll as a universal form of music, sexually unthreatening, "within which almost all tastes can be satisfied." Through his television show, *American Bandstand,* an official in the police department of New York City proclaimed, Clark supplied "a tranquilizing pill" for teenagers.

Born in 1929 in Bronxville, just north of New York City, Clark grew up in Westchester, an affluent suburban community. Educated at Syracuse University, with a major in advertising and a minor in radio, Clark landed a job in 1952 with WFIL, which owned radio and television stations in Philadelphia. Before long, he had his own radio show, "Dick Clark's Caravan of Music," and served as the announcer on Paul Whiteman's *TV-Teen Club,* the first television program to feature boys and girls dancing. Clark's big break came in 1956. Bob Horn, host of the successful TV show *Bandstand,* was arrested for drunk driving amidst rumors that he had slept with one of the young teenagers who danced on the show. A married man with three young daughters, Horn was fired by WFIL as an "embarrassment to the station." Dick Clark replaced him. Terrified by the sex scandal, he retained the show's format, including the popular "Rate-A-Record." He was also "150 percent deliberate" in cultivating a wholesome image. Donning a coat and tie on the theory that "if we looked presentable, normal, the way they [adults] think we oughta look, they'll leave us alone," Clark established on the air that he had "the most platonic of friendships" with the teenage dancers on *Bandstand.* Although, as a colleague put it, Clark "didn't know Chuck Berry from a huckleberry," he learned quickly and began booking prominent rock 'n' rollers for the show. By 1957, the ratings of Clark's *Bandstand* surpassed those of his predecessor.

That same year, when ABC provided an afternoon slot, the show got a new name, *American Bandstand,* and a national audience. At 3:00 P.M. on August 5, Clark introduced himself, read congratulatory telegrams from Pat Boone and Frank Sinatra, watched performances by Kitty Kallen, the Chordettes, and Billy Williams, and invited viewers to enter a contest, "Why I'd Like a Date with Sal Mineo." Although reviews were mixed, the national media recognized that *American Bandstand* was an alternative to the less controlled atmosphere of Alan Freed's TV program, *Big Beat.* Viewers over twenty-one might find the show "something of an ordeal" to sit through, the *New York Times* opined, but *Bandstand's* dancers were "an attractive group of youngsters . . . [with] no motorcycle jackets and hardly a sideburn in the crowd," and Clark "a well-groomed young man richly endowed with self-assurance." *Billboard* was even less enthusiastic, acknowledging but not endorsing the mainstreaming strategy the show employed: "If this is the wholesome answer to the 'detractors' of rock 'n' roll, bring on the rotating pelvises." Almost immediately, however *American Bandstand* became a hit, reaching more viewers than any other program on daytime television. Dick Clark's fortunes rose with those of the show: he became a television producer, record label and song copyright owner, promoter, distributor, discoverer and manager of performers—a force to be reckoned with in rock 'n' roll.

To "set a good example for the people watching at home," Clark promulgated a strict code of conduct for the "regulars" he recruited to dance on *American Bandstand.* Boys wore sweaters, or jackets and ties. Girls wore skirts and blouses, or sweaters over their parochial school uniforms, with white dickies sticking out of the top in what became known as "the Philadelphia collar." Girls were not permitted to wear slacks or tight sweaters. Shorts were verboten for both sexes. Dancers risked expulsion if they behaved demonstrably or impulsively, waved to the camera, or chewed gum. Clark permitted no one under fourteen or above eighteen to dance on the show: thirteen-year-olds were "too giddy and difficult to control," he thought; eighteen-year-olds might be too blasé, and the upper limit enabled Clark to keep soldiers and sailors off the set. Most important, in his on-air conversations Clark eliminated any suggestions of sexuality beyond puppy love. While he asked teenagers, "Are you going with anyone?," he never used the phrase "going steady." When a cameraman wrote a love letter to one of the dancers in 1958, Clark fired him.

Eliminated as well were controversial body movements from the dances featured on *Bandstand.* Although a writer for the *New York Herald Tribune* thought the furious pace made it "inconceivable that any dancer would have an ounce of energy left over to invest in any kind of hanky-panky whatsoever," Clark knew that many parents believed that dancing could be a form of sexual foreplay. When kids "slow-danced," he later recalled, "they could 'cop a feel.' Really sensuous girls threw the lower part of their bodies in the guy's groin; the girls would sort of backbend and chuck it right out." Such displays, of course, were out of bounds on *American Bandstand,* which preferred free-form dances, where the partners did not touch one another. Clark proved adept at introducing new dances (often adapted from African-American originals), including the Bop, the Stroll, and the Twist, accompanied by upbeat tunes, sung by cute, young, winsome performers.

American Bandstand became a weekday afternoon habit for millions of American teenagers. The show was especially popular among high school freshmen and sophomores, George Gallup reported, with three times as many girls as boys attracted. Teenagers tuned in to learn the newest dance step, and watch the latest heart-throb lip-synch his latest hit, be it Paul Anka, Frankie Avalon, Bobby Rydell, Fabian, Dion DiMucci, or Bobby Darin. They tuned in as well to check out the latest trends in grooming and fashion. Viewers wanted to know what dancer Justine Carelli used to wash her hair and how she rolled it. When Carmen and Yvette Jiminez dyed blond streaks in their bangs, so did many of their female fans; the bells and pom-poms dancers hung on their double-layered, rolled bobby sox to divert attention from the saddle shoes they wore in Catholic school became a national fad as well.

Many moms, it turned out, encouraged their teenagers to watch *American Bandstand* and, in Philadelphia, to try out for the show as dancers. When Justine was turned down because she was twelve years old, Mrs. Carelli sent her back to the studio with the birth certificate of an older sister. To the surprise of the producers of *Bandstand,* many mothers became devoted fans of the program themselves, preferring it to soaps and game shows. They wanted to see what young people looked like and what they wore. For the most part, the younger generation on *American Bandstand* pleased them. Some mothers danced to the music, with pillows named after their husbands as their partners. Clark quickly exploited this unanticipated bonanza, issuing press releases to affiliate stations boasting "Age No Barrier to *Bandstand* Beat." On the air, he addressed the "housewives" directly, inviting them to "roll up the ironing board and join us when you can."

From his position as arbiter of the cultural and social mores of teenagers, Dick Clark published his own advice book. *The Happiest Years* was almost identical to *'Twixt Twelve and Twenty* in the behavior prescribed and the topics avoided, but unlike Pat Boone, Clark assumed the tone of a knowing, sympathetic authority, rather than a peer. No one would be critical of your musical tastes, he predicted, with his own program in mind, "if you turned the volume down to normal. . . . Who knows, maybe Dad and Mom might hear some discs they enjoy, too." As had Boone, Clark addressed the initiation into sex with a message that was concise and conventional. Girls who allowed boys to "go farther than they should have while petting," he wrote, acquired a bad reputation and therefore failed to find Mr. Right. Even boys who took advantage of girls began after a while to avoid them at school and at dances. More often than not, boys who treated their teenage girlfriends "loosely" carried "this selfish attitude along with them into a disturbed and many times turbulent adult life." *The Happiest Years* was the kind of book parents—and perhaps only parents—could love. It put Dick Clark and his brand of rock 'n' roll on their side, promising to protect the kids entrusted to them by teaching them emotional maturity and sexual responsibility.

More sexually expressive brands of rock 'n' roll remained available, however, long after R&B "leerics" were scrubbed, simonized, and sanitized. Even *American Bandstand,* as we shall see, sometimes supplied a showcase for them. "There is no denying that rock and roll evokes a physical response from even its most reluctant listeners," *Time* magazine asserted, "for that giant pulse matches the rhythmical operations of the human body." *Life* magazine traced "rock 'n' roll rapture" to the "carefully calculated antics of the performer," whose bumps and grinds, glances, and gyrations triggered the emotions of "susceptible fans," setting off "a gale of screams and moans."

Whether it was expressed as puppy love, in a teenage idiom, or brought to a hot, wet climax, rock 'n' roll was masculine and macho. Women were the subjects of songs, and the objects of affection, jealousy, or betrayal. They did not sing rock 'n' roll songs; men sang about them. In the 1950s, Pete Daniel has observed, Americans would not countenance a female performer grinding against her instrument. When Cordell Jackson performed in Pontotoc, Mississippi, she recalled, "men would just walk off," muttering, "Little girls don't play guitars." Early in the decade, before rock 'n' roll, about one-third of the best-selling songs were recorded by females. By 1957, only two women reached the Top Twenty-Five, Debbie Reynolds ("Tammy") and Jane Morgan ("Fascination"), neither of them a rock 'n' roller. The result was the same in 1958, unless Connie Francis's "Who's Sorry Now" is classified as rock 'n' roll as well as pop.

Referred to in songs as "baby" or "angel," women were often idealized and invariably treated as dependent on men, as their property. "I know you're mine by the ring around your neck," Elvis sang in a typical rock 'n' roll expression of female subservience. In an interview in Amarillo, Texas, he was even more cocky. Asked if he intended to marry, Elvis reportedly asked, "Why buy a cow when you can get milk through the fence?" In "Thirteen Women (And Only One Man in Town)," the flip side of "Rock Around the Clock," Bill Haley fantasized about having female bombshells at his beck and call in the wake of a nuclear attack on the United States: "I had three gals dancin' the mambo, / Three gals ballin' the jack / And all of the rest really did their best / Boy, they sure were a lively pack."

As they projected masculine prerogatives, rock 'n' roll performers sometimes revealed an emotional vulnerability, acknowledging that women could touch or hurt them. The needs and desires of the male, however, remained paramount. Elvis might plead "Love Me Tender" (1956) and "Don't Be Cruel" (1956), but not far from the romantic lyricism was a threat. In "Baby, Let's Play House" (1955), he expressed it: "You may go to college," but "I'd rather see you dead little girl than to be with another man."

Women had a place in rock 'n' roll—in the audience. At concerts, rock 'n' rollers would have it no other way: the teenage heroes of the era were born, Thomas Morgan wrote in *Esquire,* "in the presence and at the pleasure of screaming young women." When females shook and sobbed at the seductive spectacles onstage, they in a sense endorsed the sexual status quo, reassuring their dates that they wanted only those things boys already assumed they wanted.

Although a few observers, like Morgan, concluded that rock 'n' roll singers were "safe-sex" heroes, offering vicarious thrills at no risk, many others insisted that the music impaired the morals of minors. Although he protested, "I don't do no dirty body movements," Elvis remained Exhibit A for the prosecution. After all, Ann Fulchino, the publicist for Elvis's record label, acknowledged that Presley was "the equivalent of a male strip teaser, with the exception that he doesn't take his clothes off." All across America, *Time* reported, Elvis packed theaters and fought off shrieking admirers, "disturbing parents, puckering the brows of psychologists, and filling letters-to-the-editor columns with cries of alarm." It was easy to see why. "He isn't afraid to express himself," a fifteen-year-old girl told *Life* magazine. When he performs, "I get down on the floor and scream." . . .

Using unintentionally phallic prose, *Time* averred that Elvis's appeal was more anatomical than musical: "Is it a sausage? It is certainly smooth and damp looking, but who ever heard of a 172 pound sausage. . . . Is it a corpse? The face just hangs there, limp and white with its little drop-seat mouth, rather like Lord Byron in a wax museum. But suddenly the figure comes to life. The lips part, the eyes half close, the clutched guitar begins to undulate back and forth in an uncomfortably suggestive manner. And wham! The mid-section of the body jolts forward to bump and grind and beat out a low-down rhythm. . . . As the belly dance gets wilder, a peculiar sound emerges. A rusty foghorn? A voice? Or merely a noise produced, like the voice of a cricket, by the violent stridulation of the legs?". . .

Like the clash over lyrics, the battle for Elvis's body aroused advocates of sexual containment and control. That it spread from radios, records, and concert halls to television, the bastion of traditional values, suggests that rock 'n' roll's commercial appeal provided leverage, even for its more controversial products. The contest between Elvis and his enemies ended inconclusively, an indication, perhaps, that the sexual genie was climbing out of the bottle, with the cork nowhere in sight.

On January 28, 1956, the day after RCA released "Heartbreak Hotel," Elvis made the first of six appearances on *Stage Show,* a variety program on CBS, hosted by Tommy and Jimmy Dorsey. Motivated by low ratings (*Stage Show* would be dropped after a single season), the producers were willing to book Presley when their competitors deemed rock 'n' roll too hot to handle. Although the Dorsey Orchestra had difficulty accompanying him, Elvis performed creditably, without attracting much attention from the media. As the sales of "Heartbreak Hotel" soared, Milton Berle, the original "Mr. Television," whose popularity was waning, signed Presley up for his show on NBC. In two appearances, Elvis sang "Heartbreak Hotel" and "Hound Dog," delivering the latter with a bump and grind and an erotic quiver of emotion. He also mixed it up with Uncle Miltie in comedy sketches, one of which cast Berle as Elvis's twin brother, Melvin. For the first time all season, *The Milton Berle Show* posted higher ratings than its competition, Phil Silvers's *Sergeant Bilko.* But if the NBC brass was pleased, commentators in the nation's newspapers screamed with moral outrage. Presley's "caterwauling," wrote Jack O'Brian in the *New York*

Journal-American, "has caused the most heated reaction since the stone-age days of TV when Dagmar and Faysie's necklines were plunging to oblivion." "Elvis's grunt and groin antics," agreed Ben Gross of the *New York Daily News,* were "suggestive and vulgar, tinged with the kind of animalism that should be confined to dives and bordellos." Gross was amazed that Berle and NBC had "permitted this affront."

Because Elvis was scheduled to appear on July 1 on Steve Allen's new Sunday night variety program, NBC took note of the criticism, but the network did not cancel. Recognizing that nothing boosted ratings better than a raging controversy, Allen found a way to have his guest and appear to satisfy the puritans. He assured viewers that he would not allow Presley "to do anything that will offend anyone." NBC announced that a "revamped, purified, and somewhat abridged Presley" had agreed to sing while standing reasonably still, dressed in black tie. On the air, Allen referred to the "great deal of attention" stimulated by the singer's television appearances. Interrupted by a barking sound from backstage, Allen continued, with a self-conscious laugh: "We want to do a show the whole family can watch and enjoy," so tonight, "we're presenting Elvis Presley in what you might call his first comeback. . . . Here he is." Elvis ambled out in his tux, tugging at his white gloves, and wiping his nose on his top hat. As he completed "I Want You, I Need You, I Love You," Allen appeared again, this time accompanied by a basset hound, the ostensible object of affection for "Hound Dog," a song about sex ("You can wag your tail, but I ain't gon' feed you no more"), originally recorded by Willie Mae "Big Mama" Thornton. To occasional giggles from the audience, Presley soldiered on, taking the dog in his arms, and kissing her once or twice as he sang. He completed his evening's work as "Tumbleweed Presley," in a cowboy sketch with Allen, Andy Griffith, and Imogene Coca.

The next day, as Elvis entered the RCA studios to record "Hound Dog," fans greeted him with signs that declared, "We Want the Real Elvis" and "We Want the Gyrating Elvis." In the press, critics were no kinder to the singer than they had ever been, this time pronouncing him a "cowed kid" who had demonstrated, once again, that he "couldn't sing or act a lick." But peeking through the predictable pans was some sympathy. Presley had a right to be distraught, according to John Lardner in a column in *Newsweek:* "Like Huckleberry Finn, when the widow put him in a store suit and told him not to gap or scratch," he had been "fouled" by NBC's attempt to "civilize him . . . for the good of mankind." The most important reviews, of course, came from the public. *The Steve Allen Show* annihilated CBS's powerhouse, Ed Sullivan's *Toast of the Town,* in the ratings. And "Hound Dog" became a runaway hit, eventually overtaking "The Tennessee Waltz" and "Rock Around the Clock" as the best-selling record of the '50s, with a sale of over seven million copies.

In another blow to the self-appointed arbiters of taste, Sullivan, who had vowed that he would not book Presley at any price ("He is not my cup of tea") announced that Elvis would make three appearances on his program in 1956 at an unprecedented fee of $50,000. On September 9, the season premiere of Sullivan's show, Elvis opened with "Don't Be Cruel" and then introduced "Love Me Tender," the title song from his new movie. At each movement of his body, however slight, the audience erupted in paroxysms of emotion. Later in the show, as he sang Little Richard's "Reddy Teddy" and began to move and dance, the camera pulled in, so that the television audience saw him from the waist up only. The studio audience screamed just the same, and unleashed another torrent when Elvis delivered two verses of "Hound Dog."

The show received a sensational Trendex rating of 43.7, which meant that it reached 82.6 percent of the television audience. Disc jockeys around the country began playing tapes they had made of Elvis's Sullivan-show rendition of "Love Me Tender," helping boost prerelease orders of the single to almost a million. As he wished Presley well following his third appearance on *Toast of the Town,* Ed Sullivan gave him a ringing endorsement: "I wanted to say to Elvis Presley and the country that this is a real decent, fine boy, and wherever you go, Elvis . . . we want to say that we've never had a pleasanter experience on our show with a big name than we've had with you." Sullivan had legitimized the singer with an adult audience, without in any way diminishing his standing with teenagers. Keeping Elvis's pelvis out of sight for a moment or two, moreover, was evidence not of the dominance of sexual censors but of the fact that they had been put on the defensive. In the *New York Times,* for example, Jack Gould began his review indignantly: Elvis Presley had "injected movements of the tongue and indulged in wordless singing that were singularly distasteful." Overstimulating the physical impulses of teenagers was "a gross national disservice." Gould supported common sense, not censorship, he hastened to add: "It is no blue-nosed suppression of the proper way of depicting life in the theater to expect stage manners somewhat above the level of the carnival sideshow." But Gould was discouraged by "the willingness and indeed eagerness" of businessmen to exploit teenagers. He concluded with an admission of defeat: "In the long run, perhaps Presley will do everyone a favor by pointing up the need for earlier sex education so that neither his successors nor T.V. can capitalize on the idea that his type of routine is somehow highly tempting yet forbidden fruit." Soon after this column appeared, Elvis's manager, Colonel Tom Parker, put an exclamation point on Gould's suggestion that, like it or not, television now welcomed rock 'n' roll. Two guest appearances and an hourlong TV special by Presley, he announced, would now cost the networks $300,000.

To be sure, later in his career, Elvis was often rather subdued. Intelligent and ambitious, he reached out, quite consciously, to adults as well as teenagers. Elvis's musical repertoire came to include ballads, classics, and Christmas songs, as well as rock 'n' roll, and he dutifully delivered his lines in a succession of mediocre Hollywood action romances. Nonetheless, even when he tried, the man once denounced as a "wreck and ruin artist" never lost his erotic appeal. Like Mae West, when Elvis was good, he was very good, but when he was bad, he was better. When he sneered, "If you're looking for trouble, you've come to the right place," teenage girls screamed, while bluenoses could only simmer and sigh.

For Further Study

1. The author makes a distinction between rhythm and blues, one of the important sources for rock 'n' roll, and rock 'n' roll itself. From his account, what are the most important differences between the two?

2. The author says that rock 'n' roll "was quite traditional with respect to the sex roles of males and females." What specific evidence does he offer for this conclusion?

3. Compare what the author has to say about the attacks on early rock 'n' roll with the current controversy about rap music, especially gangsta rap, and hip-hop. What is similar? What is different?

4. Try to summarize in your own words in two or three sentences the main points that Pat Boone was trying to get across to teenagers in his book *Twixt Twelve and Twenty*.

5. The author cites public opinion polls from the late 1950s that show that Pat Boone was more popular among teenagers than Elvis Presley. Yet it was Elvis who emerged as "The King" of rock 'n' roll. How do you account for this apparent discrepancy? On a related subject, to what sort of audience did Pat Boone appeal and why, and to what sort of audience did Elvis appeal and why?

For Further Reading

There are dozens of biographies of the leading figures in the early history of rock 'n' roll. Among the best are Elaine Dundy, *Elvis and Gladys* (1985), and Peter Guralnick, *Last Train to Memphis: The Rise of Elvis Presley* (1994), both on Elvis Presley, and John A. Jackson, *Big Beat Heat: Alan Freed and the Early Years of Rock 'n' Roll* (1991), on a disk jockey who played an immense role in popularizing rock 'n' roll. Among the general histories of rock 'n' roll are Charles Gillett, *The Sound of the City* (1983), James Miller, *Flowers in the Dustbin: The Rise of Rock and Roll, 1947–1977* (1999), and David P. Szatmary, *Rockin' in Time: A Social History of Rock and Roll* (1991). George Lipsitz has written two books that connect rock 'n' roll to other aspects of popular culture and to the social conditions of the time: *Time Passages* (1990), and *A Rainbow at Midnight: Labor and Culture in the 1940s* (1994).

Chapter 19

© Charles Moore/Stockphoto

Those working for civil rights, like these demonstrators in Birmingham, Alabama, were often victims of violence.

The Struggle for
Civil Rights

Doug McAdam

One can make a good argument that for most of the period since World War II the single most important domestic issue in the United States has been the struggle to achieve equality for African Americans. Slavery was destroyed after the Civil War, but it was quickly replaced by a system of "second-class citizenship" for African Americans, which included segregation, denial of equal access to education, jobs, and political power, and the general assumption by the majority of white Americans that African Americans were inherently and unalterably inferior. While challenges to this system were never entirely absent, it remained remarkably intact until well into the twentieth century, particularly in the South, where "Jim Crow," a system of laws requiring racial segregation and including the nearly universal deprivation of African Americans' right to vote, was an inescapable fact of life.

Attacks on the system began to accelerate, however, during and after World War II. Two particularly important events occurred in the mid-1950s. In 1954 the Supreme Court struck a major blow against one of the most important bastions of the whole system of Jim Crow when it held that racial segregation in public education was unconstitutional. In 1955 African Americans took another significant "stride toward freedom" with their boycott of city buses in Montgomery, Alabama. This marked a turning point in the struggle for African American equality in several ways. First, it was the occasion for the rise to national prominence and leadership of Dr. Martin Luther King, Jr., who was to remain until his assassination in 1968 the most important spokesman for the idea of the civil rights movement as a moral crusade. Second, it marked the first widespread use of direct mass action by African Americans themselves, a tactic that was to be used over and over again in the civil rights struggles of the 1960s (and in the other protest movements of that decade as well). Third, it was a direct challenge to Jim Crow in the very heart of Jim Crow country.

For the next ten years, from 1955, when the Montgomery bus boycott was begun, to 1965, when President Lyndon Johnson signed the Voting Rights Act into law, the South was the major focus of civil rights activity in the United States, direct mass action was the preferred method of attack, and the primary target was Jim Crow, that massive system of racial segregation and subordination written into the laws of the southern states. While many individuals and organizations were involved in the struggle, the spearhead of the movement in the early 1960s was SNCC (pronounced "Snick"), the Student Nonviolent Coordinating Committee. Early in its existence, it turned to the attempt to build permanent political power for southern African Americans as the shortest path to the ultimate goal of racial equality. In the summer of 1964, the leaders of SNCC conceived the idea of "Freedom Summer," during which hundreds of volunteers, mostly white college students from the North, were to conduct a massive voter registration drive in Mississippi, the poorest state in the nation and the one in which the racial situation was universally regarded as the most oppressive. The following selection by Doug McAdam tells part of the story of that summer's effort, giving an insight into the kind of opposition the civil rights movement encountered and the type of courage it took to challenge the racial status quo.

For most of the volunteers, Freedom Summer began not in Mississippi, but at the Western College for Women in Oxford, Ohio. There, in mid-June, the National Council of Churches sponsored two, week-long orientation sessions for volunteers accepted for work in Mississippi. The first session was held June 14–20 and was tailored to those who were to work in voter registration. A second session, for Freedom School teachers, was held the following week.

If the volunteers had expected a languid, leisurely week in the early summer freshness of rural Ohio, they were to be disappointed. The intensity that was to mark the entire summer was very much in evidence at Oxford. It is interesting that the volunteers interviewed have retained so few specific memories of orientation or of the summer itself. They seem to attribute this to the fact that the events in question occurred nearly twenty-five years ago. In contrast, they usually have very detailed memories of events *prior* to the summer, such as when and how they heard about the project in the first place. Possibly the reason for the lack of specific memories is simply the pace of events that summer. Things happened too quickly to allow time for the reflection required to commit specific events to long-term memory. The volunteers were feeling, seeing, experiencing too much.

Some of the intensity of the experience owed to the specific activities planned for the week. The volunteers were subjected to a daunting schedule of general assemblies, section meetings, and work groups. The general assemblies brought all the volunteers together to hear what amounted to broad orientation sessions on Mississippi or some aspect of the movement. Sometimes staff members spoke at these assemblies; more often, it was invited speakers from outside the project. Established civil right leaders, such as Bayard Rustin, Vincent Harding, and James Lawson, spoke. So too did native Mississippians, trying to give the volunteers a better understanding of their state. Jess Brown, one of only three civil rights lawyers in the state, apprised the volunteers of the "unique" quality of Mississippi justice. Long-time state civil rights leader, Aaron Henry, gave a short history of the movement in Mississippi. Even the Justice Department dispatched a representative to the orientation. In a sobering and, for many, radicalizing session, John Doar warned the volunteers not to expect federal protection while in Mississippi. "Maintaining law and order," he argued, "is a state responsibility." In the weeks to come, the volunteers would have ample opportunity to see just how Mississippi exercised that responsibility.

Section meetings were more focused planning groups involving twenty to thirty people who were expected to be engaged in the same type of work during the summer. Work groups were smaller still, consisting of between five and ten people who would actually be working with one another in Mississippi. What these smaller groups lacked in drama and emotional intensity, they made up for in relevance. It was here that the volunteers met and got to know their fellow project members and were trained in the basics of their work assignments.

The power of orientation, however, derived less from this mix of planned sessions as from the informal aspects of the experience. For many of the volunteers it was the beginning of an intensely stressful, yet exhilarating, confrontation with traditional conceptions of America, community, politics, morality, sexuality, and, above all else, themselves. What the volunteers were beginning to experience at Oxford was, to use Peter Berger's term, "ecstasy," that giddy, disorienting sense of liberation that comes from "stepping outside . . . the taken-for-granted routines of society." It was not so much of a case of the volunteers *choosing* to take this step, as being compelled to do so by virtue of their contact with a project staff that had itself become more radical and alienated as a result of three long years of struggle in Mississippi. If ever a group embodied the risks and rewards of an "ecstatic" way of life, it was the SNCC veterans. The volunteers were clearly fascinated by them and drawn to the way of life they represented. One volunteer interviewed by Sarah Evans "claimed that the first night of the orientation session in Oxford changed her life 'because I met those SNCC people and my mouth fell open'." In a letter home, another volunteer, Margaret Aley, described the SNCC staff in equally glowing terms:

> I've never known people like them before; they are so full of heart and life. They are not afraid to show their emotions, they cry when they are sad; they laugh and dance when they are happy. And they sing; they sing from their hearts and in their songs they tell of life, struggle, sadness and beauty. They have a freeness of spirit that I've

rarely seen. But I think that's because they don't worry about maintaining the status quo. When we arrived here Saturday, I had a feeling that I didn't belong. . . . [Now] somehow I feel like I've found something I've been looking for for a long time. I feel like I've finally come home. I now have no doubt that I belong here.

Ruth Steward put the matter a bit more succinctly. In a letter to her parents, she explained that "you can always tell a CORE or SNCC worker—they're beautiful." What these statements betray is a growing identification with the activist community and with a way of life that would later be dubbed the "counterculture."

Other aspects of the orientation sessions also reinforced this sense of identification. For many, the legions of reporters and television cameramen swarming over the campus had that effect. Their presence communicated a sense of "history-making" significance that was intoxicating. Not that the hypocrisy and sensationalism of the media was lost on the volunteers. This too was a part of the radicalizing process they were undergoing. In her beautiful book describing the Freedom Summer experience, another volunteer, Sally Belfrage, wrote of how the media

followed us into the classrooms and dormitories, around the lounges, out along the paths. They asked people to sing that song again for the American public. There was footage, yardage, mileage of every face in the place. "At the beginning it made me feel important," a boy from Utah said at lunch. "But they have a way of degrading everything they touch." "It's because we need them more than they need us," his neighbor returned, "and they know it." "It's just their job," commented a third. "Well, I feel unclean," the boy from Utah said.

Degrading or not, the volunteers' letters home are filled with entreaties to parents to "save the *Life* magazine picture for me," or to "watch CBS tonight; I may be on." Degrading or not, the media attention clearly reinforced the volunteers' sense of their own and the project's importance.

More than anything else, however, it was the volunteers' growing appreciation of the dangers inherent in the project that had the greatest impact on them. If they had not realized the extent of these dangers before orientation, they certainly did by the time they left Ohio. This was no accident. In planning the sessions, one of the overriding goals had been to overwhelm the volunteers with the savagery and violence of life in Mississippi. It was hoped that by doing so, the staff might be able to persuade the naive or those with lingering doubts to stay home. So in session after session, staff members recounted the litany of horror they had seen in Mississippi. In turn, the volunteers duly recorded these sessions in their journals or letters home. Margaret Rose wrote:

Last night's objective narration of facts is shot to hell by a breakdown in my defensives against fear and intimidation. The straw to break the back was the narration of a white leader here (a face mangled by scars) about a near death experience on the road coming up here. Fifteen guys in 3 cars ran them off the road (normal) and all in the car experienced the intent of the group: murder. It was somehow absolutely clear. A car full of leaders. Too good to pass over. One man, an exchange professor from Pakistan in a Mississippi university, happened to say he was a foreigner and had a passport. Some small doubt cross [*sic*] the minds of one of the 15. Somehow the mood shifted. They did not murder. He said we could expect this kind of encounter. He means it.

Another volunteer wrote:

There is a quiet Negro fellow on the staff who has an ugly scar on his neck and another on his shoulder where he stopped 45 slugs. . . . Another fellow told this morning how his father and later his brother had been shot to death. . . . I'd venture to say that every member of the Mississippi staff has been beaten at least once and he who has not been shot at is rare. It is impossible for you to imagine what we are going in to, as it is for me now, but I'm beginning to see.

Role playing sessions and lessons in how to protect oneself if attacked only underscored the growing fear the volunteers were feeling. A volunteer described the general response to one such session: "John Strickland [a volunteer] stood ashen, staring at the lad curled up on the ground. Like the rest of the crowd, he was silent. Their eyes stayed riveted to the frozen tableau of a violence that till that moment had existed for them only in grade-B movies and tabloid spreads."

But no planned simulation could ever have dramatized the dangers of Mississippi life more forcefully than the real life event that took place in Neshoba County, Mississippi, on June 21, just as the second group of volunteers were arriving at Oxford, Ohio. Less than twenty-four hours after arriving in Mississippi, one in the first group of volunteers, Andrew Goodman, climbed into a station wagon with staff members James Chaney and Michael Schwerner, and drove off to investigate a church bombing near Philadelphia, Mississippi. They never returned. Arrested in the afternoon on traffic charges, the three were held until the evening, and then released into the Mississippi night. It was the last time they were seen alive. Their burned-out station wagon was found near Bogue Chitto Swamp the next day. But it was not until August that the bodies were discovered beneath an earthen dam near Philadelphia: Chaney's showed signs of a savage beating, and Goodman's and Schwerner's, single gunshot wounds to the chest.

Back at Oxford, news of the disappearance reached the volunteers during a general assembly. Sally Belfrage describes the scene:

There was an interruption then at a side entrance: three or four staff members had come in and were whispering agitatedly. One of them walked over to the stage and sprang up to whisper to Moses, who bent on his knees to hear. In a moment he was alone again. Still crouched, he gazed at the floor at his feet, unconscious of us. Time passed. When he stood and spoke, he was something else; it was simply that he was obliged to say something, but his voice was automatic. "Yesterday morning, three of our people left Meridian, Mississippi, to investigate a church-burning in Neshoba County. They haven't come back, and we haven't had any word from them. . . ." Then a thin girl in shorts was talking to us from the stage: Rita Schwerner, the wife of one of the three. She paced as she spoke, her eyes distraught and her face quite white, but in a voice that was even and disciplined . . . Rita asked us to form in groups by home areas and wire our congressmen. . . . We composed telegrams, collected money and sent them, and tried to rub out the reality of the situation with action. No one was willing to believe that the event involved more than a disappearance. It was hard to believe even that. Somehow it seemed only a climactic object lesson, part of the morning's lecture, an anecdote to give life to the words of Bob Moses. To think of it in other terms was to be forced to identify with the three, to be prepared, irrevocably, to give one's life.

Word of the disappearance did, in fact, force the volunteers to confront the possibility of their own deaths. Some, like Stuart Rawlings, did so dispassionately:

> What are my personal chances? There are 200 COFO [Council of Federated Organizations] volunteers who have been working in the state a week, and three of them have already been killed. I shall be working in Forrest County, which is reputedly less violent than Neshoba County. But I shall be working on voter registration, which is more dangerous than work in Freedom Schools or Community Centers. There are other factors which must be considered too—age, sex, experience and common sense. All considered, I think my chances of being killed are 2%, or one in fifty.

Others expressed their fears more emotionally. "The reality of Mississippi gets closer to us everyday. We know the blood is going to flow this summer and it's going to be our blood. And I'm scared—I'm very scared.". . .

Voter Registration

Voter registration was the cornerstone of the Summer Project. This is not to say that it was necessarily the most important part of Freedom Summer. However, it did supply the strategic impetus to the project. It was the success of the Freedom Vote campaign in the fall of 1963 that led SNCC and COFO to approve Bob Moses' plan for an even more ambitious political project the following summer. Originally, the plan was simply to use large numbers of white students—à la the Freedom Vote—to register as many black voters as possible. However, as long as the state Democratic party was effectively closed to blacks, it was unclear how beneficial the simple registration of voters would be. To address the problem, SNCC spearheaded the establishment of the Mississippi Freedom Democratic Party (MFDP) at a meeting held in Jackson on April 26, 1964. The MFDP then selected and ran a slate of candidates in the June 2 Democratic Primaries for Senator and three House seats. Not surprisingly, all four of the MFDP candidates (Fannie Lou Hamer, Victoria Gray, John Houston, and the Rev. John Cameron) were soundly beaten. So, following the primary, they obtained and filed the necessary number of signatures to be placed on the November ballot as independents. The Mississippi State Board of Elections rejected these petitions. Thus stymied, the SNCC/MFDP leadership returned to the strategy that had served them so well the previous fall. If they were to be shut out of regular electoral politics in the state, they would conduct a mock election to challenge the Mississippi Delegation to the August Democratic National Convention to be held in Atlantic City.

For the volunteers, this meant they would be involved in two parallel tasks: persuading blacks to attempt to register as official voters and "freedom registering" voters on behalf of the MFDP. Freedom registration forms could be filled out in the applicant's home: official registration meant a trip to the courthouse. That made the latter process the much more difficult of the two. Neither, however, was easy.

> Canvassing is very trying, you walk a little dusty street, with incredibly broken down shacks. The people sitting on porches staring away into nowhere—the sweat running down your face! Little kids half-naked in ragged clothes *all* over the place—this is what you face with your little packet of "Freedom Forms". . . . Unfortunateley [*sic*], Freedom registration is terribely [*sic*] remote to these people. I almost feel guilty—like I'm playing for numbers only; . . . you walk up to a porch, knock on a door and enter into another world. . . . The walls are inevitably covered with a funeral hall calendar, a portrait calendar of President Kennedy, old graduation pictures. Maybe a new cheap lamp from Fred's dollar store.
>
> You meet an afraid, but sometimes eager, curious face—one which is used to . . . saying "Yes Sir" to everything a white man says. . . . You see their pain, the incredible years of suffering etched in their worn faces; and then if you convince them to sign you leave. You walk down the deteriorating steps to the dirt, to the next house—the next world and start in on your sales pitch again, leaving behind something which has broken you a little more. Poverty in the abstract does nothing to you. When you wake up to it every morning, and come down through the streets of it, and see the same old man on the ground playing the accordian [*sic*], the same man selling peaches out of [a] basket to [*sic*] heavy for his twisted body, the same children, a day older—a day closer to those men—after this everyday, poverty is a reality that is so outrageous you have to learn to . . . become jaded for the moment—or else be unable to function.

> I work in voter registration. . . . On a normal day we roll out of bed early in the morning. We may have slept in the Freedom House, or in the home of some generous and brave farmer. . . . We study the map of the county, decide where we will work for the day. We scramble for breakfast and hit the road.
>
> The work is long and hot. We drive from farmhouse to farmhouse. I have averaged almost 200 miles a day in the car. The roads are in despicable condition . . . where the pavement stops the Negro sections are likely to begin. And if there is not even gravel on the roads, we can be reasonably sure that we are in a "safe" neighborhood. Such is not always the case, though, and more than once we have been cursed and threatened by someone for knocking on a white man's door.
>
> When we walk up to a house there are always children out front. They look up and see white men in the car, and fear and caution cover their expressions. Those terrified eyes are never quite out of my mind; they drive me as little else could. Children who have hardly learned to talk are well-taught in the arts of avoiding whites. They learn "yassah" as almost their first words. If they did not, they could not survive. The children run to their parents, hide behind them. We walk up, smile, say howdy, and hold out our hands. As we shake hands I tell them my name. They tell me their names and I say Mr. ——, how do you do. It is likely the first time in the life of this farmer or housewife a white man has ever shaken hands with them, or even called them "with a handle to their names." This does not necessarily bode well with them; they are suspicious. Chances are they have heard about the "freedom riders" passing through. The news is usually greeted with mingled fear, excitement, enthusiasm and gratitude. But the confrontation is more serious and more threatening. They think, if Mr. Charlie knew . . . , and they are afraid. They have good reason to be. . . . Many . . . are sharecroppers, who must turn over a third to a half of the year's

harvest to a man who does not work at all, but who owns the land they till. They may be evicted, and have often been for far less serious offenses. Nearly everyone black in Mississippi is at least a year in debt. The threat of suspended credit and foreclosure is a tremendous burden. . . .

Freedom Schools

In planning for the Summer Project, the SNCC staff was smart enough to realize that the oppression of Mississippi's black population depended on more than restricting access to the political system. An elaborate array of caste restrictions and institutional inequities also contributed to the maintenance of the racial status quo. Among these was Mississippi's separate but clearly unequal school system. . . . State educational expenditures in 1964 averaged $81.66 per white student and $21.77 for each black student. The fact that Mississippi was one of only two states without a mandatory education law merely underscored the lack of importance accorded public education. So too did other bits of evidence. At the time of the fall cotton harvest, many of the black schools in the delta were routinely closed to take advantage of the cheap source of labor the students provided. Within the classroom, curriculum content was carefully controlled. State-selected textbooks glorified the "Southern way of life" and made no mention of significant achievements by black Americans. In some districts, school superintendents even forbade the history of the Reconstruction period from being taught in the black schools. The Freedom Schools were an effort to counter the obvious inequities and insidious political messages inherent in this system.

The chief architect of the Freedom Schools was veteran SNCC field secretary Charlie Cobb. Drafted in the fall of 1963, Cobb's proposal called for the establishment of Freedom Schools "to provide an educational experience for students which will make it possible for them to challenge the myths of our society, to perceive more clearly its realities, and to find alternatives, and ultimately new directions for action." To put the necessary curricular flesh on the bones of Cobb's proposal, the National Council of Churches sponsored a March, 1964 meeting in New York City. There, educators, clergy, and SNCC staff members hammered out a basic curriculum for the schools emphasizing four principal topic areas: (1) remedial education, (2) leadership development, (3) contemporary issues, and (4) nonacademic curriculum. This basic framework was modified again following the appointment of Staughton Lynd, a history professor at Spelman, as director of the Freedom School program. In a mimeographed packet sent out just before the start of the Summer Project, the prospective teachers were informed that "the kind of activities you will be developing will fall into three general areas: (1) academic work, (2) recreation and cultural activities, (3) leadership development." In effect, the second and third topic areas designated in the original proposal had been lumped together under the single heading of "leadership development." Judging from the letters and journals written by the teachers, most projects adhered to this modified framework in organizing their Freedom School programs. Most offered a variety of basic courses in "leadership development," or what came to be known as the core curriculum. This consisted of courses in the history and philosophy of the movement, current events, and black history. "Academic work" was represented by nearly as many courses as there were students interested in taking them. Offerings ranged from basic remedial courses in reading and math to a variety of specialized classes in such topics as French, science, dance, and debate. Finally, a variety of "recreation and cultural activities" served to round out the Freedom School program. Among the most notable of these activities were the establishment of student-run newspapers on several projects and the writing and performing of an original play by the students in the Holly Springs project.

By any standard, the Freedom Schools were a success. Where project staff had hoped to attract 1,000 or so students, between 3,000 and 3,500 showed up. This in the face of a lack of facilities, the fears of black parents, and considerable violence directed at the schools. In McComb, seventy-five students showed up for classes the morning after a bomb leveled the church that had been serving as their school. Classes were held on the lawn in front of the smoldering church while younger children played in the ruins. In the small town of Harmony, the volunteers and townspeople set to cleaning up and repairing four abandoned school buildings to be used as classrooms.

> Then the sheriff came with about six white men, who were introduced as the "Board of Education." If they weren't Klan men, then they were at least Citizen Council [a more moderate segregationist group] people. God, they hated us . . . they told us we should not use it [the school building]; it is county property. We told them it was private property. We are getting a lawyer and will fight in court. Meanwhile . . . we will teach in a nearby church and outside.

Predictably, the court ruled in favor of the "Board of Education." Undaunted, the community erected its own school/community center.

> Everyday this week . . . the men of the community hammered and poured cement. At noon, about 7 or 8 women all gathered at the center with fried chicken, fish, salad, gallons of Kool-Aid, and apple turnovers, and served them to the men, we teachers, and each other. It is a thing of beauty to see us all work together. . . . We are a living repudiation of the "too many cooks" theory. It should be up by Saturday, or at latest Tuesday.

Eventually construction was finished and classes were held in the new building, if only for the final week of the summer.

In the classroom, the volunteers discovered most of the frustrations teachers have always faced. Overcrowding was frequently a problem:

> It became evident quite early that we were going to have many more than the expected 75 students. We called Jackson and got a promise of more teachers—at full strength we will have 23. This was when we expected 150 students. On registration day, however, we had a totally unexpected deluge: 600 students! . . . After a while, as they were coming in, it changed from a celebration to a crisis. This is 26 students per teacher—much better than the local or usual ratios, but still not enough . . . to do all we want to in six weeks.

Complaints about a lack of "educational standards" or "academic discipline" were common as well:

> The . . . class tends to degenerate into discussion of anything from standards of Negro beauty to the Marxist view of private property. . . . They are eager to argue, in some ways less eager to learn; some days ago I was attempting to give some minimal account of certain facts, when one of the more brilliant and remarkable pupils, but somewhat headstrong, declared that no offense, but, all this was rather boring, and it would be better if other people got a chance to speak, and if we could have discussions. I often think of the difficulties which . . . we will (for these schools will be continued all year) have in making the transition from this school to one where solid academic discipline must be imposed.

Add to this list the problems of absenteeism, staff dissension, and teacher "burn out," and one might well be describing the generic teaching experience. But there was a difference. The volunteers also experienced the emotional rewards reserved for those teaching students who are there voluntarily and who are being taken seriously for perhaps the first time in their lives.

> I can see the change. The 16 year-old's discovery of poetry, of Whitman and Cummings and above all else, the struggle to express thoughts in words, to translate ideas into concrete written words. After two weeks a child finally looks me in the eye, unafraid, acknowledging a bond of trust which 300 years of Mississippians said should never, could never exist—I can feel the growth of self-confidence.

> The atmosphere in the class is unbelievable. It is what every teacher dreams about— real, honest enthusiasm and desire to learn anything and everything. The girls come to class of their own free will. They respond to everything that is said. They are excited about learning. They drain me of everything that I have to offer so that I go home at night completely exhausted but very happy in spirit because I know that I have given to people. . . . Every class is beautiful. The girls respond, respond, respond. And they disagree among themselves. I have no doubt that soon they will be disagreeing with me. At least this is one thing that I am working towards. They know that they have been cheated and they want anything and everything that we can given them. I feel inadequate to the task of teaching them but I keep saying to myself that as long as I continue to feel humble there is a chance that we might all learn a whole lot together.

In talking to the volunteers today it is clear that they *did* learn a lot from their experience as teachers. Some became more politically radical as a result of the courses they taught or the discussions they had with other teachers. Others altered their career plans because of the satisfaction they had derived from teaching. The schools, then, had an impact beyond the students; the teachers, too, were taught.

Life in the Black Community

While not discounting the time and energy the volunteers expended on their jobs, it may well be that work was the least demanding part of their summer experience. After all there was a certain familiarity about their work assignments. Many of those who taught either were studying to become teachers or had taught before. Those with no teaching experience had at least spent years going to school as students, so the classroom was hardly a foreign place to them. As for the voter registration workers, 76 percent had participated in some form of civil rights organizing prior to the summer.

Very few of the volunteers, however, had had experiences that prepared them for life in the black community. For one thing, few had ever lived in rural areas. Their letters capture a kind of bemused appreciation of the new experiences this afforded them.

> Man, like I don't even believe what I just did. You really had to be there to appreciate it. I took a bath. But no ordinary bath 'cause there's no running water. No, we take this bucket out in the back yard and fill it with water warmed over a fire. It's pitch black so we shine Mr. Clark's truck lights on the bucket. Then I strip down naked and stand in the bucket to wash. That is the way you take a bath around here.

> [T]here are several [chickens] and several roosters. Roosters have this habit—one sits by the window and at dawn melancholically crows in a refrain reminiscent of a man falling off a cliff. The dog outside is just thrilled by this and barks his approval. The rooster thinks about this for a while—then to show he's no party-pooper he lets go again. This sends the dog in to sheer ecstasy. A little while later they pal it up and do a duet. By this time I usually wake up for the third time convinced that someone is being murdered at the foot of my bed.

More significant and more sobering than the volunteers' introduction to rural life was their exposure to "the other America." The publicity accorded Michael Harrington's 1962 book of the same name may have made the volunteers intellectually aware of poverty, but their class advantages had insulated them from any real experiential understanding of the problem. No such comfortable distance was possible in Mississippi. The volunteers' generally optimistic, idealistic upbringing had not prepared them for the underside of the American dream.

> This was the most appalling example of deprivation ever seen by any of us who were canvassing. Upon approaching the house, we were invited on the porch which was strewn with bean shellings, rotten cotton sacks, pieces of a broken stove, and other assorted bits of scrap. . . . On a drooping cot to our right as we came in the door lay a small child (six months old). The child's eyes, nose, and mouth were covered with flies. Not being able to stand such a sight, I tried to chase them away only to be met with the reply of the mother of the child. "They will only come back again."
>
> The whole house seemed diseased, rotten, and splitting at the seams with infection. Nevertheless, the people knew what we were coming for, and the forms were filled out without our asking. . . . This is a scene that was burned into all of our minds and which will make quiet sleep impossible.

> One day has passed in Shaw and the other America is opening itself before my naive, middle-class eyes. The cockroaches draw patterns across the floor and table and make a live patchwork on the bed. Sweat covers my skin and cakes brown in my joints—wrist, elbow, knee, neck. Mosquito bites, red specks on white background.

> The four-year-old grandson is standing by my side. I wonder how our presence now will affect him when he is a man?
>
> I saw other children today who bore the marks of the Negro in rural Mississippi. One had a protruding navel the size of the stone he held in his hand. Several had distended stomachs.

Is America really the land that greets its visitors with "Send me your tired, your poor, your helpless masses to breathe free"?

There is no Golden Door in Shaw.

These images had a powerful impact on the volunteers, especially those whose upbringing had failed to provide them with even an ideological awareness of the problem. One especially sheltered volunteer, raised in an upper-middle-class suburb of Chicago, remembers "crying myself to bed at night [in Mississippi]. . . . I was just seeing too much, feeling too much. Things weren't supposed to be like this. I was just a mess. I just remember feeling sad, guilty and angry all at the same time."

In the face of these feelings—especially the guilt—the warmth, openness, and acceptance the volunteers felt from the black community was both confirming and confusing at the same time. Confirming because it communicated a kind of redemptive forgiveness that assuaged the guilt many of the volunteers were feeling; confusing because they didn't feel they deserved the special attention they were receiving. It all added up to a rich welter of feelings that left a good many of the volunteers overwhelmed. In a letter to her parents, Pam Parker struggled to communicate all she was feeling:

I am starting to ramble because there is so much in my head and heart that I want to say but cannot. It has been a big week filled with so much enthsiasm and love that I feel overwhelmed. The girls I work with . . . have accepted me completely. They have told me this in a way they have responded in class, and some have told me this directly in their essays they have written me or in actual conversations. . . . This abundance of love and gratitude and acceptance makes me feel so humble and so happy.

Even today this jumble of emotions is evident in the former volunteers' recollections of the summer. Elinor Tideman Aurthur movingly recalled the daily lunchtime ritual at the Freedom School where she taught.

[T]he women from the church everyday would bring food for all the teachers. . . . I used to look forward to it so much, and the fact that they would give this to us everyday, you know, was just wonderful . . . they had fried chicken and deviled eggs and potato salad. . . . They would spread it out on the table and they would, it was so nice [starts to cry] . . . it was so touching . . . to be cared for . . . that [way] . . . I felt like I belonged; I felt like they liked me and they wanted me to be there and I, it was so healing, you know, knowing what the divisions were . . . and yet somehow you can heal . . . I don't mean to say that they idealized us . . . because I don't think they did, but I think there was a kind of love . . . and a kind of compassion for us that they showed. It was a daily demonstration of love and acceptance . . . they were feeding us; they were giving us nourishment.

For many of the volunteers, the most immediate purveyors of this love and acceptance were the families that housed them. Sally Belfrage describes her introduction to her summer hostess: "[Mrs. Amos] hadn't planned to house summer volunteers, but Cora Lou's guest immediately became to her another child . . . she hugged me, fed me fried chicken and cornbread and installed me in the back bedroom."

Midway through the summer another volunteer described her "home life" to her mother:

I have become so close to the family I am staying with—eleven people—that Mrs. H. finally paid me a great compliment. She was introducing me to one of her Negro women friends and said, "This is Nancy, my adopted daughter!" I baby-sat for her one night and in general we have become very close friends. She is a beautiful mother. My favorite picture of her is sitting peacefully in a summer chair with her 2-year-old baby girl in her lap; the baby, sucking her bottle, with one hand inside her mother's dress resting on her bosom. It is such a human sight; such love oozes from this house I can't begin to explain.

The hospitality of the local families was all the more touching for the risks they ran in housing the volunteers. Sheltering the "invaders" was grounds for harassment, dismissal from a job, or worse. David Gelfand relates an incident that took place while he was living with a prosperous black family in Meridian:

[D]uring the five or six days I was there, there had been numerous . . . threatening phone calls and his [the black homeowner's] wife was quite upset about it. And one morning he came and woke me up. I was sleeping on the couch in the living room. And we had put a single piece of hair on Scotch Magic Tape across the hood, so you always checked before you got in the car. And the tape was broken. He had checked it. And the carport was right next to the kids bedroom—ages four to twelve. . . . And so he said, "okay, let's not do anything but release the emergency break and roll it out to the road." And we did that and then opened the hood. And there were four sticks of dynamite tied [to] . . . the ignition coil.

On occasion the volunteers were reluctantly asked to leave following incidents such as this. More often than not their hosts responded with a resiliency and toughness that impressed the volunteers. In his journal, Gren Whitman recounted the following early-morning encounter with the woman in whose house he was living:

I am writing this at 6 A.M. Just now coming down the hall from the bathroom. I met Mrs. Fairley coming down the hall from the front porch carrying a rifle in one hand [and] a pistol in the other. I do not know what is going on. . . . [All she said was] "You go to sleep; let me fight for you."

Nor was this volunteer's experience unique. In their journals, letters, or interviews, many of the volunteers recounted similar incidents. For a group not raised around guns, it was yet another eye-opening aspect of the summer, and one that would lead a number of the volunteers to rethink strongly held pacifist convictions. . . .

Confrontation with White Mississippi

During the course of the summer, COFO compiled a running chronology of "hostile incidents.". . . The list is twenty-six mimeographed pages long and covers everything from threatening phone calls to the disappearance of the three workers. Oddly, instead of being viscerally powerful, the list is curiously unaffecting.

The sheer number of incidents simply overwhelms the reader, leaving one emotionally numb to the specifics of any given incident. A summary of violence during the summer has much the same effect. So that the following statistics:

      4 project workers killed
      4 persons critically wounded
     80 workers beaten
   1000 arrests
     37 churches bombed or burned
     30 black homes or businesses bombed or burned

fail to inform in an emotional sense. To gain some empathetic understanding of these events, one really has to read the volunteers' own accounts of them. Only then does one begin to appreciate the combination of shock, anger, disillusionment, and fear the volunteers felt in the face of the violence and terror they were witnessing.

> I really cannot describe how sick I think this state is. I really cannot describe the feeling in my stomach when I hear a typical story of injustice. . . . I cannot describe the real courage it takes to stay down here. I cannot describe the fears, the tensions and the uncertainties of living here. When I walk I am always looking at cars and people: if Negro, they are my friends; if white, I am frightened and walk faster. When driving, I am always asking: black? white? It is the fear and uncertainty that is maddening. I must always be on guard. . . . When confronted with a crisis, then the action is clearly defined. But when I do not know what to expect, but always know to expect something, then the tensions mount and I think of courage and of how deep my commitment has to be, and I think of getting the hell out of this sick state. I live day to day. I wake up in the morning sighing with relief that I was not bombed, because I know that "they" know where I live. And I think, well, I got through that night, now I have to get through this day, and it goes on and on. Even as I write this letter we are told that our office might be bombed by an anonymous voice, "to get rid of it once and for all."

> Yesterday while the Mississippi River was being dragged looking for the three missing civil rights workers, two bodies of Negroes were found—one cut in half and one without a head. Mississippi is the only state where you can drag a river any time and find bodies you were not expecting . . . Negroes disappear down here every week and are never heard about. Things are really much better for rabbits here. There is a closed season on rabbits when they may not be killed. Negroes are killed all year round. So are rabbits. The difference is that arrests are made for killing rabbits out of season . . . Jesus Christ, this is supposed to be America in 1964.

> Tonight the sickness struck. At our mass meeting, as we were singing "We Shall Overcome," a girl was shot in the side and in the chest. We fell to the floor in deathly fear; but soon we recovered and began moving out of the hall to see what had happened. . . . When I went out I saw a woman lying on the ground clutching her stomach. She was so still and looked like a statue with a tranquil smile on her face. I ran to call an ambulance.

While the presence of so many reporters in the state muted the violence to a degree, there was still no shortage of celebrated atrocities. In Greenwood a local activist, Silas McGhee, was shot in the head while he sat in his car out in front of a local club. Three volunteers raced him to the hospital only to be told they couldn't bring him in because they didn't have shirts on. They had taken their shirts off to bandage McGhee's head. On the evening of July 8, the front wall of the McComb Freedom House was destroyed by eight sticks of dynamite. Miraculously, the workers sleeping inside sustained only minor injuries. In Hattiesburg, two days later, five voter registration workers (including a rabbi visiting from Ohio) were attacked and severely beaten by two local men armed with lead pipes. And so it went, day in and day out, an endless string of incidents that lent a brutal and frightening texture to the volunteers' lives.

Had the volunteers been in their home states, they would invariably have turned to the police for protection from such incidents. Obviously, this was not practical in Mississippi. Often the police were implicated in the very incidents they were called to investigate. For instance, it turned out that Neshoba County Deputy Sheriff Cecil Price had coordinated the kidnapping and murders of Chaney, Goodman, and Schwerner. Even acting in their official capacity as law enforcement officers, the police spared few opportunities to harass or terrorize the volunteers. The following two affidavits filed by project volunteers recount typical incidents:

> On July 9, 1964 Mary Lane, George Johnson and I accompanied Phillip Moore to the Greenwood Police Station. His purpose was to swear out a warrant against one of the local whites who had beaten him on the street. While Moore was thus occupied in another room, Miss Lane (Negro), Johnson (white) and I waited in the station room. There were three officers present—Desk Sergeant Simpson, Officer Logan and another unidentified officer. Logan was not in uniform—evidently off duty.
>
> Logan took a long knife out of his pocket and started to sharpen it, [directing] a running stream of threats at the three of us. He asked Johnson how he liked "screwing that nigger" (indicating Miss Lane). Then he said, while sharpening the knife: "sounds like rubbing up against nigger pussy." He poked the knife against my ribs a few times; then he held it out toward me, told me to put my hand on it and asked: "Think it's sharp enough to cut your cock off?" Then he looked at Officer Simpson and said "You'd better get me out of here before I do what I'd like to do." At no time did Simpson or the other officer make any move to restrain him or protect us.
>
> Shortly thereafter, he walked over behind the desk and took out a pistol from his trousers pocket. He brandished it in our direction and spun the chamber, then tucked it in his shirt front. He walked over to the door. Miss Lane was standing about eight feet from the door in front of him with her back turned to him. He took out his gun again, pointed it at Miss Lane for a few seconds and put it in his pants pocket. Then he opened the door with his left hand and simultaneously reached out and gave Miss Lane a shove with his right fist, knocking her several feet across the room. He swore at her; then Officer Simpson joined in and told Miss Lane: "Nigger, you get your ass away from that door." Miss Lane refused to move, explaining that she wasn't in the doorway, especially since Logan had knocked her practically across the room. Both the officers shouted threats at her, threatening to throw her in jail if she didn't move.
>
> We went out about 15 minutes later and found that the tires of my car had been slashed. We went back in and reported the vandalism to the police but to no avail.

I pulled over and stopped, even though I heard no siren and had no definite knowl-edge that the following car contained police . . . and waited until the man in the car arrived. He came up to the truck and told me to get out. I asked for identification. He didn't show me anything, but told me to get out of the truck. I got out . . . and he and I walked to his car. Eric also got out and we received a . . . lecture while he was writing a ticket for speeding. . . . A highway patrol car arrived. . . . A third car then pulled up, which was unmarked and contained one man not in uniform. We could tell he had been drinking because of his actions and because we could smell the liquor.

After a short interchange between him and the first man, the first man left and the third man took me back to the car of the highway patrolman. He opened the car and told me to get inside. I got inside and sat on the back seat. He told me to move over and got in. All the doors and windows were shut. He said, "I can't kill you, but you know what I'm going to do to you." I answered, "No, sir." At this time he pulled his gun out of his holster and started to hit me on the head with the gun butt. I put my hands up to protect my head and rolled into a ball on the seat. Over a period of about a minute he hit me about four times on the head and about eight to ten times on the left hand. He also hit me about three times on the left leg, twice on my right hand, and once on my left shoulder. All or this was with the gun butt. . . . Three of them then went up to Eric. They had a conversation with Eric which I could not hear and one of the men raised a gun and struck Eric, knocking him down. He got up and was knocked down again. I had been sitting in the car through all of this. I felt the blood on my face and on my arm. The man who had beaten me then came back to the car and sat down in the back seat. He picked up a flashlight and hit me across the mouth with it. I then rolled into a ball again and he put the gun to my temple and cocked it. He said, "If you move, I'll blow your brains out."

Arrest often held a special kind of terror for the volunteers. As generations of Mississippi blacks had learned, there was virtually no end to the physical and psy-chological brutality Southern jailers could inflict upon a prisoner. In this the vol-unteers achieved equality. The police accorded them the same treatment.

Upon entering [the] cell block we were taken to "nigger bull pen." Then [we] were shoved inside and officers said, "Here they are, get 'em boys." This is very unusual practice for whites to be put into the Negro section. The Negroes expressed confu-sion and fear. They were moved to beat us. Five minutes later, two officers took us into a white cellblock. This was about 12:30 A.M. Wednesday. At the white cell, the of-ficers tried to incite white prisoners to take out their aggressions on the volunteers. ("It's wooping [*sic*] time.") The officers left and white prisoners gathered about. R————opened a conversation with one, and eased some of the tension. At this point, a Mexican spoke up and R————spoke to him in Spanish to help develop a rapport. After several minutes, a Mississippian announced that he hated all niggers and nigger-lovers and that COFOers were there to be beaten by the whites. However he was going to let us go.

We lay down and listened to the argument, that lasted about three hours, on whether or not to beat us up. Sporadically, police officers and trustees would enter argument, attempting to incite white prisoners to "do justice." Morning arrived with-out real incident.

About 10 A.M. officers took us out of the cell into fingerprinting rooms. As they were fingerprinting and [taking mug shots of] me, the officers told————sordid stories about brutality that had been imposed upon fellow COFOers since the day before . . . and that a fellow white girl worker had been brutally raped and was on her death bed. At this point R———fainted. Upon awakening, the back of his head bleeding, we both were escorted to the lobby where attorneys from COFO in Jackson were waiting. . . . Local police refused to return personal papers, mainly handwritten notes, and denied they had even taken them. . . . In a subsequent interview, FBI agents expressed no interest in the mental harassment which occurred during the 12 hours spent in jail. . . . When taken to jail, R———had been told he was being arrested on a vagrancy charge. The following morning the sheriff said there were no charges.

Even when nothing happened, the possibility that something might could turn an evening alone in jail into an exhausting experience. In a letter home, William Hodes described his feelings during just such an evening.

> So there I was: alone in a Southern jail. First thing I did was check the layout of the cell in case I had to protect myself. I pulled the mattresses halfway off the beds so that I wouldn't hit any sharp corners as I went down. I planned to stay on one of the beds in the corner, so that I could get between two beds and a wall, and make myself hard to get at, except maybe by kicking. I was very jumpy, and was terrified at every door slam, phone call, and particularly key ring jingle jangle. My pulse was . . . over a hundred the whole three hours or so that I was in jail. . . . Then I was sure they would suddenly decide to drop charges and put me out into the hostile night. That would be really bad, because I knew that trouble was brewing all over the city. I could see the big police wagon outside my cell window, all ready to go. Cops with gas masks and sheriffs with rifles jump into cars and zoom off. I heard dogs barking, police dogs. I figured that I would refuse to leave the station until they gave me a phone call: "You didn't let me have one when I came in, so you might as well give it to me now," I imagined myself saying. Could I hit a cop to get rearrested, or would that beating be worse than the possibility of getting caught by a mob? You can see why my pulse wasn't normal. . . .
>
> I went home to bed, absolutely exhausted. The mental strain of being in there alone was just too much. While I slept, the office was shot into.

The cumulative effect of these confrontations with the enemy was to wear the volunteers down. As the summer wore on, the physical and emotional strain grew progressively worse. "Fear *can't* become a habit," wrote one volunteer to a friend. But in fact it had. The quality of Mississippi violence—random, savage—necessitated the habit. It was a means of survival. But it was achieved at the cost of physical and psychological exhaustion. Writing late in the summer, Sally Belfrage acknowledged that "there are incipient nervous breakdowns walking all over Greenwood." Tensions within the projects only added to the strain. . . .

All things considered, it had been a remarkable summer for a remarkable group of people. As it drew to a close, the volunteers found themselves exhausted and exhilarated in equal measure. There simply had been no letup in intensity from the time they had arrived at Oxford. For the better part of two months they had been subjected to one emotionally draining experience after another. They had confronted their own mortality, experimented with new lifestyles, reveled in transcendent community, known terror, lived in poverty, felt the sting of racial hostility, and experienced the development of a radical new political consciousness. Theirs was an interesting dilemma. As much as they wanted the psychic barrage to stop, so too did they want the "high" to continue. In letters home the volunteers acknowledged the strong and conflicting feelings they were having:

> All I have to do is sit and the world piles in on me. I would like something simple, to go swimming once, or see a movie, or walk in a field, or go for a drive without having to look out the back window or just to sit somewhere cool and quiet with a friend. Only once might work. . . . I'm simply exhausted. I yell at everybody. No, I don't yell at anyone at all, I only think I do, but I can't. Madness, a constant agitation, unrest. It could all be explained by fatigue. . . . But there's a strange mechanism at work on us at night . . . when the children are gone, the chicken eaten, the mass meeting over, then there are still all of us left to egg each other on, everyone full and fed up with it but somehow longing for the next disaster. . . . All I've got is a fabulous depression, split in two—I can't bear another moment of it but it's impossible to believe that it can end in three weeks. How can I leave? How can I leave people I love so much? What made me think I could accomplish anything in this length of time? There's nowhere else I want to be.

The volunteers resolved this conflict in very different ways. At least eighty decided to stay in Mississippi indefinitely. While there had been little encouragement from SNCC to do so and no official mechanism set up to retain people, these volunteers were not ready to leave in August. Their letters home reflected both their resolve and the anguish they were causing their families.

> I have been here nearly two months. I know the drudgery, the dangers, and the disappointments. I know what it's like to eat meatless dinners, to be so exhausted you feel as though you will drop, to have five people show up at a meeting to which 20 should have come. Yet I also know what it's like to sing, "We Shall Overcome" with 200 others till you think the roof will explode off the church. I know what it's like to see the organization which you have nurtured come to life and begin to function and create. I know what it's like to have a choir of little girls sing out, "Hi, Ellen," as I walk down the road and envelop me in their hugs.
>
> Only now that I know these things can the decision to stay be mature and meaningful.
>
> Furthermore, maturity does not develop from facing a familiar routine from year to year. Maturity comes from having to face new situations, from making new decisions, from coming to terms with a new world. . . .
>
> This summer is only the briefest beginning of this experience—both for myself and for the Negroes of Mississippi. So much of it will seem pointless if it ends now, or if it is taken up again in two years. A war cannot be fought and won if the soldiers take twelve-month leaves after every skirmish. . . . I have considered your parental qualms; really I have. But I'm afraid they cannot counterbalance the feelings of my duty here.

> Many people, including those who supported my going to Mississippi as part of the Summer Project, and those who believe that the Summer Project has been an important thing, have expressed shock and disapproval at my decision to go back to Mississippi, and have attempted to dissuade me from returning. I have been amazed at this response.

There is a certainty, when you are working in Mississippi, that it is important for you to be alive and to be alive doing just what you are doing. And whatever small bit we did for Mississippi this summer, Mississippi did ten times as much for us.

I guess the thing that pulls me back most are the people who made us a part of their community. People I knew in Mississippi could honestly and unselfconsciously express affection in a way that few people I know in the North are able to do. They did not have to be "cool" or "one up" or "careful.". . . In Mississippi I have felt more love, more sympathy and warmth, more community than I have known in my life. And especially the children pull me back.

The majority of the volunteers *did* go home. However, for many the decision to do so was just as wrenching as it had been for those who remained behind.

August 6

I had a very hard time . . . convincing myself that I should leave Mississippi. . . . It is so necessary that people stay, especially northern white students. Holly Springs has so much potential and could really develop into something much greater than it already is if there are the right leaders here. I would love to be a part of making the Freedom School into a real ongoing concern with the adults and kids of the community doing most of the teaching and leading themselves. However, I have come to realize that there is still a great deal that I need to learn. I feel that I still have a lot of growing up to do. But most of all I see what this kind of life can do to you and I think that I need a rest and a change of environment to prepare myself for a life-long commitment wherever I might be needed.

Even harder than the decision to leave was the painful sense of dislocation many of the volunteers felt once they were out of Mississippi. They had arrived in the state in groups, buoyed by the exhilarating sense of community they had felt at Oxford. Now they trickled out of Mississippi one by one, alone and exhausted, without ever having an opportunity to process or come to grips with all they had seen and felt. If Oxford had oriented them to life in Mississippi, nothing prepared them for life after Mississippi. For many the transition was rough. Barely three weeks after writing the previous letter, Pam Parker struggled to express how she was feeling:

I have been putting off writing my concluding thoughts on my experiences in Mississippi because I have been unable to sort out my thoughts and feelings since leaving. I will try to at least give you a picture of the reactions of one girl on entering the free, white world of her past once again. No one can go through an experience such as Mississippi without coming out changed. I do not believe that many of those who spent their summer in Mississippi will be able to go back to their old way of living.

I am out of Mississippi and glad to be out for a while. I have always loved to take walks at night but never have I felt so grateful for the opportunity to take peaceful walks as these last few days. I could sit for hours on the porch of our friends' place in New Hampshire, soaking in the peacefulness and the quiet of the countryside. I feel so relaxed . . . but I am not relaxed, not completely. I wonder if I will ever relax fully again. . . .

I have found that instead of Mississippi seeming distant from my life, it and all that it exemplifies in a magnified form of our society has become unbearably real to me.

She was not alone in what she was feeling. On the very same day, another volunteer in another state echoed her sentiments: "I've felt depressed since I've returned. I don't know how much is personal, and how much it is a reaction to that place and the people I've left behind, and a heightened awareness of so much that is wrong up here." Contrast the underlying tone of these two letters with that expressed in a third letter written the same day by a volunteer who had stayed on in Mississippi:

> We were sitting on the steps at dusk, watching the landscape and the sun folding into the flat country, with the backboard of the basketball net that is now netless sticking up into the sunset at a crazy angle. Cotton harvesters went by—and the sheriff—and then a 6-year-old Negro girl with a stick and a dog, kicking up as much dust as she could with her bare feet. As she went by, we could hear her humming to herself, "We shall overcome."

The psychic and geographic distance from Mississippi was great indeed. Even greater was the gulf between the volunteers' summer experiences and their previous lives. Bridging that gap would prove difficult for many, impossible for some. For many the old adage, "you can always go home," would prove a lie. For some of the volunteers there would be no "going home" except in a geographical sense. They had simply seen and felt too much to ever experience their world in the same way again. They had been changed in some very fundamental ways. The extent and significance of these changes would become apparent over the next few months.

 ## For Further Study

1. What were the specific obstacles that the summer volunteers faced in Mississippi in getting African Americans registered to vote?

2. Why was it thought necessary or desirable to establish Freedom Schools? What were the schools intended to do?

3. In 1964, Mississippi ranked at or near the bottom of all the states in various measures of economic health and prosperity. In addition to being among the poorest states, if not absolutely the poorest, Mississippi also probably had the worst record with regard to racial oppression and violence. What evidence do you find in the selection that these two conditions may have been connected? What other connections may there have been between poverty and racial oppression?

4. What were the effects on the volunteers, positive and negative, of their experiences in Mississippi?

5. The selection clearly shows that those involved in Freedom Summer felt a curious mixture of hope and fear about what they were doing. To what extent was this mixture of feelings prevalent in the rest of the civil rights movement of the 1950s and 1960s? To what extent were the violence and threat of violence that marked Freedom Summer characteristic of the rest of the movement?

For Further Reading

John Hope Franklin's *From Slavery to Freedom* (1978) is a general history of African Americans. C. Vann Woodward, *The Strange Career of Jim Crow* (1974), is a relatively brief but very rich account of race relations in the South from the end of the Civil War to the recent past. Harvard Sitkoff, *The Struggle for Black Equality: 1954–1980* (1981) is a very good short history of the civil rights movement. Taylor Branch's *Parting the Waters: America in the King Years, 1954–1963* (1988) tells a part of that story in much greater detail. Martin Luther King, Jr. expressed his own views in *Stride Toward Freedom: The Montgomery Story* (1958) and *Why We Can't Wait* (1964). For another perspective on racial issues in the United States, *The Autobiography of Malcolm X* (1965) is essential reading. The history of SNCC is related by Clayborne Carson in *In Struggle: SNCC and the Black Awakening of the 1960's* (1981). There are many autobiographical accounts of life in the civil rights movement in general and Freedom Summer in particular that are valuable sources of information. Among them are Cleveland Sellers with Robert Terrell, *The River of No Return: The Autobiography of a Black Militant and the Life and Death of SNCC* (1973), by an African American man, Mary King, *Freedom Song: A Personal History of the 1960's Civil Rights Movement* (1987), by a white woman, and Anne Moody, *Coming of Age in Mississippi* (1968) by an African American woman who was also a native of Mississippi.

Chapter 20

Wayne Miller/Magnum Photos

The Haight-Ashbury section of San Francisco was the headquarters of the counterculture.

The Counterculture

Jay Stevens

The 1960s were many things, most certainly a decade of tumult and up-heaval, marked by the emergence of a number of protest movements—the civil rights movement, the student movement, the women's rights movement, the antiwar movement, the environmental movement. Those who enlisted in these causes were, of course, demonstrating their unhappiness with the exist-ing state of affairs and their desire to change it in some way. We may distin-guish two broad types of protest or rebellion: One type—the civil rights move-ment and the protests against the Vietnam War for example—was directed toward social change through political action. The other type—for example the "consciousness raising" efforts of the women's movement, trying to make women aware of the disadvantages they faced solely because of their gen-der—might be called cultural rebellion, in that the action was not directed so much against particular laws, policies, or institutions, but against the values and ways of thinking out of which those laws, policies, and institutions grew. The goal was not to get laws repealed or policies revised but to change the way people thought.

Another example of cultural rebellion is the counterculture. In the 1950s, a small group of artists and intellectuals known as the Beats, including such people as the poet Allen Ginsberg and the novelists Jack Kerouac and William Burroughs, had begun to argue that American society and culture were intel-lectually and spiritually sterile. Throughout the 1950s the Beats were little more than a curiosity to most Americans, more ridiculed for their strange ap-pearance or reviled for their use of drugs than listened to for their ideas. By the 1960s, increasing numbers came to share the Beats' notion that America was deeply flawed in fundamental ways and that drastic revisions were nec-essary. The counterculture was born out of the resulting search for alterna-tives to the dominant culture.

The term "counterculture" is difficult to define with precision, for the peo-ple who comprised it were a diffuse group with divergent ideas and goals. In general, however, one can say that they were united by a common belief that modern America was materialistic, overcentralized, competitive, conformity-ridden, and riddled with conflict and anxiety. In its place, they hoped to construct a new culture based on individual freedom and love. Frequently, perhaps even usually, these ideas were so vague as to be nearly meaningless, and many of those who eventually became involved in the counterculture were self-indulgent sensation-seekers. This was true in large part because of the central place drugs held in the counterculture experience. To prophets of the drug culture, such as the maverick psychologists Timothy Leary and Richard Alpert, drugs were a means by which individuals could "expand their consciousness" and achieve important insights about the universe, themselves, and their place in it. All too often, however, the drug experience degenerated into a quest for nothing more profound than a good time, immediate gratification, "kicks". In the following selection Jay Stevens tells the story of the counterculture, where it came from, what it was all about, and what happened to it.

There is no simple way to explain what went on in the Sixties, no easily identifiable event, like the assassination at Sarajevo, which one can point to and say, "there, tensions might have been growing for decades, but that's the spark that touched off the explosion." Indeed, the more thoroughly you study the Sixties, the more comforting becomes a concept like the *zeitgeist*. Strip away the decade's thick impasto of sex, drugs, rebellion, politics, music, and art, and what you find is a restless imperative to change, a "will to change," if you will, and one that could be as explanatory for the latter half of this century as Nietzsche's "will to power" was for the first.

Change jobs, spouses, hairstyles, clothes; change religion, politics, values, even the personality; try everything, experiment constantly, accept nothing as given. It was as though the country as a whole was undergoing a late adolescence, and not just the 20 million Baby Boomers whose leading edge began turning eighteen in 1964. Either that or the Boomers, the largest generation ever, possessed enough mass of their own to alter the normal spin of things.

But alter it in what direction? Somehow the satire of *Mad* magazine and the kinetic electricity of Elvis, the surreal dailyness of Beaver Cleaver and the fear of the Bomb; somehow the awful drabness of Dad in his official corporate uniform, the gray flannel suit, and the awful sameness of the suburbs, those theme parks of the good safe life; somehow all these had combined into a combustible outrage. It was an almost obscene irony, but the kids who had enjoyed the richest, most pampered adolescence in the history of the world had now decided that it was all crap. "We've got so many things we could puke," they said. "We live in the most manipulated society ever created by man."

Since infancy (or so it seemed to the Boomers) their minds had been measured, their psyches sculpted, their emotions straitjacketed, and for what? Why, to preserve the good old Corporate American Way of Life!

The corporations, so omnipotent during the Fifties, were vilified as the source of most of what was wrong with America, whether it was the imperialism that had brought on the Vietnam War or the subtler neurosis that caused people to measure their self-worth in terms of the number and quality of the consumer items they were able to surround themselves with. The same throwaway culture that the parents found convenient and liberating was dismissed by the children as ugly, trashy, and stupid when measured against the ecological cost of living in such a manner.

But the kids also realized that the corporations were only the visible tip of the iceberg, that the real menace was less tangible, although by the late Fifties it already had a number of provocative names: *the military-industrial complex, the power elite, the Garrison Society,* and—the ultimate winner in terms of usage—*the Establishment.*

What these terms attempted to describe was a conspiracy of money and power whose tentacles stretched into every nook and cranny of daily life. Corporations were members of the Establishment. But so were labor unions. Politicians were valued players, of course, but so were teachers, reporters and generals. Republicans and Democrats were merely different frequencies in the Establishment spectrum, while liberalism was nothing more than a clever way of allowing the illusion of change while maintaining the perquisites of power. Uniting these disparate elements was an overt commitment to anticommunism and American hegemony abroad, together with a domestic brand of democracy that sounded more like a well-run corporation than the noble experiment of the Founding Fathers. Instead of "the people," Establishmentarians talked about the managed and the managers, a formula that was not too dissimilar to the one followed in the Establishment's archenemy, the USSR.

Reflecting upon this woeful state of affairs, the Baby Boomers decided that not only didn't they want to be managed, but they could do without the occupation of manager as well. Norman Mailer caught their mood exactly when he wrote that "the authority had operated on their brain with commercials, and washed their brain with packaged education, packaged politics. The authority had presented itself as honorable, and it was corrupt, corrupt as payola on television, and scandals concerning the leasing of aviation contracts—the real scandals as everyone was beginning to sense were more intimate and could be found in all the products in all the suburban homes which did not work so well as they should have worked, and broke down too soon for mysterious reasons. The shoddiness was buried deep. . . ."

Of course not every Sixties kid accepted this critique. For each one who wanted to seize power, dismantle the Establishment, and redistribute the wealth, there were at least ten others who just wanted to get through school, get laid, get a job, and get out of going to Vietnam; for every kid who grew his hair long, smoked dope, listened to rock music, and proclaimed an urgent longing to make a clean break with American society, there was a corresponding kid who drank beer, worshiped the local football team, and measured his personal worth by the car he drove. The differential between silent majority and noisy minority probably varied little for the kids of the Sixties from that of their parents. But it didn't seem that way, if only because the silent majority is never news. And they are even less so when the *zeitgeist* is changing rapidly.

Compared to the quiescent teens of the Fifties, the Baby Boomers seemed a generation of Jacobins, a rude, unwashed, overeducated mob who, if not precisely endangering the State, certainly threatened one's peace of mind.

One of the difficulties in writing about the Sixties is deciding when the story began. Was it the day President Kennedy was assassinated in Dallas, a day imprinted on every Baby Boomer the way Pearl Harbor was for their parents? Kennedy was the Establishment's best salesman; with programs like the Peace Corps he almost managed to sell liberalism to the Baby Boom. But his death left a vacuum that was soon filled with anger and cynicism.

Or was it during the first freedom marches in Mississippi, when the kids learned just how loath the Establishment was to extend basic rights to the Blacks? Reflecting on what had happened to the consciousness of those kids who went South in the summer of 1964, Michael Novak later wrote: "Enough young people have been beaten, jailed and even killed while trying to bring about simple constitutional rights to American Negroes to have altered the inner life of a generation. The young do not think of law enforcement as the enforcement of justice; they have experienced it as the enforcement of injustice."

Or did it begin in the fall of 1964, when a group of Berkeley students staged a spontaneous sit-in that quickly grew into the Free Speech Movement?

The seeds of the FSM were sown in early September, when Berkeley Chancellor Clark Kerr, perhaps acting upon the liberal assumption that politics in the old sense was dead, banned all politicking outside Berkeley's main gate on Bancroft Way. For years Bancroft Way had been an ideological flea market, with groups of every persuasion soliciting funds and dispersing literature. Although Kerr's decision drew protests from nearly every student group, from the fledgling Students for a Democratic Society to Youth for Goldwater, Kerr refused to relent and in late September suspended eight students for political activities.

Then, on October 1, a young mathematics graduate student named Jack Weinberg was arrested for refusing to abandon the table he was manning for CORE—the Committee on Racial Equality. A campus squad car was dispatched and when it arrived Weinberg went limp, a technique he had acquired the previous summer during the freedom marches in Mississippi. As the security guards dragged him to the car, an outraged crowd began to form, effectively blocking the exit. For the next thirty-two hours, speaker after speaker climbed atop the car's hood, exhorting the students to seize the moment and strike. It was as though somebody had touched a match to a mood that had been building for years, not just a few weeks.

I felt "torn open, everything boiling in me," wrote Michael Rossman in *The Wedding Within the War*, his memoir of the Sixties. A colleague of Weinberg's in the Berkeley mathematics department, and a fellow radical, Rossman described the aftermath of the cop car siege as "the Tearing Loose—the active beginning of the end of my life within the old institutions."

On December 2, 1964, four hundred members of the Free Speech Movement seized Sproul Hall and held it until they were dragged out singing by hundreds of helmeted riot police. Five days later, an audience of eighteen thousand gathered at Berkeley's Greek Theatre to listen as Clark Kerr poured forth his vision of the true academic community as a "knowledge factory" whose purpose lay in creating socially productive individuals. Now this was the wrong tack to take with students who increasingly resented the factory analogy, but the real mistake came after the speech. As the meeting ended, Mario Savio, a young philosophy major who had become one of the leaders of the FSM, stepped to the rostrum. He intended to invite everyone to a mass rally where Kerr's speech could be debated, but before he could open his mouth to speak he was grabbed by two policemen and wrestled to the floor. A wave of anger swept the crowd. As Godfrey Hodgson later wrote, "one minute Clark Kerr, the champion of liberalism, had been talking about the powers of persuasion against the use of force, and the next moment armed agents of the University were choking his opponent, the symbolic representative of free speech."

The next afternoon the faculty voted 824–115 to accede to the FSM's demands. The Baby Boom had received its first taste of political power.

Not surprisingly, the facts attending the birth of the FSM were drowned in an ocean of learned speculation, as journalists and political scientists rushed to explain this momentary aberration. Although few of the commentators could see beyond their own ideological categories—Lewis Feuer, a reputed expert in left-wing political phenomena, dismissed the FSM as "intellectual lumpen-proletariats, lumpen beatniks, and lumpen agitators" who espoused a "melange of narcotics, sexual perversion, collegiate Castroism and campus Maoism"—most divined the central theme of the protest, which was a hearty dislike of the liberal ideal of a rationally managed society. It was a revolt against the depersonalization implied by the factory analogy that Kerr was so fond of, which was why the IBM card, with its ubiquitous warning "do not fold, spindle or mutilate," became the symbol of all they despised. Rossman described the target of the FSM as the Big Daddy Complex, which was his name for the species of liberal paternalism that had banished political diversity not only from Bancroft Way, but from the University curriculum as well. The motto of the Big Daddy Complex, he wrote, was the phrase "for your own good," and its "effect is to inhibit autonomous adulthood."

This last was a crucial point: instead of adopting the definition of psychological maturity that the mental health movement had proposed in the Fifties, with its emphasis on conformity and responsibility to the larger ideals of society, the Baby Boomers were moving in the opposite direction. The ability to let go, to explore the depths of one's own psyche, to conform to individual rather than social imperatives—these were the new benchmarks of psychological maturity.

Another element that the commentators completely ignored was the exhilaration that came from collective action. During the fifteen-hour occupation of Sproul Hall, life had been lived in a wholly new key. It was, to bend Maslow's term, a collective peak experience whose import lay not so much in the demands that had brought them together, as in the fact that they *were* together. The protesters had turned Sproul Hall into a carnival, with Chaplin movies on the walls and folksingers in the stairwells. "We ate terrible baloney sandwiches and then established the first Free University, conducting some dozen classes cross-legged atop the Civil Defense disaster drums stored in the basement," remembered Rossman. "People smoked grass in the corners . . . and at least two women had their first full sexual experiences under blankets on the roof, where walkie-talkies were broadcasting news to the outside." . . .

The word *hippie,* indeed the whole phenomenon of the Haight-Ashbury, first came to light in September 1965, in the course of a San Francisco *Examiner* article about a coffeehouse called the Blue Unicorn.

The Unicorn, which advertised the cheapest food in the city, was a little hole in the wall on Hayes Street, near Golden Gate Park, in the midst of a twenty-five-block district that derived its name from two intersecting streets—Haight Street, which ran in a flat line toward the Pacific Ocean; and Ashbury, a much shorter thoroughfare which climbed up Mt. Sutro and stopped. Like the Unicorn, the Haight-Ashbury was something of a hole-in-the-wall district, full of ornate but shabby Victorian houses dating back to the Teens, when so many politicians had built themselves mansions above Haight Street that the area had been nicknamed "politicians' row."

But in the intervening years the Haight-Ashbury had tumbled so far down the socioeconomic ladder that during World War II it had been considered an appropriate spot for worker housing. After the war refugees from Eastern Europe and a small population of Orientals had tried to resuscitate its former splendor, but when Blacks began moving into the district—encouraged by urban renewal, which was razing their traditional ghetto to the west—these homesteaders had packed up, leaving the Haight in the curious position of offering lavish living for dirt cheap prices. For a few hundred dollars it was possible to rent a whole house, complete with leaded windows and ballroom.

Now it happened that this abandonment coincided with the disintegration of the North Beach Beat scene, due to a combination of rising rents, police harassment, and obnoxious tourists who flocked to see the beatnik in his native habitat. The Haight was an obvious solution, and by the time the *Examiner* tumbled to what was happening, it supported a thriving bohemian community, of which the Unicorn was the heart and soul.

This, then, was the gist of what journalist Michael Fallon had to report to his readers: the Beat movement, far from being dead, was alive and flourishing in what had once been one of San Francisco's tonier neighborhoods. But if the Haight was where the Beat movement had fled to, then something had happened in the passage. Compared to the moody, nihilistic beatniks of old, those clichéd cave creatures in their black turtlenecks, the patrons of the Unicorn were like vivid butterflies in their pink striped pants and Edwardian greatcoats. They were sunny and cheery, and the word *love* punctuated their conversation with alarming frequency: all kinds of love, elevated ethereal love and plain old physical love. And on nights when LEMAR—the acronym for the legalize marijuana movement—wasn't meeting at the Unicorn, the Sexual Freedom League was.

Like any scientist fortunate enough to discover a new class of fauna, Fallon's first instinct was to give it a name, which he did by borrowing Norman Mailer's hipster and contracting it into hippie, a word that caught some of the Unicorn's buoyancy, but one the hippies themselves were never fond of. From their perspective, hippie was just another example of the subtle derogation practiced by the mainstream media whenever it was confronted by something outside its usual ken. Hadn't Fallon's fellow journalist, Herb Caen, done something similar when he tagged Ginsberg & Co. with the diminutive beatnik?

But whether they liked it or not, hippie it was and would be.

Oddly, Fallon's inventiveness later served to obscure the fact that in many respects the hippies were second-generation Beats. This was clearer in the early days, when it was still easy to trace the connection between the old Beat fantasy of creating an alternative culture—the word "counterculture" was still years off—and what was aborning in the Haight. "We have a private revolution going on," wrote Bob Stubbs, the owner of the Unicorn, in one of the policy statements he used to distribute to his customers. "A revolution of individuality and diversity that can only be private. Upon becoming a group movement, such a revolution ends up with imitators rather than participants."

A very private revolution: at the time of Fallon's article, there were probably only a dozen houses scattered throughout the Haight that could have been characterized as hippie. And yet the district pulsed with energy. "Even if you lived elsewhere, your forays to the neighborhood were always important," wrote one frequent visitor. "The Haight-Ashbury had four or five grapevines cooking at all times . . . and the two words that went down the wire most often in those days were *dope* and *revolution*. Our secret formula was grass, LSD, meditation, hot music, consolidation, and a joyous sexuality."

Had you lived in any of those houses in the autumn of 1965, it would have been immediately clear that the key ingredient in that formula, the reason why the Haight was not the North Beach six years later, was LSD. LSD was the Haight's secret weapon, with emphasis on secret. "Taking it was like being in a secret society," remembers one pioneer. "Hardly anything was being said about it publicly . . . [although] not an illegal drug, people acted as if it were; it seemed illegal."

It also seemed intensely serious. In the compelling phrase of one hippie, LSD was hard kicks: "hard kicks is a way of looking at your existence, not like mistreating your body or throwing your mind to the crows. It's a way of extending yourself [so that] something spectacular and beautiful can be available to you."

It was axiomatic, in the beginning, that hard kicks were dangerous. They were not a game for the timid or insecure. But insofar as they offered a way out of the white suburban world that so many of the early hippies had been born into, they were worth the risk. . . .

According to the hippies, LSD was "one of the best and healthiest tools available" for the examination of consciousness. "Acid opens your door, opens the windows, opens your senses. Opens your beam to the vast possibilities of life, to the glorious indescribable beauty of life." You could "drop down into your unconscious to see the pillars and the roots of the tree which is your personality. . . . You see what your hangups are; you might not even overcome them but you cope with them, and that's an amazing advance."

The Haight then, in its earliest incarnation, was a kind of sanitarium, an indigenous Baden Baden that offered a therapeutic regime of good vibes and drugs, rather than mountain air and mineral springs. . . .

By June 1966, an estimated fifteen thousand hippies were living in the Haight, an increase that baffled the hippies about as much as it did everyone else. "God has fingered that little block system between Baker and Stanyon Street," they told the curious. "And we spend all our time, verbally and nonverbally, trying to discover why." Helen Perry, one of the first of the social scientists to arrive on the scene, likened the Haight to "the delta of a river," where all the unrooted sediment of America was washing ashore. But even Perry was unclear as to why the undercurrents of American life should be sweeping so many into this odd backwater . . . asked why they had chosen the Haight, the hippies murmured vague things like, "I fell in with some vibrational energies and ended up here.". . .

Although the Summer of Love officially began on June 21, the summer solstice, its actual beginning occurred the previous fall, specifically on October 6, 1966, the day the California law making possession of LSD a misdemeanor went into effect.

Declaring that the long arm of the State was reaching into their psyches, the hippies welcomed the new law with a sort of Boston tea party—plenty of drugs, free food, and music—which took place in a narrow strip of park paralleling Haight Street known as the Panhandle. The get-together had a name, the Love Pageant Rally, and to everyone's surprise and delight, several thousand extravagantly garbed hippies turned out, prompting one middle-aged tourist to remark to a local journalist: "Why, you don't see anything like this in Philadelphia."

Nor, discounting the Trips Festival, which already seemed ancient history, had anything like it been seen in San Francisco before. For the first time, surrounded by fellow freaks, it dawned on the hippies that their ruling fantasy might really be correct, that the evolutionary tides might really be flowing in their direction. Perhaps it was a consequence of all the LSD, but from the Love Pageant on, a naive optimism permeated the Haight, combined with a mystical faith that whatever was needed would be provided. Almost overnight the Haight found itself with its own newspaper, the San Francisco *Oracle*, its own police force, the Hells Angels, and its own radio station, KMPX, whose lobby usually included a hippie or two in full lotus; its own Chamber of Commerce in the HIP [Haight Independent Proprietors] merchants and its own social workers in the Diggers. And there was talk of a hip employment agency, a hip hotel, and a hip cafeteria that would serve food grown on communal farms run by hippies tired of the urban grind. . . .

The first Diggers—the name originally belonged to a group of seventeenth-century religious communists who made the mistake of demanding access to the uncultivated land in Cromwellian England, and were exterminated—were actors. They belonged to a theatrical enterprise known as the San Francisco Mime Troupe, which performed a kind of political *commedia dell'arte* wherever there was space for stage and audience. The Mime Troupe specialized in street theater, which was perhaps why a few of the company began to see the Haight as a wonderful context for a perpetual theater of the absurd.

The Diggers announced their presence in a series of anonymous broadsides that mocked the smell-the-flower fatuousness of so many of the hippies. Cosmic was fine, LSD was fine, they said, but when you came back down you still had to cope with outrageous rents and bad food and all the temptations of the established culture, particularly money. "Money lust is sickness," the broadsides said. "It kills perception . . . almost all of us were exposed to this disease in childhood, but dope and love are curing us." Not surprisingly, the HIP merchants were a frequent target of Digger critiques. "How long will you tolerate people [straight or hip] transforming your trip into cash?" And they even went so far as to picket one festival, the First Annual Love Circus, because admission was a steep $3.50.

From broadsides the Diggers progressed to street theater: the Birth and Death ritual, the New Year's Wail, the Invisible Circus, the Death of Money parade. This last, consisting of six pallbearers wearing enormous papier-mâché animal heads and carrying a black-draped coffin down Haight Street, was a spectacle worthy of the surrealists. Gradually, however, the Diggers began talking less and doing more. They set up shop in an old garage known as the Free Frame of Reference, which was a reference to the huge yellow frame that they lugged around, largely so they could make the pointed joke of inviting onlookers to "step into our frame of reference now." They opened a Free Store that was full of cast-off clothes and housewares scrounged in daily forays around San Francisco. And the goods really were free. More than one Samaritan watched in astonishment as the Diggers, after ceremoniously accepting a contribution, proceeded to light their cigarettes with it. And if anyone demanded to see the person in charge, the Diggers always replied, "You are!"

The Diggers made their most substantial contribution, however, with the food feeds. Every afternoon at 4 P.M. their Dodge truck arrived in the Panhandle loaded with big aluminum garbage cans of soup, the fruits of the sort of artful hustling that the Beats had perfected back in the Fifties. . . .

One reason this was happening was because the Haight-Ashbury was about to undergo an ambiguous fifteen minutes of fame as the most notorious street-corner in the world. Every national magazine and major newspaper in the country would send a reporter to do a standard "I Was a Hippie for a Day" story. Some, like the *Chronicle*'s man, stayed undercover for a couple of weeks, and Washington *Post* reporter Nicholas Von Hoffman took in the whole three-act play that summer. But most donned blue jeans and a paisley shirt and spent a day or two standing around outside the Drugstore, trying not to sound like a narcotics agent, asking things like. "Why do you wear your hair so long?" *Because I think I'm beautiful.* "Why are your clothes so colorful?" *Because I have self-respect. Say, have you ever stopped to think that writing STOP on a sign is a pretty silly way to communicate that concept? It'd be much better if stop signs had God's eyes on them, don't you think. People would stop for God's eyes.* And so on, until you asked how he knew what God's eyes looked like, and he'd wink and say, "cause I looked into them, baby."

There was something about the psychedelic temperament that couldn't resist baiting the straights. They were so nervous about life; all you had to do was walk up to them on the street and hand them a flower and they'd freak, as though you'd just given them a joke flower that was about to spray them with *eau de deviant.* Perhaps the best put-on, the grandest, was the Great Banana Conspiracy, which first broke in the Berkeley *Barb* that March. A new psychedelic had been discovered, the *Barb* reported, one anyone could obtain, since the only ingredient was dried banana peel. Dry the peel, scrape off the inner portion, and smoke it. The high, according to cognoscenti quoted in the *Barb,* was comparable to opium, with some nice psilocybin shadings.

From the *Barb* the banana hoax bounced to the wire services and thence across the country. Students held banana smoke-ins and grocery stores experienced a repeat of the run on morning glory seeds a few years earlier, as scraggly young kids began appearing at the checkout counters with carts full of bananas. Was America going to have to ban the banana? Or require licenses before people could buy them? A congressman from New Jersey jokingly introduced two new acts to Congress: the Banana Labeling Act of 1967 and the Banana and Other Odd Fruit Disclosure and Reporting Act of 1967. But not everyone was laughing. United Fruit was more than a little alarmed. They asked Sidney Cohen to find out whether bananas really were hallucinogenic, a question that the FDA [Food and Drug Administration] also was taking very seriously. And after a lengthy and sober evaluation, it was announced that bananas were good sources of potassium and fiber, and definitely not hallucinogenic.

When it came to the hippies, the country alternated between "we are amused" and "we are not amused." A hippie is someone who "dresses like Tarzan, has hair like Jane, and smells like Cheetah," quipped the newly elected governor of California, Ronald Reagan, while in another speech he described the Bay Area as a hotbed of evil that he intended to stamp out. *Look* described the archetypical hippie pad as "a filthy litter strewn swarming dope fortress that was a great deal less savory and sanitary than a sewer," while *Time* praised its occupants as leading "considerably more virtuous lives than the great majority of their fellow citizens. This, despite their blatant disregard for most of society's accepted mores and many of its laws—most notably those prohibiting the use of drugs." But others detected, in their talk of pushing evolution and creating a new Man, the aroma of fascism. The hippies are a "fascistic reservoir" because "they are a rootless community that makes a fetish of having no leaders [and thus] may easily be mobilized by an unscrupulous leader.". . . Would they be rejected, or would the hippies, their internal compasses skewed by the drugs, follow like a slavish mob? Writing in the *Nation,* poet Karl Shapiro described the hippies as the "perfect cultural broth for fascism. The Beat people had a marginal politick and a sense of community; their drug was weed. The new generation has no need of politick or community or poetry. They have acid.". . .

There were the usual fulminations against LSD as a dry rot in the American soul and the usual symposiums of experts asking themselves why the kids of America were rejecting the time-honored stimulants of their parents. Sociologist Kenneth Kenniston attributed it to "psychological numbing." Part of the price of living in an advanced industrial society, he explained, was a deadening of the senses. "Our experiences lack vividness, three dimensionality and intensity. Above all, we feel trapped or shut in our own subjectivity." The hippies were using LSD as "a chemical sledgehammer for breaking out of [their] shell," Kenniston wrote, and while he deplored the means, he couldn't help but acknowledge the legitimacy of the search.

But that didn't console the San Francisco city fathers. Drug abuse was costing the city an estimated thirty-five thousand dollars a month; since the beginning of the year San Francisco General had been seeing an average of four bad LSD trips a day, many of them runaway adolescents barely out of puberty; and in two years the city-wide venereal disease rate had risen by a factor of six. The Haight was an open sore, and now these misguided deviants had the chutzpah to invite the youth of America to join them in a summer-long orgy of drugtaking and loitering. Mayor Shelley, in March, issued a statement that said, in effect, not in my city, you don't. "I am strongly opposed to any encouragement of a summer influx of indigent young people who are apparently being led to believe by a certain element of society that their vagrant presence will be tolerated in this city," said the mayor.

A few days later a platoon of health inspectors descended on the Haight, accompanied by a full complement of reporters. No doubt they were expecting a confirmation of filth and degradation thesis, since the adjective *dirty* had attached itself to the hippies like a birthmark. However, as public health director, Dr. Ellis D. ("LSD") Sox was forced to admit, "The situation is not as bad as we had thought." Of the fourteen hundred buildings examined, only sixty-four had violations, and only sixteen of those housed hippies.

But the raid presaged an increasingly active policy of official harassment. Police began daily raids in the Haight, sweeping the streets, demanding proof of age, arresting runaways, busting careless hippies for possession of pot and LSD, and in general wreaking havoc with the private revolution.

Paranoia, which was the shadow side of the kind of ecstatic energy that seemed to accompany prolonged LSD experimentation, began to build. A fascist putsch was being planned, went the whispers, every hippie in prison by July. "All spring the Haight shook with premonition," remembers Michael Rossman, "the airways of gossip were incessant with flashes of apocalypse . . . deep fear throbbed in the Haight."

As the Summer of Love approached, the Haight quivered in a contagion of first-night jitters.

Charles Perry, in his history of the Haight-Ashbury, describes the Haight in the summer of 1967 as "part old Calcutta with beggars squatting on the sidewalk, part football stadium crush, with people selling programs—the *Oracle,* the *Barb* and two new papers, the Haight-Ashbury *Tribune* and the Haight-Ashbury *Maverick.*" The street scene was a visual equivalent to the posters Bill Graham was commissioning to advertise the Fillmore, a swirling, colorful anarchy whose bizarre calligraphy, indecipherable at first, soon became second nature. So it was with the Haight. What to outsiders appeared demented madness was perfectly clear to anyone who was *attuned.*

Take clothes. An astute observer could date the various hippie fauna just by the cut of their clothes. The earliest residents were dandies, partial to cowboy outfits and Edwardian rigs, complete with bowlers and canes. Then came the Day-Glo superhero collages that the Pranksters had pioneered, followed by the ethnic borrowings, the serapes and desert robes, the peasant blouses, the Tibetan prayer costumes. Standing on Haight Street during the Summer of Love, an astute observer could pick out the older hippies, moving like peacocks through a monotonous sea of gray sludge: faded denim was the dominant hue that summer, blending into the fog that came rolling up Haight Street, mingling with the garbage smell and the dirt, accentuating the loneliness and despair—by midsummer it was clear that the yin had arrived to balance out the yang of the Be-In glow.

Haight Street, said the *Oracle,* had become the "abstract vortex for an indefinable pilgrimage . . . walking barefoot with hair askew, hand-made robes over torn blue jeans, the young people wander from noon until nearly two. Wandering aimlessly up Haight St., over to the free store at Carl and Cole, then back to Masonic for a cream pie and coke or to the Panhandle for Digger stew." And these wanderers weren't the true brothers of the post Be-In visions; rather they were the imitators that Bob Stubbs had warned about. They weren't beautiful, they had bad teeth and acne scars and it was easy to see they hadn't been voted homecoming king or queen back in Oshkosh or Biloxi, or wherever they'd come from. These kids were rejects; they'd come here because they were losers, and while that had a certain Christian appropriateness, it was not what the Council for the Summer of Love had expected. And along with the sheep came the usual complement of wolves, the hustlers and petty criminals. For the first time crimes other than shoplifting became a problem. One day Jerry Garcia was strolling down Haight Street when he came across a chilling bulletin:

> Pretty little 16-year-old-middle-class chick comes to the Haight to see what it's all about & gets picked up by a 17-year-old street dealer who spends all day shooting her full of speed again & again, then feeds her 3000 mikes & raffles off her temporarily unemployed body for the biggest Haight Street gang bang since the night before last.

Garcia was amazed. Why would anyone print such a depressing piece of news? "That was the point," he recalls, "where I thought, this scene cannot survive with that in there. It just goes all wrong."

Complicating the problem were the tourists, who crawled down Haight Street, bumper to bumper, windows shut, doors locked, as though passing through one of those zoos where the animals roam free and it is the humans who're encaged. In March, the Gray Line, a bus company that had operated a similar tour during the heyday of the beatniks, began advertising the Hippie Hop: for six dollars it would take ordinary Americans beyond the "bearded curtain," on the "only foreign tour within the continental limits of the United States. . . . Among the favorite pasttimes of the hippies, besides taking drugs, are parading and demonstrating, seminars and group discussions about what's wrong with the status quo; malingering; plus the ever-present preoccupation with the soul. . . ."

The hippies devised various strategies to deflect this boorish scrutiny. At first they loped into the traffic and distributed mocking handbills which read, "Middle Class Brothers! Loosen Up, let God flow through you. Remember we are with you as you drive through the valley of the shadow of death." Then they discovered the mirror game. In one of their scrounges the Diggers came across a bin of broken mirrors. The next time the Gray Line buses arrived, the hippies ran alongside holding up mirrors to the windows so the tourists could take a good look at themselves. But then the Diggers thought up the walk-ins, which involved hundreds of people walking across the street in geometric patterns, snarling traffic for miles, and generally ending with the arrival of a vanload of police.

Then in early July a small riot broke out, as a group of frustrated hippies began jumping up and down on car bumpers, banging on hoods, terrifying the tourists. The police arrived, twenty carloads of them, and a fight broke out amid cries of "fascist bastards" and "police brutality." Although numerous bones were broken, the only fatality was a dog, clubbed to death by an overexcited policeman.

Malnutrition, overcrowding, a few bad apples, paranoia, bad drugs, big egos, the absence of any leaders who were willing to call themselves leaders, the constant police harassment—there were dozens of reasons why it was going bad. Meetings were called to try to puzzle out a strategy. . . . There was no dearth of suggestions, things like: "We have to say the Ommm sound. Every day there should be a procession down Haight Street to bring the good vibes back." Or: "I think it would be a good idea to open a cathouse because there's lots of straight guys on the street who're always asking where they can get laid. And when they can't get laid their energy gets very negative." Everyone knew the vibes were turning sour, could sense it with that awakened third eye. Whenever they took LSD it was all black apocalypse and visions of the bloody crucified Christ flying across the immense nothingness of the universe.

Bad trips became the most frequent trips (San Francisco General was treating an average of 750 panic reactions a month), and for the first time the LSD psychotic became something more than a media favorite. William Irwin Thompson, a historian who was teaching at MIT, ran into the dark side of the hippie dream one night at Esalen: "His hair was very short, and it was clear from his looks that he had not been with the movement very long. Zen and the *I Ching* meant nothing to him, but the weeks of grass, speed and acid seemed to be taking him into a hell that increased his contempt and resentment for the hippies who surrounded him with talk of love." As Thompson watched, appalled, the kid began to chant to himself, "Blood, Blood, Blood, Hate, Hate, Hate." It was one thing, Thompson realized, to celebrate, à la Leary, the death of the mind. But it was something quite different "to stare unperturbed into the violent eyes of a person who has gone out of his mind."

Ralph Metzner, who had moved to California and was working up the coast from San Francisco at Mendocino State Hospital, had some equally grim visitations, as casualties from the Haight-Ashbury began arriving at the hospital. One told him, "It's coming so fast I can't function at that speed." Another said, "You, Leary and Alpert started this whole mess. That's why I took acid. Now I'm going straight to hell. I can't stop it."

Three days later he slit his wrists and bled to death.

Instead of coming together as one beautiful tribe, the Haight was getting zooier. Those who could, got out of town, like hosts abandoning their own party; others, like the Diggers, began carrying guns.

A miscalculation had been made, perhaps as far back as the gray November day when Leary, over hot milk, had rejected Huxley's elitist perspective in favor of Ginsberg's *pro bono publico* perspective. And this, with a generous nod to Kesey and the Pranksters, was the result: kids gobbling LSD wherever and whenever they could, completely ignorant of set and setting, without the least bit of interest in the Unspoken Thing. As Nicholas Von Hoffman, who was perhaps the most astute journalist to visit the Haight that summer, observed, "Their own genius for manipulating the mass media and dominating the youth culture undid them. The taste and demand for acid increased exponentially; the programming diminished. People didn't prepare themselves for dropping it; they didn't take it within the bounds of the little millennarian communities of the Haight . . . they just swallowed pills anywhere because they wanted to get stoned and see colors."

LSD wasn't a trip to the Other World for these kids: it was mind-blowing fun, better than a fast car or a quick orgasm. When there wasn't any acid around, they were equally willing to shoot up methedrine (which had the added byproduct of decreasing hunger) or heroin. The cliché that nobody who grokked (understood) the meaning of LSD could poison their body with speed or heroin turned out to be just that, a cliché. The older hippies ran around putting up signs saying "Speed Kills" but it didn't do any good. Instead of creating a taste for enlightenment, LSD was promoting a love of sensation, the more intense the better, and it began to dawn on the hippie leadership that there were a lot of kids in the Haight that summer who were going to keep sledgehammering at their shells until there was nothing left but the ubiquitous dust. . . .

It was rumored that the Mafia was moving in on the psychedelic trade, circulating bad acid so that the hippies would turn to more lucrative habits, like heroin and speed. Signs appeared saying "Boycott Syndicate Acid," but how could you tell?

It was a classic case of projection. The problems were not out there—they were at the heart of the Haight itself, and perhaps even at the heart of the psychedelic experience. There was a point, during every LSD user's career, when the trips to the Other World became negative. In a therapeutic sense, this was good. It meant that the subject was finally confronting the various repressions and neurotic clusters that were inhibiting the smooth evolution of the self. And provided the therapist or guide was skilled, the subject could usually pass through this personal Dark Wood and continue the journey. But what happened with individuals also happened with groups. There was a period when the group mind also passed through the shadow, as it were, and it was here, as the Pranksters learned during the Watts Acid Test, when the urge to erase all limits, to annihilate everything was overwhelming.

The Haight had reached this point in its collective journey, and one of the reasons it was unable to summon the wisdom to guide itself past this darkness was STP.

People took STP and went on three-day trips, many of them terrifying. "I saw myself on fire and then I began to feel the pain of fire . . . I was in hell." It was the ultimate macho trip and descriptions of it sounded like war stories, people exploding through the envelope and burning, or filled with a cold wind that wouldn't stop blowing through the hollows of their mind. STP didn't stay a secret for long. The authorities knew about the new superpsychedelic ("the next step," enthused the chemists, the first of many new combinations) almost immediately because as soon as STP hit the street the emergency rooms filled with nervous, flipped-out kids who quickly became screaming, sobbing kids when the thorazine (the traditional antidote for a bad LSD trip) took effect. Apparently thorazine acted as a booster to the STP, pushing the horror up a few more notches.

That wasn't the whole story, by any means, although it was the one that the average citizen received. What happened to most STP users was subtler, and perhaps even more profound. When Dick Alpert took it, he generally liked it and predicted a useful future. But he also made a curious remark: "I felt I had lost something human. I felt that I had lost my humanity." Alpert wasn't particularly bothered by this . . . but it really worried Ken Kesey. Kesey took STP and "forgot something. I lost a thing we take for granted, something that's been forged over I don't know how many thousands of years of human effort, and it's now in us. All I knew when this high was over was that I'd forgotten it, and it was the most important thing I'd ever known and I'd known it since I was a kid." Kesey had a hard time articulating exactly what this was ("a way of relating that, when it's gone, leaves you mighty bleak") but finally he settled for "the tiller." STP had burned away his tiller.

For the first time people were examining the fine print of the psychedelic contract, and one of the clauses they found most troubling was the possibility that besides burning away their "tillers," psychedelics were also altering their chromosomes. In March *Science* had reported that LSD, introduced to a test tube of chromosomes, caused significant breaks. And follow-up studies seemed to confirm that the white blood cells of people who had used LSD frequently showed a high percentage of breaks. The *New England Journal of Medicine* suggested that the effects of psychedelics might be similar to those of radiation, which was a sobering thought to the hippies, particularly since they were so fond of saying that God had given them LSD to counteract the Bomb. Although most scientists were quick to question the validity of the chromosome research (aspirin, thorazine, and the common cold affected chromosomes) and the underground newspapers published long (and ultimately valid) critiques of the work, it didn't diminish the anxiety that clutched at every hippie's heart: hadn't Leary always talked about LSD releasing cellular energies? What if it did? What if they really were becoming mutants? Or was it just another fusillade in the propaganda battle, an ingenious reply to Leary's thousand-orgasm gambit?

These were subtle psychological currents whose movements became clear only months later. At the time it was much simpler and much more satisfying to blame the government (the fascist putsch rumors had yet to abate) and the press. "This wasn't a Summer of Love" the hippie called Teddybear told one reporter. "This was a summer of bull and you, the press, did it. The so-called flower children came here to find something because you told 'em to, and there was nothing to find."

For the first time the next step was obvious. The Haight-Ashbury should die, so the rest of the country could be reborn. "I think it might be a good idea for us to get a pocketful of acid and go to Topeka, Kansas, and begin the work of turning people on," said Allen Cohen at one of the final strategy meetings. "There's a lot of turned-on people in New York and here, but in between is a tribal wasteland."

In a few days it would be a year since the California law criminalizing LSD had taken effect; a year since the Love Pageant Rally. It was a good time to say good-bye, so thousands of black-bordered notices were printed up:

> Hippie in the Haight-Ashbury District of this city
> Hippie, devoted son of Mass Media
> Friends are invited to attend services beginning at sunrise, October 6,
> 1967, at Buena Vista Park.

At noon on the sixth, a fifteen-foot coffin was solemnly paraded down Haight Street followed by some two hundred mourners in elaborate costumes shaking tambourines. Ten sweating pallbearers carried the giant box once around the entire Haight-Ashbury, ending in the Panhandle, where it was ceremoniously set alight. But someone had called the fire department and within minutes a couple of engines came screaming up. "The remains," someone yelled. "Don't let them put it out."

But they did, their giant hoses turning the coffin into a charred soggy mass. All that was left of hippie was a hissing cloud of steam that drifted off toward the center of the country.

For Further Study

1. Stevens says that the sixties were characterized by a widespread "will to change." How was this desire for change manifested? Where did it come from? Since most aspects of American life in the sixties seemed pleasant on the surface, how do you explain the apparent discontent of so many people?

2. Many Americans deplored the hippies and what they stood for. What exactly did they find deplorable? Do you think their opinions were justified?

3. Describe the relationship between the hippies and the media. What was the impact of the media on the counterculture?

4. What role did drugs play in the counterculture? Why were they as important as they were? What effects did drugs have on the nature and development of the counterculture? How, if at all, was the use of drugs among the hippies different from the ways drugs are used today?

5. Most of those involved in the counterculture (and the other protest movements of the 1960s, too, for that matter) were relatively young, in their teens and twenties. Why do you suppose this was the case? What effects did the relative youth of its participants have on the counterculture?

For Further Reading

William O'Neill's *Coming Apart: An Informal History of America in the 1960s* (1971), is a very good place to start looking for understanding of that tumultuous decade. Morris Dickstein concentrates on its cultural history, including its popular culture, in *Gates of Eden: American Culture in the Sixties* (1977). Young people played a large role in giving the sixties a distinctive character. Landon Y. Jones, *Great Expectations: America and the Baby Boom Generation* (1980), details the impact they had. W. J. Rorabaugh, *Berkeley at War, the 1960s* (1989), tells the story of the Free Speech Movement. On the Beats, Bruce Cook, *The Beat Generation* (1971), gives a general treatment, but the writings of the Beats themselves are indispensable to understanding them. Jack Kerouac's novel *On the Road* (1957) is an autobiographical account of Beat life in which most of the prominent Beats appear as thinly disguised characters. Allen Ginsberg's poem *Howl* (1956) shows what the Beats found repellent about American civilization. On the counterculture itself, Theodore Roszak, *The Making of a Counter Culture* (1970), is a generally sympathetic scholarly account; Charles Perry, *The Haight-Ashbury* (1984), is a readable treatment of hippie life in its chief capital; and Tom Wolfe, *The Electric Kool-Aid Acid Test* (1969), paints a very vivid picture of one particular group, the Merry Pranksters, which gathered around the novelist Ken Kesey, and provides many insights into the nature of and the reasons behind the counterculture.

Chapter 21

Donald McCullin/Contact Press Images

Many of the American troops in Vietnam were not happy about what they were doing there and made no attempt to hide their feelings.

Vietnam—and After

Loren Baritz

There is still widespread disagreement about the Vietnam War: what or who was responsible for our failure there, what we might have done to achieve better results, and what lessons we should learn from it. What seems abundantly clear is that the war traumatized the nation, both while it was going on and afterwards. We got into it without knowing precisely how, fought it for goals that were never entirely clear, argued among ourselves about it while it was in progress, and got out telling ourselves that we had won but knowing we really had not. As a consequence, when the war ended, most Americans seemed to want to forget the whole unpleasant experience as quickly as possible. That included, although no one said so in so many words, forgetting the men who had actually fought—the "grunts" as they called themselves.

However much the nation as a whole may have suffered from the war, certainly the ordinary soldiers suffered most. They risked, and 58,000 of them lost, their lives. Even more were wounded, and some of the wounds meant a lifetime in a wheelchair. Thousands suffered serious psychological wounds, and psychologists began to speak about a new kind of mental disturbance that some vets exhibited: Post-Traumatic Stress Disorder. In addition, some vets suffered long-term damage to their health as a result of exposure to Agent Orange, a chemical compound used in defoliants in Vietnam. And initially, all the veterans suffered from what seemed to them, and others, to be the indifference, ingratitude, or outright hostility of the general public.

An indication that things were changing was the dedication of the Vietnam Veterans' Memorial in Washington, D.C. in November, 1982, slightly less than ten years after the withdrawal of American troops from Vietnam. Although there were bitter debates about the Memorial's design when it was first made public, it has become a focal point for healing many of the psychological and social wounds left by the war and a force for helping to reconcile the still existing conflicts about it.

In the following selection, Loren Baritz describes the conditions that the ordinary "grunts" faced in Vietnam, how their experiences were rendered especially painful by the peculiar conditions surrounding the Vietnam War, and the problems with which they had to contend once they returned to the United States.

The drafted grunts who humped the boonies came from all over America. Street-smart ghetto kids, raised in the basketball wars, became battlefield buddies with dewy farm kids from Minnesota, patriotic, wide-eyed innocents who choked up a little when they sang "God Bless America." Hispanics, passionately ambivalent about Anglo culture, fought and drank alongside their closest war pals, the steelworkers, gas station attendants, and high school dropouts who never had a steady job. The entire nation went or was sent to war, except for the rich, the middle class, the vast majority of college students, and individuals who objected to war, or who objected to that war.

After LBJ decided to send combat troops, and after the draftees were moved into combat, the Vietnam War was fought by working-class teenagers. The draft was designed to produce that result. The average age of the American soldiers in Vietnam was just over nineteen. In World War II, the average age of the GIs who were in for the duration was about twenty-six. It was said that the military brass understood that Vietnam was a teenage war, that the kids were unruly, and that there was not much that could be done about actually imposing discipline on these post-adolescents, strong boymen who were juicers and drank too much, or were smokers on skag or pot, and were too irreverent to obey by instinct or tradition. . . .

As in Korea, the army, navy, and air force rotated individuals out in twelve months, and, until 1969, the marines in thirteen. They were almost always replaced one by one by new meat, or twinks, or cherries, or FNGs (fuckin' new guys) who were twelve or thirteen months younger than they were on their DEROS (date eligible for return from overseas).

When these kids enlisted or were drafted, at least after the American invasion in 1965, they knew that the so-called crazies were protesting the war, running away to Canada, hiding in colleges. Many of these soldiers had not thought much about the war, disliked the long hair of the hippies, and were offended by TV pictures of braless young women. Like most of the rest of the nation, they rejected the war protesters without thinking much about the war. Some men enlisted to get a better deal than the draft offered, or to get a new start in their young lives, or because a close friend signed up, or to escape the family, or to see the world, or to combat Communism. Some did not know why they enlisted. For some, it was an article of faith that the President knows best, and when he calls, you go.

"The Warriors" from *Backfire: A History of How American Culture Led Us into Vietnam and Made Us Fight the Way We Did,* by Loren Baritz. Copyright © 1985 by Loren Baritz. Reprinted by permission.

George Ryan enlisted after he graduated from high school in Virginia. He had only read girlie magazines, sports magazines, and racing-car magazines. "If Vietnam was such a mistake," he asked, "how come the leaders of our country, the wisest men we have . . . how come they sent us in? None of the doves I ever met had any answers to *that*."

A student of the army collected more of these reactions:

I know one thing. Before I went in, my brother could kick my ass, but now he can't. . . . He ain't nothing no more.

The only thing I used to read was sports. . . . So I didn't have any feelings one way or the other. I figured it was more or less right, because why would I be going if it wasn't right?

I knew almost nothing about it. The war, I thought was like they taught us in high school, you know, you're fighting communism, you know, it was just the good guys against the bad guys.

A majority of the kids who were drafted thought of the draft as an event like measles, a graduation, the weather, something that happened to people. Young men got drafted as their fathers had in earlier wars. Sometimes brothers were already in. You had to do it because it had been done before, and probably would always be done, and you had to take your turn. It was usually more intimate and domestic than patriotism, although occasionally that too played a role. More often it was an unwillingness to let someone down, to hold up your end, and to do the right thing, as that was defined in the family and in the small circle of good friends. There is not much soul-searching required to honor so simple an obligation. Someday you have to earn a living, probably marry and have children, pay taxes, but first you get drafted.

There were more enlistees than conscripts, but the draftees were especially vulnerable. They were more likely than the enlistees to find themselves in the shooting war. The draftees made up 16 percent of the battle deaths in 1965; in 1969, they were 62 percent. Draftees represented 88 percent of infantry riflemen in 1970. The army apparently considered the draftees disposable—throw-away, non-returnable men.

The Vietnam draft was an ideal model of discriminatory social policy. It kept the middle class from creating political pressure on the war administrations. So the draft was biased by level of income. The higher the income, the less chance of being drafted, importantly but not exclusively because of educational deferments. Poor young Americans, white as well as black and Hispanic, were twice as likely to be drafted and twice as likely to be assigned to combat as wealthier draft-aged youth. The draft rejected many blacks, but it was more likely to accept poor men than richer men with the same qualifications, or the same lack of qualifications. As a result, poor black Americans were swept into the fighting war in disproportionate numbers. Economic class, even more than race, except that people of color were more likely to be poor, was what determined who fought and who died. . . .

Education in this country is a badge of class. One study of Chicago neighborhoods found that kids from areas with low educational levels were four times as likely to be killed in Vietnam than those from more schooled neighborhoods. It was as if the war had been designed to digest America's victims, the men President Eisenhower called the "sitting ducks" for the draft. Class and education also shaped the experience of the young men who enlisted. Two staff officials of President Ford's clemency board showed that a college graduate who enlisted had about a 40 percent chance of being sent to Vietnam, while a high school graduate's chance was about 65 percent, and that of a high-school dropout was 70 percent. . . .

Survival was the strategy of the American GI, not different from soldiers in earlier wars. But, for the great majority of Vietnam grunts, there was no external purpose to the war—not defending national goals, not resisting an evil enemy, not defending motherhood and apple pie. As a result, there was no animating justification for combat or for risk. The best way to survive was to keep away from danger. This absence of external purpose made it difficult for some to develop a sense of shared enterprise with other GIs outside their own unit. Because the replacements were inserted into the war as individuals, not as members of a unit, these GIs were in fact movable parts, separate cogs in the war's machinery. Such separateness induced a sense of fragility, probably more intense and widespread than in other wars. The separate arrivals and departures, along with the absence of shared purpose, emphasized the individuality of the grunt, even while they formed the life-saving bonds of brotherhood in their small squads or platoons. It is touching and painful to hear how often the veterans felt alone.

The grunt was the instrument of General Westmoreland's "strategy" of attrition. For entirely different reasons, the grunts' war plan became identical with the general's. There was no real estate that had to be taken and held, there were no objectives to be seized. The plan was to kill the enemy, wherever and whoever he or she was. Because the body count was the scorecard, killing supposedly proved progress. This made war sense from the grunt's perspective because it was simply based on the desire to live, not necessarily callousness or moral collapse, but war through the eyes of the walking conscripts.

That is why the "other war," the ideological war, meant nothing to most of them. It did not seem, at least in the short run, the time that really mattered, to protect their lives. So they mocked the entire effort to "win the hearts and minds" of the Vietnamese by referring to it as WHAM and embroidering it even further: "Grab 'em by the balls and their hearts and minds will follow."

Luis Martinez, a Puerto Rican marine, decided he would learn something about the Vietnamese and treat them with respect because "if the Viet Cong is going to do something, he remembers you and you have a better chance of surviving." In this sense, winning hearts and minds might help him to return home in one piece. It was like money in the bank that could produce interest in the future. But in this war's twists, respect and friendship for the Vietnamese could backfire. For example, a sergeant became friends with a Vietnamese woman and her daughter. They were both killed by the NLF [National Liberation Front: Viet Cong] because they had associated with him. He decided that from then on he would leave them all alone. For most, the "other war" would take too long, was out of focus, and was therefore not a good shield for the vital or fatal 365 days they would be targets.

The grunts hated bloody fighting to take a fire base, perhaps losing buddies in the process, and then being ordered to abandon the base to fight or patrol somewhere else, and then having to endure another fire fight to recapture the first base. Some bases were retaken three or four or more times. One GI put it this way: "We don't take any land. We don't give it back. We just mutilate bodies. What the fuck are we doing here?" It seemed senseless to risk everything over and over for the same piece of turf. There was no achievement to show for the mutilations and deaths. Except the numbers. They had to train themselves to think of achievement by the numbers. Many, probably most, could not do it. They could not think of what they were doing only in terms of the body count. Even in war, death was supposed to be for something, not a thing in itself.

They recognized that the body counts were being hyped to satisfy, or shut up, corrupt officers who kept demanding higher numbers. The men could deliver any number any REMF, "rear echelon mother fucker," wanted. Of course that made the killing even more pointless. If the brass would accept fake numbers, and if the whole point of the war was numbers, why risk your life to get real kills? The war could have been fought over the radio, with a squad or company reporting whatever number was wanted. That is what sometimes happened. The grunts knew it was fraudulent and they became contemptuous of their officers. For example, after one fire fight, Herb Mock, a rifle-squad leader, said: "General Westmoreland flew in. All the news outfits and everything. It was the most hilarious thing. As these son of a bitches came out there, the GIs started lying. The newsmen would walk up to just anybody and say, 'What did you do?' 'I single-handedly killed three hundred thousand with my bowie knife.'" Lieutenant Robert Santos spoke for many when he said, "You come home with the high body count, high kill ratios. What a fucking way to live your life.". . .

Some grunts were stunned by the open hostility of some South Vietnamese, the people they had come to defend. When they had to run up chicken wire to block the objects, including grenades, that some South Vietnamese threw at them, there was no way they could avoid wondering what they were doing there. It was maddening to discover that the food or medicine they gave to friendlies would be handed to the guerrillas after dark. It was a shock to march past an aged mama-san selling Coca-Cola on the road and notice her head nodding as each grunt passed; she was counting them. What for? What could you make of the fact that the friendlies who washed your clothes or cut your hair were found dead in your ambush of the NLF during the night? And what about the mama-san who brought you things right into your fire base and hung around a little while so she could memorize where your bunkers were so the guerrillas that night could zero in with their mortars? What about the local whores telling you where you were going next, before your own officers had announced it? This war was not like others. You could never identify the enemy. That created constant danger, not merely at the front—there was no front—but everywhere, and not merely during a battle, but anytime. Any Vietnamese could be the one. A T-shirt worn by the grunts displayed the message: KILL THEM ALL! LET GOD SORT THEM OUT!

Having no larger external purpose, there were also often no external constraints. The line beyond which an action would become a transgression was a matter of individual conscience, a Protestant formula. This was as true for the officers as for the troops. The moral formlessness of the bureaucratic war necessarily emphasized technique and means, not goals or purpose. Bureaucracies typically do not do as well at expressing where they wish to go as they do at expressing how to get there. "If you're lost, drive faster; that way you'll get it over with sooner." This left the teenage warriors to their own moral devices, such as they were. Group pressures formed one code of conduct; a watchful officer might sometimes form another. Unlike earlier wars, the Vietnam rule was the moral independence of the foot soldier and his officers.

The rapid turnover of their immediate officers—usually every six months, often less—led to the conviction that the grunts knew better than anyone else, especially better than the six-month wonders, the shake-'n'-bake lieutenants, how to stay alive. These teenage warriors were therefore thrown back into themselves in a way unusual in war. They had to take care of each other if they were to make it. After a while they could wear earrings, write almost anything they liked on their helmets and flak jackets, shoot up on drugs, get drunk, and more often than not get away with it, especially when they were in the field, which everyone called Indian country. They enjoyed getting away with it, and hated "chicken shit officers" who worried about shined shoes; but getting away with it also taught some of them that the brass did not care, and that they were on their own both as a unit and as individuals. . . .

The grunts understood that they were endangered by the guerrillas, the regular army of North Vietnam, and their own temporary, rotating officers, in no particular order of threat. They knew that the home front did not support what they were doing. If no one cared about them, they could not care about the rules or established authority. Occasionally, around 1970, grunts would scribble UUUU on their helmets: the unwilling, led by the unqualified, doing the unnecessary, for the ungrateful. Other helmets proclaimed POWER TO THE PEOPLE, KILL A NONCOM FOR CHRIST, or NO GOOK EVER CALLED ME NIGGER. It was finally as if all they could believe and remember were pain and death. One young man from the Bronx, for example, was cited for heroism:

> They gave me a Bronze Star and they put me up for a Silver Star. But I said you can shove it up your ass. I threw all of the others away. The only thing I kept was the Purple Heart, because I still think I was wounded.

A wound is the most intimate souvenir.

It cannot be surprising that the grunts found ways to resist corrupt officers in a war that could not be understood. Desertions, excluding AWOLs, in the army alone rose from 27,000 in 1967 to 76,634 in 1970, a rate increase of 21 per thousand to 52 per thousand. The marines were even worse with 60 desertions per thousand. According to the Department of Defense, the rate of desertion in Vietnam was higher than in either Korea or World War II, and the rate increased as the intensity of the fighting declined and absurdity increased. As President Nixon began withdrawing troops, many of the grunts remaining on the ground lost even more conviction about why they should stay and fight. The desertion rate from 1965 to 1971 increased by 468 percent.

Fragging, defined as an attempt to murder by using a grenade, reached astonishing levels in Vietnam. It was usually a result of the fear and hatred felt by the workers toward their bosses. For example, marine Private Reginald Smith testified in a court-martial that his lieutenant was so slow in setting up a listening post that by the time he sent three marines out, the NLF was waiting and killed two of them. The troops were discussing the incompetence of this lieutenant just before he was killed by a fragmentation grenade. It was frequently said that combat squads raised a bounty to be awarded to anyone who would "waste" a particularly hated officer. The Criminal Investigating Department of the Third Marine Amphibious Force said there were more than 20 fraggings in eight months of 1969, according to the transcript of a court-martial. The Defense Department admits to 788 fraggings from 1969 to 1972. This figure does not include attempts to kill officers with weapons other than "explosive devices," such as rifles. Richard Gabriel calculated that "as many as 1,016 officers and NCOs may have been killed by their own men," but he points out that this figure includes only men who were caught and tried. There is no precedent in American military history for violence against officers on anything like this scale.

Another response of the "workers" was to "strike," that is, to disobey a combat order, that is, to commit mutiny. The Pentagon kept no records of mutinies, but Senator Stennis of the Senate Armed Forces Committee said that there were 68 mutinies in 1968 alone.

Yet another form of resistance by grunts was the pandemic use of hard drugs. In the spring of 1970, 96 percent pure white heroin appeared in Saigon; by the end of the year it was everywhere, sold in drugstores and by Vietnamese children on street corners. This junk was so pure and cheap that the troops smoked or sniffed, with only a minority reduced to injection. Its use was not remarkable in Vietnam because smoking was usually a group activity, accepted by almost everyone, and common for clean-cut midwestern boys as well as for city kids. Nothing in all of military history even nearly resembled this plague. About 28 percent of the troops used hard drugs, with more than half a million becoming addicted. This was approximately the same percentage of high school students in the States who were using drugs, but they were using softer stuff. In Vietnam, grass was smoked so much it is a wonder that a southerly wind did not levitate Hanoi's politburo.

The failure of senior officers is partly reflected in the fact that they knew what was going on and did nothing to stop it, and did not protest. Richard Gabriel and Paul Savage concluded that "the higher officer corps was so committed to expedience that the organized distribution of drugs was accepted as necessary to the support of the South Vietnamese government, which often purveyed the drugs that destroyed the Army that defended it." The CIA and the diplomatic corps in Vietnam prevented other governmental agencies from getting at the truth, while individuals with the CIA, if not the Agency itself, helped to fly drugs into Vietnam from Laos.

Despite an occasional attempt to do something—usually punishing the troops—about the blizzard of skag, neither the U.S. government nor the military ever accomplished anything worth mentioning. The much advertised urine testing (to be conducted in what the GIs called The Pee House of the August Moon) was ineffective because the tests were unreliable, the troops who were not hooked could flush their bodies before the tests, and no one was prepared actually to help the soldiers who were addicts. One scholar concluded that "in not rooting out the sources of heroin in Laos and Thailand, the government had simply made a calculation that the continued political and military support of those groups profiting from the drug traffic was worth the risk of hooking U.S. soldiers." General Westmoreland, as usual, blamed everyone but his own senior officers: "The misuse of drugs . . . had spread from civilian society into the Army and became a major problem. . . . A serious dilution over the war years in the caliber of junior leaders contributed to this. . . ."

Racial conflict was suffused throughout the war, from 1968 until the end. Every service, including the previously calm air force, had race riots of varying magnitude. As some of America's cities burned, or rather as the ghettos in some cities burned, the domestic rage found its counterpart in the military. Fraggings were sometimes racially motivated. One battalion commander said, "What defeats me is the attitude among the blacks that 'black is right' no matter who is right or wrong." One black soldier said, "I'd just as soon shoot whitey as the VC." In one incident that is what actually happened: Two white majors were shot trying to get some black GIs to turn down their tape recorder.

White officers were sometimes offended by expressions of black solidarity, including ritual handshakes, the closed fist, swearing, black jargon, and, especially, blacks arguing that they were being forced to fight "a white man's war." (The North Vietnamese and the NLF often tried to exploit that theme through various forms of psychological warfare.) The weight of the military justice system was lowered on black GIs far out of proportion to their numbers. The congressional Black Caucus did a study in 1971 that showed that half of all soldiers in jail were black. The next year, the Defense Department learned that blacks were treated more harshly than whites for identical offenses. The occasional race riots were invariably triggered by the increasing militance of American blacks in general, the peculiarly obtuse social attitudes of many older military officers, the frustrated hopes of the Great Society, the sense of an unfair draft, and an unfair shake in Vietnam.

Trying to make it to DEROS, that miraculous day one year after they had stepped foot onto Vietnam's red soil, the foot soldiers did what they could to survive the guerrillas or North Vietnam's army or their officers. For most of them, the point of the war was the clock ticking toward the shortening of their time, and, finally, the last day, the wake-up call, and home. Others, in a daze of battle, tried to put home out of mind. Many others, probably most, became increasingly cautious as their "sentence" wore down, and the ingenuity expended by the short-timers in avoiding combat, occasionally simply by threatening a hard-driving officer, was inspirational, almost enough to revive the American dream of self-reliant citizens. No one wanted to die with only hours, or days, or weeks, or months, left to serve. No one wanted to die in any case, but it was even more unbearable to think about with only a short time to go. The idea of home, the idea of making it, became increasingly real as the war became increasingly surreal.

They left Vietnam as they came, suddenly, by air, usually alone, and engulfed by impressions and anxieties that were too cascading to sort out. "We went to Vietnam as frightened, lonely young men. We came back, alone again, as immigrants to a new world," William Jayne, a marine rifleman, wrote. "For the culture we had known dissolved while we were in Vietnam, and the culture of combat we lived in so intensely for a year made us aliens when we returned." They were aliens for a great variety of reasons, some because they had grown up while their former buddies who had not gone to Nam seemed as if they had been frozen in time; they were still late adolescents whose lives revolved around six-packs, cars and chasing girls. Others because they were stunned by the nation's refusal to welcome them home as returning warriors. Others because of the continuing pain of flesh and memory. Yet others because the war had destroyed their earlier faith in "the World," in American institutions. . . .

. . . Thomas K. Bowen thought when he got home that the entire war had been a "mistake," and said, "I mean I have no—absolutely no—respect for my government." Still others could not get jobs, and some resented the women and the non-vets who were working. Joe Boxx finally decided that "bein' a Vietnam vet didn't mean shit." Skip Sommer had re-upped to survive, but finally could not endure the army and deserted; he eventually gave himself up and was later dishonorably discharged. He was a haunted, enraged man even twelve years later. But, he said, "I don't remember anything I really am ashamed of, besides the fact that I survived." Alberto Martinez was losing his mind and in despair killed himself. Edmund Lee became an expatriate in Australia. Frank Goins, back home in south Georgia, remembered the democracy of races in the foxholes, but discovered, "When we got home, they still didn't want us to go to Mr. Charlie's cafe by the front door. . . ." David Brown was not even given the usual four or five days off the line at the end of his tour; one day he was in combat and the next night the freedom bird landed him in San Francisco. He drank too much for a year or two. Charles Rupert said: "I risked my life for my country, and now nobody gives a shit. If I have a son, I won't let him go. I'll send him to Canada first." J. C. Wilson: "We were fools."

On the other side, Lieutenant Robert Kennish, a commander of Charlie Company: "I did pretty well. No problems at all, really, that are going to afflict me for the rest of my life. I think I gained more from my experience in the military and in Vietnam than I lost." What mattered to him most was that he grew in his own self-esteem as a man. An anonymous veteran grunt said that he simply grew up in the war. David Rioux, a devout Catholic who was blinded in the war, understood and approved the war as a struggle against Communism, one that he was proud to have fought. Michel, David's brother, fought in David's company and feels that David's faith prevented him from committing suicide. David said about himself and his brother: "We both knew why we were in Vietnam, and the men around us didn't, for the most part, or saw it only confusedly, but we saw why we were there and we were proud to be there, defending a people who were being oppressed by Marxist Communism. We were doing something that was commendable, in the eyes of God, our country and our family."

The stereotypes at loose in the nation when the troops began returning were largely shaped by the reports of My Lai as well as television reports of the heroin nightmare. Many Americans assumed the returning vets were junkies. Some vets were persistently asked how it felt to kill a human being. All the vets were subjected to an embarrassed national attitude about the war, and about their role in it. It got worse when the North overran Saigon, and television showed the pictures of the scramble to evacuate the remaining Americans. Then the question became even more insistent: What did we accomplish by fighting? For the veterans who had believed in the cause, Saigon's surrender was a terrible blow. Both the Rioux brothers, along with other traditionalists, believed that "giving up" was the mistake, not intervening in the first place. For the others, those who had decided the war was not worth fighting while they were fighting it, the fall of Saigon confirmed their opinion. In any case, the veterans faced an unprecedented social and political fact when they finally made it back: The nation did not know what to do with them, and would just as soon forget, or try to forget, the entire sorry "episode." None of the vets could forget.

They were not only not welcomed home, some of them were abused for their uniforms, their decorations, and their short hair. There was a revealing false rumor that antiwar critics were shooting vets as they climbed out of their planes. It is a mass delusion, of course, but thousands of vets claim that they were spat upon when they first arrived home. . . .

Most of the veterans returned home reasonably whole, as whole as returning veterans from earlier wars. The majority were not dopers, did not beat their wives or children, did not commit suicide, did not haunt the unemployment offices, and did not boozily sink into despair and futility. Yet, some prisons are still populated with black vets; the VA [Veterans Administration] hospitals still do their bureaucratic thing too often and fail to help. Some vets, more than a decade later, have not yet recovered, and some never will. The government has done less for these veterans than for those of other wars. The vets had to build their own monument. Now they are struggling to force the reluctant government to face up to the hideous question of the degree to which our war technology had poisoned our own men with Agent Orange. More than a decade after most of them had come home, the government in 1984 began to make small progress in admitting its responsibility in this issue.

Nonetheless, the majority returned home and found there was life after Vietnam. Tim O'Brien, a former grunt and prize-winning novelist, thought the adjustment was too good. He feared that the vets' experience was becoming too mellow, too nostalgic. He had hoped their recoil from war would have been more of a brake on national saber-rattling. He wished they could have retained the passion and convictions that sustained them while they were boonie-rats. He wrote, "We've all adjusted. The whole country. And I fear that we are back where we started. I wish we were more troubled."

When some grunts in Vietnam heard the news that the war was over, everyone began shouting. "They were ecstatic." One of them finally asked, "Who won?" They were told the NLF won. "They didn't care."

For Further Study

1. How did the conditions the grunts faced in Vietnam differ from what American soldiers had to deal with in previous wars? How did the reception they got at home differ?

2. Baritz's account implies that many in the Army itself, particularly those on the higher levels of command, were not as concerned as they should have been with the welfare of the troops under their command. Do you think this implication is correct? If so, how do you explain it?

3. It has been suggested that the problems within the armed forces in Vietnam, drug use, racial tension, lack of respect for authority, and so forth, were simply reflections of these problems within American society. Others argue, on the contrary, that these problems originated in the conditions in Vietnam itself. Which explanation makes more sense to you? Why?

4. How are the conditions Baritz describes, both in Vietnam and the United States, related to the psychological problems some Vietnam veterans have experienced?

5. Does the information in Baritz's account give you any insights into why the United States was not able to achieve its objectives in Vietnam?

For Further Reading

The literature on the war in Vietnam is enormous and still growing. The following items represent only a tiny sample. One might begin by reading *The Pentagon Papers,* published in many editions, including one in paperback (1971), edited by Neil Sheehan et al. of *The New York Times.* Volumes dealing with the war within the larger context of social and political developments within the United States include Alexander Kendrick, *The Wound Within: America in the Vietnam Years, 1945–1974* (1974); David Halberstam, *The Best and the Brightest* (1972), a study of the false pride that Halberstam feels led to this and other national tragedies; William J. Lederer, *Our Own Worst Enemy* (1968), a look at the self-deception and ignorance of the American people regarding the war in Vietnam; and Frances FitzGerald, *Fire in the Lake* (1972), an account of how cultural differences divided Americans from Vietnamese and led to mutual misunderstandings that contributed to the debacle. Stanley Karnow, *Vietnam, a History* (1983), is a general history of the war derived from a television series made for the Public Broadcasting System. Accounts of the war by those who experienced it firsthand are numerous. They include Alan Dawson, *55 Days: The Fall of South Vietnam* (1977), and Michael Herr, *Dispatches* (1977)—both by journalists—and Ron Kovic, *Born on the Fourth of July* (1976), and Tim O'Brien, *If I Die in a Combat Zone, Box Me Up and Ship Me Home* (1973)—which tell the story of the war from the soldiers' point of view. Al Santoli has collected soldiers' reminiscences in *Everything We Had: An Oral History of the Vietnam War by Thirty-Three American Soldiers Who Fought It* (1981). Christian G. Appy, *Working-Class War: American Combat Soldiers and Vietnam* (1993), is a recent historical work that summarizes much of the existing information about the experiences of soldiers in Vietnam. The commanding general, William C. Westmoreland, gives his view of the war in *A Soldier Reports* (1976). Robert Jay Lifton, *Home from the War* (1973), discusses the impact of the war on the veterans. Harrison E. Salisbury, ed., *Vietnam Reconsidered: Lessons from a War* (1984), contains the conflicting opinions of several people on the meaning and impact of the war and the lessons that we should draw from it.

Chapter 22

R. Ferrell Friend/Charleston Gazette

A rally protesting the introduction of new text books into the schools of Kanawha County, West Virginia.

Culture War

William Martin

The social movements of the 1960s had a number of long-term effects on the United States besides getting laws passed and policies adopted. One was to make new forms of protest and direct action seen feasible and desirable. Another was to awaken social groups that had previously been regarded—and possibly had regarded themselves—as marginal to the possibilities of social and political action on their own behalf. A final effect was to generate a series of conflicts and controversies that by the end of the decade had created a deeply polarized society and established the foundations for what are often referred to as the "culture wars" of contemporary society.

One specific manifestation of these effects has been the emergence in recent years of the religious right. Previously in the twentieth century, except for a brief flurry in the 1920s, there was little obvious connection between people's religious beliefs and their political preferences and actions. The effects of religion on politics were indirect, covert, or completely nonexistent. This situation began to change in the 1970s. Many people were deeply disturbed by what they saw as the excesses committed by the various social protest movements of the 60s and by the ways those movements had changed and were changing America. Some responded by reasserting their commitment to traditional values, including religious values, and the result was a powerful resurgence of political and cultural conservatism, culminating in the election of Ronald Reagan as president in 1980 and his reelection in 1984. In this process, a prominent role was played by ministers like Jerry Falwell and Pat Robertson who used television to spread views that combined religion and politics into a potent mixture. For many devout followers of these and other ministers, political activism became a way of bearing witness to their religious beliefs.

The following selection describes one particular conflict in one county in West Virginia, but it is representative of many others that became and have remained a significant feature of the nation's social and political landscape. It is also a clear example of how religious belief was wedded to political action in the emergence of the religious right.

Alice Moore read about the Battle of Anaheim [over a proposed sex-education program in the public schools] in the *Saturday Evening Post* in 1969, while sitting in a beauty shop in St. Albans, West Virginia. "I was shocked at some of the things I read," she recalled, "but I wasn't that concerned about it, because I knew this was West Virginia, not a radical state like California. I thought, 'It's not going to happen here.' " Not long afterward, however, she saw a newspaper story announcing that sex education was going to be introduced in Kanawha County schools. "That concerned me a little bit," she said, "but not all that much. And then I noticed that there was going to be a parents' meeting in a little restaurant in South Charleston, so I decided I'd go." That simple decision set Alice Moore on a course of action that erupted into a full blown "culture war," a violent and prolonged upheaval that laid bare deep fissures in the county's social structure.

In 1969, Kanawha County, West Virginia, was predominantly white, Anglo-Saxon, and Protestant—folks who, one would think, should find it easy to get along. But cutting across those broad categories were divisions of religion, class, and world-view that made real community for whites, much less for whites and blacks together, all but impossible. By its residents' own account, the county had at least two distinct populations of whites: the reasonably well-educated middle-class citizens of Charleston and the rural Appalachians who worked in the chemical plants and refineries of Nitro, St. Albans, and Dunbar, or carved a living out of the sometimes wild, coal-filled mountains gorged by hollows and creeks that drain into the Kanawha River. The social and cultural chasm between the capital city and the surrounding Upper and Lower Valleys is sufficiently wide that, at times, some have thought the county should be divided into two. Just about the only governmental jurisdiction that treated the area as a single unit was the Kanawha County school district, and in the 1970s that could serve more to divide than to unite. The closing of dozens of small schools during the 1950s and '60s has thrown more rural children into contact with urban culture, thereby undermining their own folkways. The changes wrought by the upheavals of the sixties also threatened the fragile peace that masked quite different ways of perceiving reality.

Alice Moore was a relatively new resident of the area, having moved there when her husband became minister of the fundamentalist Church of Christ in St. Albans, an industrial suburb south of Charleston. Though she had no deep roots

---

in the county, she did have a great concern for children and strong convictions about how they should be reared. Nevertheless, while the leaders of the meeting in South Charleston were uneasy about the proposed sex-education program, Mrs. Moore tried to keep an open mind. "When I listened to some of the things they were saying," she remembered, "I still wasn't convinced that everything was necessarily true, because people get excited about things sometimes. So I decided I would go to the Board of Education and just ask to see the materials myself. Many of the pictures I had seen at the meeting simply weren't there. Many of the things they had said were in the materials, I didn't see." Later, she alleged, she learned that some of the more controversial materials had been withdrawn after the first flurry of objections. Even with those items removed, however, she still found the proposed curriculum disturbing. "What concerned me was that this wasn't just a sex-education course. It dealt with every aspect of a child's life. It dealt with their attitudes. In fact, the stated purpose of the course was to teach children how to think, to feel, and to act. And it covered everything, from their re-lationship with their parents, to their attitudes toward the use of drugs and social drinking, to their attitudes toward sexual conduct. So that concerned me."

The curriculum, a comprehensive health education program, had been pre-pared with the aid of a U.S. Office of Education grant and approved by the Kanawha County Board of Education and a Curriculum Advisory Committee of interested citizens—none of whom represented the county's more conservative rural population. To express her concern, Moore called Superintendent of Schools Walter Snyder and explained her feeling that the proposed curriculum would intrude into "our relationship with our children, what we wanted to teach them, what we wanted them to believe, how we wanted them to behave." His reply, by her account, amounted to little more than, "I'm sorry, Mrs. Moore, but there's absolutely nothing you can do about it."

Alice Moore did not accept Snyder's reading of the situation. Instead, she be-gan speaking to various groups around the county and lobbying members of the state legislature to look into the matter. When her efforts seemed ineffectual, Moore and a few of her friends decided she should run for the single contested spot on the Board of Education. "We went down there with just minutes to spare and signed up to run," she recounted with a laugh. "It was really a spur-of-the-mo-ment decision." A newspaper poll conducted a week before the election gave the incumbent nearly a third of the vote and Moore about eighteen percent, with the remainder split among seven or eight other candidates. Moore credits the news-paper poll, which indicated she had at least some chance, with rallying much of the anti-incumbent sentiment behind her. . . . [S]he took thirty-four percent to the incumbent's thirty-three, defeating him by approximately four hundred votes.

Within months of taking office in early 1970, Moore managed to overcome op-position to her view that the sex-ed curriculum was anti-Christian, anti-American, and indoctrinated students with an "atheistic and relativistic view of morality" that ran counter to her own firm conviction that "God's law is absolute." She acknowl-edged, "We pretty well won our case. Everything wasn't exactly to my liking, but we no longer had a program that was as disturbing to people as that one had been." In the course of this conflict, Superintendent Walter Snyder resigned and was replaced by Kenneth Underwood. These accomplishments made Alice Moore a champion in some circles. When she ran for re-election in 1976, she received 25,000 votes, two-and-a-half times her total in 1970 and 7,500 more than the nearest competitor. Moreover, she pointed out, most of the eight or nine people running against her shared her basic stand on most issues. Clearly, the rural "creekers" and factory workers, as well as a substantial number of white-collar city folk, felt they now had a voice on the Board of Education.

"Sweet Alice," as both friends and critics came to call her, though with different inflections, next made big news in 1974, when the school board sought to adopt 325 titles for its K–12 language-arts curriculum. In standard fashion, the books had been chosen by a school-system textbook committee. Under Superintendent Underwood, the Curriculum Advisory Committee had become dormant, so the textbook committee's recommendation reached the board in March and received rubber-stamp preliminary approval at a meeting Alice Moore missed. In keeping with the times, the books included substantial selections from black, Hispanic, and other minority writers, as well as a much greater than usual variety of other materials, all designed to help teachers create individualized programs of instruction that recognized differences in student interests, outlooks, and aptitude. The board followed established policy and put the books on display at the Kanawha County Library, to allow any citizen who wished to look them over to do so. They apparently drew almost no attention. When the time came to finalize adoption, however, Moore complained that not enough time had been allowed for inspection and persuaded her colleagues to extend the period of inspection until the June board meeting.

Mrs. Moore was particularly concerned about a growing toleration of "non-standard English" and had read articles, she explained, "to the effect that it was as important for a child who spoke standard English to learn to speak ghetto English as it was for a child of the ghetto to learn to speak standard English. That was an outrageous idea. If that's the case, why do we hire English teachers? Why do we even bother?" She listened to English teachers tell the board about a broadening approach to teaching, and, she recalled, "The more they talked, the more I realized they were talking about teaching non-standard English. So I suggested we postpone the adoption."

Objection to "non-standard English" can be a coded way of registering dislike of blacks and other minorities. It can also be precisely what it purports to be: objection to non-standard English. Those to whom the substitution of "lay" for "lie" and the use of nominative pronouns after prepositions sound worse than fingernails on a blackboard need not be racist to hope their children will not "axe" such questions as "Do he have your grammar book?" Whatever Alice Moore's true motivation on that score, she soon found even more substantial problems with the new books. Indeed, moments after the April board meeting adjourned, her husband, who had been leafing through some of the books, said, "I want you to look at what you just adopted." The selection he handed her, she remembered, "was written by a man who said, 'Thank God' he had gotten out of the South, because if he hadn't, he'd 'still be a blankety-blank Christian.' ". . .

[C]omplaints about the textbooks fell into categories familiar to anyone who . . . was aware of similar struggles in other states. The objecting parents sought to shield their children from anything that smacked of a lack of patriotism or, in their oft-used phrase, "disregard for government authority." Mike Edds, an inner-city youth pastor who rallied to Moore's side early in the protest, explained that, "Those books challenged the sacredness of everything that we believe about America. I'm sure America's wrong at times, but we believe it's the best thing we've come across in this world. They never brought out what America did do that was good. They said the flag was just a piece of cloth. Well, that's not what we believe. We have a lot of relatives who died under that banner. To us, it's like a sacred symbol. You don't burn the flag; you don't challenge what our Founding Fathers have done, or the Constitution. If there're things that're wrong, you work to change [them] and make it better." Closely related to changes of a lack of patriotism were complaints that the books contained criticism of the free-enterprise system. Elmer Fike [a local businessman], regarded some of the readings as "obviously liberal, socialist, even communist-inspired." Alice Moore was less inclined to think actual communists were involved, but she did believe the books bore the marks of "people in our country who are maybe leftist leaning, who think socialism is a better system than we have. They were radical books."

In addition to these fears, Mrs. Moore voiced concern that the books might create "more race consciousness than they would otherwise have had." Numerous parents were disturbed by material written by such black writers as Nikki Giovanni, Alice Walker, James Baldwin, and Gwendolyn Brooks. Ruth Davis, an English teacher who was also active in the local NAACP chapter, recalled her pleasure at seeing the work of black and Hispanic authors in the series: "I felt we had moved forward. We had faced integration and here we were now, teaching all students, and we were going to be able to have the black students see some of their culture within the textbooks for once in our career." Repeatedly, however, these writers were criticized for profane or negative language, for depressing content, and for exposing children to realities from which they should be shielded. Ms. Davis felt this was a transparent effort to hide the fact that many white parents did not want their children exposed to black influences, even in books.

Although selections by black authors contained some strong language and gritty scenes, racism could not account for all the discomfort over "realism" in the books. Board-member Matthew Kinsolving acknowledged that the books contained some "cuss words" and such terms as "tits" and "piss," which some parents found objectionable, but Alice Moore thought it more serious than that. "The books were filled with all kinds of profanity," she insisted. "It wasn't just an occasional thing." She felt the stories not only contained inappropriate vocabulary, but their content was often quite unsuitable for youngsters. "There was a play in a junior high book," she recalled, "to be acted out in a classroom, and it was a story of a fifteen-year-old boy's first visit to a prostitute. Now this was a book for junior high children! It was almost as if they were stretching the limits, to see how far they could go, to see what they could do."

Echoing a common . . . objection, Moore and her backers charged the books with being pervaded by a "morbid," "negative," "depressing" tone. "There's more to life than negative things," said Mike Edds. "The sun shines sometimes; it's not always rain and clouds and darkness and sadness. They said, 'We want to introduce you to real life.' Well, I thought I was living real life. Most of us were happy people. Maybe we were happy in our ignorance, but we were happy people. We were happy in our homes; we were happy with what we were teaching our children. I wasn't really concerned with what was taking place on the streets of New York City."

James Moffett, the editor-in-chief of a collection of books called *Interaction*, which comprised 172 of the 325 books on the adoption list, thought the matter more complicated. He noted that much literature and drama, including the ballads of Appalachian folk culture, has long dealt with dark subjects. He said, "We had a book called *Monologue and Dialogue* that had a lot of old chestnuts of English literature in there—Robert Browning, William Blake, Matthew Arnold, T. S. Eliot. But they said 'Trash, trash from beginning to end' about this book. They said it was 'morbid.' That criticism—that things were 'negative,' 'morbid,' 'depressed'— made me do a lot of thinking about what was in their mind. The psychological research on the authoritarian personality indicates that it's based on a very negative view of the world—'The world is a fearsome place and I'm not going to make it'— and on low self-esteem, low self-confidence, a view that mankind is evil, a feeling of being unable to cope. I think that comes out in their criticisms."

Since one aspect of a fearsome world is the absence of reliable road signs, the textbook critics assailed readings that smacked of moral relativity, that is, the belief that there are no definite right and wrong answers. Closely related was a distaste for symbolism, irony, satire, ambiguity, or role-playing, since all these invite interpretations that diverge from a literal reading of the text. In their view, schoolbooks—like the Bible—should have one meaning and one only, and it should be obvious to all. Cultivating a taste and talent for multiple interpretations can only increase the likelihood of thought and behavior that call into question the settled and dependable nature of one's community and religion. . . .

By the time of the June 27 school board meeting, Alice Moore had convinced most parent-teacher groups and numerous conservative white churches to line up against the textbooks. On the other side, the West Virginia Human Rights Commission and the chapters of the NAACP and YWCA endorsed the adoptions, as did the *Charleston Gazette,* the *Charleston Daily Mail,* WCHS television, and most black churches. A coalition of clergy representing the West Virginia Council of Churches, Roman Catholic churches, Jewish synagogues, most Episcopal, Presbyterian, and Methodist churches, and some Baptist congregations, issued a statement acknowledging that any wide-ranging set of books is likely to stir controversy but asserting that their own investigation had found the books "not nearly as bad as portrayed." The issues objected to, they said, must be discussed openly if students are to be prepared to face the challenges of living in a multifaceted world. "We know of no way to stimulate the growth of our youth if we insulate them from the real issues. We feel this program will help our students think intelligently about their lives and our society." In response, a conservative coalition organized by a Baptist pastor and members of the Dunbar Ministerial Association issued statements critical of the books. And in the most impressive show of opposition, the Magic Valley Mother's Club gathered twelve thousand signatures of Kanawha County citizens urging the board to rescind the adoption.

The June school-board meeting drew more than one thousand people. In the end, the five-member board voted three-to-two to approve the original list, with the exception of eight books from the *Interaction* series. Joining Alice Moore in casting a negative vote was Matthew Kinsolving, who admits he was less concerned about the content of the books than about peace in the county. "On the basis of what she had upstirred," he said, "I voted against adopting those books at that time." Kinsolving's apprehensions were to prove more than justified.

Some citizens expected the objectors to accept their defeat with resignation, if not with grace. The response, however, involved neither. During July and August, an organization called Christian-American Parents initiated a letter-writing campaign, bought newspaper ads, held a large public rally, picketed a board member's company, and held a demonstration in front of the governor's mansion. (Eventually, a different group of parents came together and called themselves Non-Christian American Parents, to make the point that people other than fundamentalists opposed the books.) Another new group, Concerned Citizens, picketed the Board of Education. And various parties . . . continued to circulate copies of material calculated to stir anger even further.

Some of the most inflammatory material, blatantly sexual in nature, was not even in the books that had been adopted, but few bothered to check; some of those who did check, and did not find the controversial passages, concluded that a deceitful administration was hiding the material until the furor died down. Because nearly all attacks on the books emphasized the profanity and sexual content, the entire collection soon came to be known as "the dirty books."

As summer wore on, Alice Moore began to urge parents to hold their children out of school in September if the board tried to force them to use the new books. On Labor Day, September 2, the day before schools were scheduled to open, Concerned Citizens sponsored a rally at which fundamentalist preacher Marvin Horan fervently urged the crowd of eight thousand to boycott the entire school system the next day. Tuesday morning, with national news media on hand to watch, approximately twenty percent of the district's forty-five thousand students stayed home. In the Upper Valley, where Horan and other fundamentalist preachers had been most vociferous in their objections to the books, some schools had absentee rates above eighty percent. Some parents doubtless kept their children home out of fear of what the protesters might do to those who violated the call for a boycott—this was, after all, strong union territory—but most observed the boycott because they believed it was a righteous cause.

The following day, the boycott received a tremendous boost when an estimated thirty-five hundred coal miners struck in a show of solidarity with the protesters, despite orders from United Mine Workers officials not to do so. Within a week, the number of striking miners in Kanawha County and seven surrounding counties ran as high as ten thousand. Meanwhile, protesters picketed schools, school-bus garages, businesses, and various other sites, sometimes erecting barricades to keep people and vehicles from passing through. Thousands of people mounted daily demonstrations at the school district's main administration building. On September 10, Charleston bus drivers honored the picket lines, leaving more than ten thousand regular riders without service.

On September 11, the school board caved in, announcing it would withdraw the disputed books from use and submit then to examination by a new Textbook Review Committee, to which each board member would be allowed to name three individuals of his or her choosing. . . .

Perhaps to Moore's surprise, the troops she had mobilized were not content with a partial victory. At a large rally on the evening of the board's concession, the crowd jeered when she called the agreement "the best we can expect." Marvin Horan, who had signed the agreement on behalf of Concerned Citizens, reversed himself and joined the crowd's call to continue the boycotts and pickets until the offending texts were permanently removed from the schools and the superintendent and school board members who approved them swept out of office.

The protests not only continued after the rally, but quickly turned to ugly violence over the next few weeks. While the Textbook Review Committee formed and began its work, one school was dynamited, two others were firebombed, and several were damaged by gunfire and vandalism. Two men were wounded by gunfire, one as he tried to cross a picket line and the other, a protester, shot through the heart by a pro-book demonstrator who said he thought he was being attacked. CBS News reporter Jed DuVall and his television crew were badly roughed up. School buses were fired upon while returning from their rounds, and at one point most of the buses in the upper part of the county were disabled by vandals. Protesters stoned the houses and broke car windows of parents who defied the boycott and sent their children to school. Teachers and administrators were repeatedly threatened. Shots were fired into a car belonging to the president of the Classroom Teachers Association. And someone set off fifteen sticks of dynamite under the gas meter at the school board building just minutes after Underwood and the board had left.

Supporters of the books were also guilty of violence. The car of one protester was destroyed by fire. Alice Moore was repeatedly threatened, guns were fired in front of her house, sugar was put in her gas tank, and police bodyguards stayed with her during times of greatest threat. At one point, concern for student safety moved Superintendent Underwood to cancel all classes and extracurricular activities for several days, during which he and several board members, including Mrs. Moore, left town for reasons of personal safety. All attacks on schools and school buses occurred when no children were present, but one man eventually convicted in the bombings testified that he and others had considered bombing carloads of children as a way to stop "people that was sending their kids to school, letting them learn out of books when they knew they were wrong.". . .

The renewal of hostilities triggered by the boycott drew new adversaries into the arena. Joining Marvin Horan were three other fundamentalist preachers—the Reverends Avis Hill, Ezra Graley, and Charles Quigley—who quickly assumed leading roles in court-defying mass protests at school headquarters, which resulted in their being arrested, jailed, fined, or released on bail, and accorded martyr status among their followers. Quigley gained early notoriety when he declared, "I am asking Christian people to pray that God will kill the giants [the three board members who voted for the books] who have mocked and made fun of dumb fundamentalists."

On the other side of the aisle, the Reverend James Lewis, rector of St. John's Episcopal Church in Charleston, emerged as a key leader of pro-textbook forces. Lewis was a newcomer to Charleston who had paid little attention to the textbook controversy before the boycott began. At the request of several student council leaders who objected when the new texts were withdrawn, Lewis, along with a rabbi and a Baptist minister, met with a group of students to see what might be done to get the books back into the classrooms. That meeting led to others and, soon, to the formation of the Kanawha County Coalition for Quality Education, which sought both to defend the new books and also to avoid further damage to the social fabric. One of the coalition's first steps was to hold meetings throughout the country to give citizens the opportunity to examine the books for themselves, to show that much of what they had been told about the books was simply not true. "Everyone was so frightened," Lewis said, "as though somehow the children would die if they read these books."

Lewis's meetings were reasonably effective in easing the minds of some parents, particularly those primarily concerned with the presence of graphic sexual material, but they did little to mollify those who disagreed with the overall multicultural thrust and innovative approach of the books. . . .

"What we saw in that struggle," he said, "was a real religious crusade. If you stepped in front of it and challenged it in any way, you were immediately demonized and seen as the enemy, as the Antichrist. When you move into that kind of demonization, you are just a hair away from killing the person or people associated with that view, because to kill something evil becomes something good. That was the aura and the mood of that whole struggle. A woman stepped up to me at a meeting one time and put her face up against mine, quoting Scripture in my face as though somehow I didn't read Scripture, and she said to me, 'We shouldn't cast our pearls before swine' as though I were swine. There's a sense in which this passion turned into a terrible crusade that got violent very quickly in a self-righteous way. That's the thing you could feel in that valley all the time: you could be killed 'for Christ's sake.'"

Following a telephoned death threat, Lewis's family and friends urged him to step away from the controversy, but he felt that was not an option. Comparing the struggle to an explosion outside the church door, he said, "You have to go to it. People were warring with one another. This was Bosnia. This was a deeply tribal struggle, and there was no way to stay out of it." Lewis consistently described the conflict as a clash between cultures. "It was a struggle," he said, "of people from lots of different persuasions. My concern was always, 'How can all of us in this valley study and work and live together and not kill one another, particularly over these textbooks?' It was crystal-clear to me from the very beginning that we were in a major struggle with folks who saw life from a different perspective. The seeds had been there for a long time, but something new was happening." In an article carried by newspapers across the country at the time, Lewis wrote, "The anti-textbook people of Kanawha County are confused and angry about everything from marijuana to Watergate. Feeling helpless and left out, they are looking for a scapegoat. They are eager to exorcise all that is evil and foul, cleanse or burn all that is strange and foreign. In this religious war, spiced with overtones of race and class, the books are an accessible target."

Like James Lewis, evangelical youth pastor Mike Edds also felt he had no choice but to take a stand. "We'd been taught in the Bible Belt," he explained, "that there is a higher law, that if the civil law is contrary to biblical law, then we have to obey the higher law. I felt something great was at stake. That's where the majority of parents and many of the educators who grew up in West Virginia were. Our whole belief system was at stake, and we had to take a stand. That was the first time in my life I had ever known Christian people to march in a protest or resist something. Before that, Christians did nothing; whatever came down the pike—fine, good, bad, or in-between—it was 'Just don't bother me.' But this was striking at their very soul."

Edds agreed with Jim Lewis's assertion that the struggle over the books stemmed from cultural differences, but viewed it from a different angle. Recalling a report that Superintendent Underwood had remarked in exasperation, "These fundamentalists: How can we live with them?," Edds said, "That's where the split came. There was an elitism in the central office that saw the majority of the county's population as ignorant, uneducated folks. I'm sure some of the folks didn't use proper English; I speak with a little bit of hillbilly lingo and slang. Some of these folks maybe didn't finish high school, maybe some of them didn't go on to college, but that's not a mark of a person's intelligence. People in Kanawha County are very pro-American, very patriotic—it's apple pie, Mom, the flag, and the church. These textbooks struck at every area of that belief system, and parents felt like, 'We cannot just avoid this conflict; we have to face it; we have to do something about it.' It was a terrible time. It was almost like a civil war. The community was just split down the middle." . . .

Given the emotional climate, tensions ran high in anticipation of a public meeting the school board scheduled for November 8, at which time it planned to reach a final decision on the Textbook Advisory Committee's recommendations. Expecting a huge turnout, the board rented the Charleston Civic Center and had thousands of seats set up. To discourage violence, guards armed with metal detectors and guns were stationed at entrances; additional guards kept watch on the auditorium floor from positions in the rafters. These elaborate preparations proved to be superfluous. Alice Moore and a minister from the pro-book forces had both used radio and personal contact with various groups to urge citizens not to attend the meeting, lest trouble break out. As a result, the board conducted its deliberations in the huge hall before an audience of no more than fifty people. By a four-to-one margin, with Moore as the lone dissenter, it ruled that the books would be returned to the schools, but that no school or child would be forced to use them. Parents would have to provide written permission for their children to be assigned the books, and children whose parents objected would continue to use the old books or some acceptable alternative. Some books, including James Moffett's *Interaction* series, would be restricted to library use. Two weeks later, the board agreed that future texts would have to meet criteria set forth in a set of restrictive guidelines Alice Moore had prepared . . .

One might imagine that both sides would conclude they had done about as well as could be expected. Traditional parents could protect their children from the new books, and future books would be more to their liking. The children of more progressive parents could use the controversial books until they wore out and, if not too many of them turned into communists or criminals, a future board might relax some of the restrictions it had placed on itself. Ideological struggles, however, seldom end quite so peacefully, especially when they involve fundamentalists, for whom half-measures and partial victory are regarded as little better than defeat. . . .

On December 1, the Reverend Avis Hill led a demonstration in which two thousand people marched through the Charleston shopping district waving flags and carrying placards that read, "Trash Is for Burning," "No Peaceful Coexistence with Satanic Communism," and "Wish We Had More People Like Sweet Alice." A few days later, Hill and fellow fundamentalist preacher Ezra Graley went to Washington to discuss their concerns with conservative Indiana Congressman Roger Zion, who registered their complaints in the *Congressional Record*. On December 12, during a televised school-board meeting, protesters physically assaulted Superintendent Underwood and all the board members except Alice Moore. And on Christmas Eve, worshipers leaving a family service at St. John's Episcopal Church, which had backed the pro-book forces, found the church door decorated with stickers that announced, "You Have Been Paid a Visit by the Klan." On the other side, the National Educational Association held hearings and issued a report that criticized the board both for not being more sensitive to the concerns of a significant part of its constituency and also for caving in to most of the objectors' demands. . . .

On January 17, a grand jury indicted preacher Marvin Horan and five others for "conspiracy to blow up two elementary schools and other School Board property." The next day, nearly two hundred protesters, including Horan, welcomed several delegations of the Ku Klux Klan who gathered on the steps of the state capitol for a full-hood rally, followed by a larger gathering at the Civic Center, where Imperial Wizard James Venable darkly predicted that the "Communist, socialist, nigger race is going to dominate this nation," and other Klansmen declared their support of the protesters and invited them to join the Klan.

With the exception of some of the fundamentalist preachers, most leaders of the anti-textbook forces professed to be disturbed by such support. Elmer Fike . . . [said of] the Klan, "We didn't want anything to do with them. We wouldn't touch them with a ten-foot pole." Mike Edds was even more pointed: "We're not ignorant people. We felt like we were fully capable of representing ourselves. I was appalled when the Klan got involved. They just found a good thing going, that was getting some national attention, and they jumped on board. A lot of us dropped out toward the end. We were tired of other groups wanting to speak for us, trying to promote their organization's agenda, which wasn't the agenda that had us out on the streets. There is a religious right and a political right, and they're not one and the same."

The intrusion of uninvited outside forces and the arrest of Marvin Horan and his coconspirators, together with the increased presence of West Virginia State Police, soon brought an end to the boycotts and demonstrations and violence. After Horan was found guilty of conspiring to bomb the schools, the Reverend James Lewis appealed to the federal judge to give Horan a probated sentence, so he could remain in the community and use his influence to help try to heal fractures and restore peace to the valley. The judge sentenced Horan to three years in the federal penitentiary; his five accomplices received various lesser sentences.

By some accounts, the pro-textbook forces won the Kanawha County textbook wars; most of the offending books were restored to the classrooms and the most vociferous of their enemies went to jail or prison. The apparent victory, however, proved hollow. In schools where opposition ran high, the books were typically not used at all. When opinion was mixed, as was often the case, teachers found it difficult to devise comparable assignments and often abandoned attempts to use the new materials at all.

Because the Kanawha County conflict created such upheaval and was so widely publicized, its effects were felt throughout the country. To avoid similar problems in their own districts, many school boards and administrators refused even to consider adopting the controversial *Interaction* series, and competing publishers' salespeople quite happily spread the word that the books had been condemned as immoral in West Virginia. As a result, books languished and died before their time. Since then, publishers have been unwilling to produce books containing the range of subjects and ideas found in the books vilified and crippled in the Kanawha County struggle.

Though no battle has come close to the Kanawha County episode in intensity or scope, hundreds of school districts throughout the nation have experienced protests, usually initiated by small groups of conservative Christian parents, against textbooks and other books assigned in classes or available to students in school libraries. The protests are part of a general campaign. "They're the same old books all the time," James Moffett noted, referring to such titles as John Steinbeck's *Of Mice and Men,* J. D. Salinger's *The Catcher in the Rye,* Mark Twain's *Huckleberry Finn,* Shel Silverstein's *A Light in the Attic,* Judy Blume's *Forever,* Judith Guest's *Ordinary People,* Madeleine L'Engle's *A Wrinkle in Time,* and Maya

Angelou's *I Know Why the Caged Bird Sings*. "I can think of much worse books to censor, but they're on a standard list that circulates throughout the censorship network. These parents just pick these books off the lists, look for them in their schools, and then complain."

As evidence of the growing power of the Religious Right, book banning efforts intensified after Ronald Reagan's election in 1980. A 1981 survey by the Association of American Publishers, the American Library Association and the Association for Supervision and Curriculum Development estimated that more than twenty percent of the nation's school districts and thirty percent of school libraries experienced challenges to literary works and textbooks. Four years later, in 1985, *USA Today* reported a thirty-seven percent increase in censorship efforts over the previous academic year, with incidents occurring in forty-six states.

The textbook controversy spurred another development that has had many counterparts throughout the country: the growth of private Christian day schools and an increase in home schooling. Kanawha County teacher Ruth Davis regarded this as an unfortunate turn for American education. "Students are segregated," she said; "We need to expose students to all types of literature and to people working together. They need to be able to see how people in different cultures can come together and work together and live together and go to school together." James Moffett agreed. While appreciating the desire to protect one's culture against a perceived invasion, he felt that establishing private schools tailored to subcultural preferences "sets a time bomb for the future" and "will seriously deepen community and national divisions. Children who grow up apart will probably fight as adults. Not having grown up learning to share resources despite personal differences, they will be unable to live, let live, and unite to solve common problems. Not speaking the same language, they will not talk together." . . .

 ## For Further Study

1. Detail the specific objections that Alice Moore and the other protesters had to the proposed new educational materials.

2. Many of the objections that the anti-book protesters had to the new materials were rooted in their religious views, yet many of those who supported the new materials were also religious. What, if anything, is different in the religious beliefs of the pro-book and anti-book forces?

3. Describe the methods used by the protesters in their campaign against the proposed books. How are those methods similar to and different from the methods used by civil rights protesters in the 1960s?

4. One of the defenders of the books said that the protesters' objections were a result of their feelings of "low self-esteem, low self-confidence, a view that mankind is evil, a feeling of being unable to cope." What do you think of this argument? Do you agree with it? Why or why not?

5. The protesters believed that school textbooks have the power to shape the minds of children and thus determine the nation's future. Do you think that the influence of schoolbooks is that great?

6. What connections do you see between the growth of protests like that described in the selection, the rise of the so-called religious right, and the upsurge of political conservatism in the 1970s and 1980s?

7. Relate the conflict described in the selection to contemporary "culture wars" over issues such as abortion, school prayer, flag burning, gay rights, and so forth. What similarities do you see in the lineup of contending forces and in the arguments advanced by each of the two sides?

For Further Reading

Leo Ribuffo, *The Old Christian Right: The Protestant Far Right from the Great Depression to the Cold War* (1983) is a critical look at the religious right in the period before it became politically powerful. The book from which this selection was taken, William Martin, *With God on Our Side: The Rise of the Religious Right in America* (1996) takes the story from the 1950s into the 1990s. James Moffett, *Storm in the Mountains* (1982) is a detailed account of the Kanawha County book controversy by one of those on the pro-book side. Jeffrey K. Hadden and Anson Shupe, *Televangelism: Power and Politics on God's Frontier* (1988) shows how some evangelical ministers have learned to use television as a way of spreading their religious and sometimes their political views. Jerry Falwell, *Listen America!* (1980) is by a leading televangelist, the founder of the Moral Majority, one of the more powerful organizations on the religious right. James Davision Hunter, *Culture Wars: The Struggle to Define America* (1991) details and analyzes the ideas of those involved in current controversies over such issues as abortion, gay rights, and prayer in schools.